THE GUARDIAN Vol.2

By KÔSEN

~ We also Present ~

Reluctant Savior

STORY BY MISA IZANAKI, ART BY YISHAN LI
LETTERS BY LAILA REIMOZ, EDITED BY XAVIERA PALLARS

www.yaoipress.com

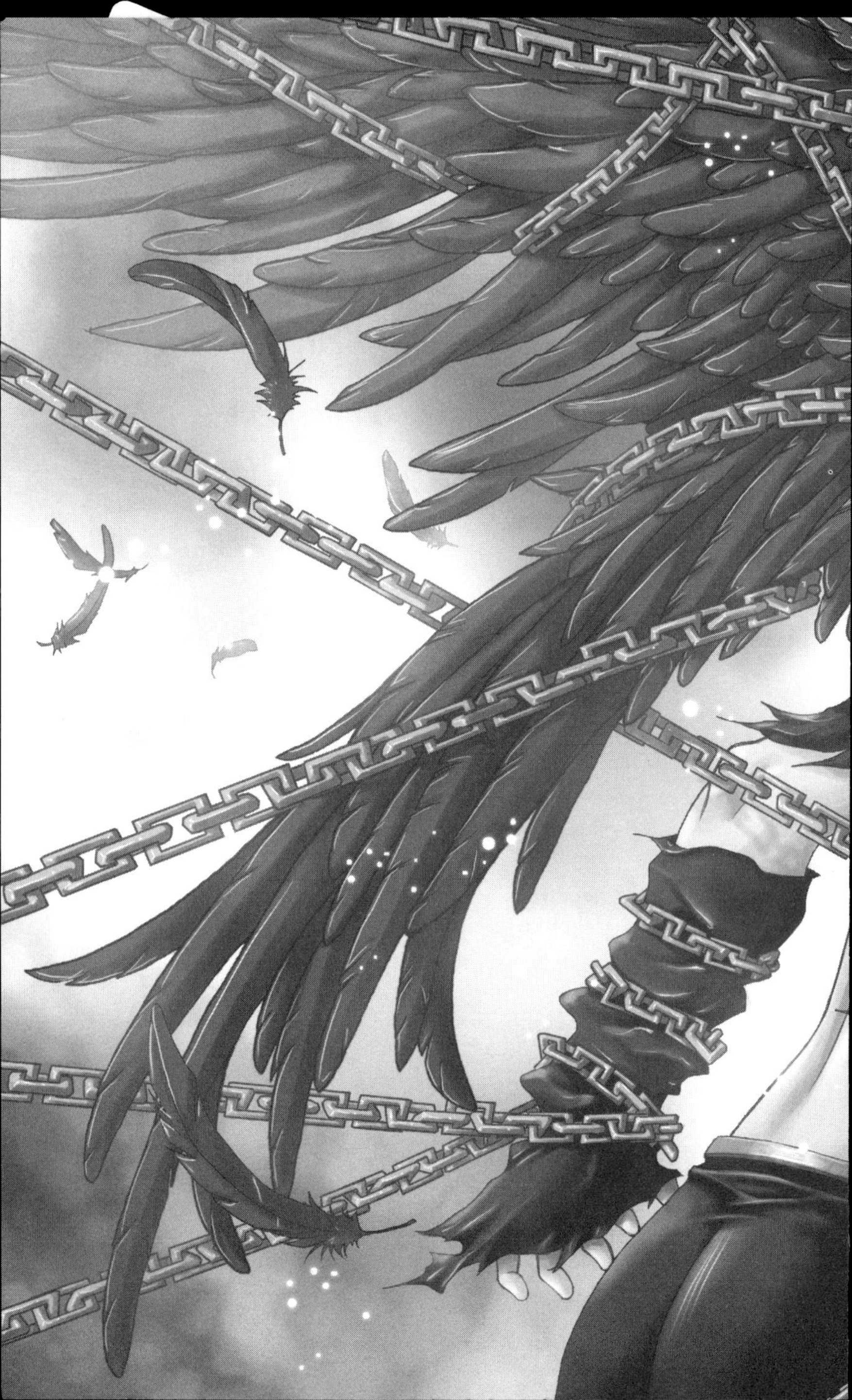

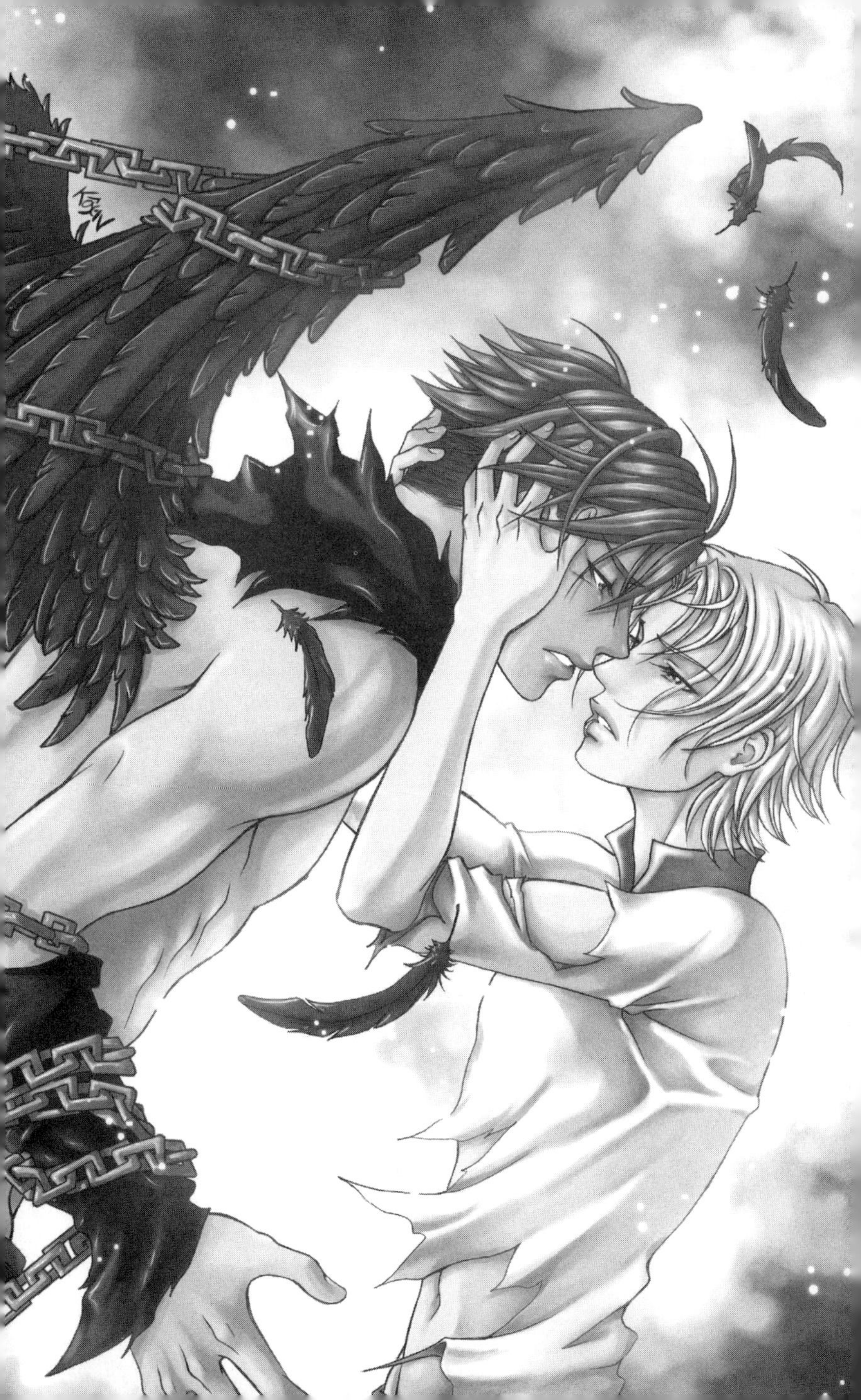

Saihôshi the Guardian Volume 2
Story and art by KÔSEN

Reluctant Savior
Story by Misa Izanaki, Art by Yishan Li, Letters by Laila Reimoz

Edited by Xaviera Pallars and Yamila Abraham.

Printed in the United States of America

ISBN: 1-933664-06-1

ISBN 13: 978-1-933664-06-4

Published by Yaoi Press Ltd. First printing September 2006.

www.yaoipress.com

10 9 8 7 6 5 4 3 2 1

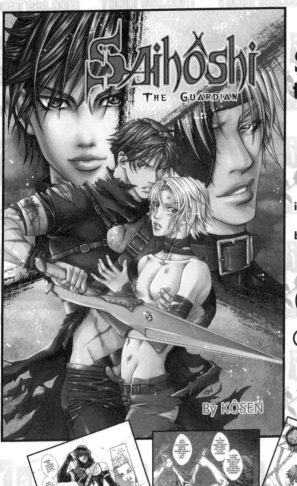

Available Now!

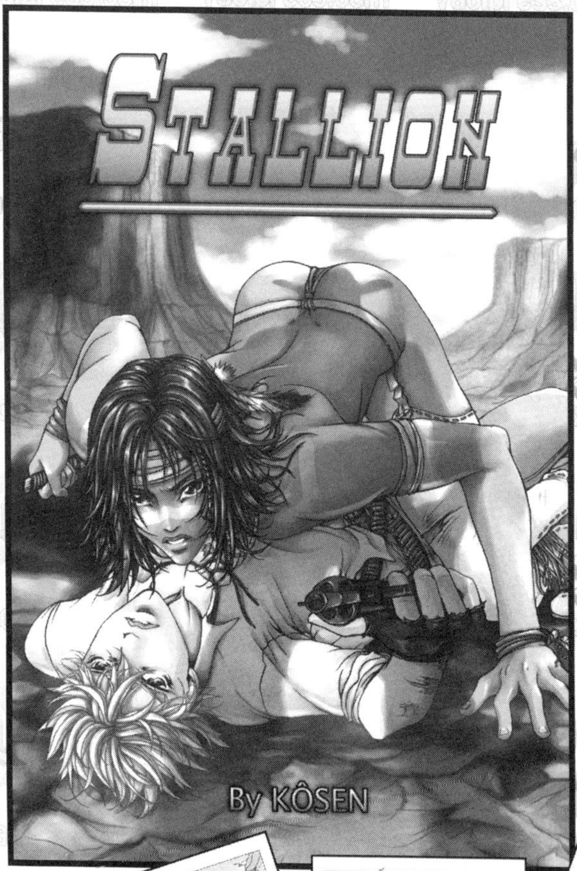
STALLION
By KÔSEN

Stallion

by KÔSEN

Native American Stallion is out for revenge on the cowboy who ruined his life, but has competition from another one of cowboy Bill's victims. Enemies at first, they unite and learn they share a tragic bond due to what they both suffered in the past.

ALSO BY STUDIO KÔSEN! FREE STICKERS INSIDE!

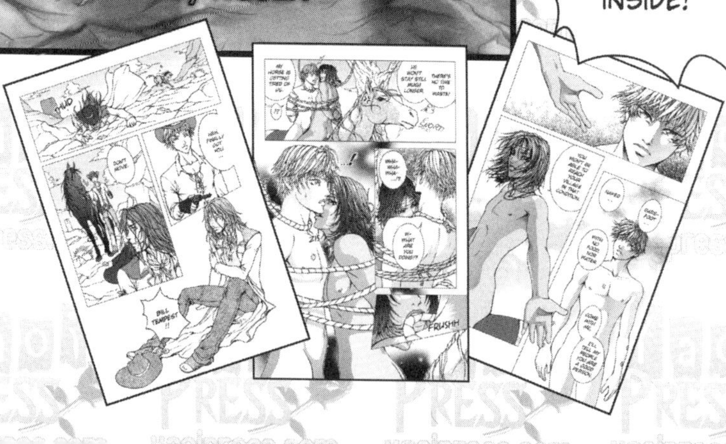
THUD
DON'T MOVE.
BILL TEMPEST !!
FRUSHH

Available Now!

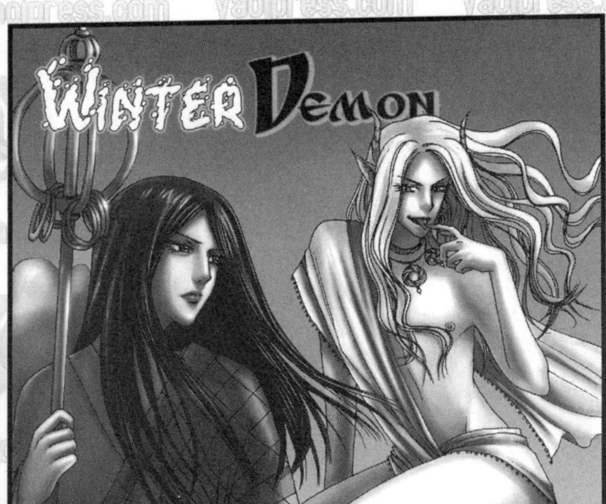
Winter Demon
Yamila Abraham • Studio Kosaru

Winter Demon

by Yamila Abraham and Studio Kosaru

Three fire demons cause the monk Hakuin to seek help from Fuyu, the demon who tormented him the year before. Fuyu will fight the demons, but only if Hakuin becomes his willing slave. Alas, the fire demon leader is too strong...and he's hot for Fuyu.

See a Preview at the end of this book!

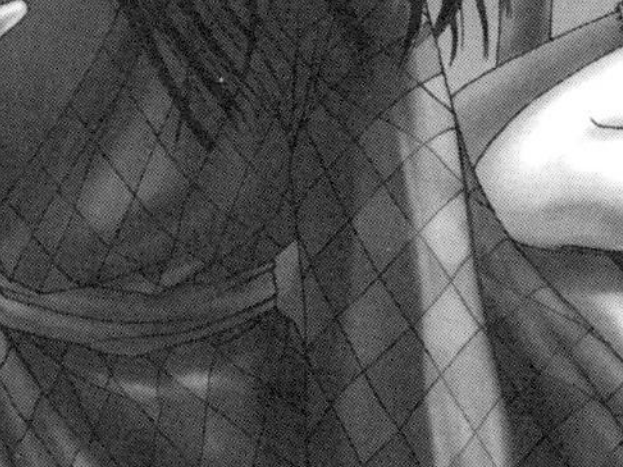

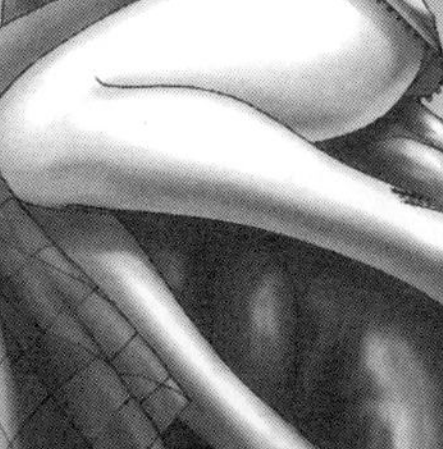

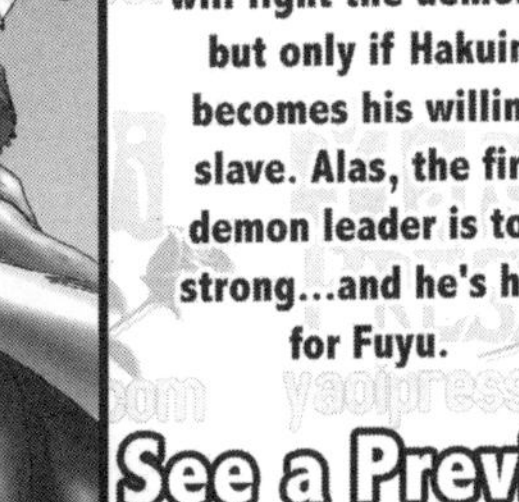

Coming Nov 2006!

Surge
by Kyle Green and Studio Kosaru

Gorgeous surfer Shawn needs to pass a test or he'll flunk out of school. Luckily, the cute nerd Alan wants to learn how to surf so they strike a deal. Romantic sparks fly for the very mismatched couple, but Shawn's jealous ex warns Alan he's just being used.

Kyle Green
Studio Kosaru

Saihôshi
THE GUARDIAN

Story and art by KÔSEN

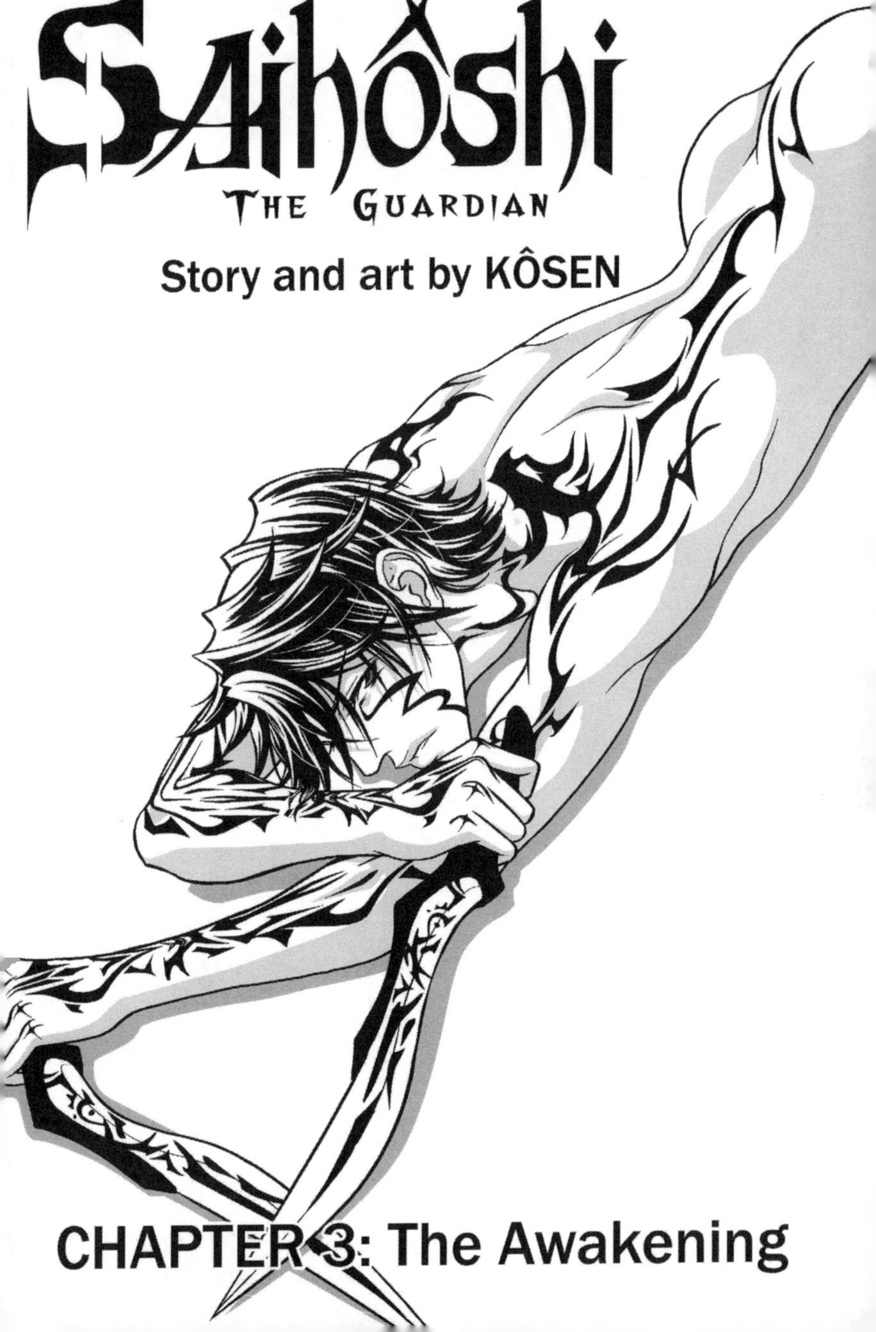

CHAPTER 3: The Awakening

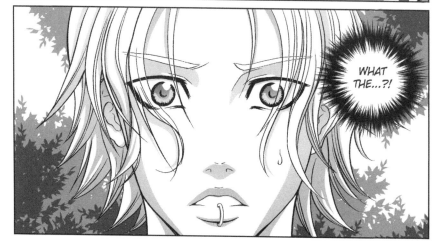

WHAT THE...?!

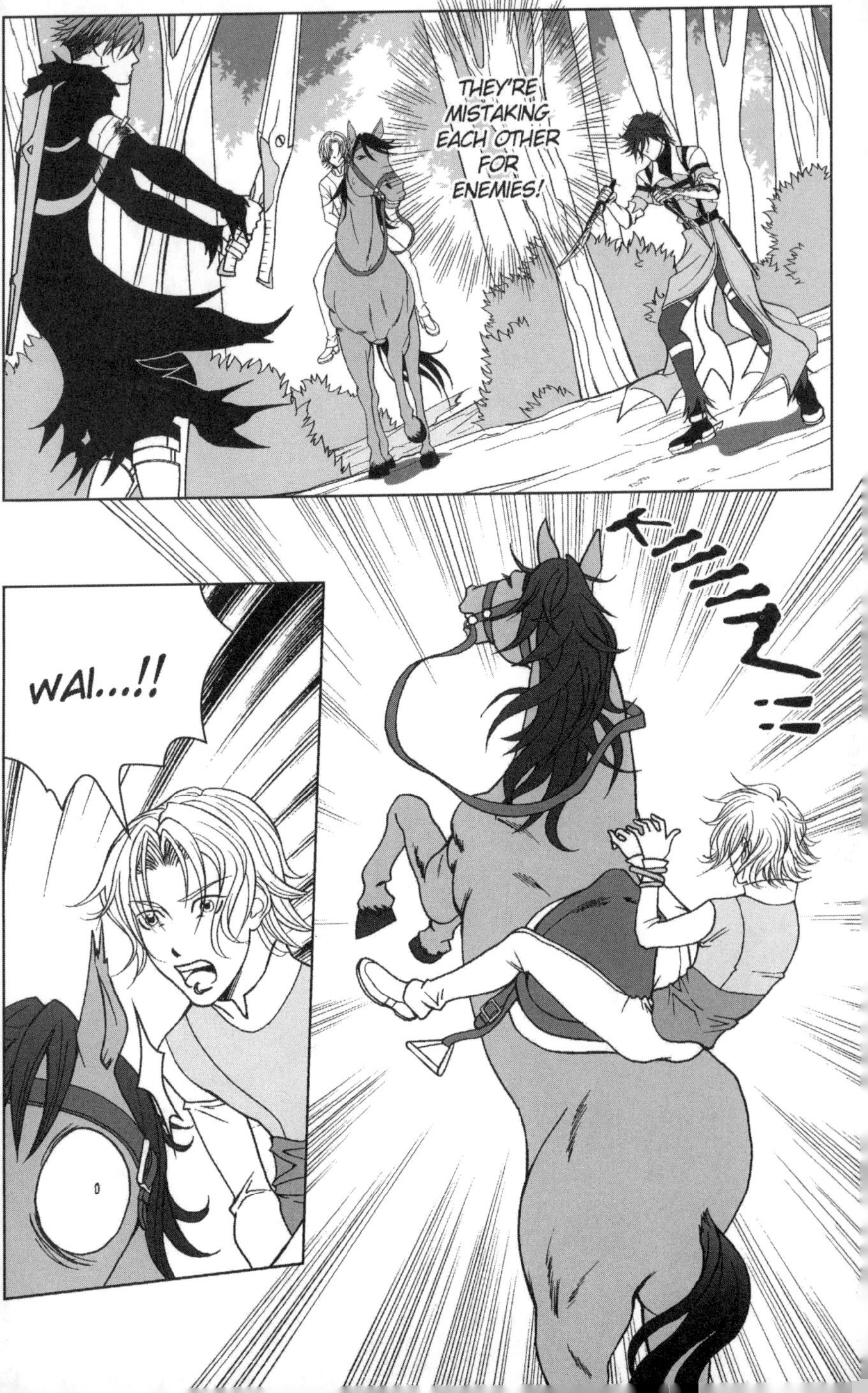
THEY'RE MISTAKING EACH OTHER FOR ENEMIES!
WAI...!!

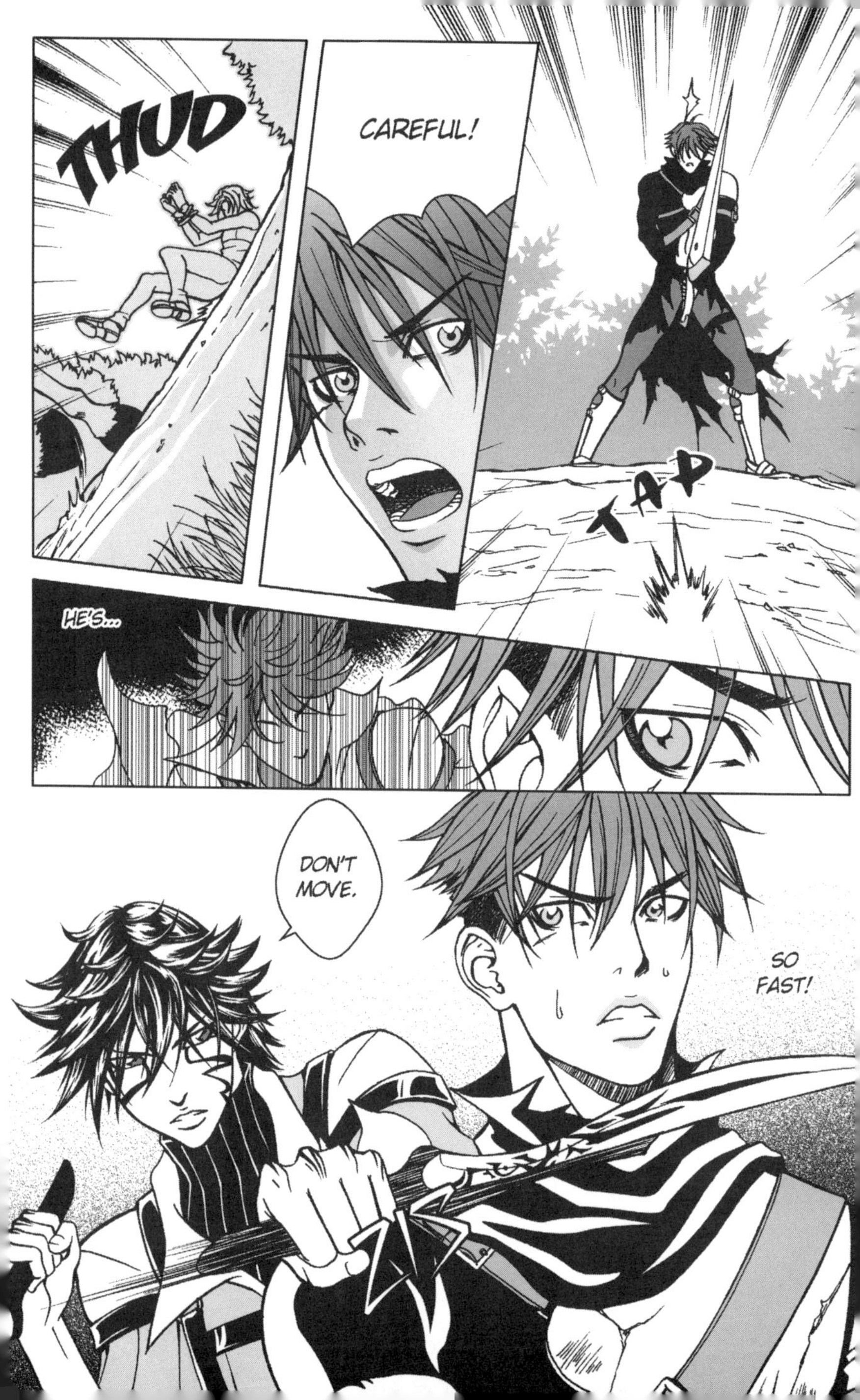
THUD
CAREFUL!
TAP
HE'S...
DON'T MOVE.
SO FAST!

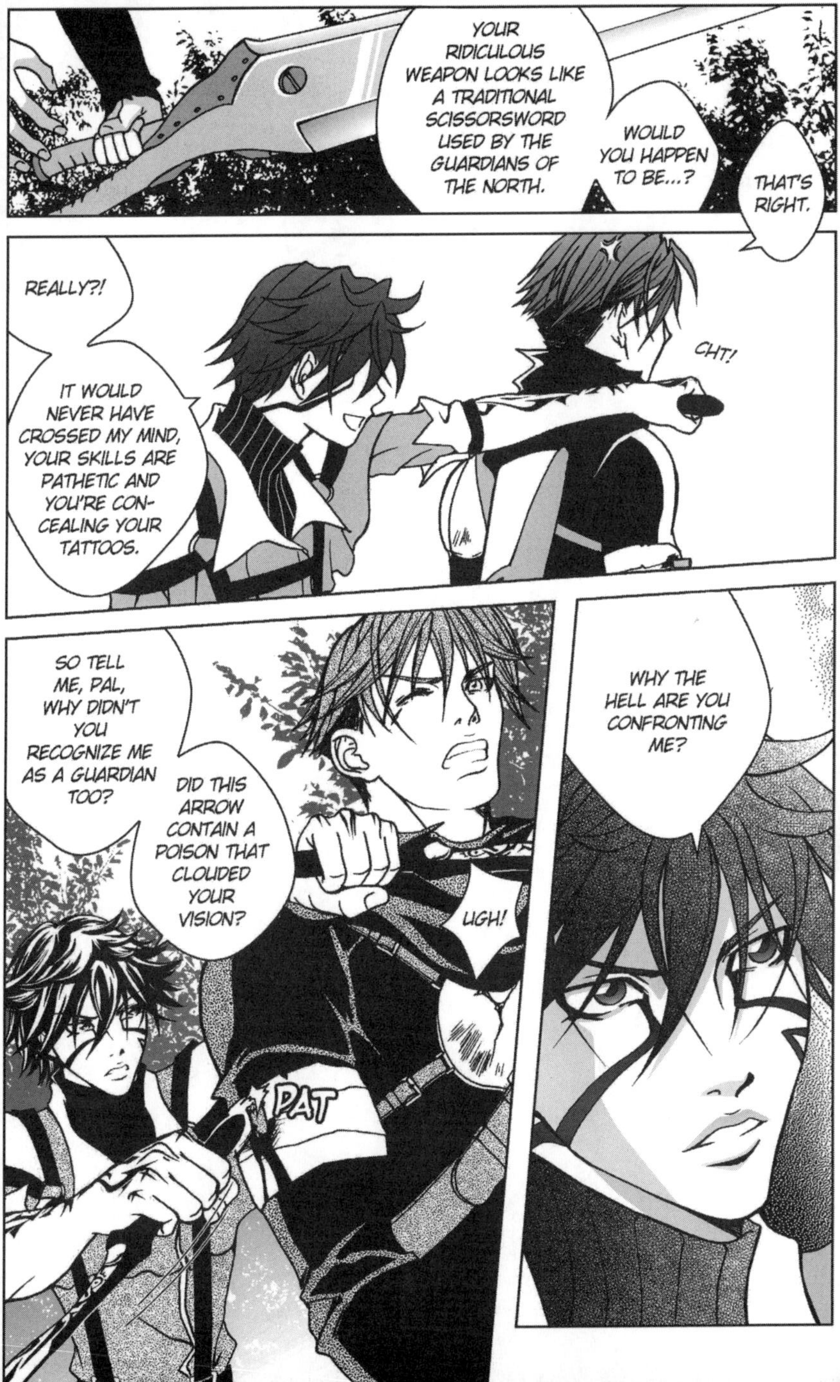
YOUR RIDICULOUS WEAPON LOOKS LIKE A TRADITIONAL SCISSORSWORD USED BY THE GUARDIANS OF THE NORTH.
WOULD YOU HAPPEN TO BE...?
THAT'S RIGHT.
REALLY?!
IT WOULD NEVER HAVE CROSSED MY MIND, YOUR SKILLS ARE PATHETIC AND YOU'RE CON-CEALING YOUR TATTOOS.
CHT!
SO TELL ME, PAL, WHY DIDN'T YOU RECOGNIZE ME AS A GUARDIAN TOO?
DID THIS ARROW CONTAIN A POISON THAT CLOUDED YOUR VISION?
UGH!
WHY THE HELL ARE YOU CONFRONTING ME?
PAT

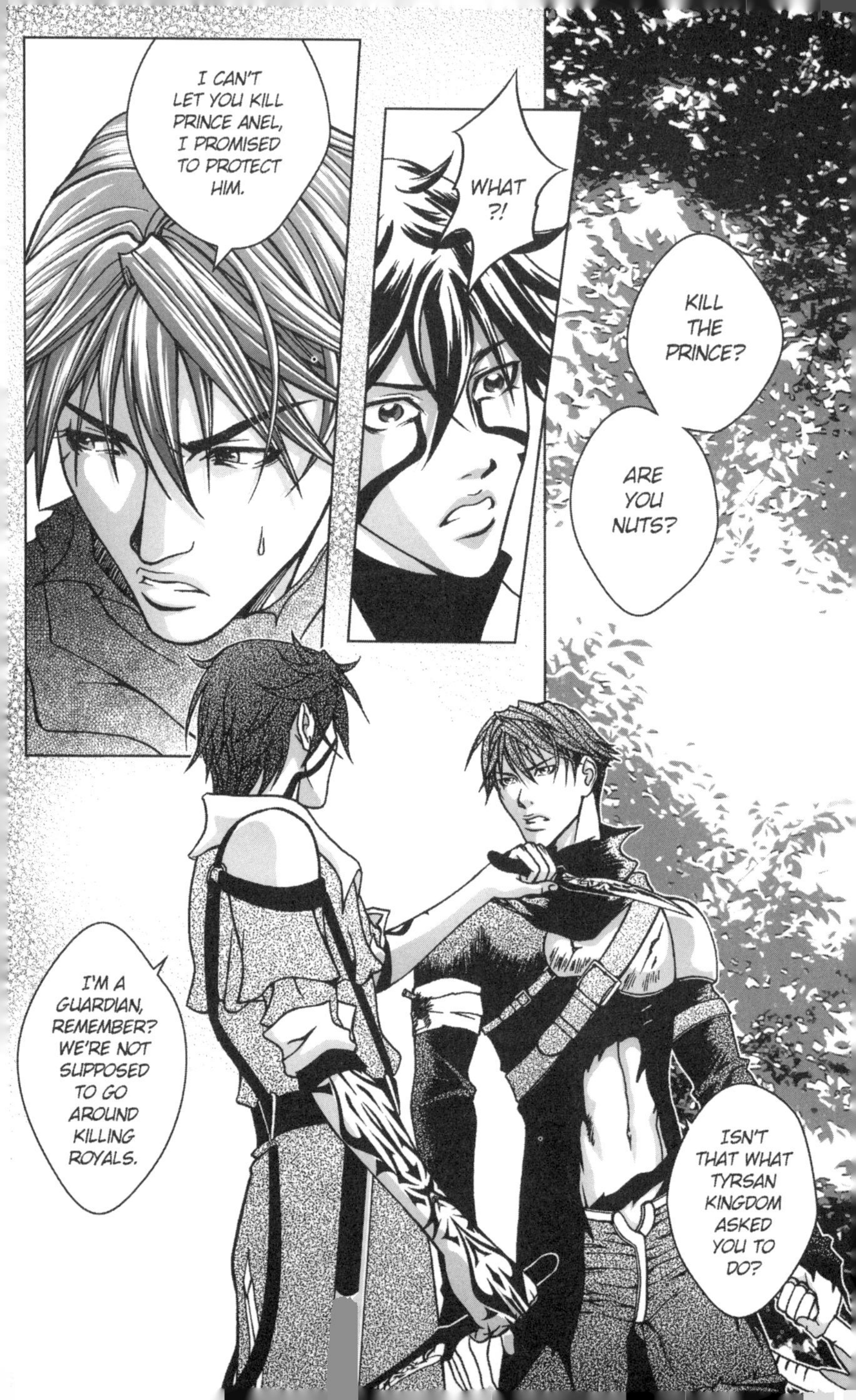
I CAN'T LET YOU KILL PRINCE ANEL, I PROMISED TO PROTECT HIM.
WHAT ?!
KILL THE PRINCE?
ARE YOU NUTS?
I'M A GUARDIAN, REMEMBER? WE'RE NOT SUPPOSED TO GO AROUND KILLING ROYALS.
ISN'T THAT WHAT TYRSAN KINGDOM ASKED YOU TO DO?

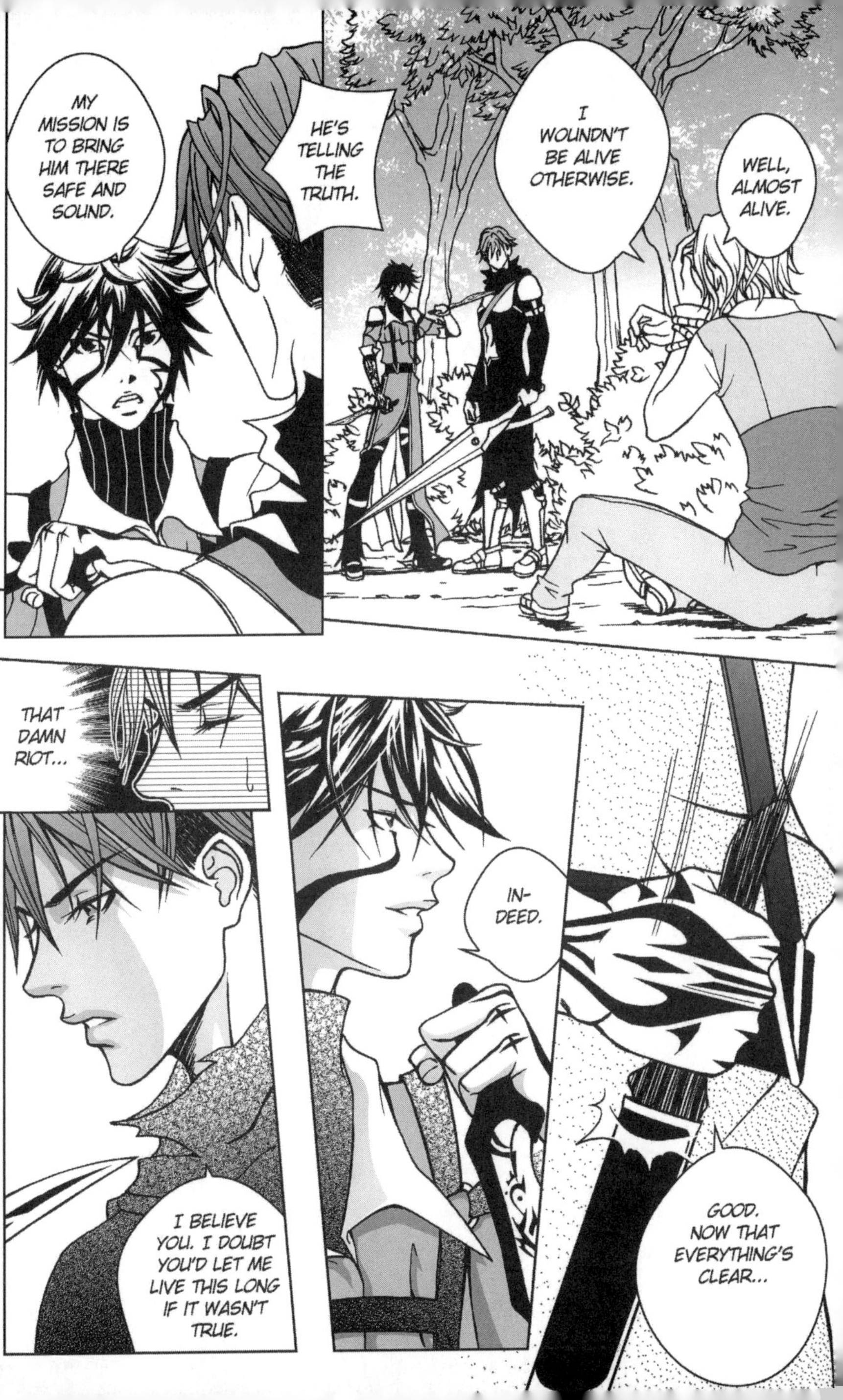
MY MISSION IS TO BRING HIM THERE SAFE AND SOUND.
HE'S TELLING THE TRUTH.
I WOUNDN'T BE ALIVE OTHERWISE.
WELL, ALMOST ALIVE.
THAT DAMN RIOT...
I BELIEVE YOU. I DOUBT YOU'D LET ME LIVE THIS LONG IF IT WASN'T TRUE.
IN-DEED.
GOOD. NOW THAT EVERYTHING'S CLEAR...

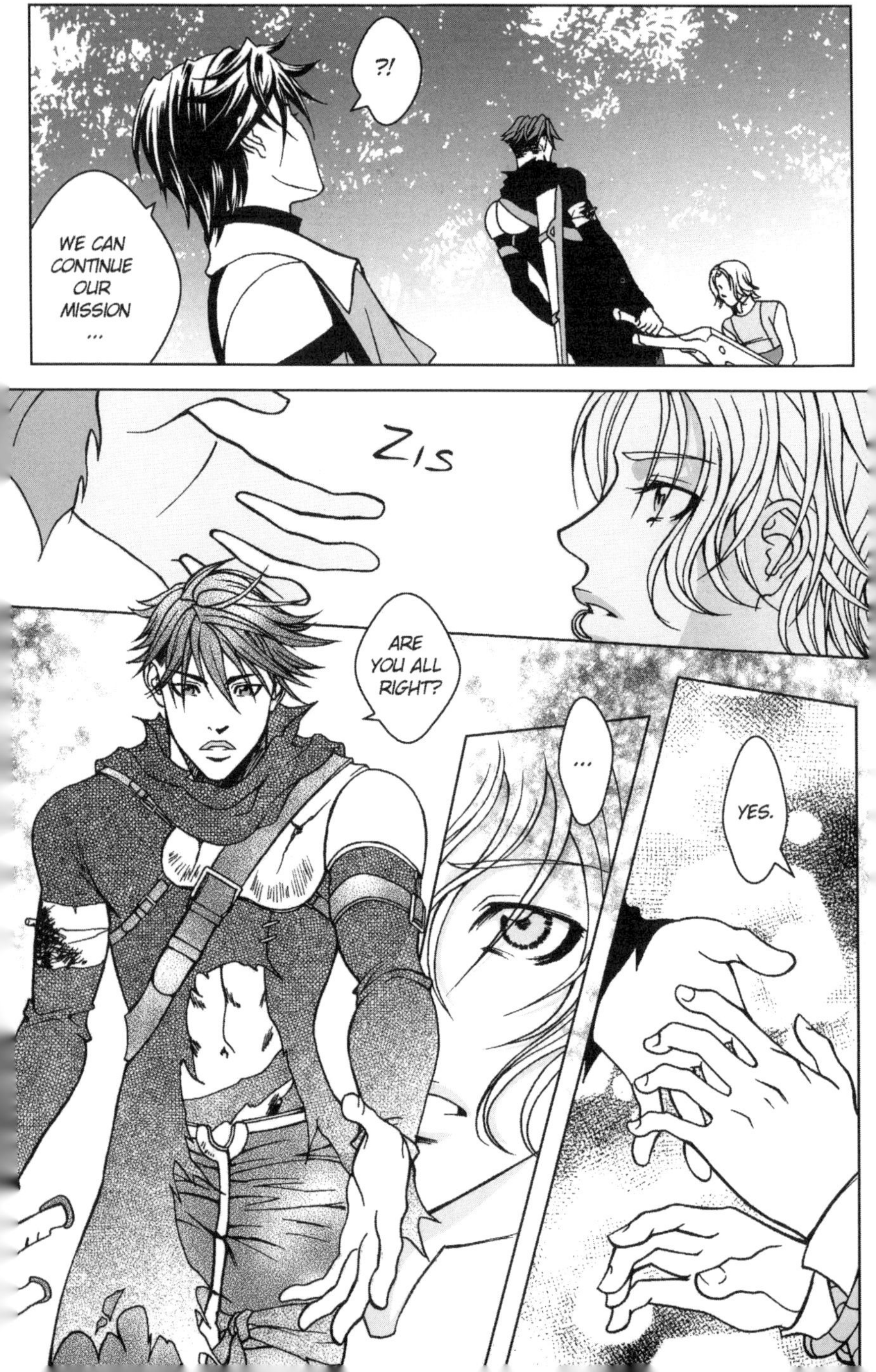
WE CAN CONTINUE OUR MISSION ...
?!
ZIS
ARE YOU ALL RIGHT?
...
YES.

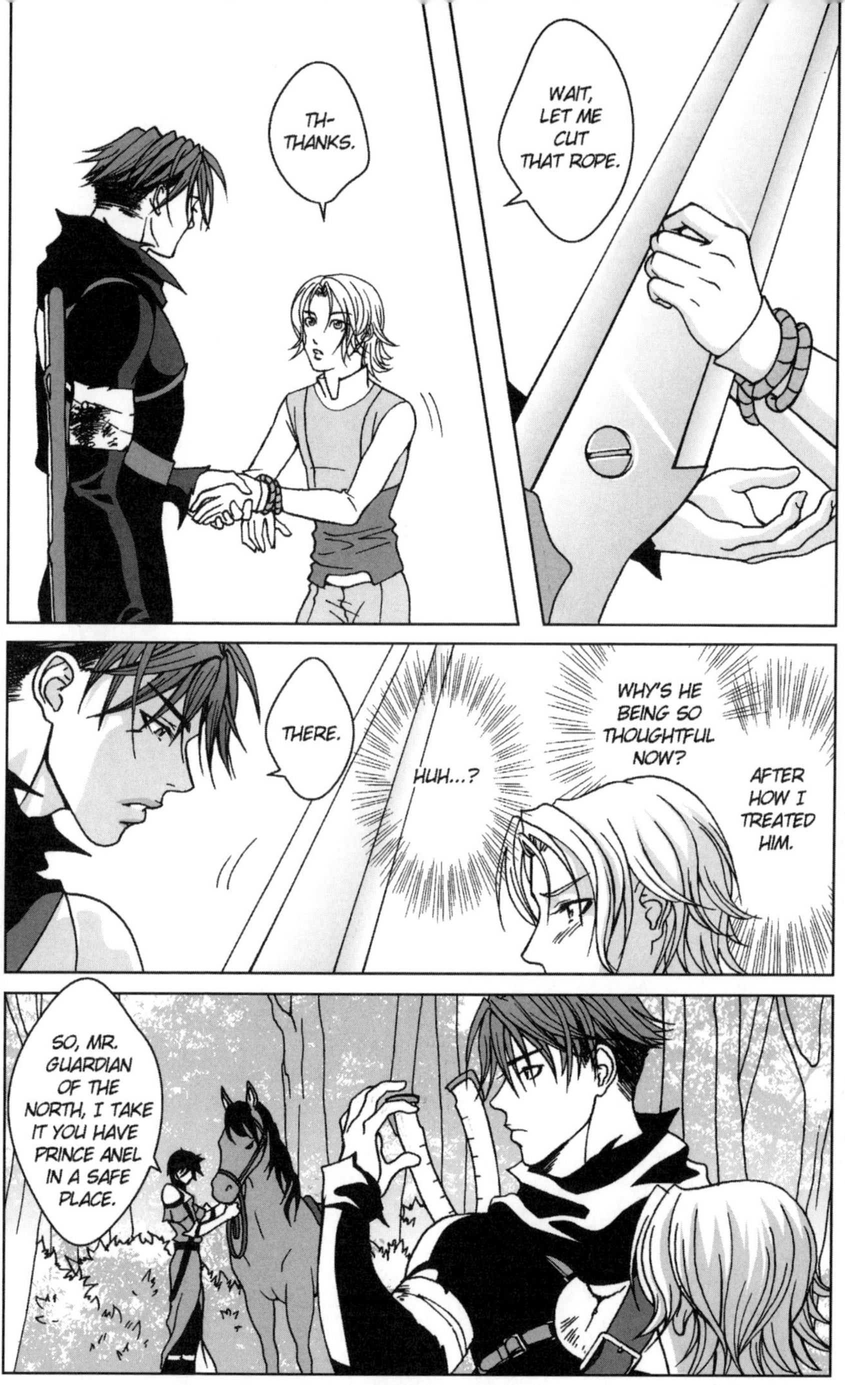
WAIT, LET ME CUT THAT ROPE.
TH- THANKS.
WHY'S HE BEING SO THOUGHTFUL NOW?
AFTER HOW I TREATED HIM.
HUH...?
THERE.
SO, MR. GUARDIAN OF THE NORTH, I TAKE IT YOU HAVE PRINCE ANEL IN A SAFE PLACE.

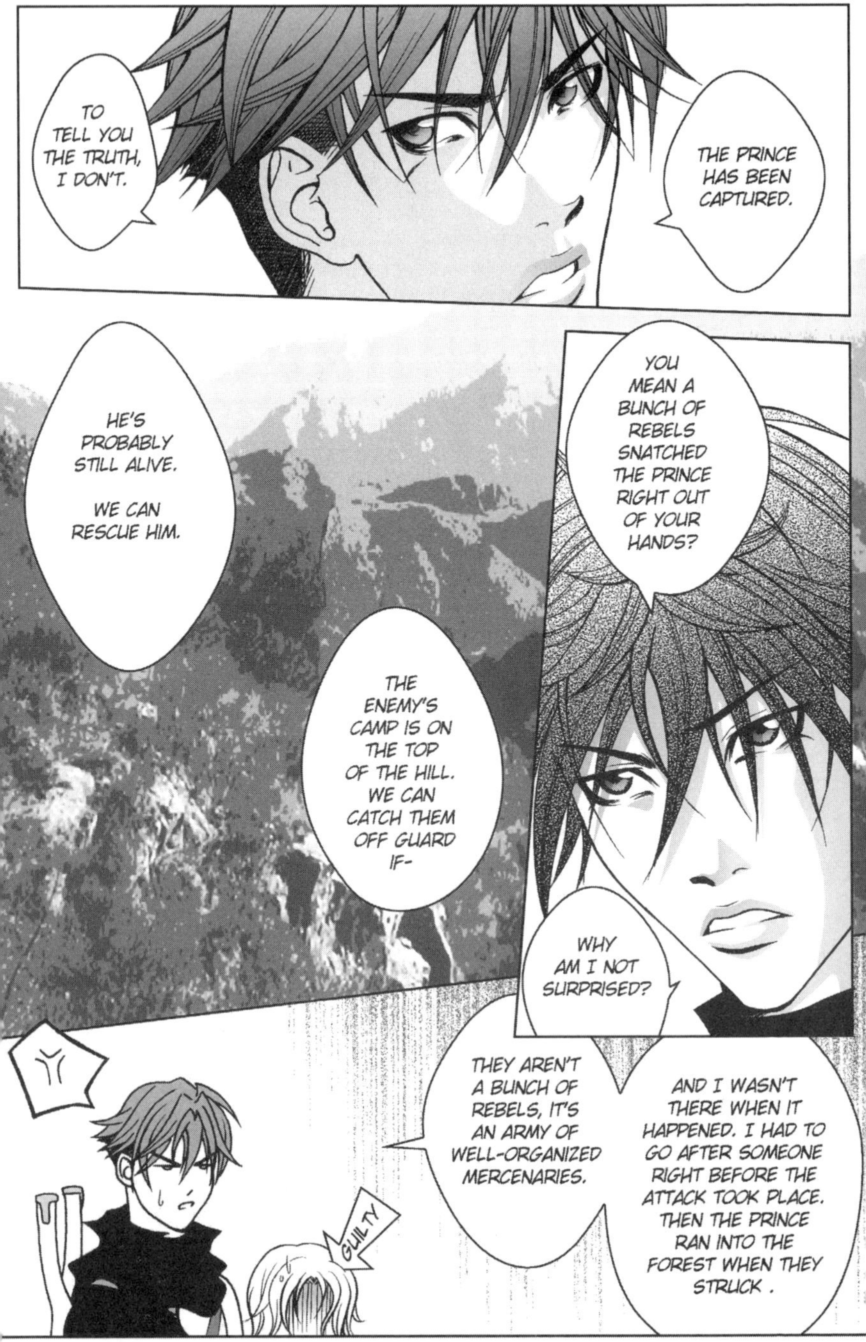

TO TELL YOU THE TRUTH, I DON'T.
THE PRINCE HAS BEEN CAPTURED.
HE'S PROBABLY STILL ALIVE.
WE CAN RESCUE HIM.
YOU MEAN A BUNCH OF REBELS SNATCHED THE PRINCE RIGHT OUT OF YOUR HANDS?
THE ENEMY'S CAMP IS ON THE TOP OF THE HILL. WE CAN CATCH THEM OFF GUARD IF-
WHY AM I NOT SURPRISED?
THEY AREN'T A BUNCH OF REBELS, IT'S AN ARMY OF WELL-ORGANIZED MERCENARIES.
AND I WASN'T THERE WHEN IT HAPPENED. I HAD TO GO AFTER SOMEONE RIGHT BEFORE THE ATTACK TOOK PLACE. THEN THE PRINCE RAN INTO THE FOREST WHEN THEY STRUCK .
GUILTY

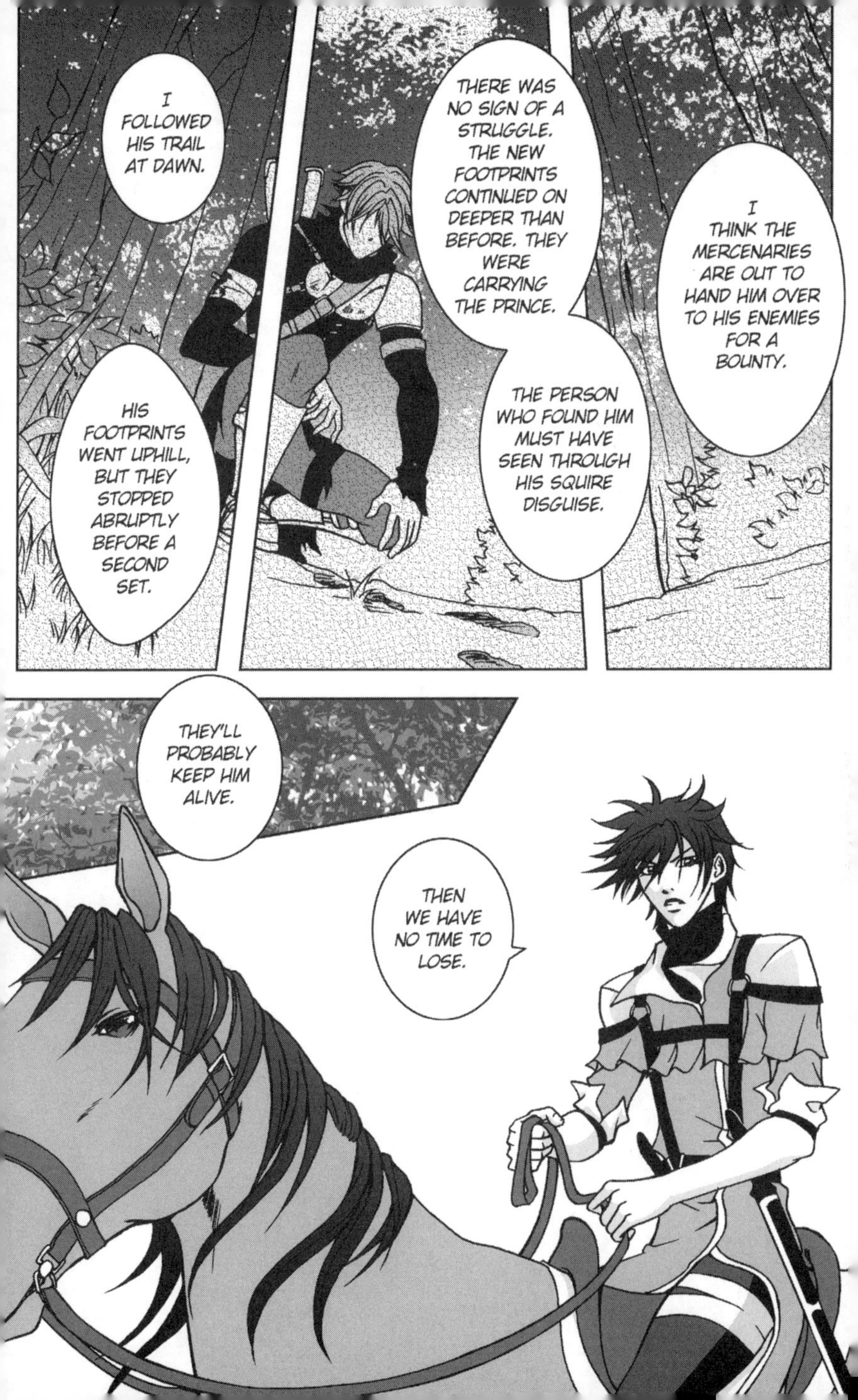
I FOLLOWED HIS TRAIL AT DAWN.
HIS FOOTPRINTS WENT UPHILL, BUT THEY STOPPED ABRUPTLY BEFORE A SECOND SET.
THERE WAS NO SIGN OF A STRUGGLE. THE NEW FOOTPRINTS CONTINUED ON DEEPER THAN BEFORE. THEY WERE CARRYING THE PRINCE.
THE PERSON WHO FOUND HIM MUST HAVE SEEN THROUGH HIS SQUIRE DISGUISE.
I THINK THE MERCENARIES ARE OUT TO HAND HIM OVER TO HIS ENEMIES FOR A BOUNTY.
THEY'LL PROBABLY KEEP HIM ALIVE.
THEN WE HAVE NO TIME TO LOSE.

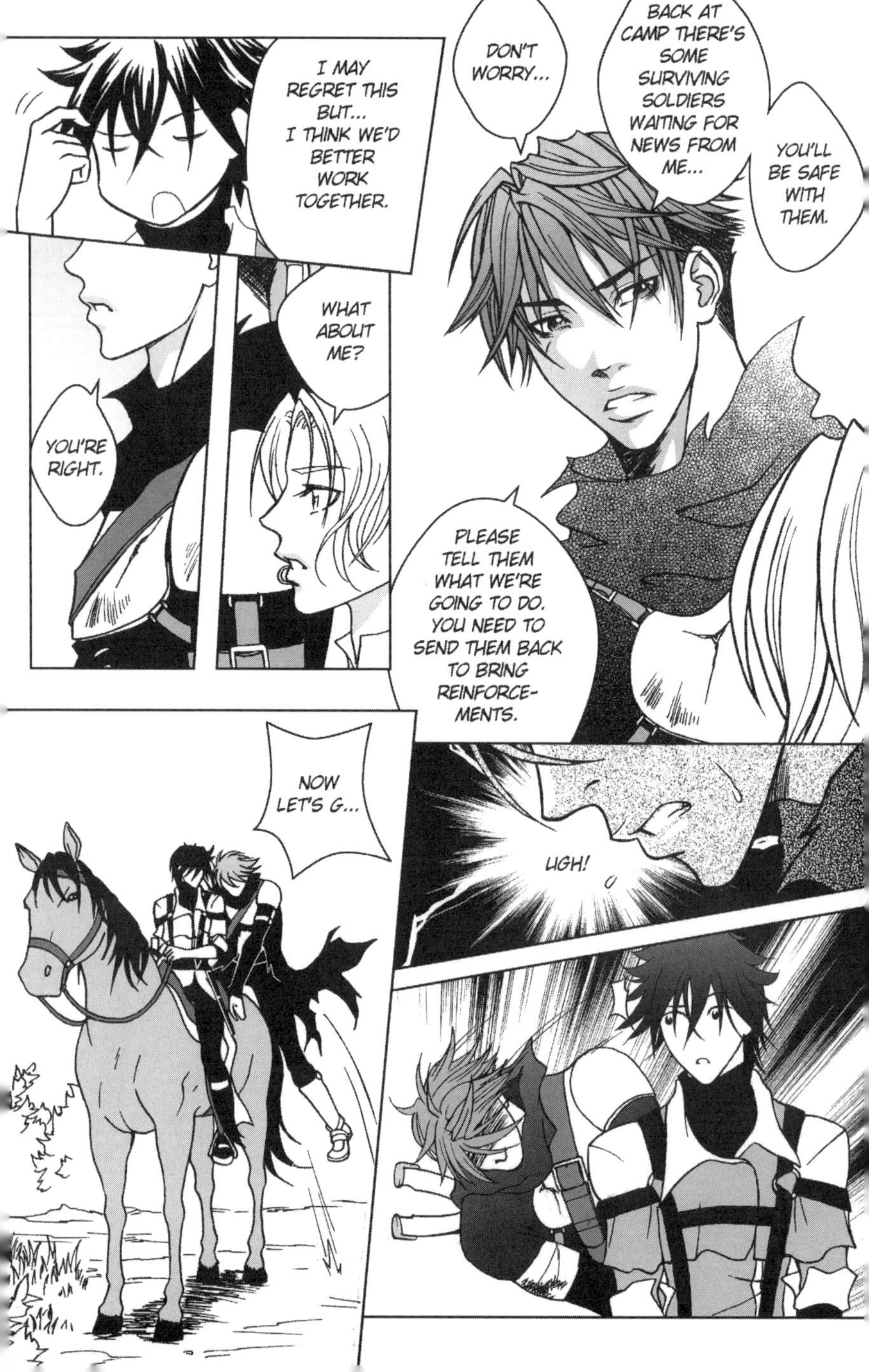

I MAY REGRET THIS BUT... I THINK WE'D BETTER WORK TOGETHER.
YOU'RE RIGHT.
WHAT ABOUT ME?
DON'T WORRY...
BACK AT CAMP THERE'S SOME SURVIVING SOLDIERS WAITING FOR NEWS FROM ME...
YOU'LL BE SAFE WITH THEM.
PLEASE TELL THEM WHAT WE'RE GOING TO DO. YOU NEED TO SEND THEM BACK TO BRING REINFORCE-MENTS.
NOW LET'S G...
UGH!

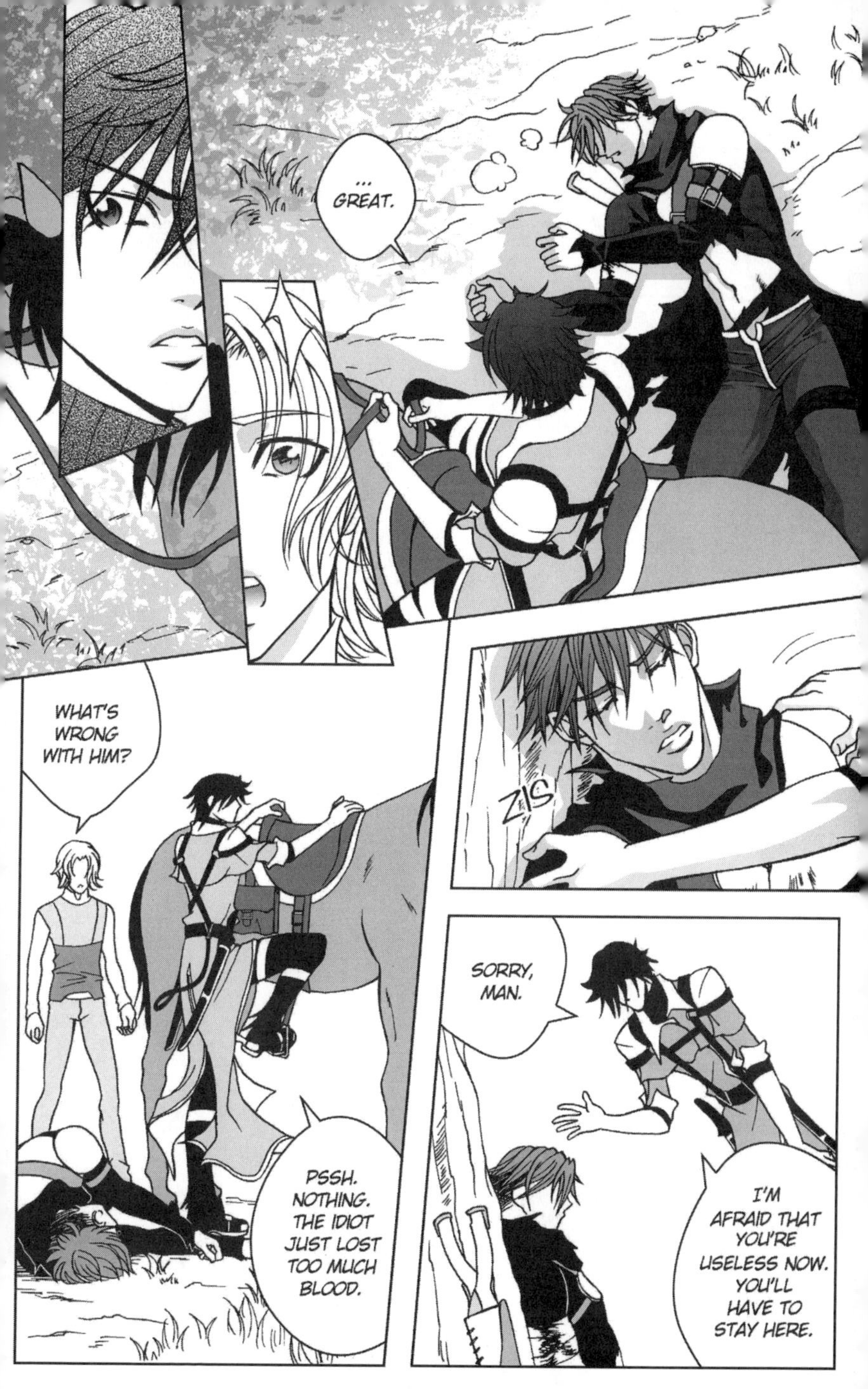
... GREAT.
WHAT'S WRONG WITH HIM?
PSSH. NOTHING. THE IDIOT JUST LOST TOO MUCH BLOOD.
ZIS
SORRY, MAN.
I'M AFRAID THAT YOU'RE USELESS NOW. YOU'LL HAVE TO STAY HERE.

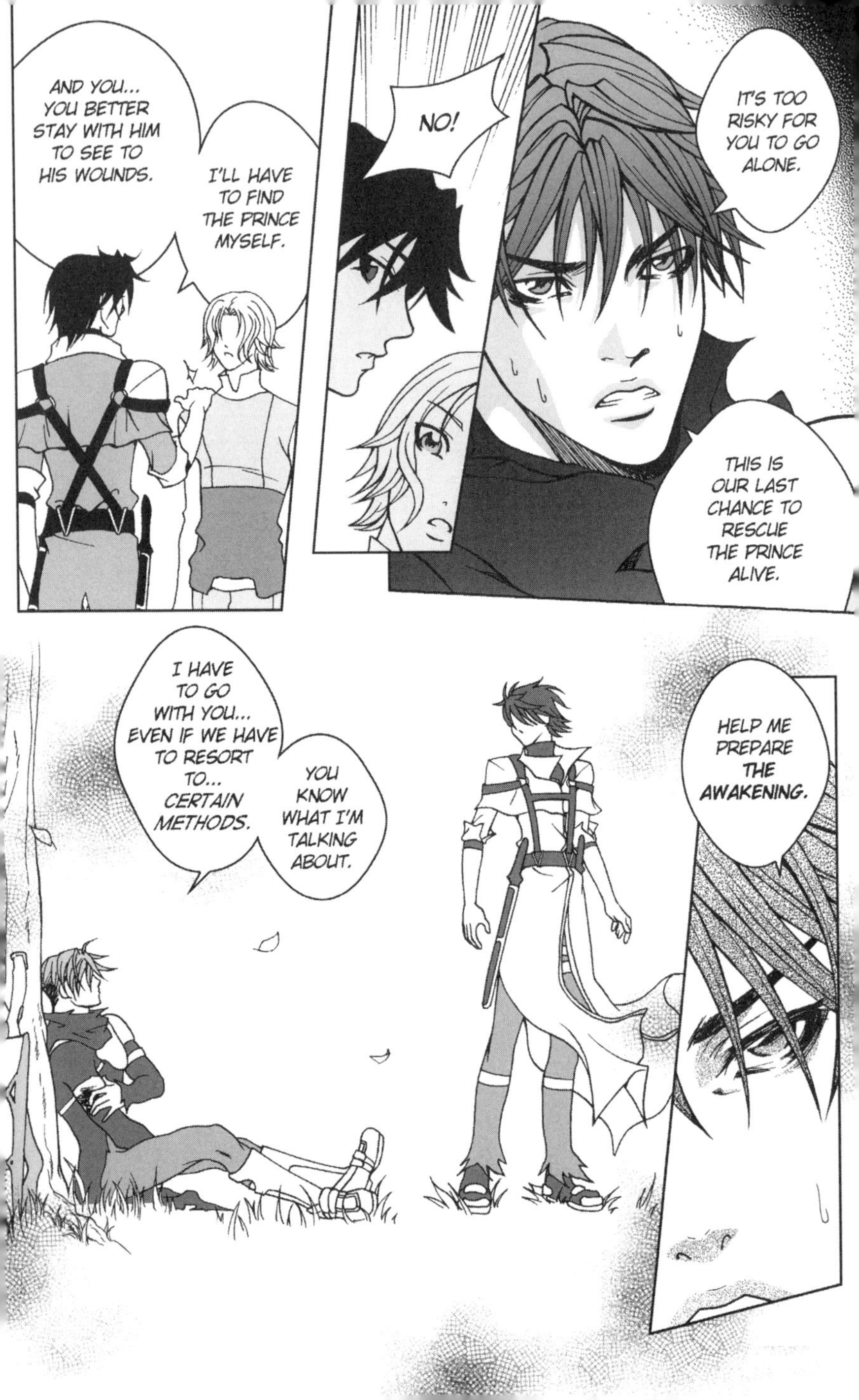
AND YOU... YOU BETTER STAY WITH HIM TO SEE TO HIS WOUNDS.
I'LL HAVE TO FIND THE PRINCE MYSELF.
NO!
IT'S TOO RISKY FOR YOU TO GO ALONE.
THIS IS OUR LAST CHANCE TO RESCUE THE PRINCE ALIVE.
I HAVE TO GO WITH YOU... EVEN IF WE HAVE TO RESORT TO... CERTAIN METHODS.
YOU KNOW WHAT I'M TALKING ABOUT.
HELP ME PREPARE THE AWAKENING.

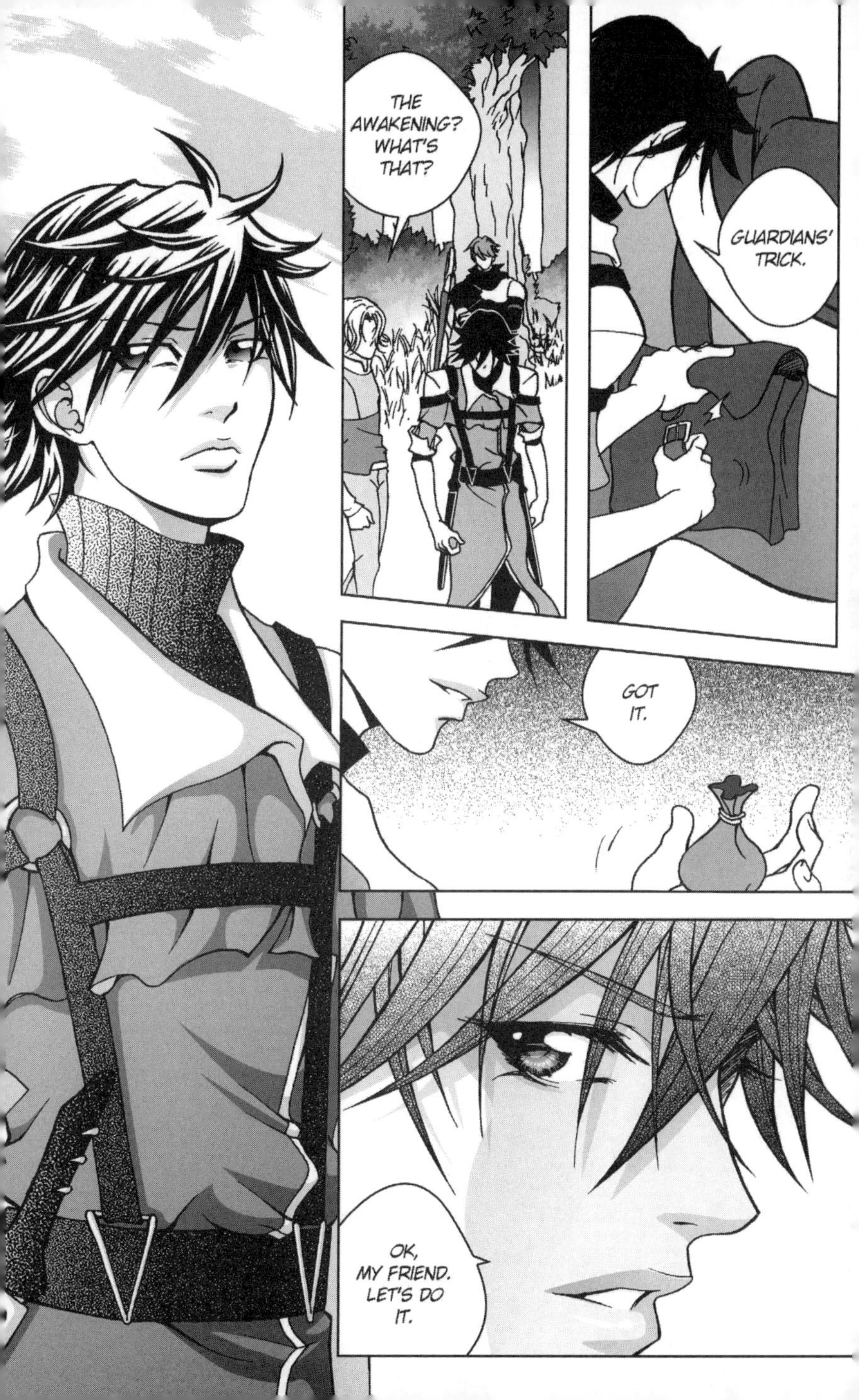
THE AWAKENING? WHAT'S THAT?
GUARDIANS' TRICK.
GOT IT.
OK, MY FRIEND. LET'S DO IT.

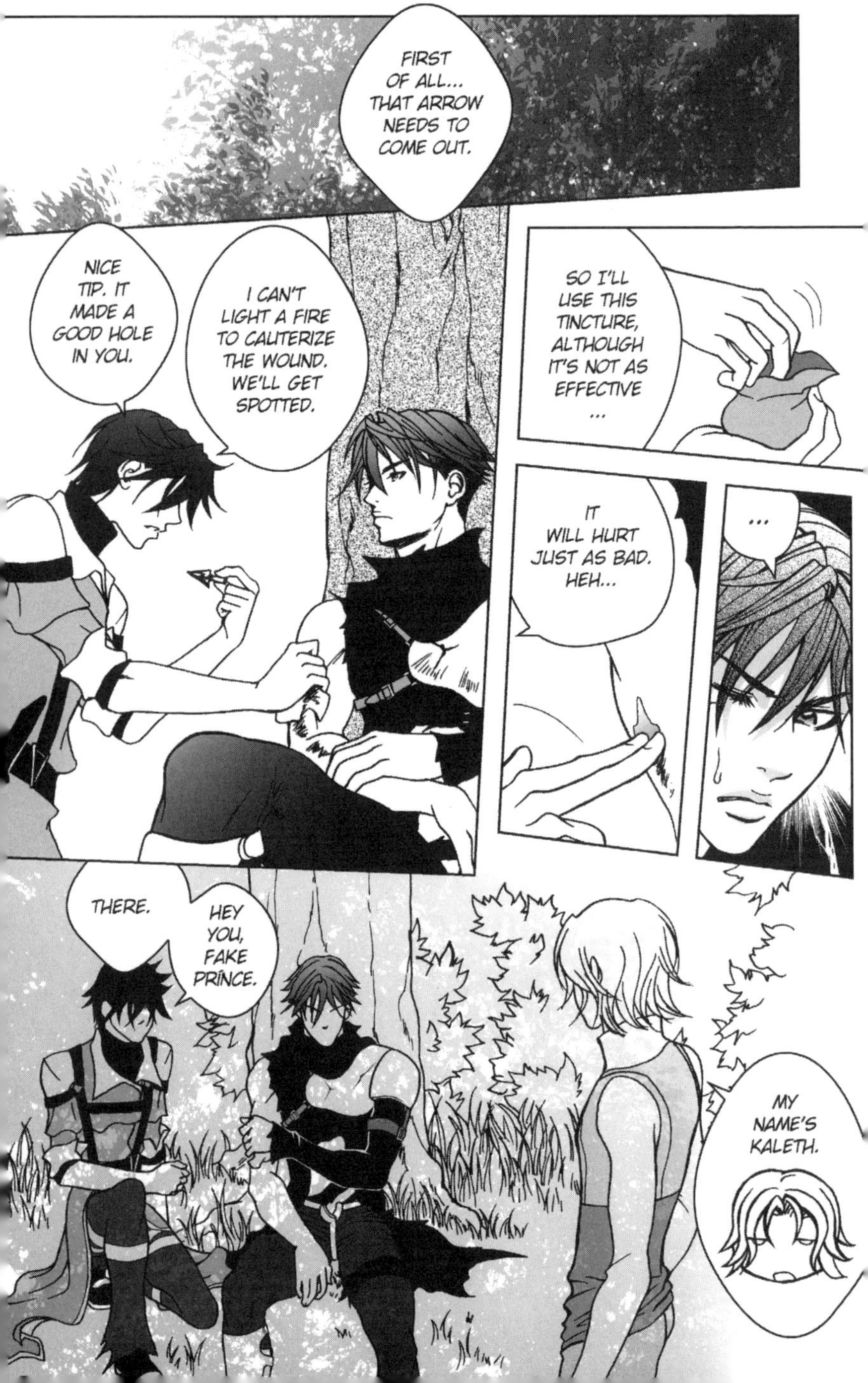
FIRST OF ALL... THAT ARROW NEEDS TO COME OUT.
I CAN'T LIGHT A FIRE TO CAUTERIZE THE WOUND. WE'LL GET SPOTTED.
NICE TIP. IT MADE A GOOD HOLE IN YOU.
SO I'LL USE THIS TINCTURE, ALTHOUGH IT'S NOT AS EFFECTIVE ...
...
IT WILL HURT JUST AS BAD. HEH...
THERE.
HEY YOU, FAKE PRINCE.
MY NAME'S KALETH.

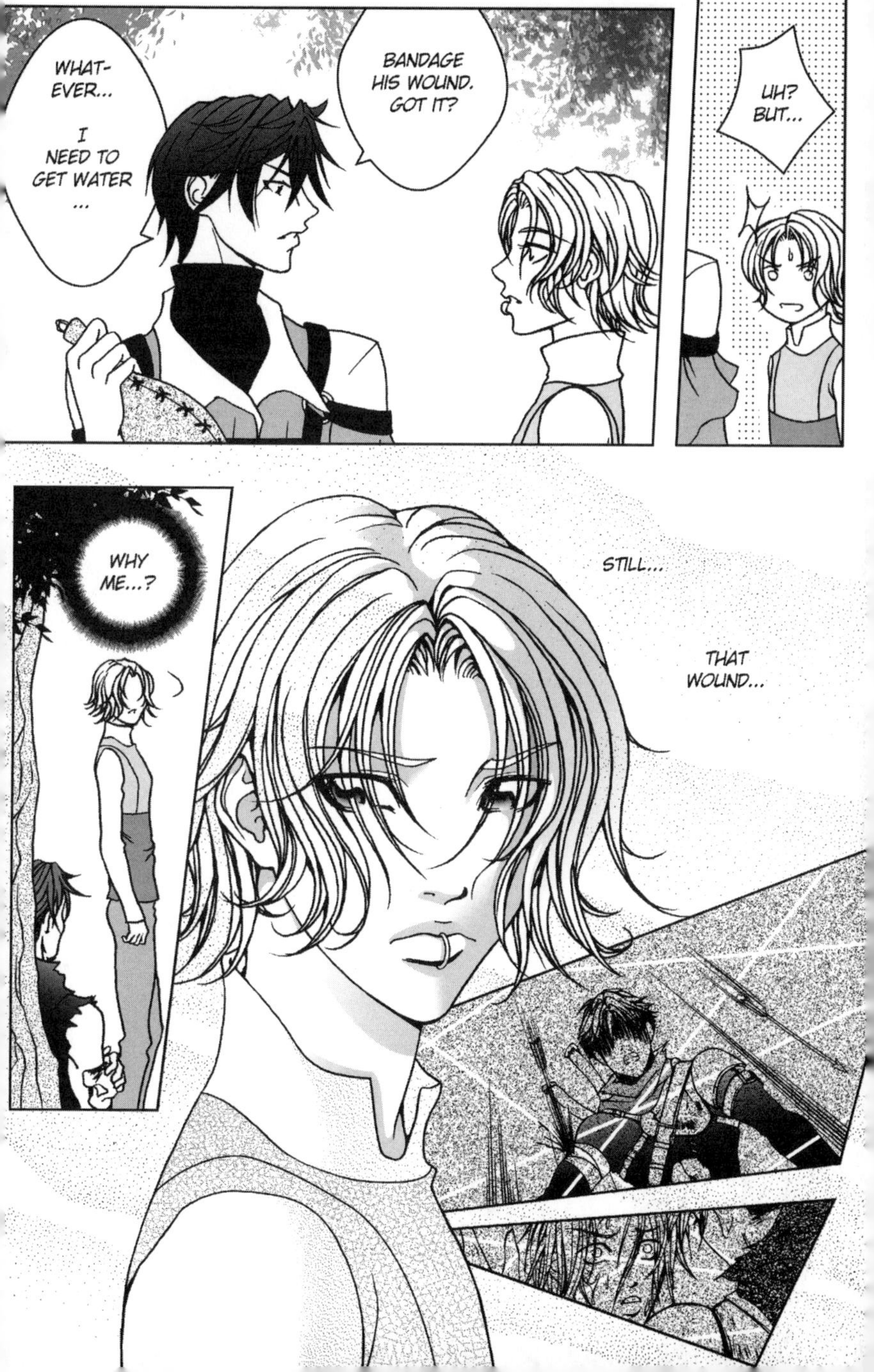
UH? BUT...
BANDAGE HIS WOUND. GOT IT?
WHAT-EVER...
I NEED TO GET WATER ...
STILL...
THAT WOUND...
WHY ME...?

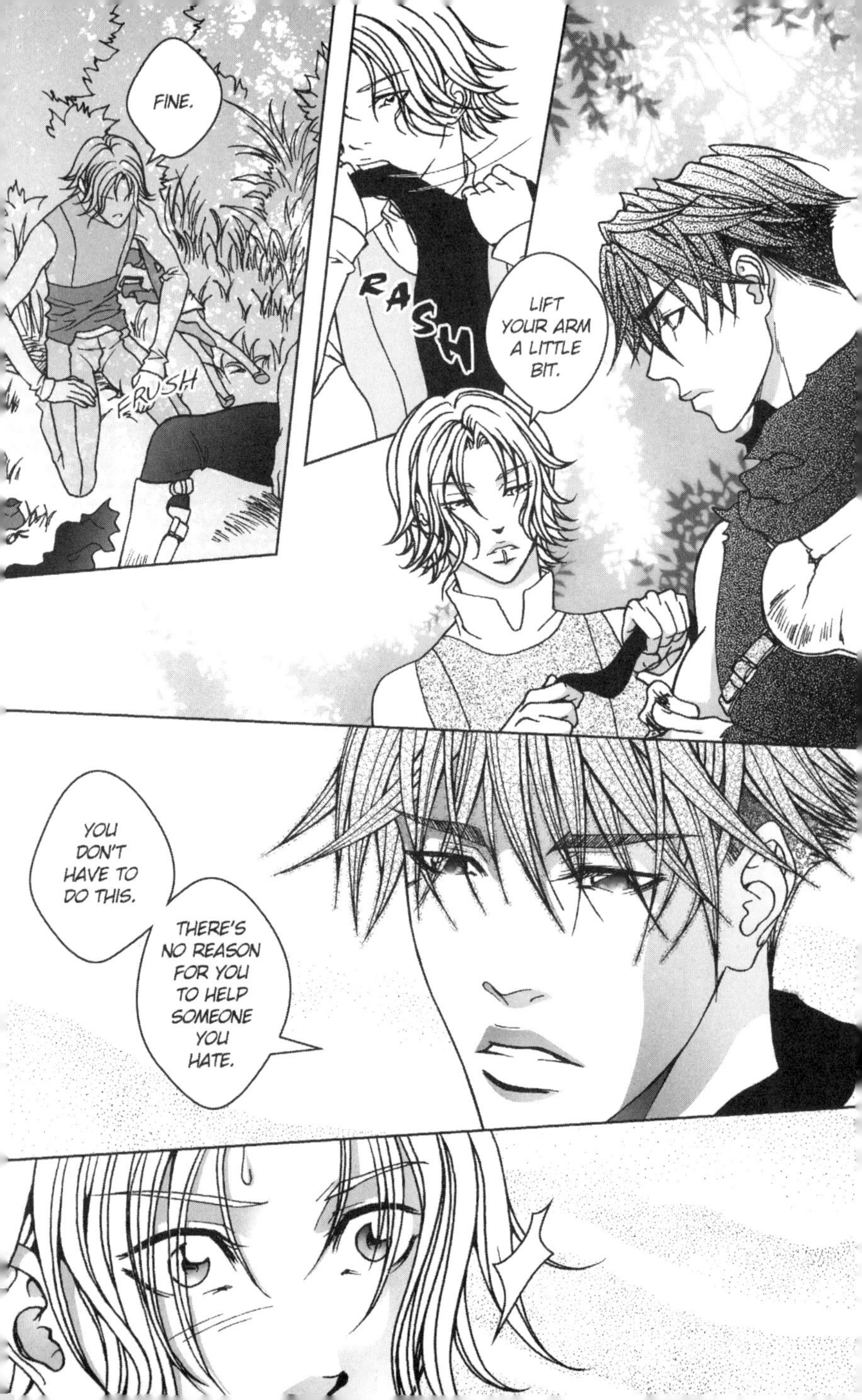
FINE.
FRUSH
RASH
LIFT YOUR ARM A LITTLE BIT.
YOU DON'T HAVE TO DO THIS.
THERE'S NO REASON FOR YOU TO HELP SOMEONE YOU HATE.

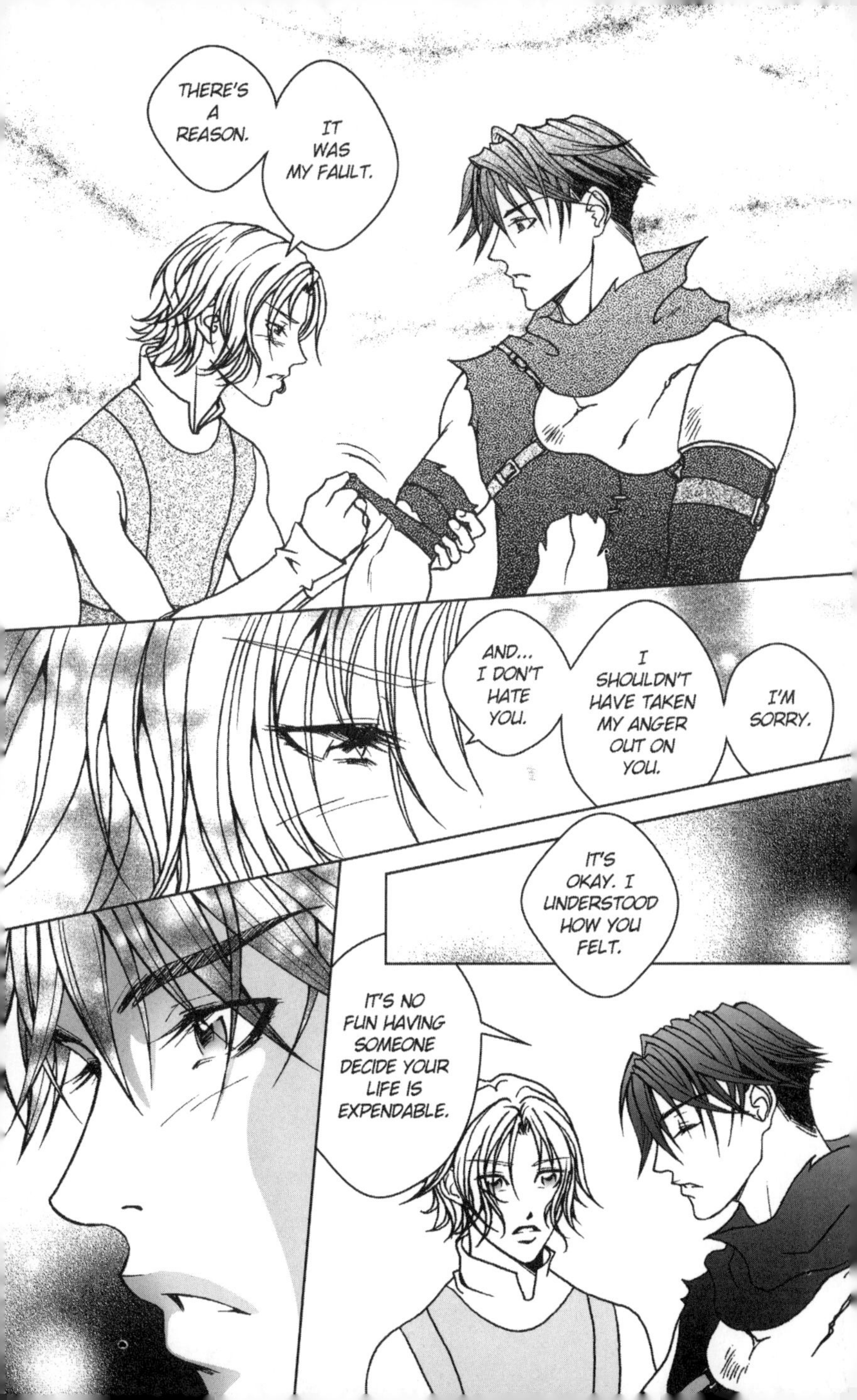
THERE'S A REASON.
IT WAS MY FAULT.
AND... I DON'T HATE YOU.
I SHOULDN'T HAVE TAKEN MY ANGER OUT ON YOU.
I'M SORRY.
IT'S OKAY. I UNDERSTOOD HOW YOU FELT.
IT'S NO FUN HAVING SOMEONE DECIDE YOUR LIFE IS EXPENDABLE.

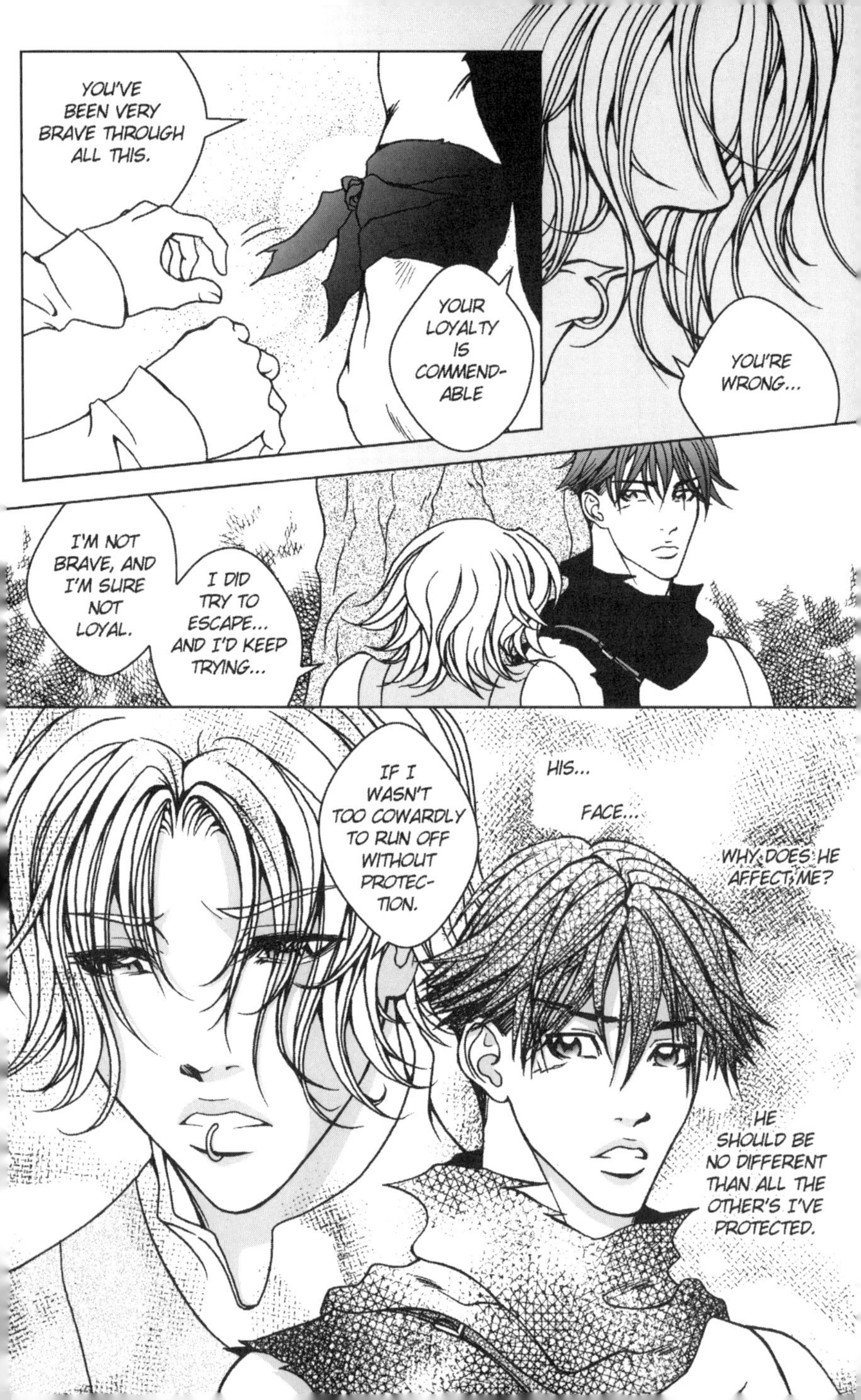
YOU'VE BEEN VERY BRAVE THROUGH ALL THIS.
YOUR LOYALTY IS COMMEND-ABLE
YOU'RE WRONG...
I'M NOT BRAVE, AND I'M SURE NOT LOYAL.
I DID TRY TO ESCAPE... AND I'D KEEP TRYING...
IF I WASN'T TOO COWARDLY TO RUN OFF WITHOUT PROTEC-TION.
HIS...
FACE...
WHY DOES HE AFFECT ME?
HE SHOULD BE NO DIFFERENT THAN ALL THE OTHER'S I'VE PROTECTED.

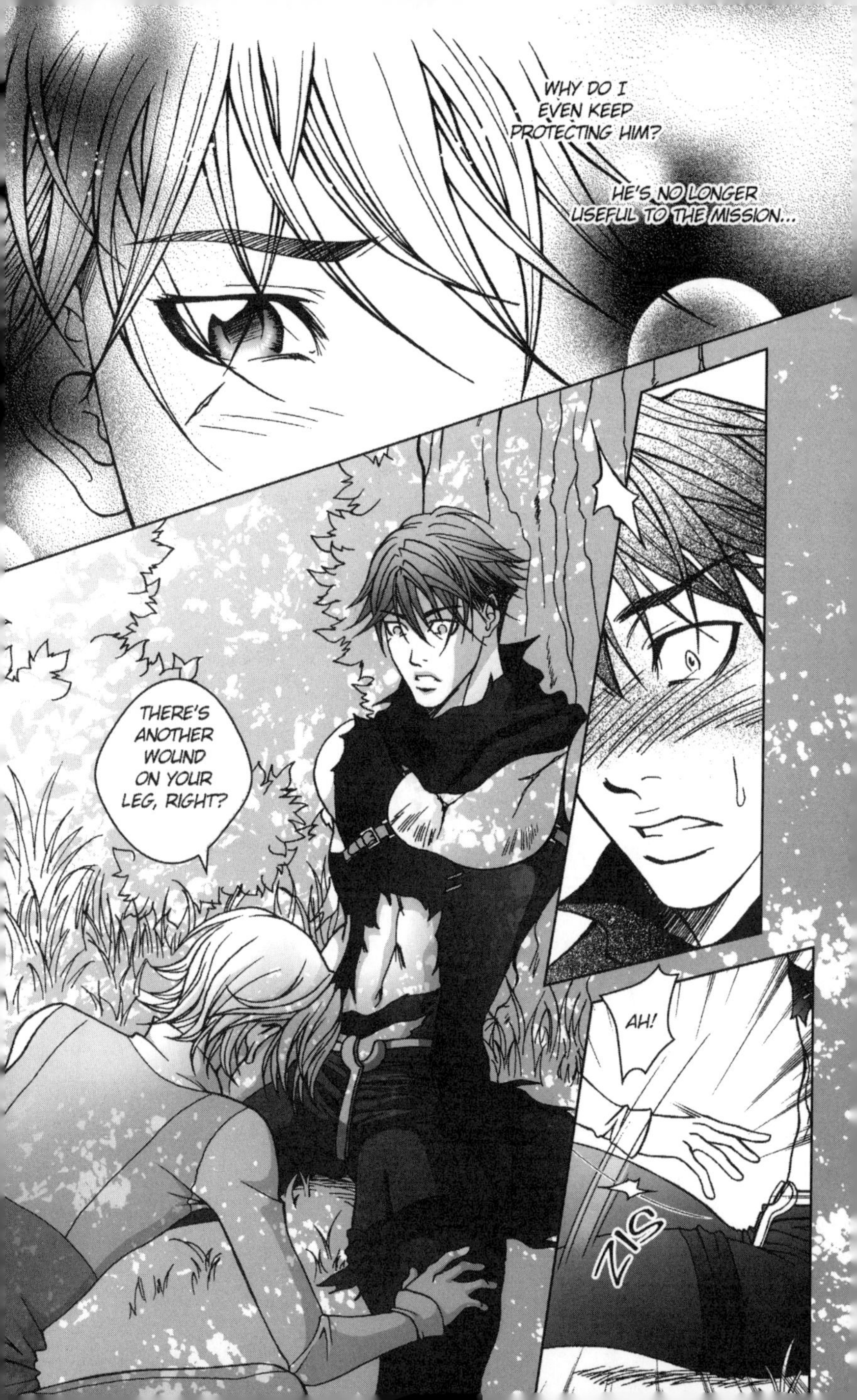
WHY DO I EVEN KEEP PROTECTING HIM?
HE'S NO LONGER USEFUL TO THE MISSION...
THERE'S ANOTHER WOUND ON YOUR LEG, RIGHT?
AH!
ZIS

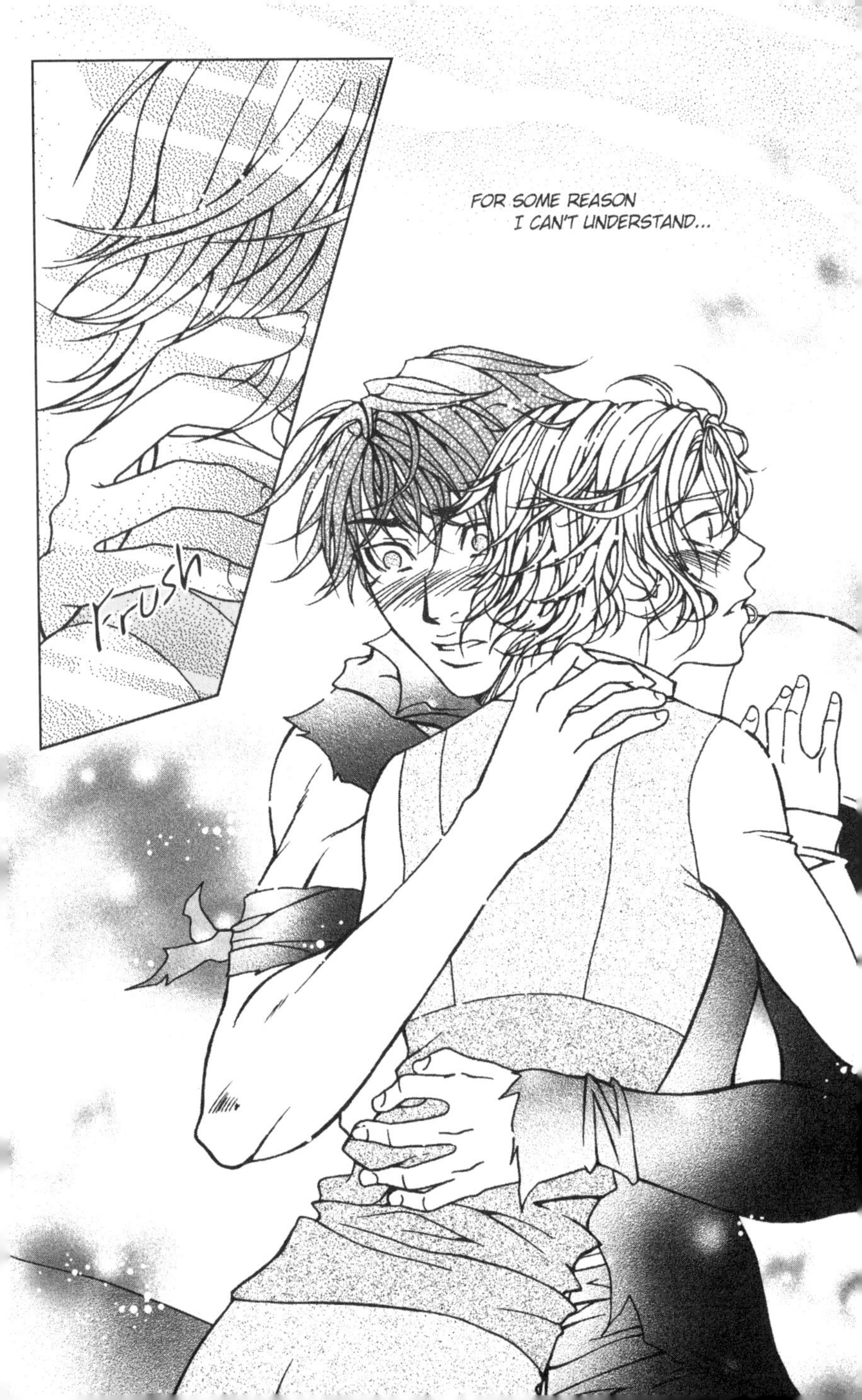

FOR SOME REASON
I CAN'T UNDERSTAND...
KRUSH

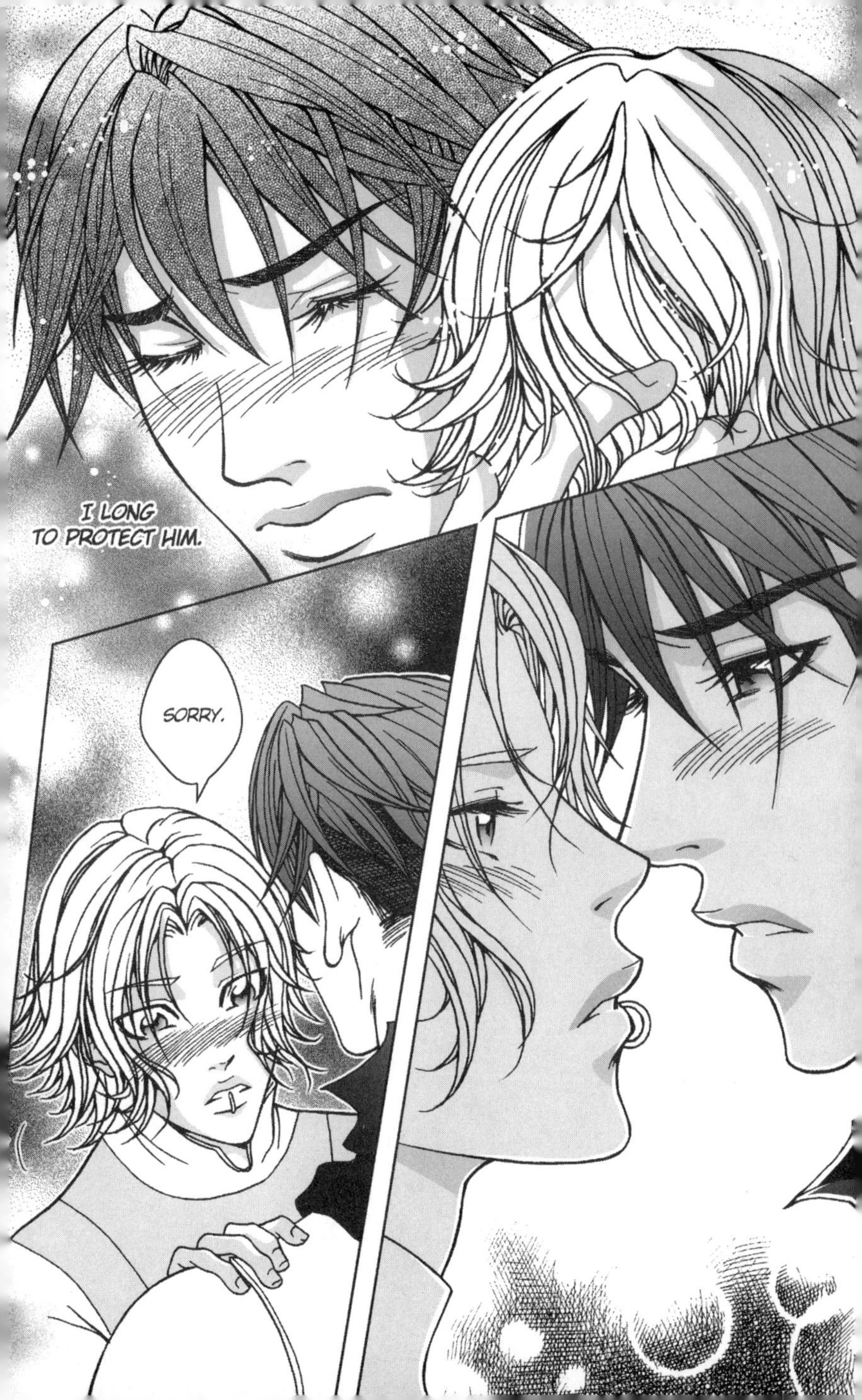
I LONG
TO PROTECT HIM.
SORRY.

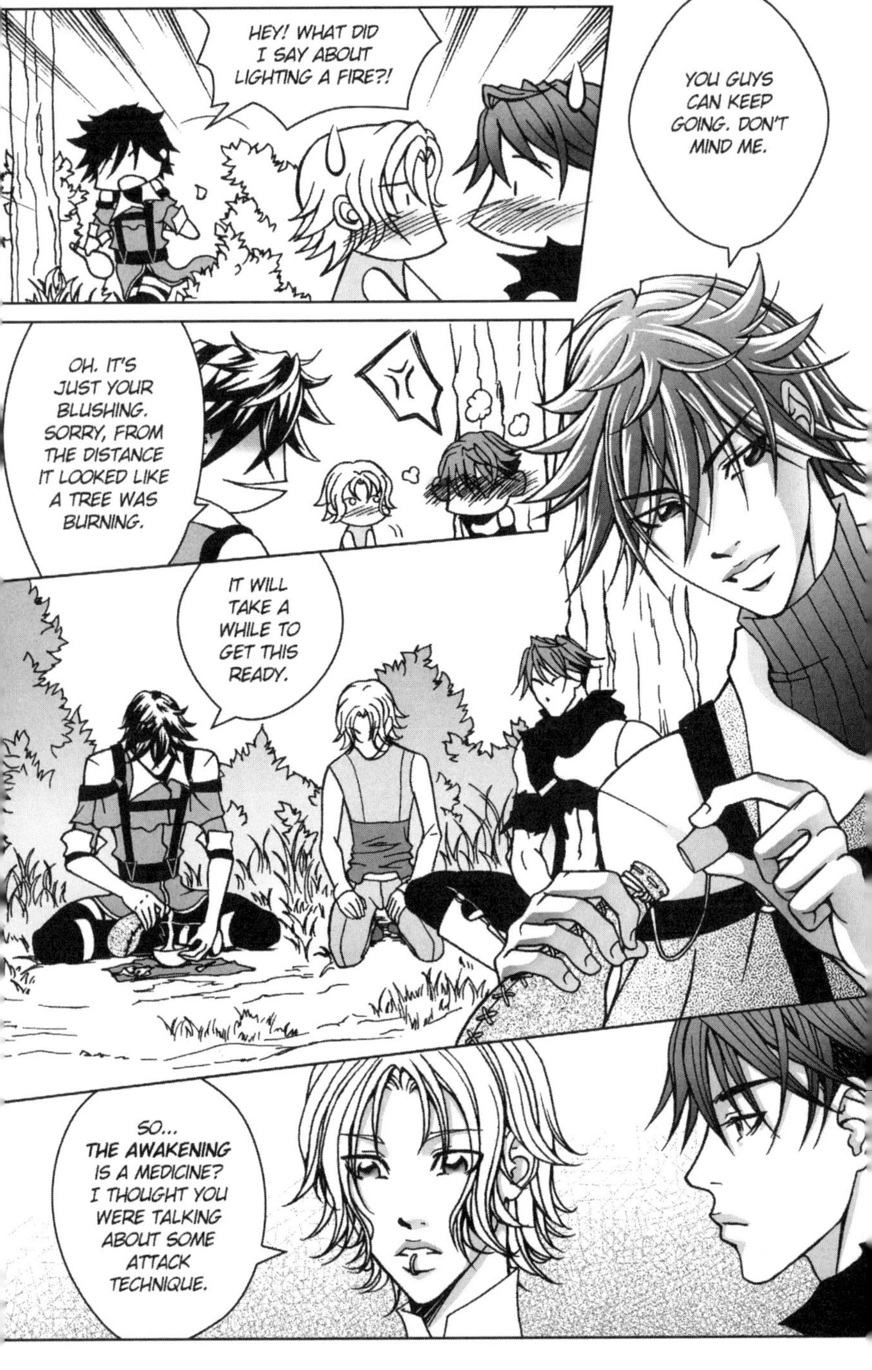

HEY! WHAT DID I SAY ABOUT LIGHTING A FIRE?!
YOU GUYS CAN KEEP GOING. DON'T MIND ME.
OH. IT'S JUST YOUR BLUSHING. SORRY, FROM THE DISTANCE IT LOOKED LIKE A TREE WAS BURNING.
IT WILL TAKE A WHILE TO GET THIS READY.
SO... THE AWAKENING IS A MEDICINE? I THOUGHT YOU WERE TALKING ABOUT SOME ATTACK TECHNIQUE.

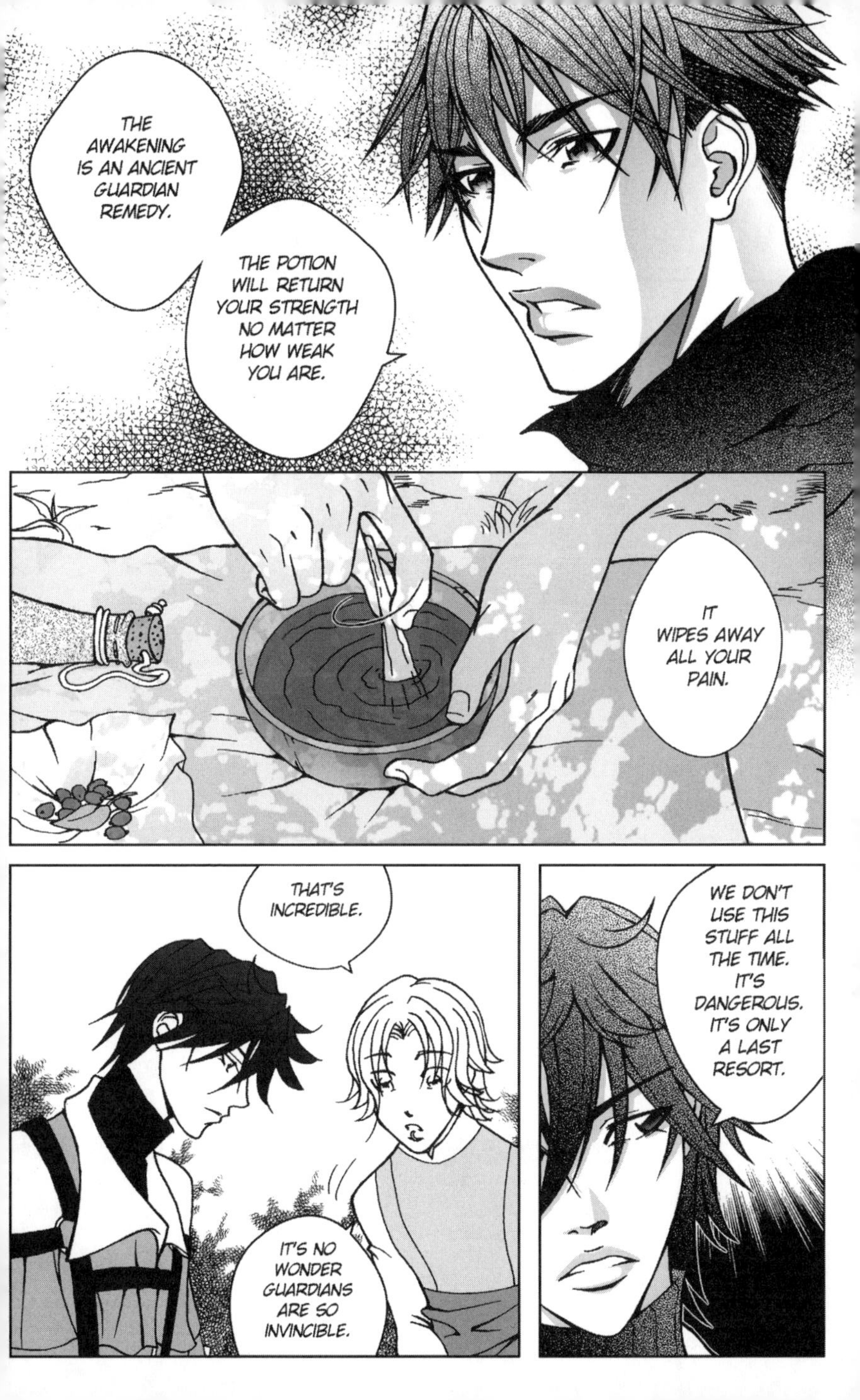
THE AWAKENING IS AN ANCIENT GUARDIAN REMEDY.
THE POTION WILL RETURN YOUR STRENGTH NO MATTER HOW WEAK YOU ARE.
IT WIPES AWAY ALL YOUR PAIN.
THAT'S INCREDIBLE.
IT'S NO WONDER GUARDIANS ARE SO INVINCIBLE.
WE DON'T USE THIS STUFF ALL THE TIME. IT'S DANGEROUS. IT'S ONLY A LAST RESORT.

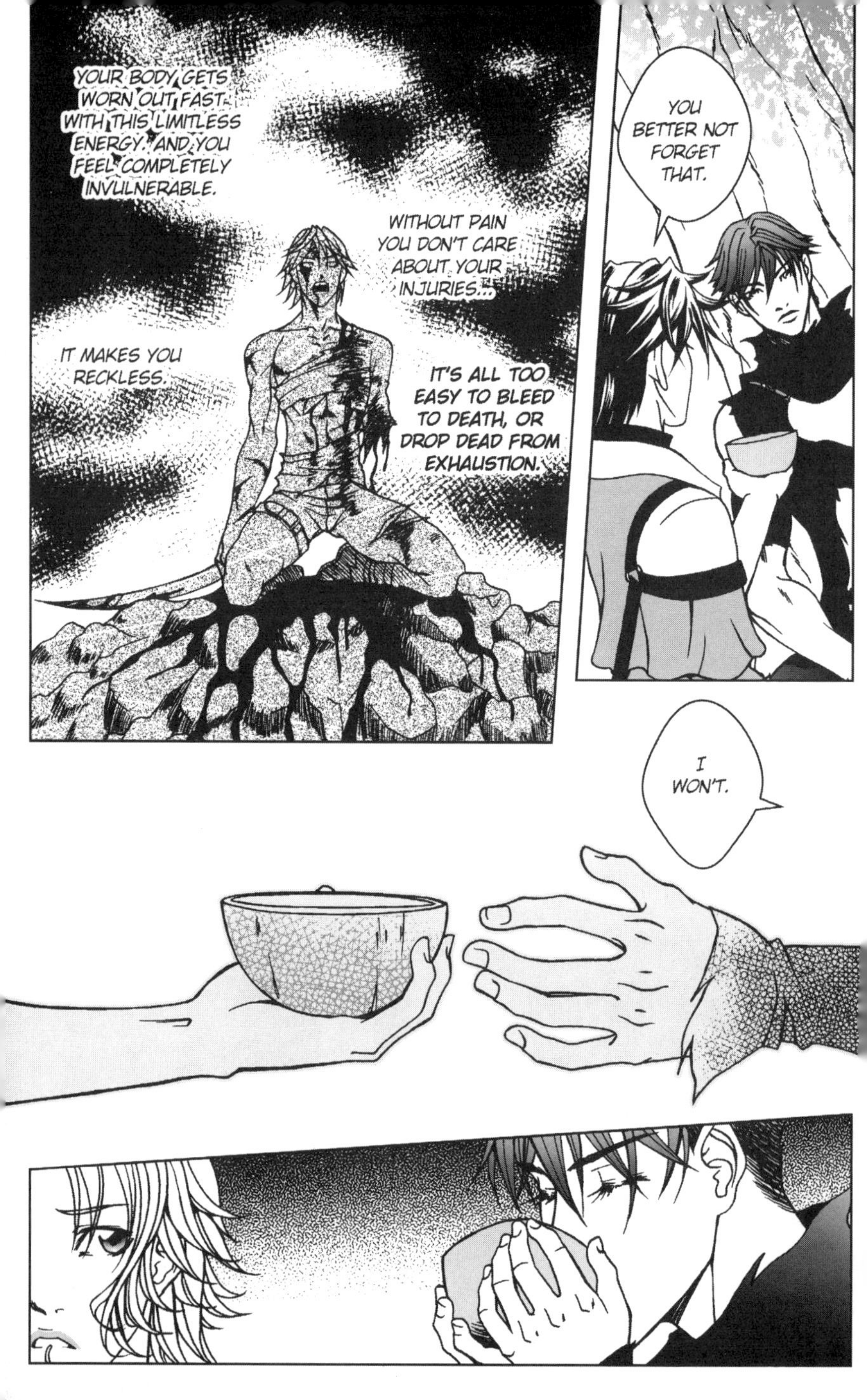
YOU BETTER NOT FORGET THAT.
YOUR BODY GETS WORN OUT FAST WITH THIS LIMITLESS ENERGY. AND YOU FEEL COMPLETELY INVULNERABLE.
WITHOUT PAIN YOU DON'T CARE ABOUT YOUR INJURIES...
IT MAKES YOU RECKLESS.
IT'S ALL TOO EASY TO BLEED TO DEATH, OR DROP DEAD FROM EXHAUSTION.
I WON'T.

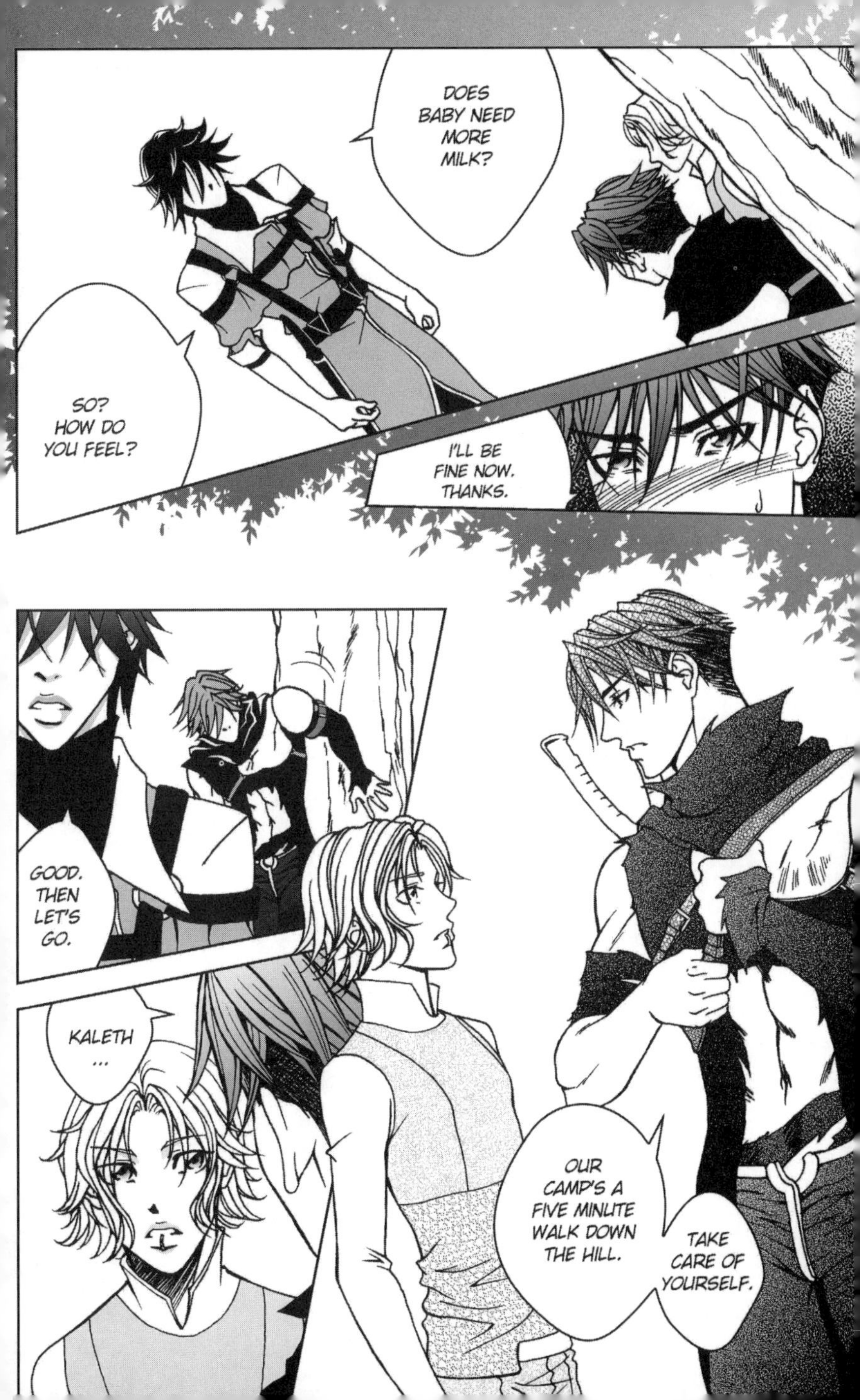
DOES BABY NEED MORE MILK?
SO? HOW DO YOU FEEL?
I'LL BE FINE NOW. THANKS.
GOOD. THEN LET'S GO.
KALETH ...
OUR CAMP'S A FIVE MINUTE WALK DOWN THE HILL.
TAKE CARE OF YOURSELF.

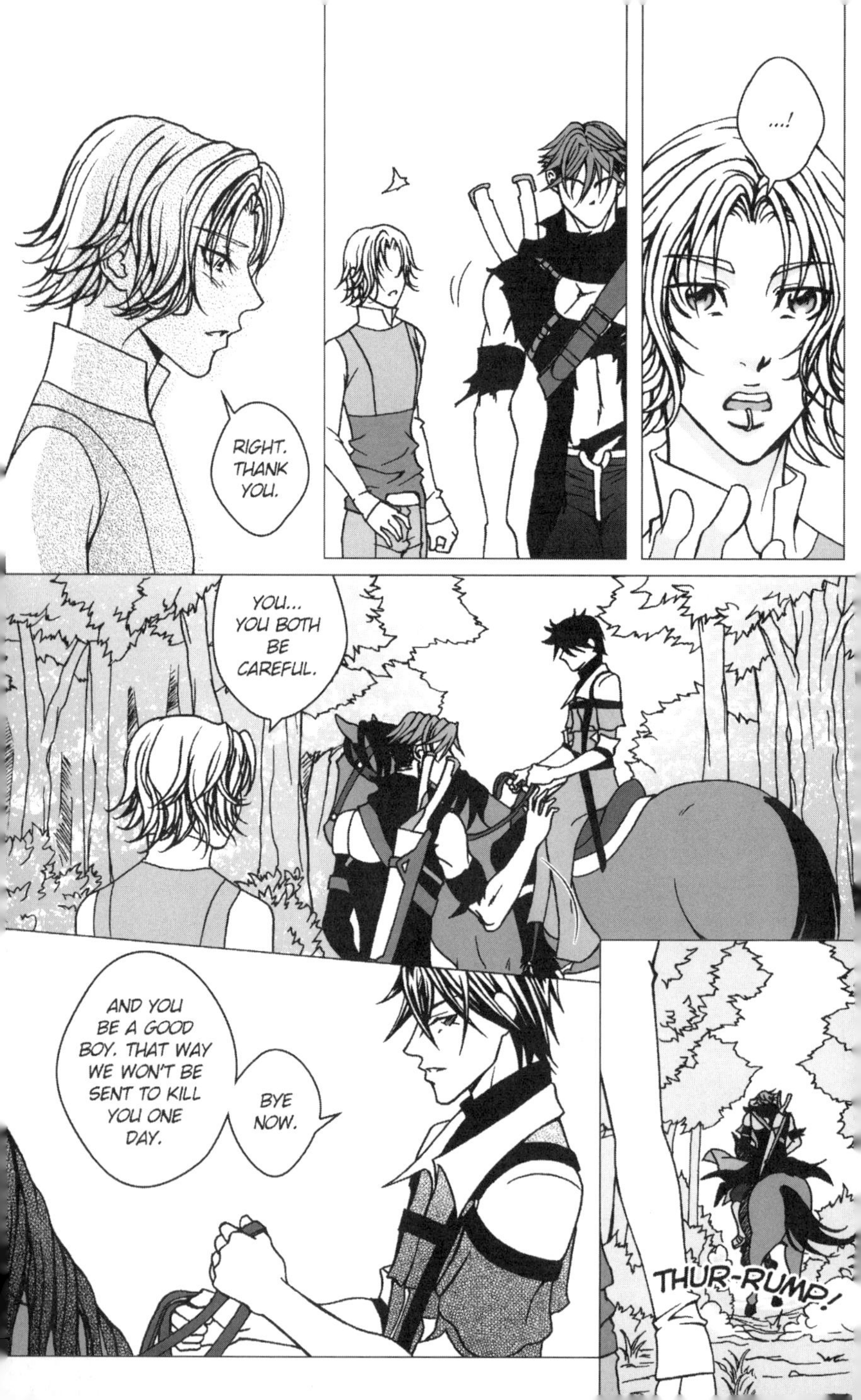
RIGHT. THANK YOU.
...!
YOU... YOU BOTH BE CAREFUL.
AND YOU BE A GOOD BOY. THAT WAY WE WON'T BE SENT TO KILL YOU ONE DAY.
BYE NOW.
THUR-RUMP!

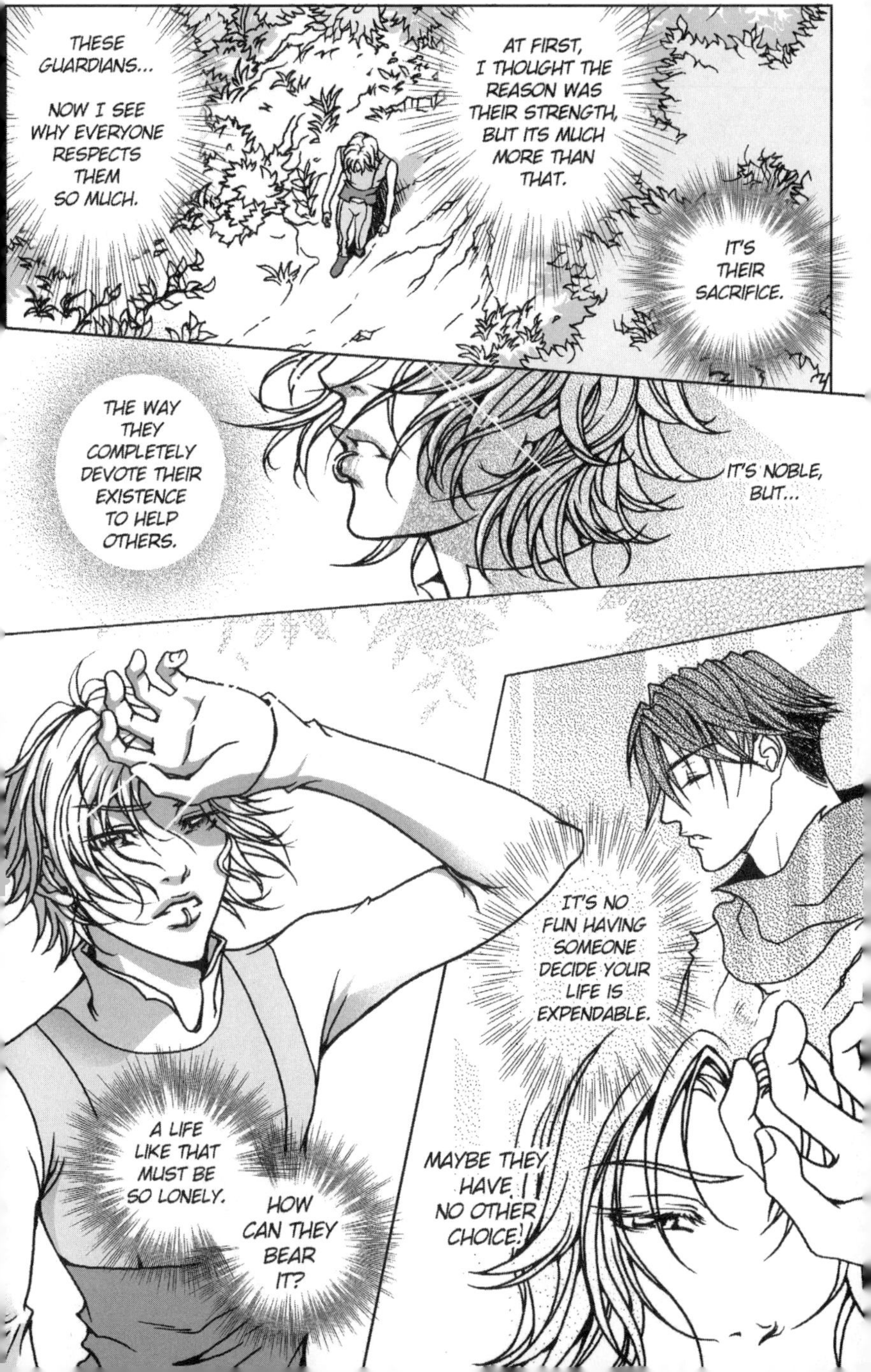
THESE GUARDIANS...
NOW I SEE WHY EVERYONE RESPECTS THEM SO MUCH.
AT FIRST, I THOUGHT THE REASON WAS THEIR STRENGTH, BUT ITS MUCH MORE THAN THAT.
IT'S THEIR SACRIFICE.
THE WAY THEY COMPLETELY DEVOTE THEIR EXISTENCE TO HELP OTHERS.
IT'S NOBLE, BUT...
A LIFE LIKE THAT MUST BE SO LONELY.
HOW CAN THEY BEAR IT?
IT'S NO FUN HAVING SOMEONE DECIDE YOUR LIFE IS EXPENDABLE.
MAYBE THEY HAVE NO OTHER CHOICE!

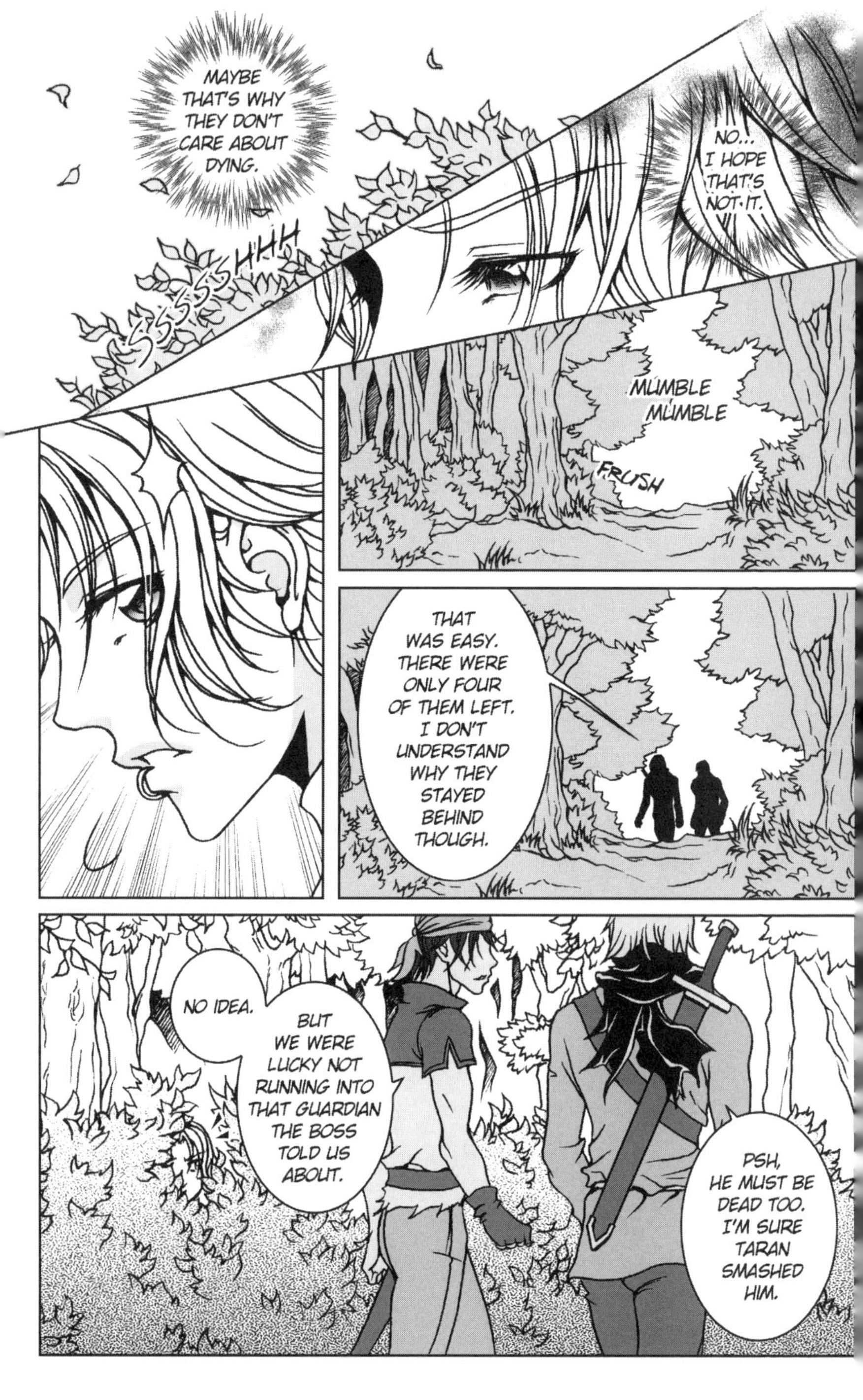
MAYBE THAT'S WHY THEY DON'T CARE ABOUT DYING.
NO... I HOPE THAT'S NOT IT.
SSSSSHHH
MUMBLE MUMBLE
FRUSH
THAT WAS EASY. THERE WERE ONLY FOUR OF THEM LEFT. I DON'T UNDERSTAND WHY THEY STAYED BEHIND THOUGH.
NO IDEA.
BUT WE WERE LUCKY NOT RUNNING INTO THAT GUARDIAN THE BOSS TOLD US ABOUT.
PSH, HE MUST BE DEAD TOO. I'M SURE TARAN SMASHED HIM.

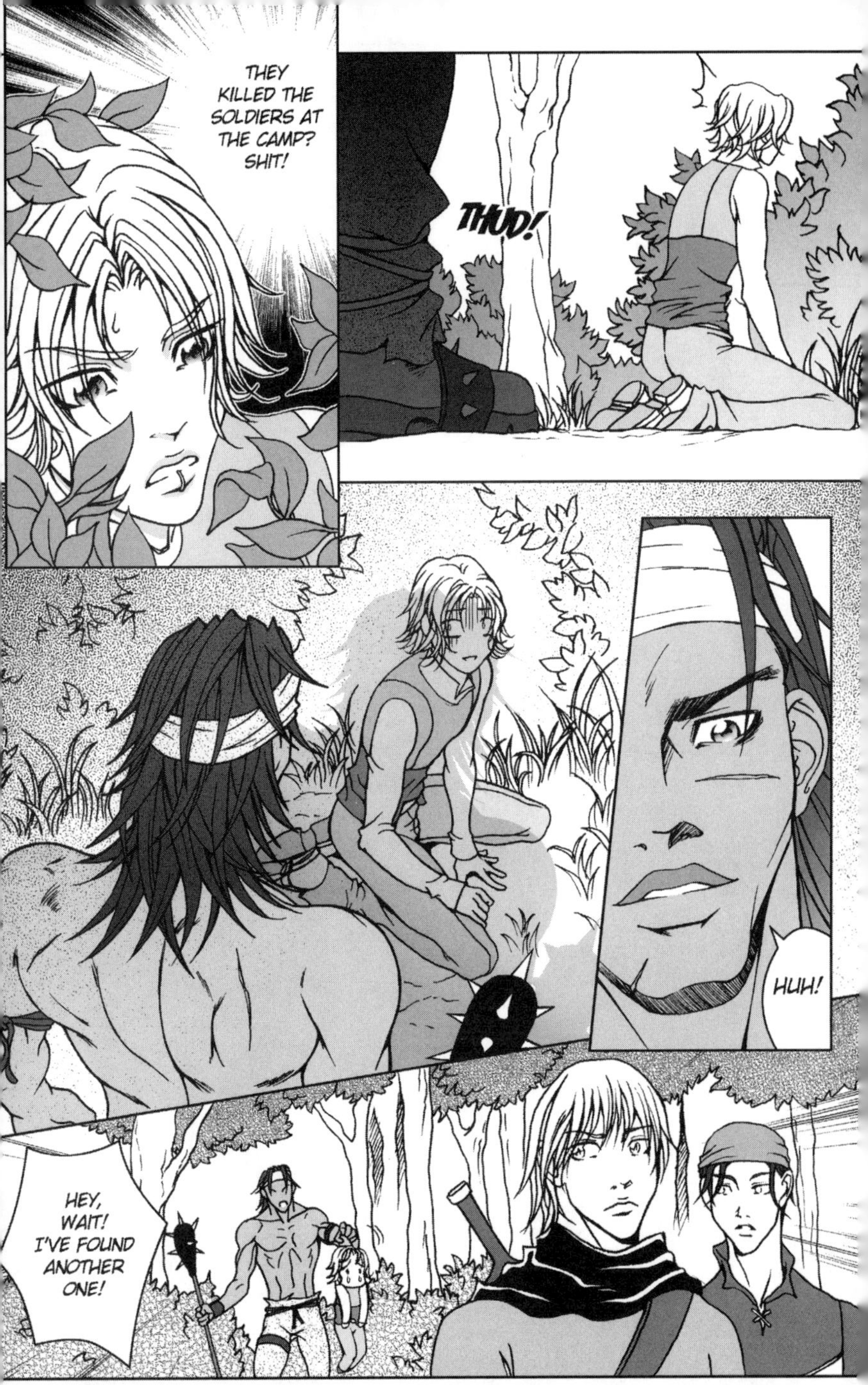
THEY KILLED THE SOLDIERS AT THE CAMP? SHIT!
THUD!
HUH!
HEY, WAIT! I'VE FOUND ANOTHER ONE!

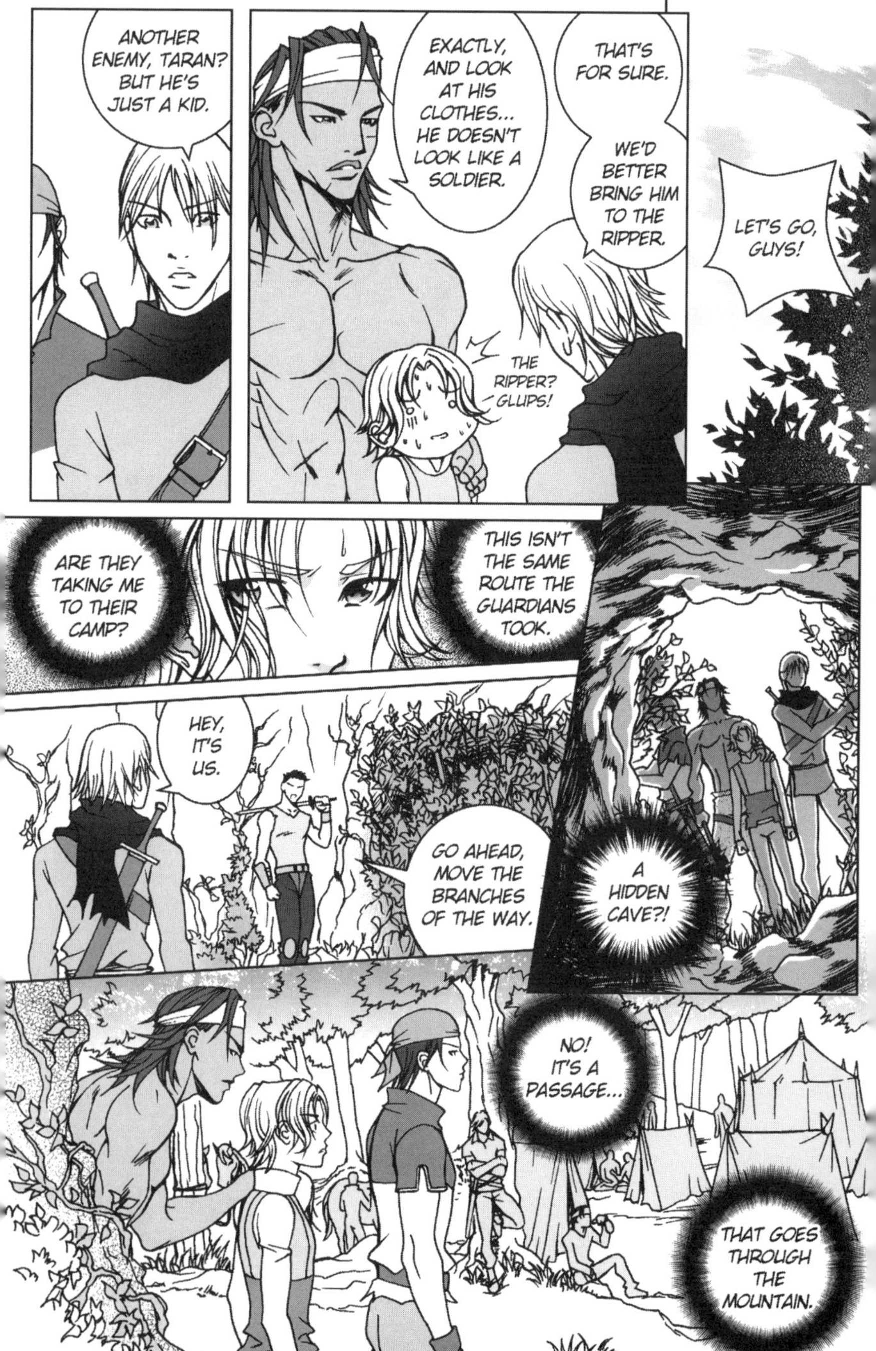
ANOTHER ENEMY, TARAN? BUT HE'S JUST A KID.
EXACTLY, AND LOOK AT HIS CLOTHES... HE DOESN'T LOOK LIKE A SOLDIER.
THAT'S FOR SURE.
WE'D BETTER BRING HIM TO THE RIPPER.
THE RIPPER? GLUPS!
LET'S GO, GUYS!
ARE THEY TAKING ME TO THEIR CAMP?
THIS ISN'T THE SAME ROUTE THE GUARDIANS TOOK.
HEY, IT'S US.
GO AHEAD, MOVE THE BRANCHES OF THE WAY.
A HIDDEN CAVE?!
NO! IT'S A PASSAGE...
THAT GOES THROUGH THE MOUNTAIN.

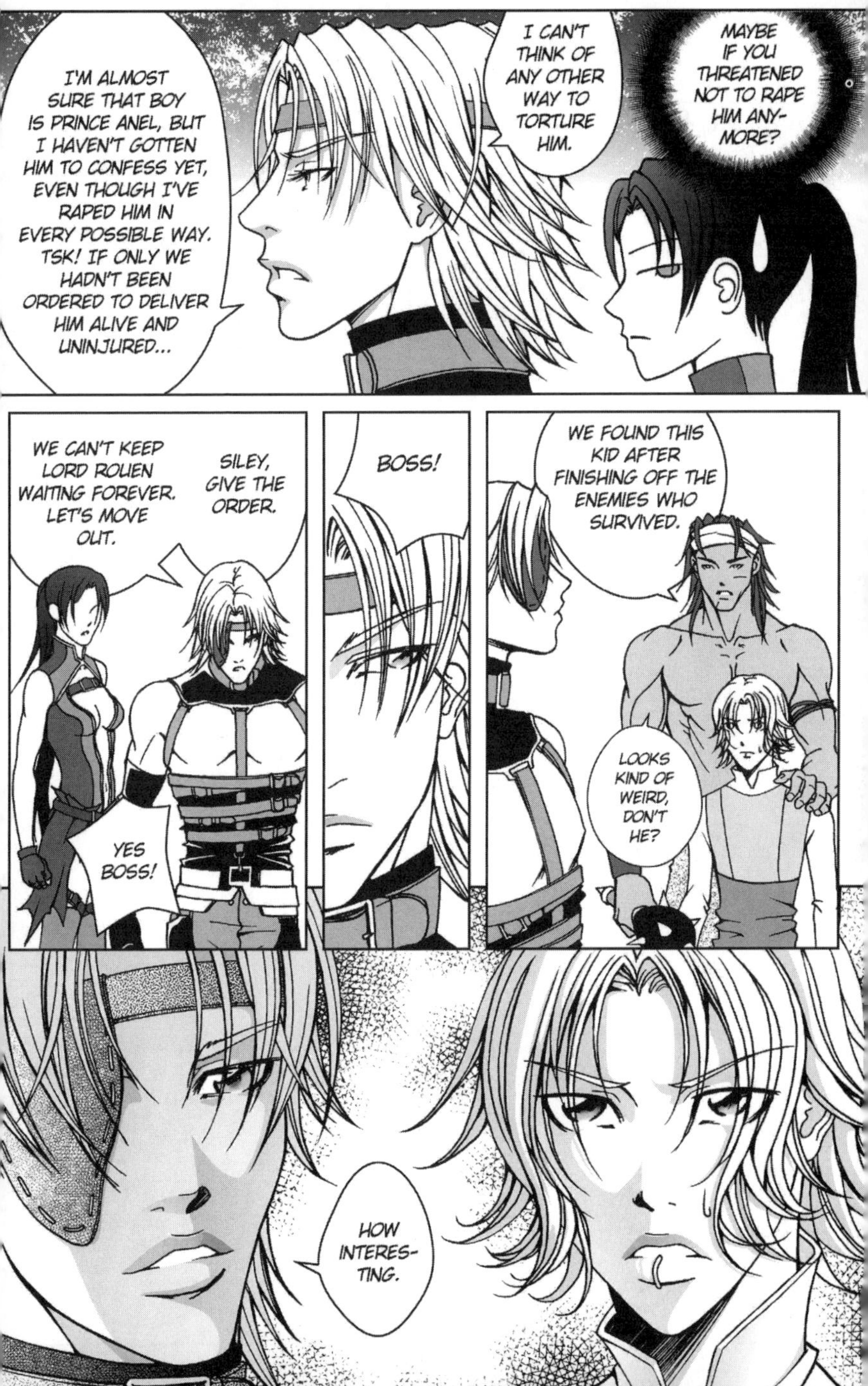
I'M ALMOST SURE THAT BOY IS PRINCE ANEL, BUT I HAVEN'T GOTTEN HIM TO CONFESS YET, EVEN THOUGH I'VE RAPED HIM IN EVERY POSSIBLE WAY. TSK! IF ONLY WE HADN'T BEEN ORDERED TO DELIVER HIM ALIVE AND UNINJURED...
I CAN'T THINK OF ANY OTHER WAY TO TORTURE HIM.
MAYBE IF YOU THREATENED NOT TO RAPE HIM ANY-MORE?
WE CAN'T KEEP LORD ROUEN WAITING FOREVER. LET'S MOVE OUT.
SILEY, GIVE THE ORDER.
YES BOSS!
BOSS!
WE FOUND THIS KID AFTER FINISHING OFF THE ENEMIES WHO SURVIVED.
LOOKS KIND OF WEIRD, DON'T HE?
HOW INTERES-TING.

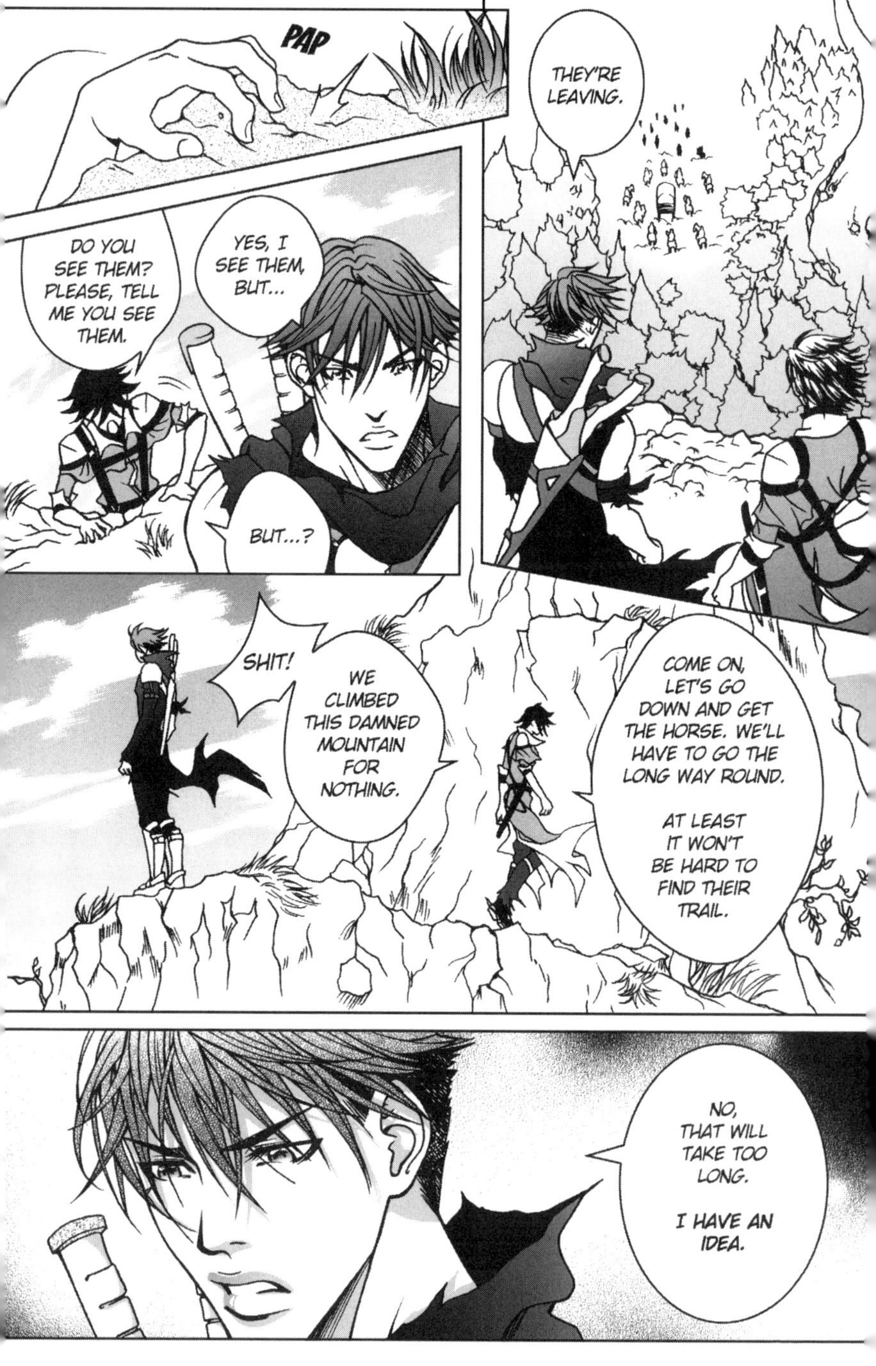
PAP
THEY'RE LEAVING.
DO YOU SEE THEM? PLEASE, TELL ME YOU SEE THEM.
YES, I SEE THEM, BUT...
BUT...?
SHIT!
WE CLIMBED THIS DAMNED MOUNTAIN FOR NOTHING.
COME ON, LET'S GO DOWN AND GET THE HORSE. WE'LL HAVE TO GO THE LONG WAY ROUND.
AT LEAST IT WON'T BE HARD TO FIND THEIR TRAIL.
NO, THAT WILL TAKE TOO LONG.
I HAVE AN IDEA.

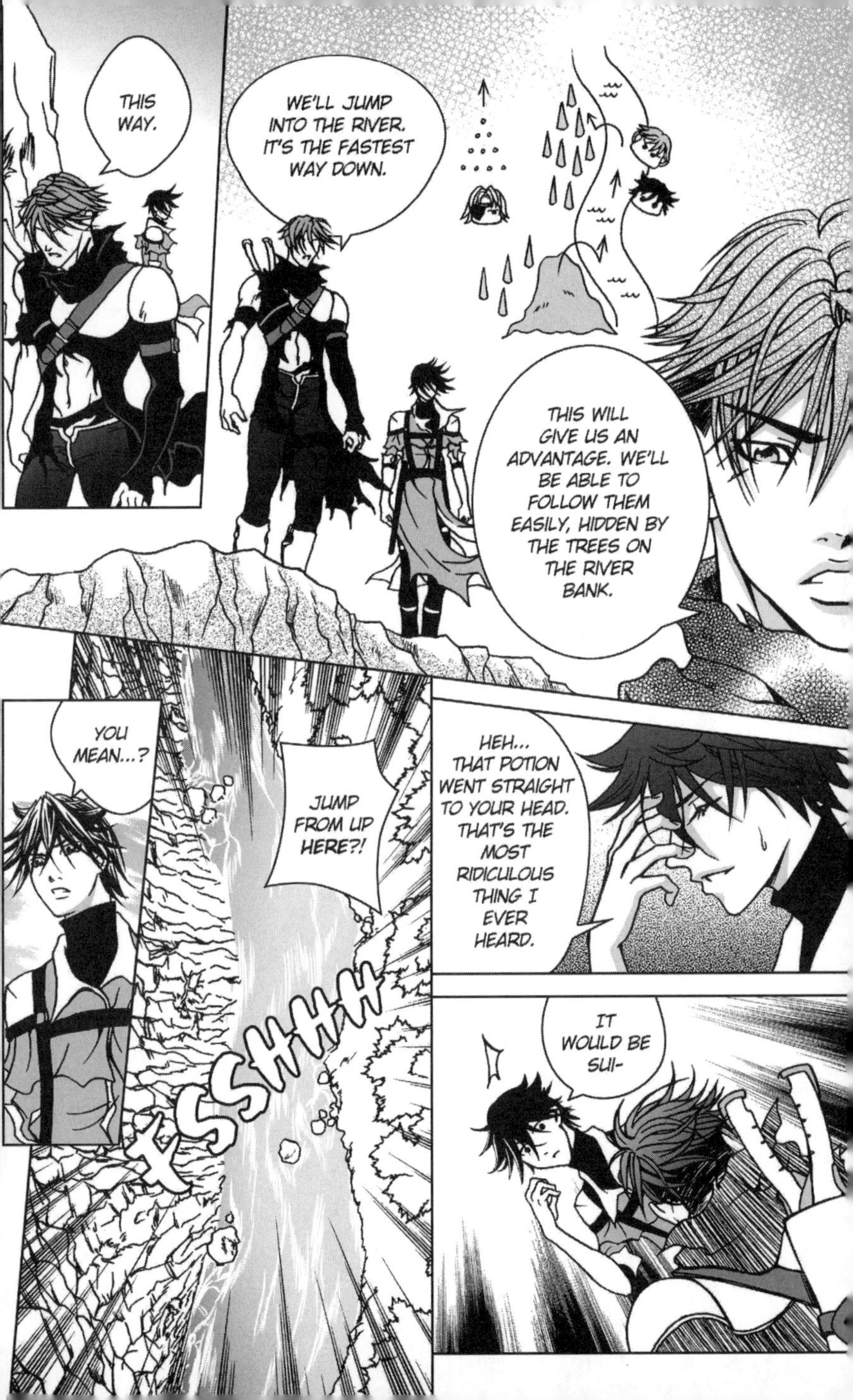
THIS WAY.
WE'LL JUMP INTO THE RIVER. IT'S THE FASTEST WAY DOWN.
THIS WILL GIVE US AN ADVANTAGE. WE'LL BE ABLE TO FOLLOW THEM EASILY, HIDDEN BY THE TREES ON THE RIVER BANK.
YOU MEAN...?
JUMP FROM UP HERE?!
HEH... THAT POTION WENT STRAIGHT TO YOUR HEAD. THAT'S THE MOST RIDICULOUS THING I EVER HEARD.
IT WOULD BE SUI-
XSSHHH

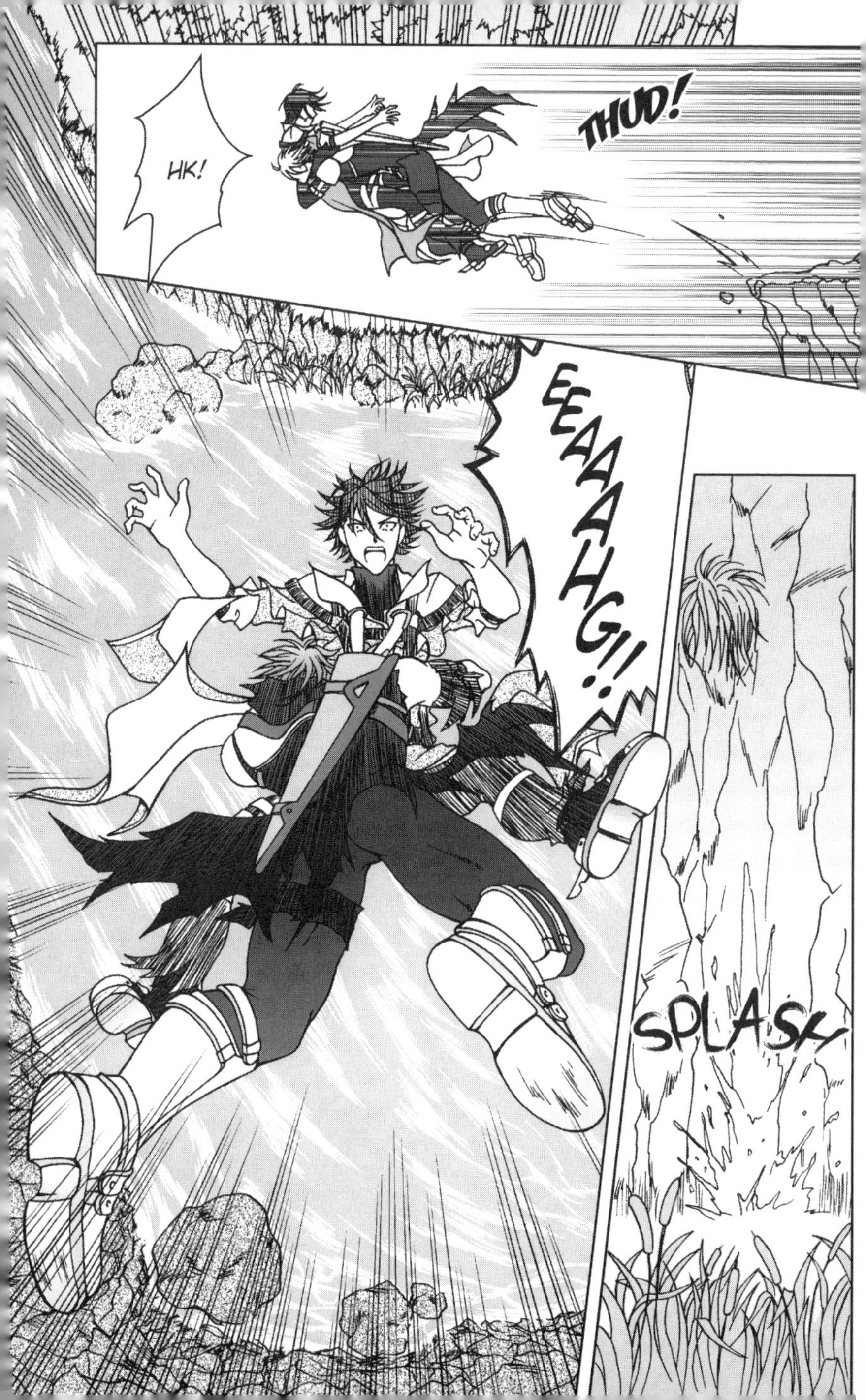
HK!
THUD!
EEAAAAHG!!
SPLASH

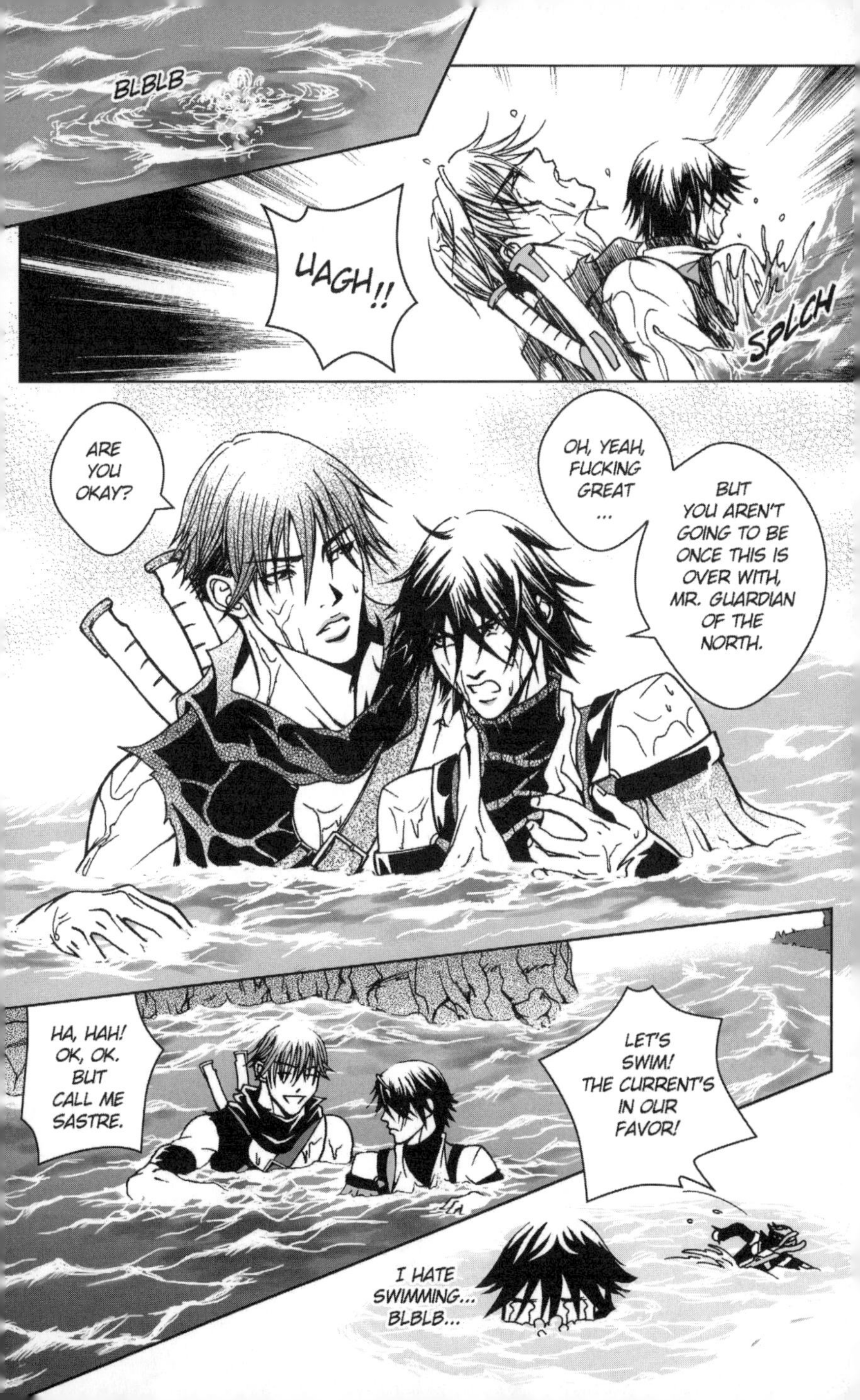
BLBLB
UAGH!!
SPLCH
ARE YOU OKAY?
OH, YEAH, FUCKING GREAT ...
BUT YOU AREN'T GOING TO BE ONCE THIS IS OVER WITH, MR. GUARDIAN OF THE NORTH.
HA, HAH! OK, OK. BUT CALL ME SASTRE.
LET'S SWIM! THE CURRENT'S IN OUR FAVOR!
I HATE SWIMMING... BLBLB...

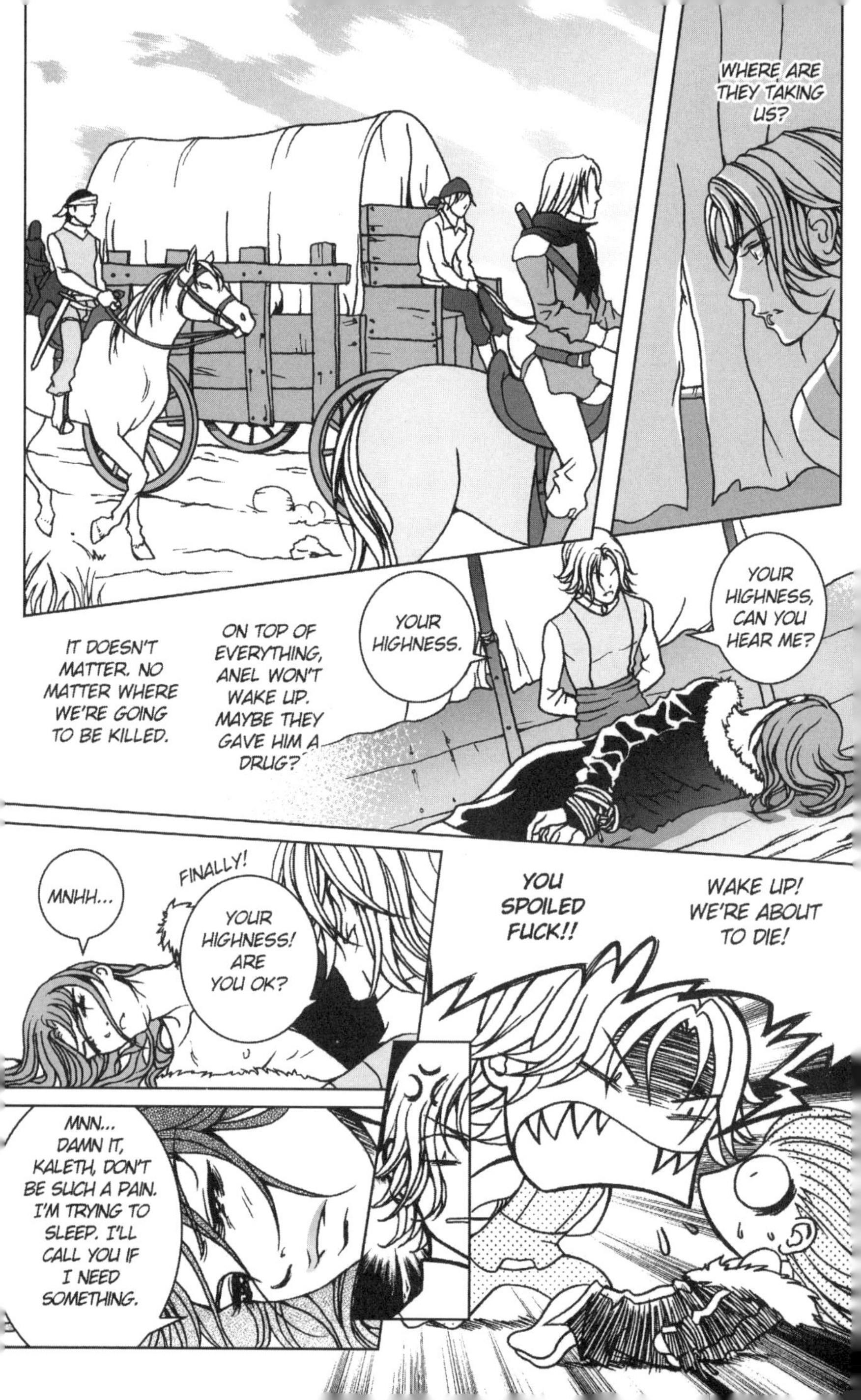
WHERE ARE THEY TAKING US?
IT DOESN'T MATTER. NO MATTER WHERE WE'RE GOING TO BE KILLED.
ON TOP OF EVERYTHING, ANEL WON'T WAKE UP. MAYBE THEY GAVE HIM A DRUG?
YOUR HIGHNESS.
YOUR HIGHNESS, CAN YOU HEAR ME?
MNHH...
FINALLY!
YOUR HIGHNESS! ARE YOU OK?
YOU SPOILED FUCK!!
WAKE UP! WE'RE ABOUT TO DIE!
MNN... DAMN IT, KALETH, DON'T BE SUCH A PAIN. I'M TRYING TO SLEEP. I'LL CALL YOU IF I NEED SOMETHING.

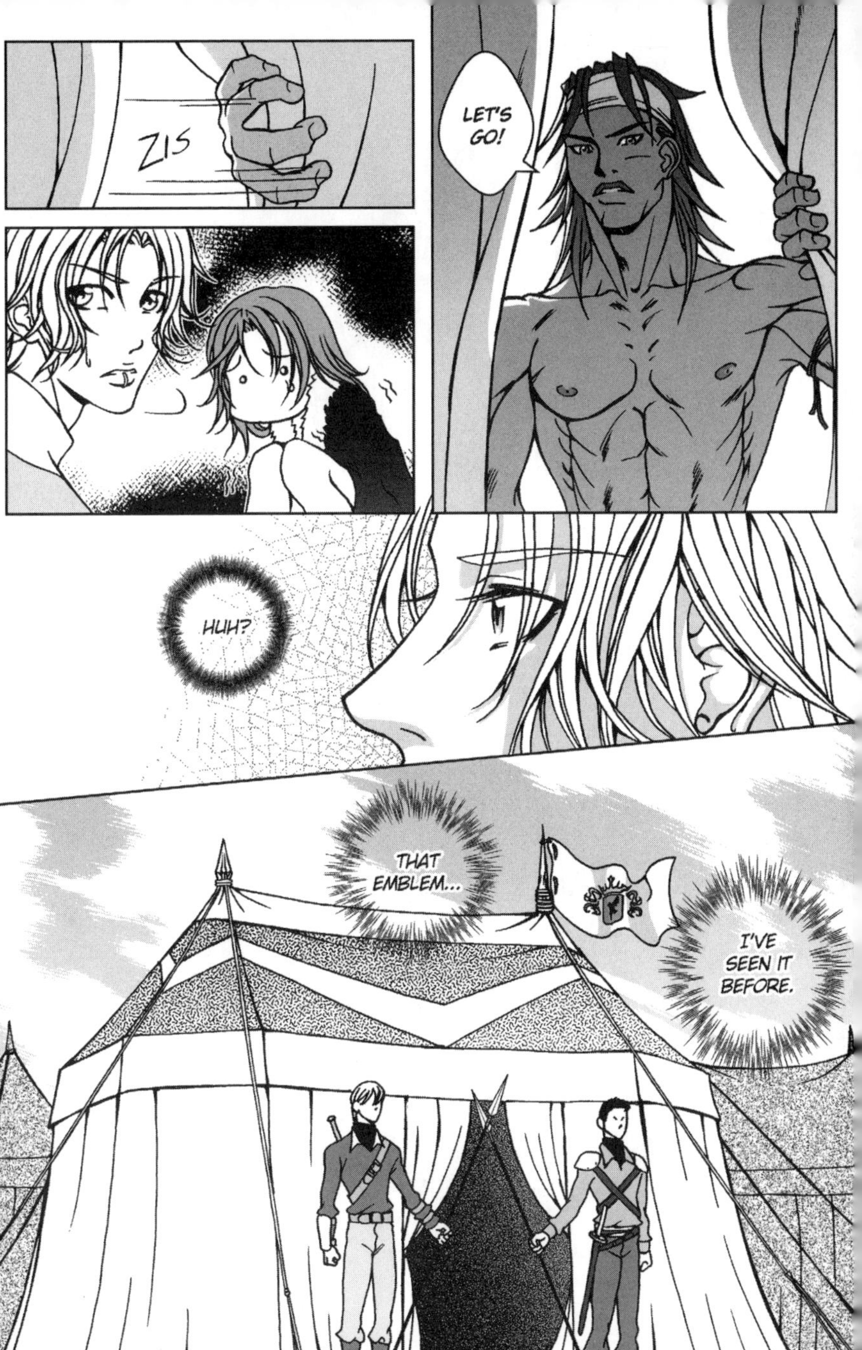
ZIS
LET'S GO!
HUH?
THAT EMBLEM...
I'VE SEEN IT BEFORE.

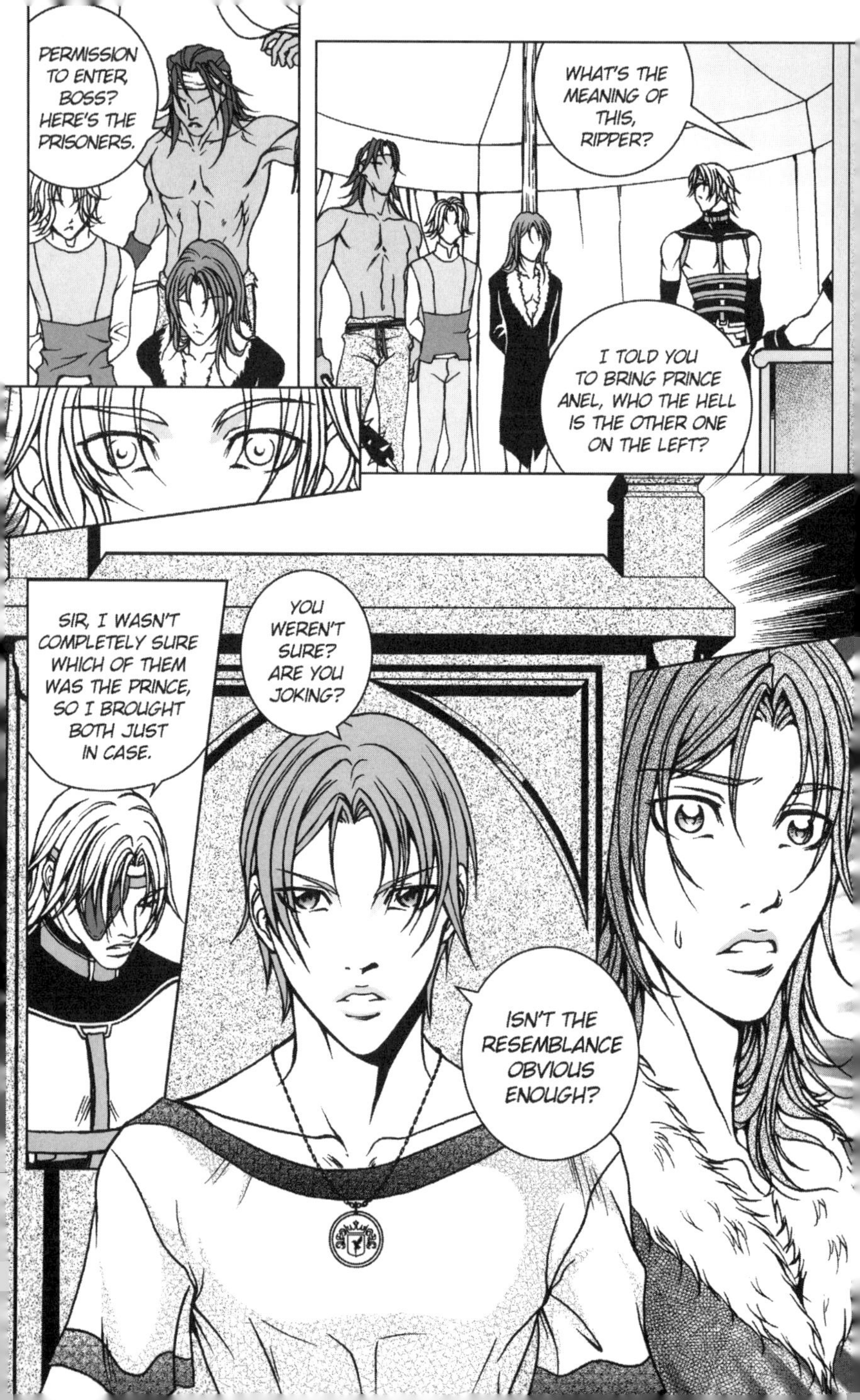
PERMISSION TO ENTER, BOSS? HERE'S THE PRISONERS.
WHAT'S THE MEANING OF THIS, RIPPER?
I TOLD YOU TO BRING PRINCE ANEL, WHO THE HELL IS THE OTHER ONE ON THE LEFT?
SIR, I WASN'T COMPLETELY SURE WHICH OF THEM WAS THE PRINCE, SO I BROUGHT BOTH JUST IN CASE.
YOU WEREN'T SURE? ARE YOU JOKING?
ISN'T THE RESEMBLANCE OBVIOUS ENOUGH?

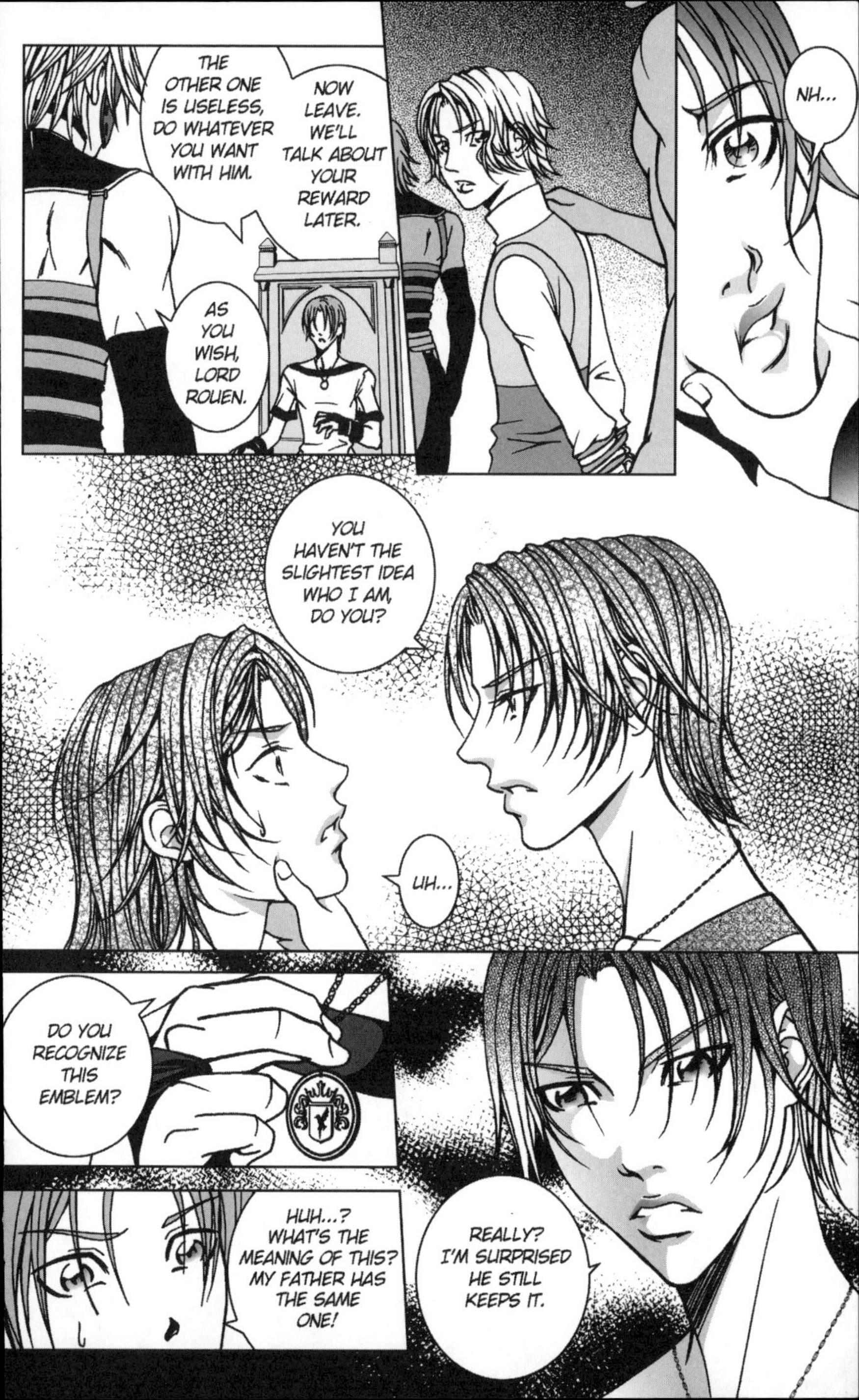
THE OTHER ONE IS USELESS, DO WHATEVER YOU WANT WITH HIM.
NOW LEAVE. WE'LL TALK ABOUT YOUR REWARD LATER.
AS YOU WISH, LORD ROUEN.
NH...
YOU HAVEN'T THE SLIGHTEST IDEA WHO I AM, DO YOU?
UH...
DO YOU RECOGNIZE THIS EMBLEM?
HUH...? WHAT'S THE MEANING OF THIS? MY FATHER HAS THE SAME ONE!
REALLY? I'M SURPRISED HE STILL KEEPS IT.

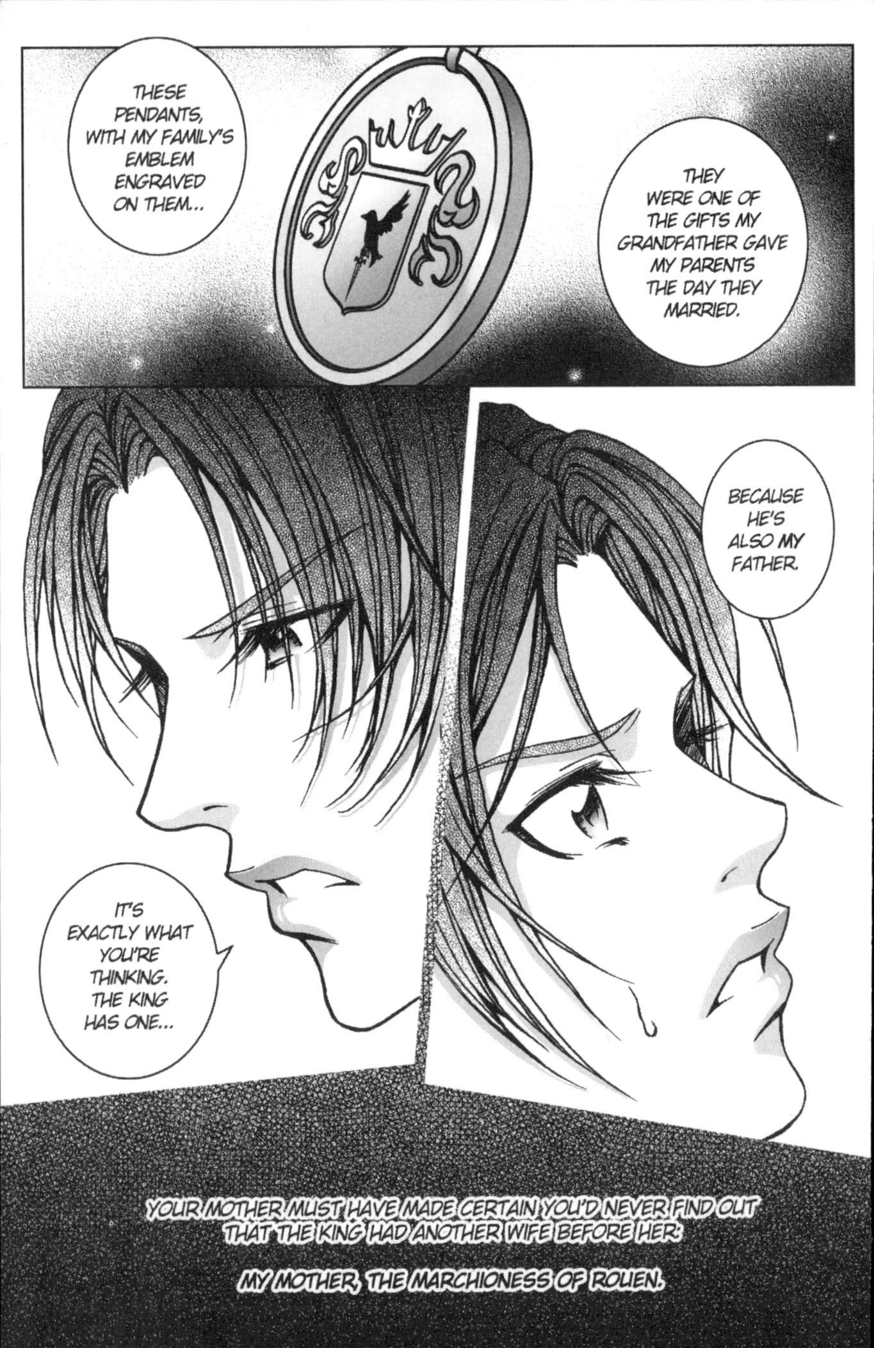
THEY WERE ONE OF THE GIFTS MY GRANDFATHER GAVE MY PARENTS THE DAY THEY MARRIED.
THESE PENDANTS, WITH MY FAMILY'S EMBLEM ENGRAVED ON THEM...
BECAUSE HE'S ALSO MY FATHER.
IT'S EXACTLY WHAT YOU'RE THINKING. THE KING HAS ONE...
YOUR MOTHER MUST HAVE MADE CERTAIN YOU'D NEVER FIND OUT THAT THE KING HAD ANOTHER WIFE BEFORE HER:
MY MOTHER, THE MARCHIONESS OF ROUEN.

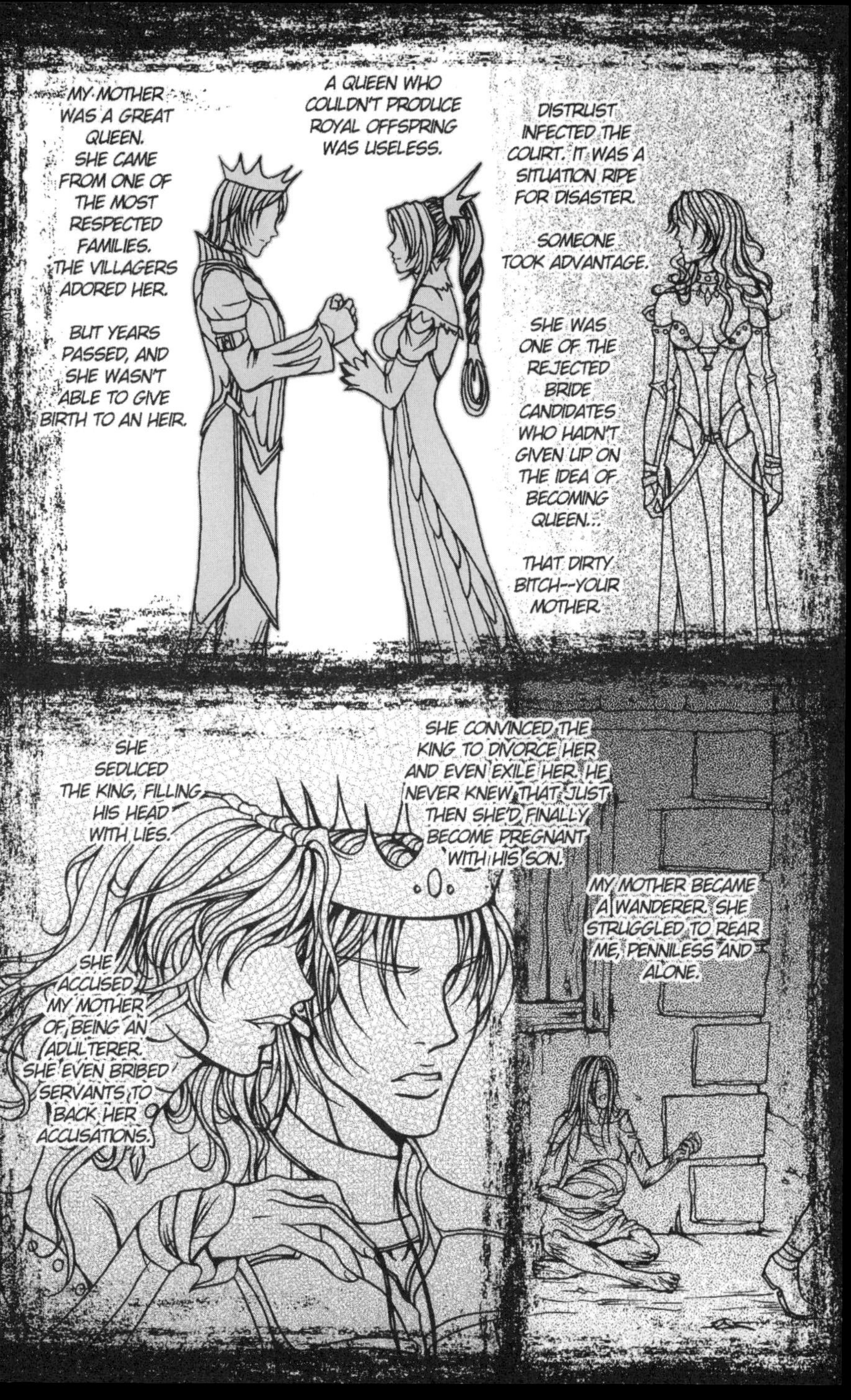
MY MOTHER WAS A GREAT QUEEN. SHE CAME FROM ONE OF THE MOST RESPECTED FAMILIES. THE VILLAGERS ADORED HER.
BUT YEARS PASSED, AND SHE WASN'T ABLE TO GIVE BIRTH TO AN HEIR.
A QUEEN WHO COULDN'T PRODUCE ROYAL OFFSPRING WAS USELESS.
DISTRUST INFECTED THE COURT. IT WAS A SITUATION RIPE FOR DISASTER.
SOMEONE TOOK ADVANTAGE.
SHE WAS ONE OF THE REJECTED BRIDE CANDIDATES WHO HADN'T GIVEN UP ON THE IDEA OF BECOMING QUEEN...
THAT DIRTY BITCH--YOUR MOTHER.
SHE SEDUCED THE KING, FILLING HIS HEAD WITH LIES.
SHE CONVINCED THE KING TO DIVORCE HER AND EVEN EXILE HER. HE NEVER KNEW THAT JUST THEN SHE'D FINALLY BECOME PREGNANT WITH HIS SON.
SHE ACCUSED MY MOTHER OF BEING AN ADULTERER. SHE EVEN BRIBED SERVANTS TO BACK HER ACCUSATIONS.
MY MOTHER BECAME A WANDERER. SHE STRUGGLED TO REAR ME, PENNILESS AND ALONE.

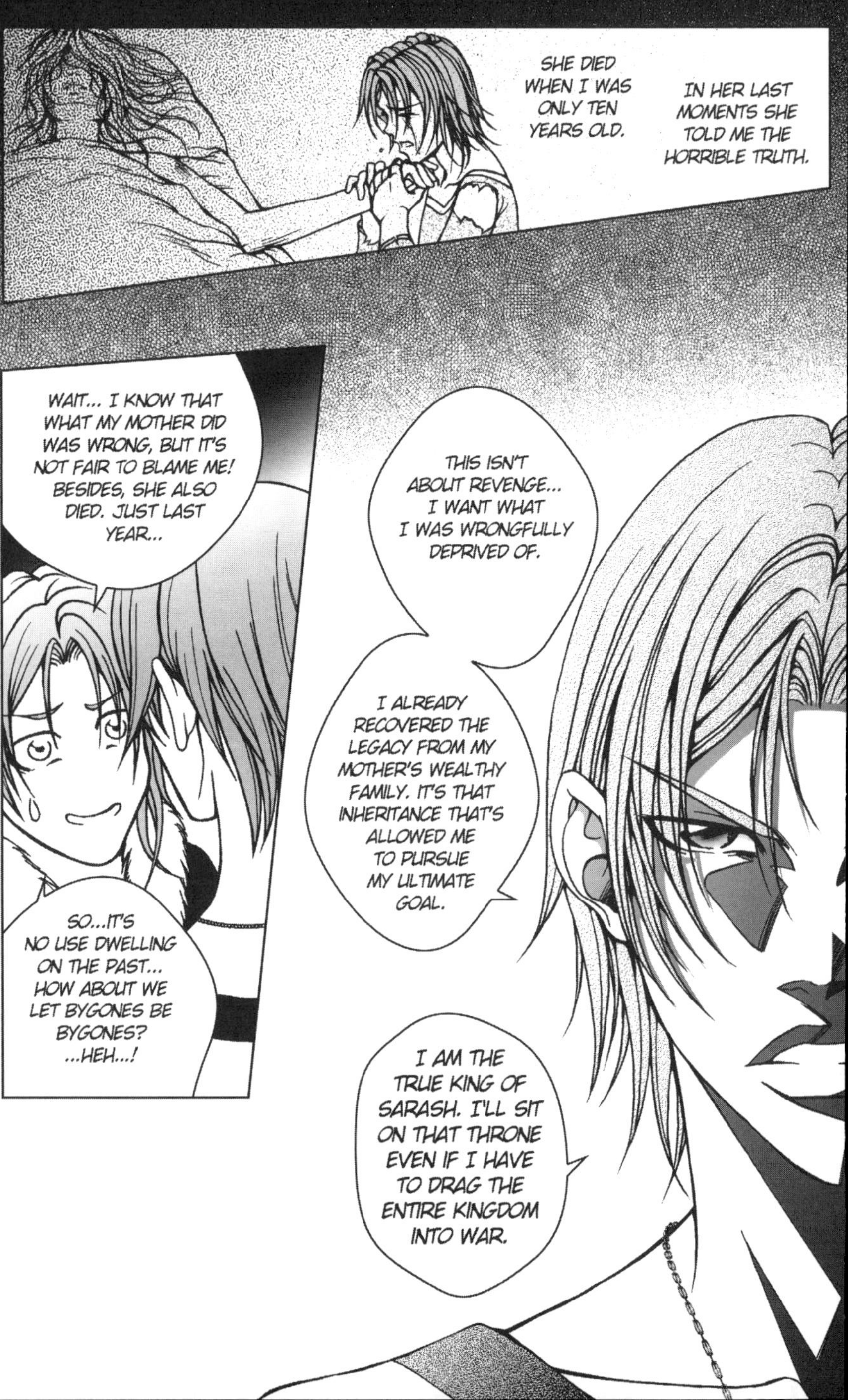
SHE DIED WHEN I WAS ONLY TEN YEARS OLD.
IN HER LAST MOMENTS SHE TOLD ME THE HORRIBLE TRUTH.
WAIT... I KNOW THAT WHAT MY MOTHER DID WAS WRONG, BUT IT'S NOT FAIR TO BLAME ME! BESIDES, SHE ALSO DIED. JUST LAST YEAR...
SO...IT'S NO USE DWELLING ON THE PAST... HOW ABOUT WE LET BYGONES BE BYGONES? ...HEH...!
THIS ISN'T ABOUT REVENGE... I WANT WHAT I WAS WRONGFULLY DEPRIVED OF.
I ALREADY RECOVERED THE LEGACY FROM MY MOTHER'S WEALTHY FAMILY. IT'S THAT INHERITANCE THAT'S ALLOWED ME TO PURSUE MY ULTIMATE GOAL.
I AM THE TRUE KING OF SARASH. I'LL SIT ON THAT THRONE EVEN IF I HAVE TO DRAG THE ENTIRE KINGDOM INTO WAR.

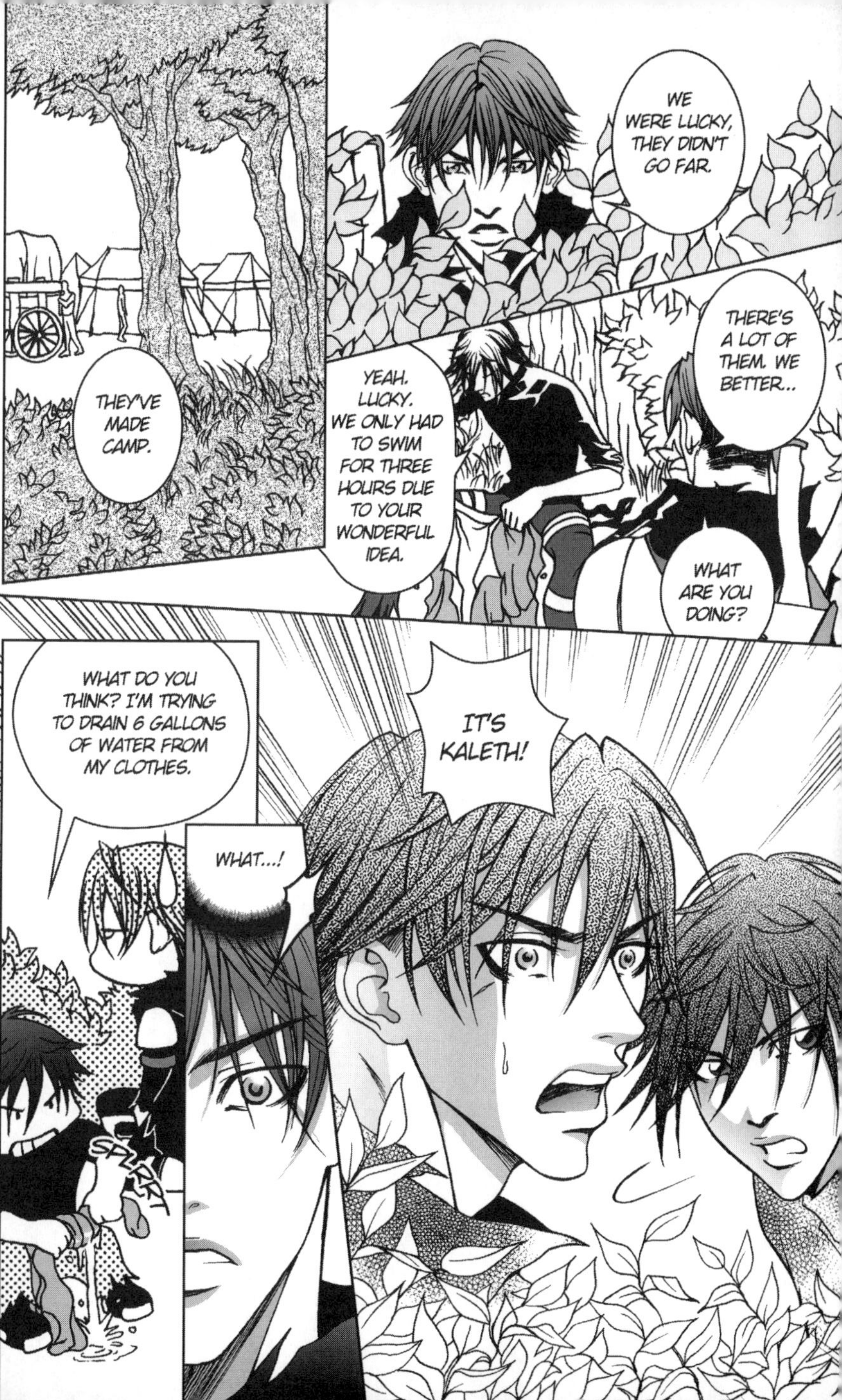
THEY'VE MADE CAMP.
WE WERE LUCKY, THEY DIDN'T GO FAR.
YEAH. LUCKY. WE ONLY HAD TO SWIM FOR THREE HOURS DUE TO YOUR WONDERFUL IDEA.
THERE'S A LOT OF THEM. WE BETTER...
WHAT ARE YOU DOING?
WHAT DO YOU THINK? I'M TRYING TO DRAIN 6 GALLONS OF WATER FROM MY CLOTHES.
WHAT...!
IT'S KALETH!

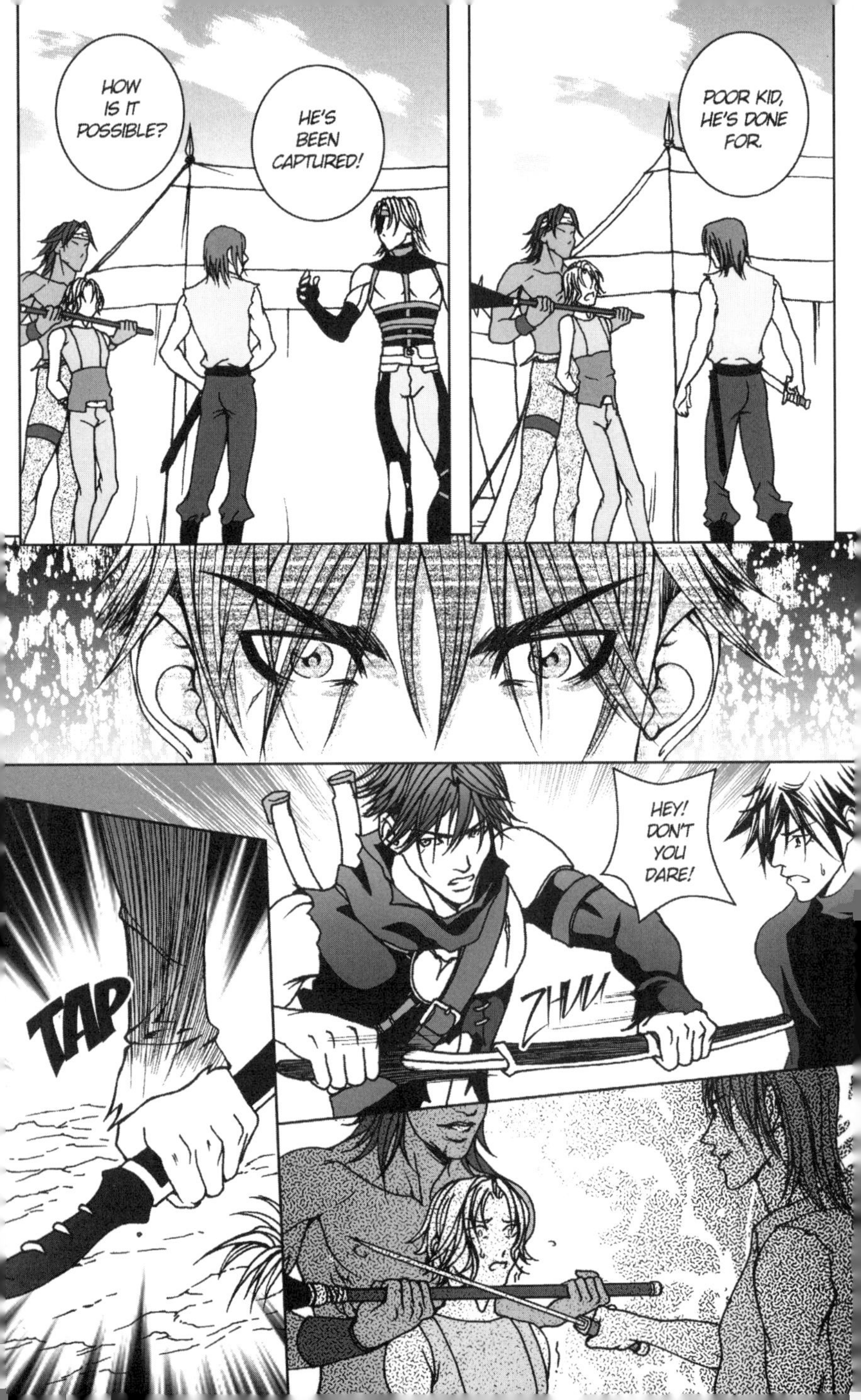
HOW IS IT POSSIBLE?
HE'S BEEN CAPTURED!
POOR KID, HE'S DONE FOR.
TAP
ZHUU
HEY! DON'T YOU DARE!

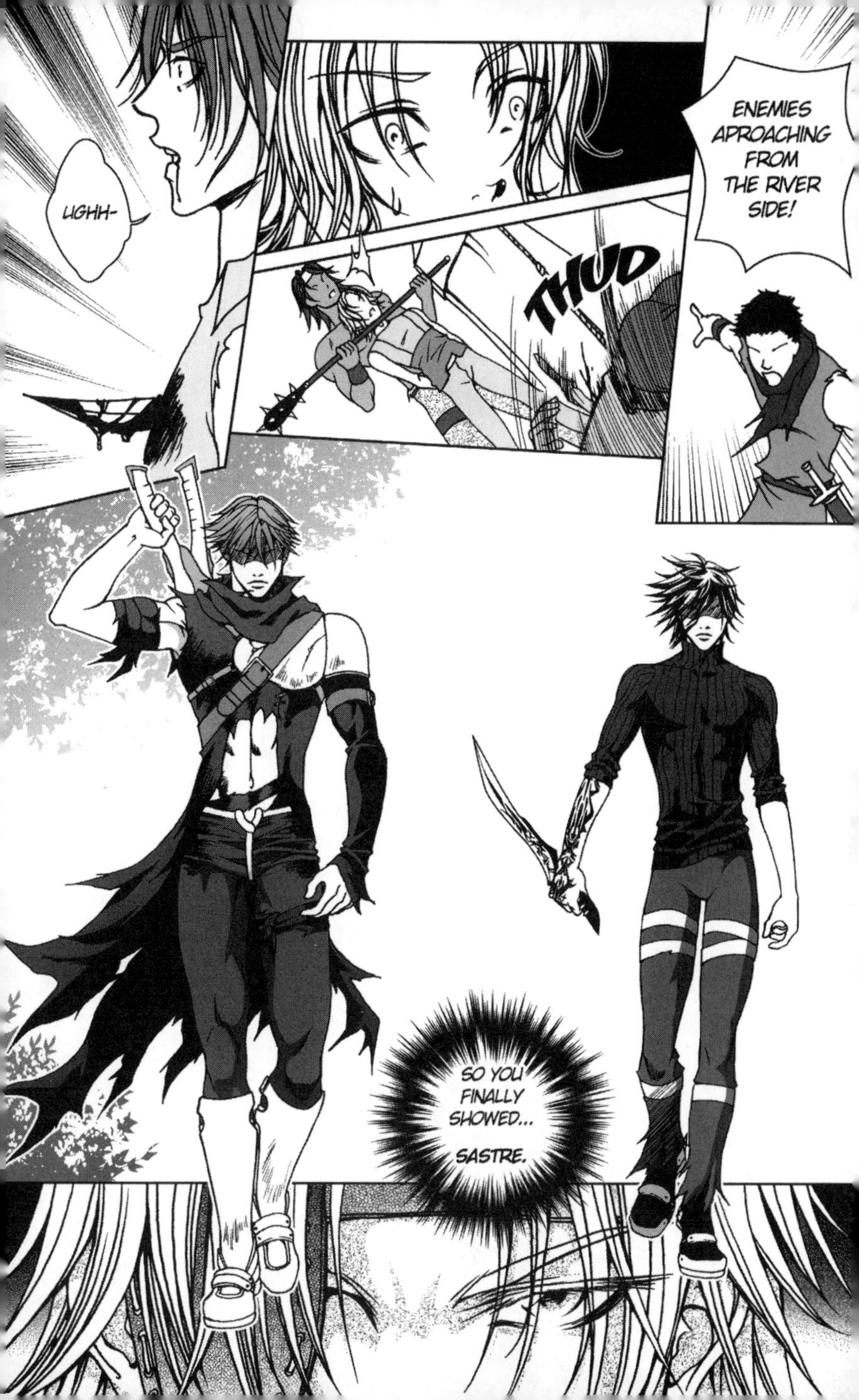
ENEMIES APROACHING FROM THE RIVER SIDE!
THUD
UGHH-
SO YOU FINALLY SHOWED...
SASTRE.

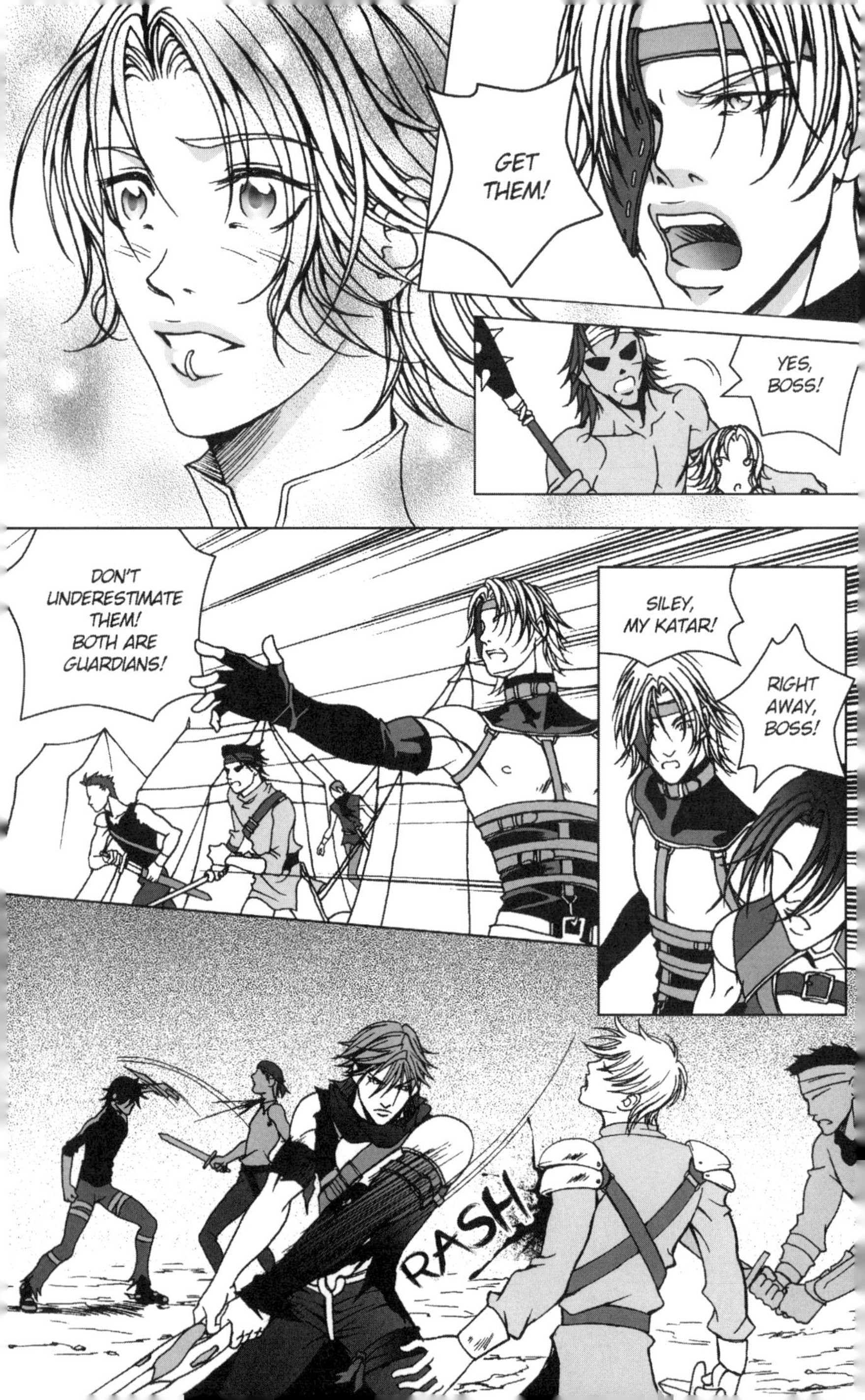
GET THEM!
YES, BOSS!
DON'T UNDERESTIMATE THEM! BOTH ARE GUARDIANS!
SILEY, MY KATAR!
RIGHT AWAY, BOSS!
RASH

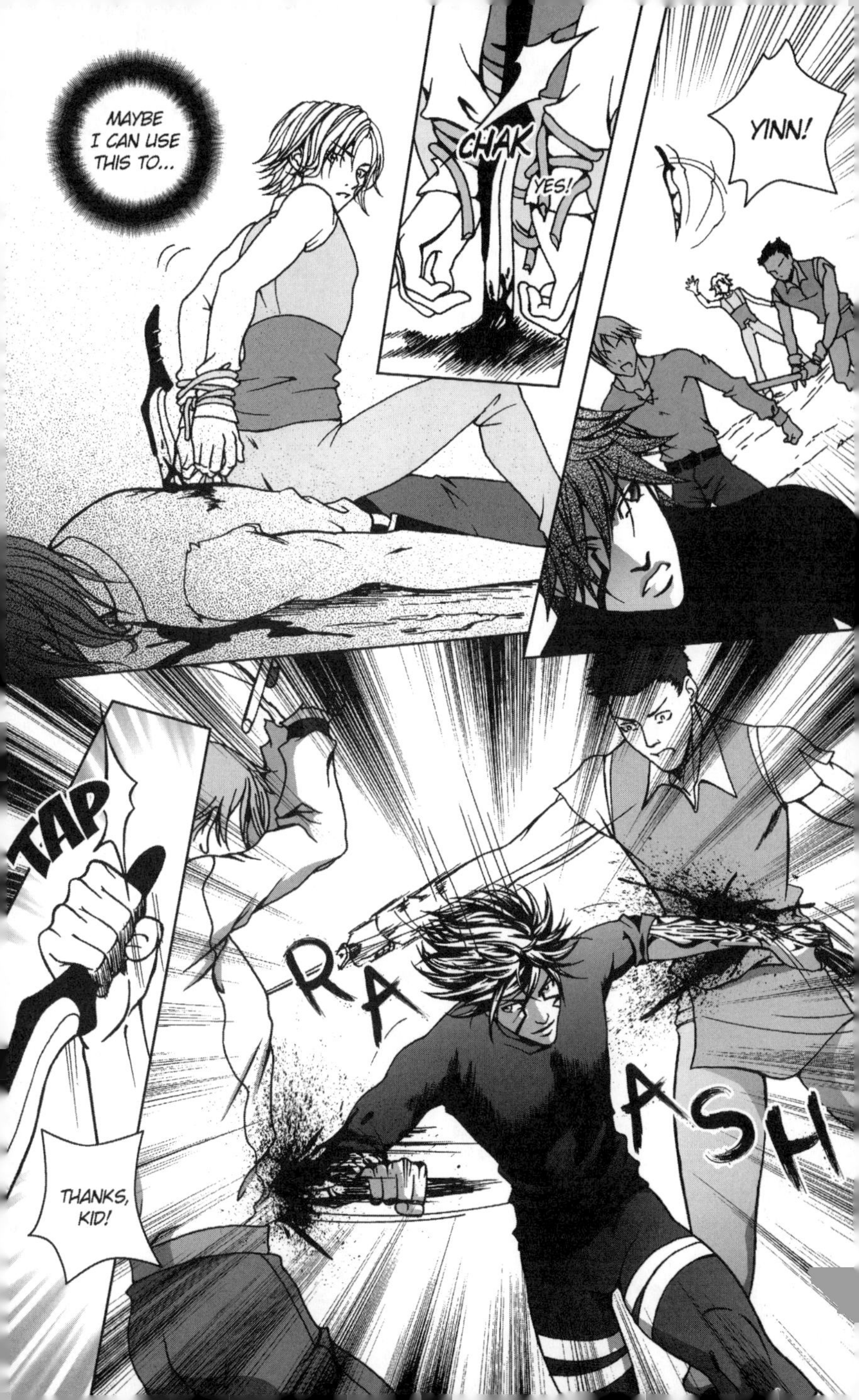
MAYBE I CAN USE THIS TO...
CHAK
YES!
YINN!
TAP
RA
ASH
THANKS, KID!

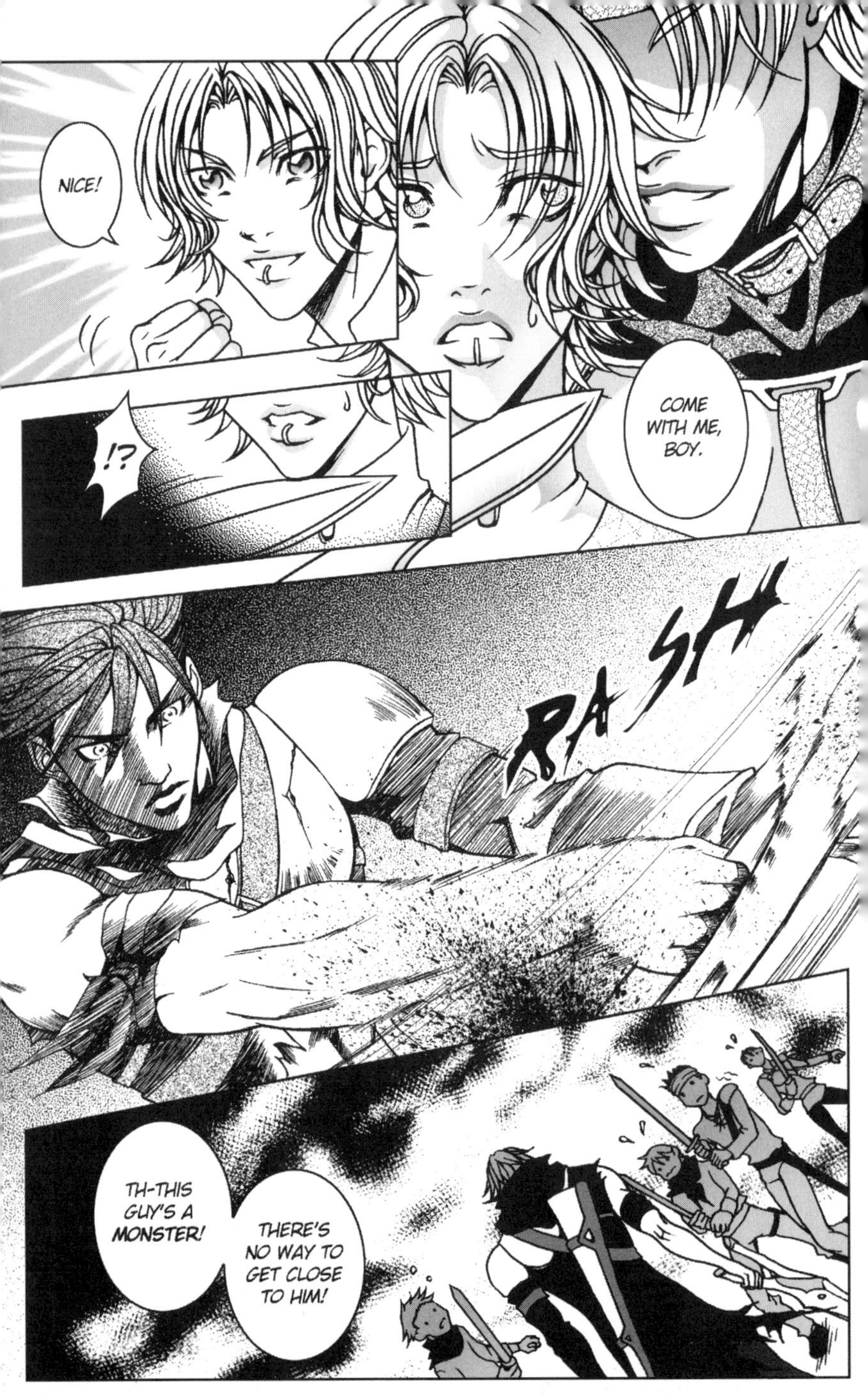
NICE!
!?
COME WITH ME, BOY.
PASH
TH-THIS GUY'S A MONSTER!
THERE'S NO WAY TO GET CLOSE TO HIM!

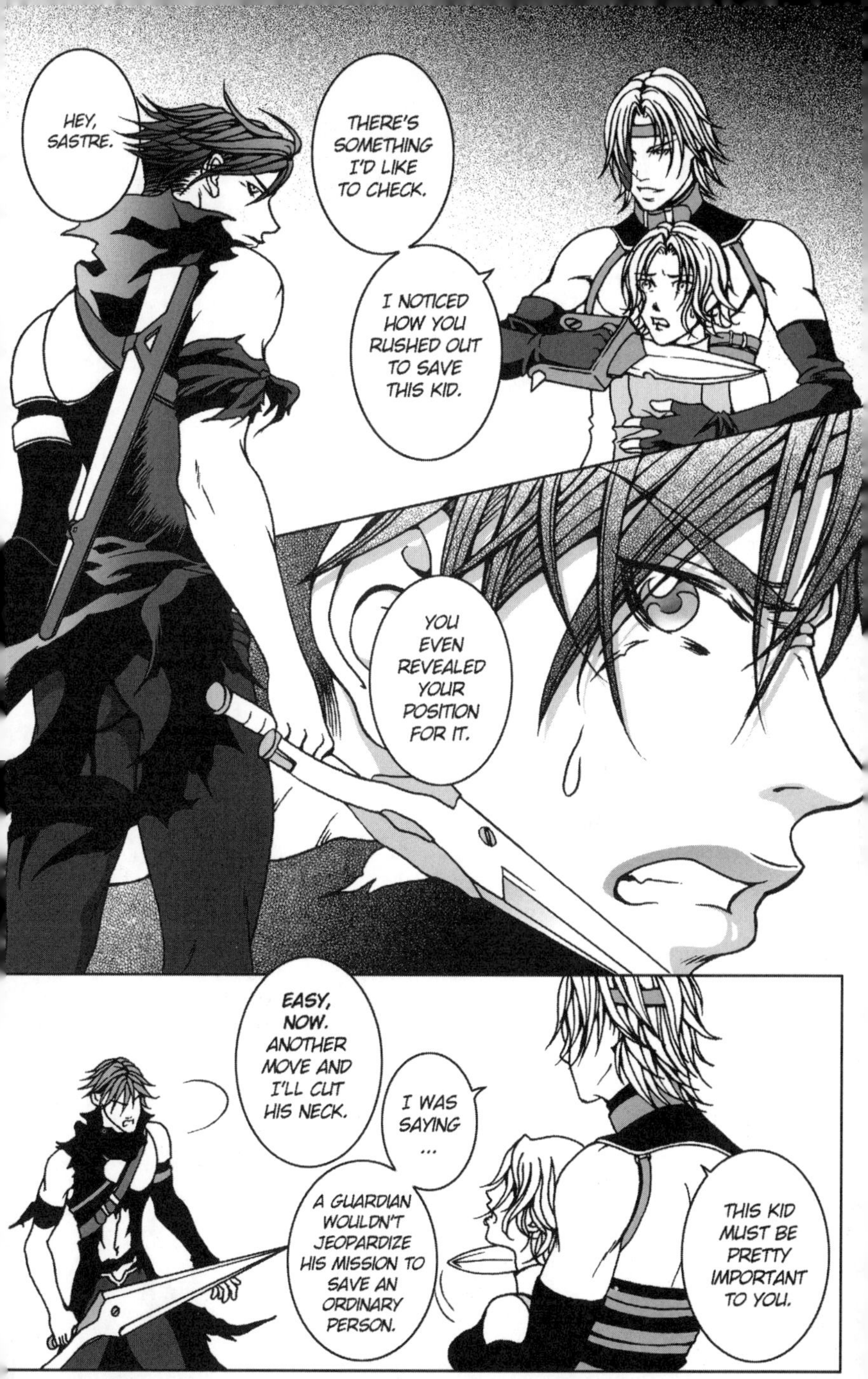
HEY, SASTRE.
THERE'S SOMETHING I'D LIKE TO CHECK.
I NOTICED HOW YOU RUSHED OUT TO SAVE THIS KID.
YOU EVEN REVEALED YOUR POSITION FOR IT.
EASY, NOW. ANOTHER MOVE AND I'LL CUT HIS NECK.
I WAS SAYING ...
A GUARDIAN WOULDN'T JEOPARDIZE HIS MISSION TO SAVE AN ORDINARY PERSON.
THIS KID MUST BE PRETTY IMPORTANT TO YOU.

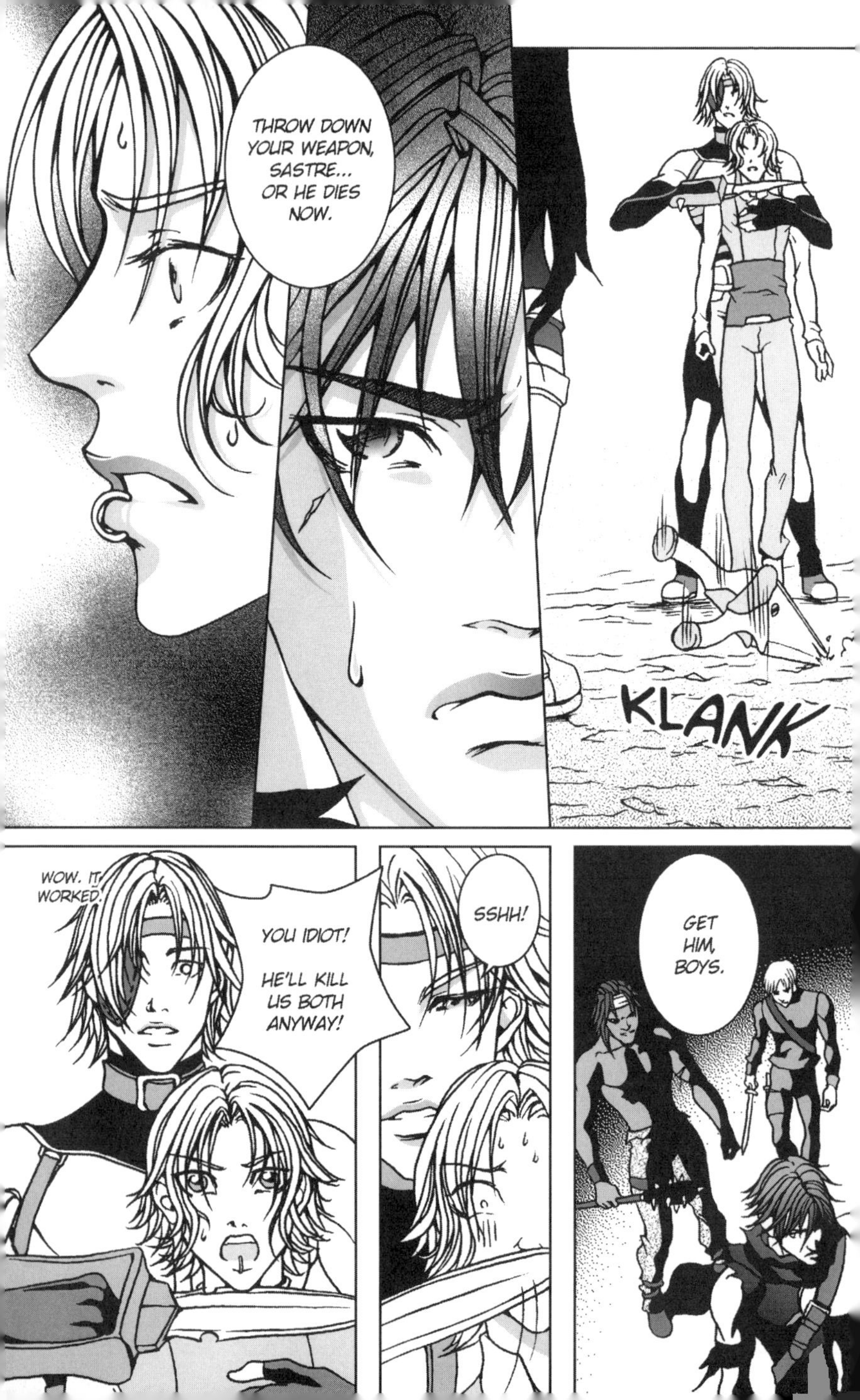
THROW DOWN YOUR WEAPON, SASTRE... OR HE DIES NOW.
KLANK
WOW. IT WORKED.
YOU IDIOT!
HE'LL KILL US BOTH ANYWAY!
SSHH!
GET HIM, BOYS.

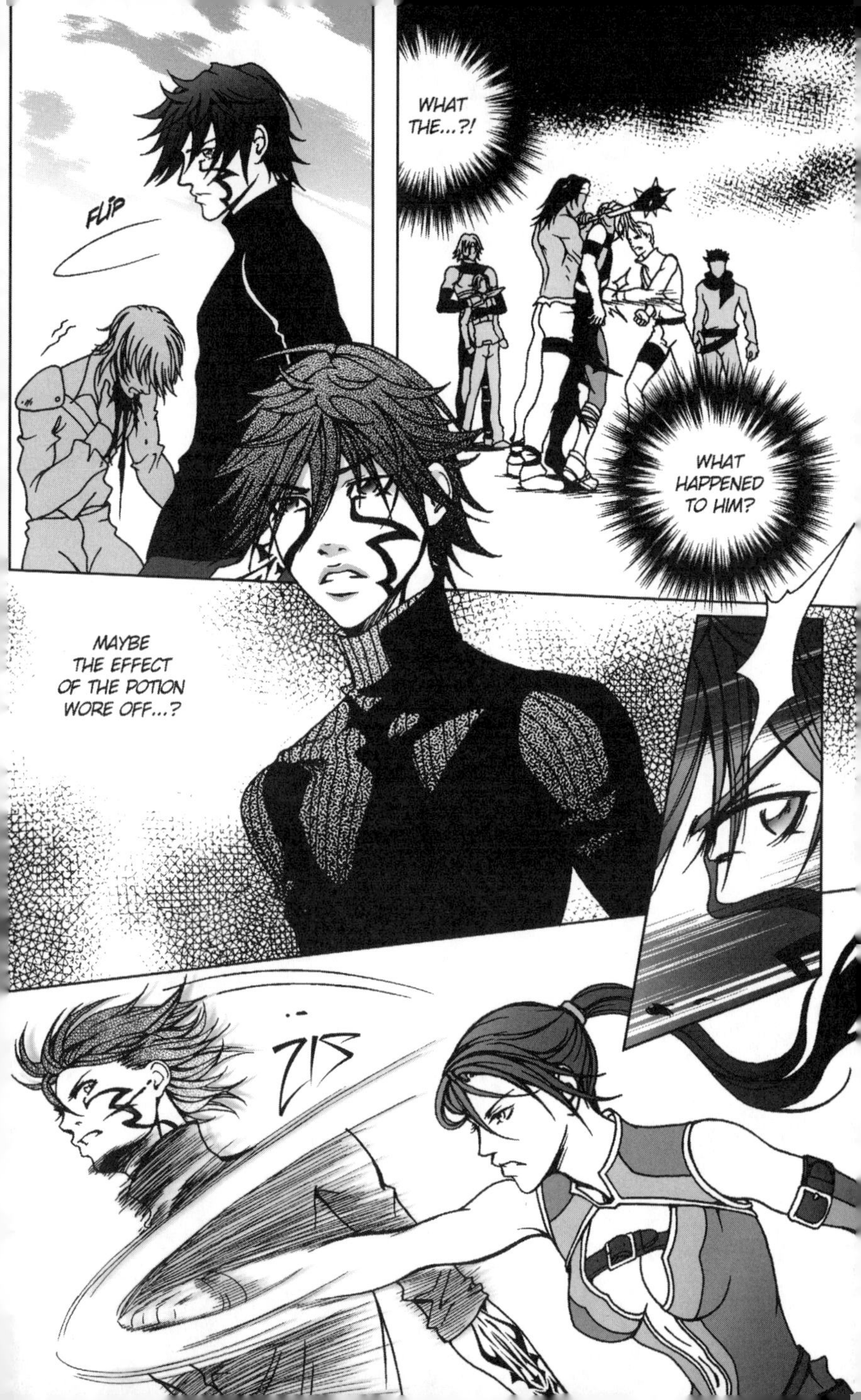
FLIP
WHAT THE...?!
WHAT HAPPENED TO HIM?
MAYBE THE EFFECT OF THE POTION WORE OFF...?

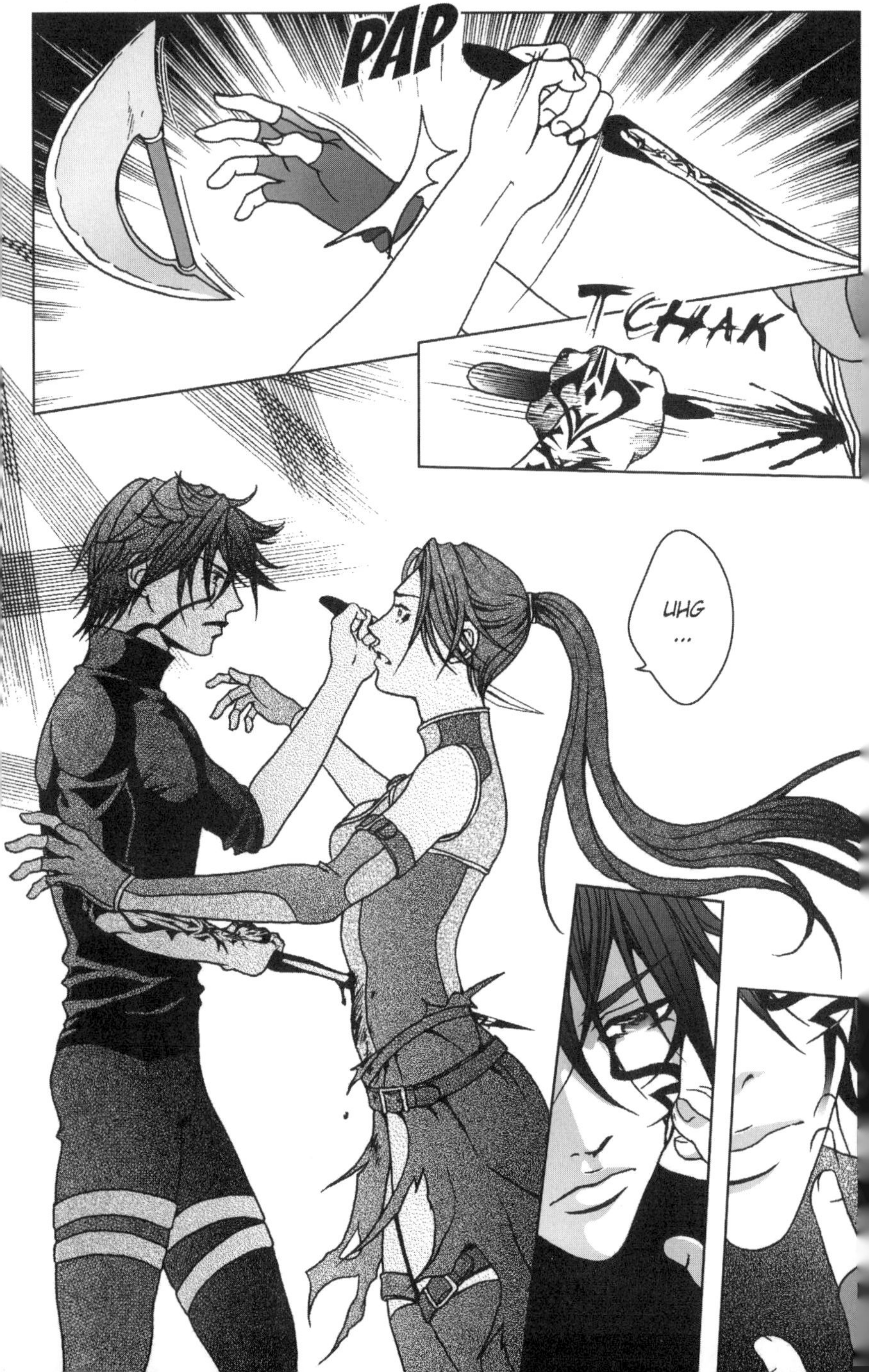
PAP
T-CHAK
UHG
...

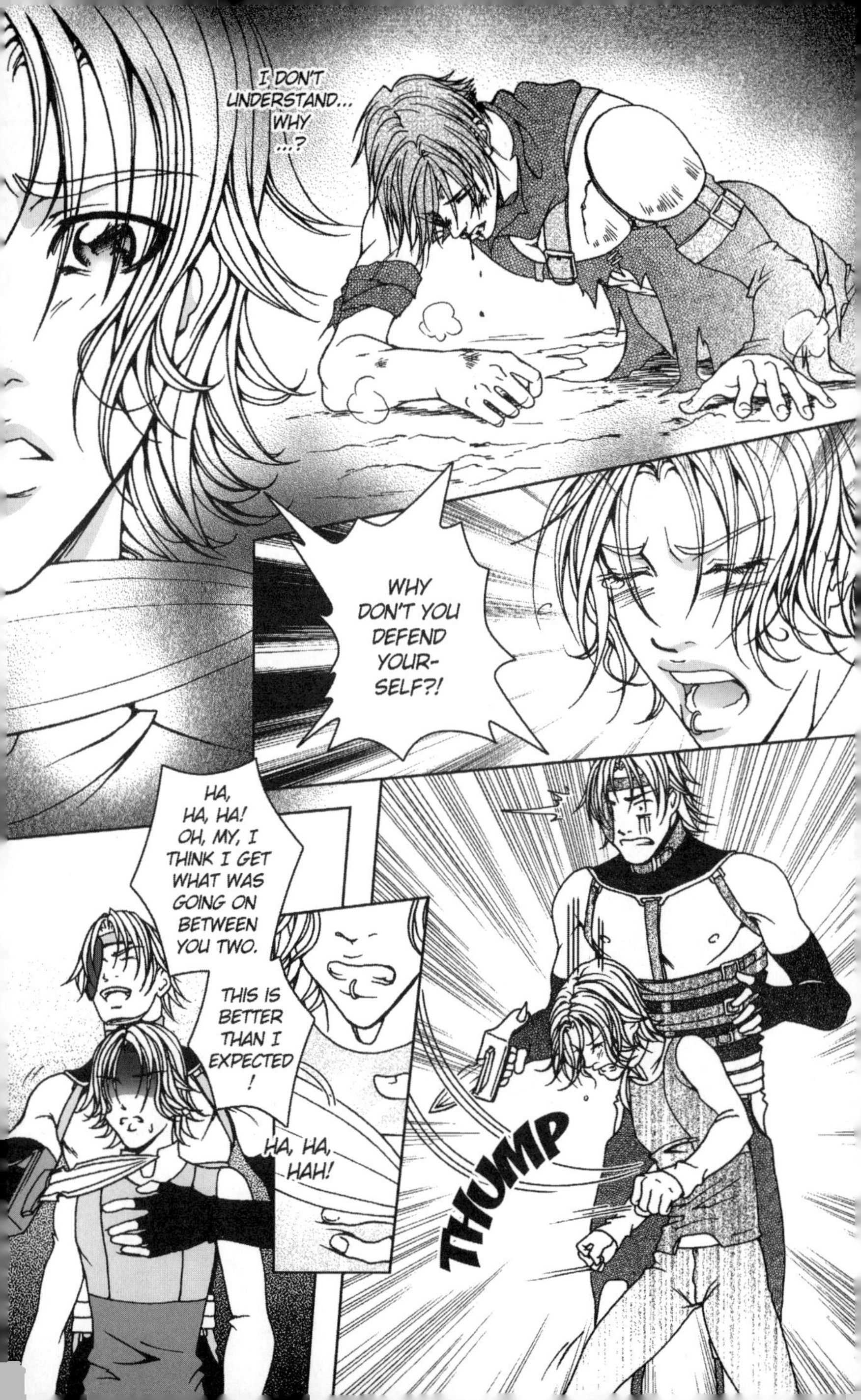
I DON'T UNDERSTAND... WHY ...?
WHY DON'T YOU DEFEND YOUR-SELF?!
HA, HA, HA! OH, MY, I THINK I GET WHAT WAS GOING ON BETWEEN YOU TWO.
THIS IS BETTER THAN I EXPECTED!
HA, HA, HAH!
THUMP

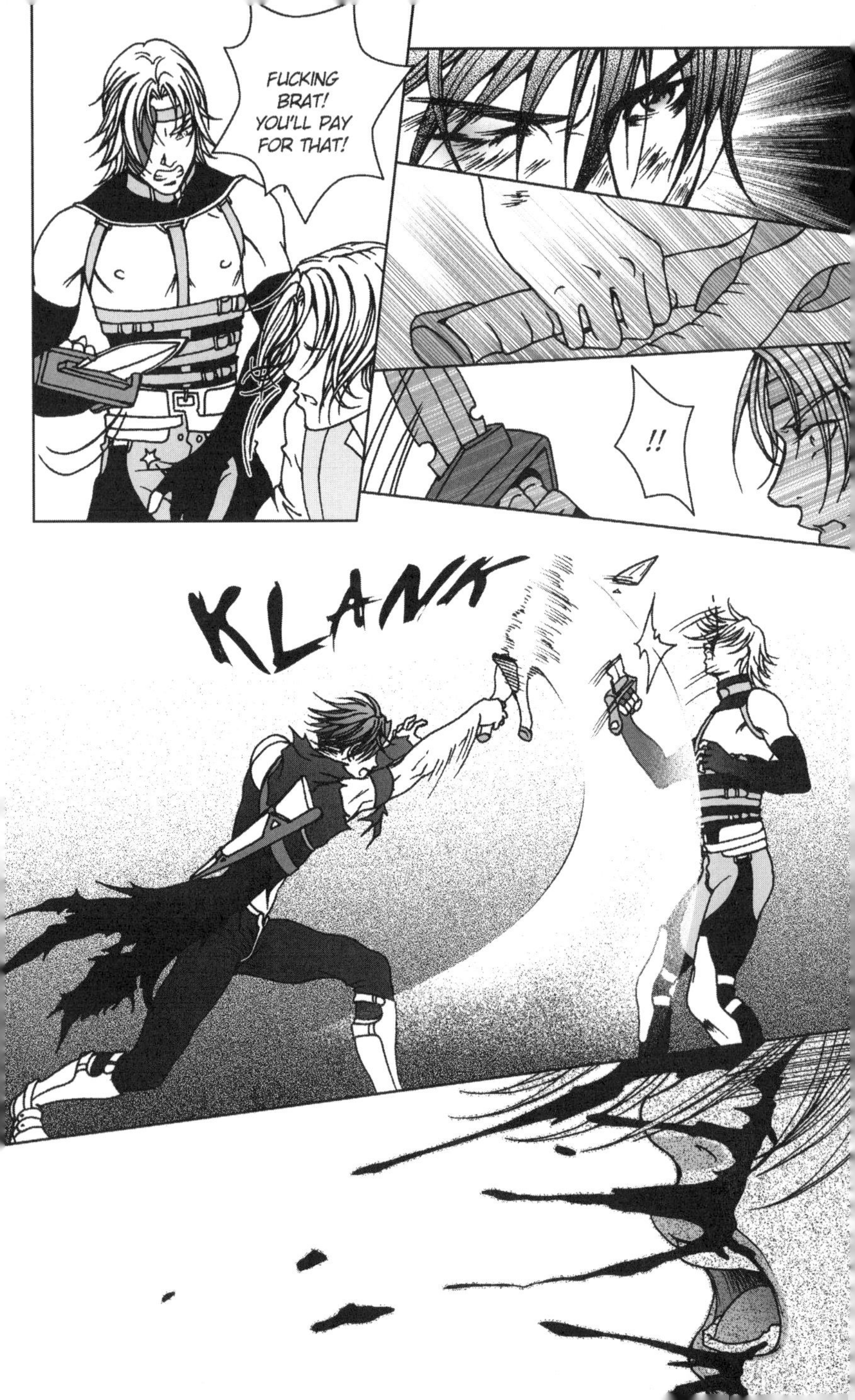
FUCKING BRAT! YOU'LL PAY FOR THAT!
!!
KLANK

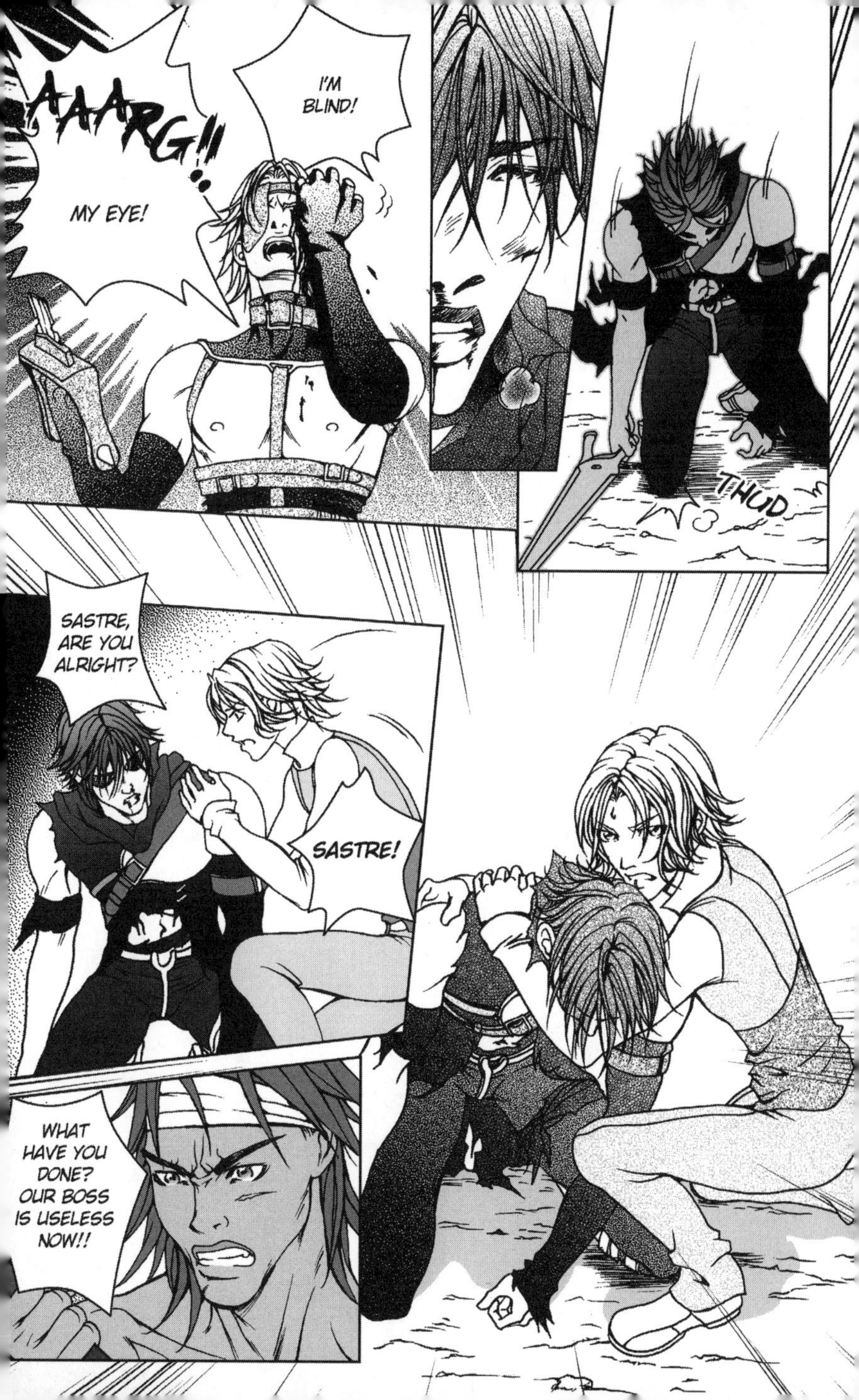
AAARG!!
MY EYE!
I'M BLIND!
THUD
SASTRE, ARE YOU ALRIGHT?
SASTRE!
WHAT HAVE YOU DONE? OUR BOSS IS USELESS NOW!!

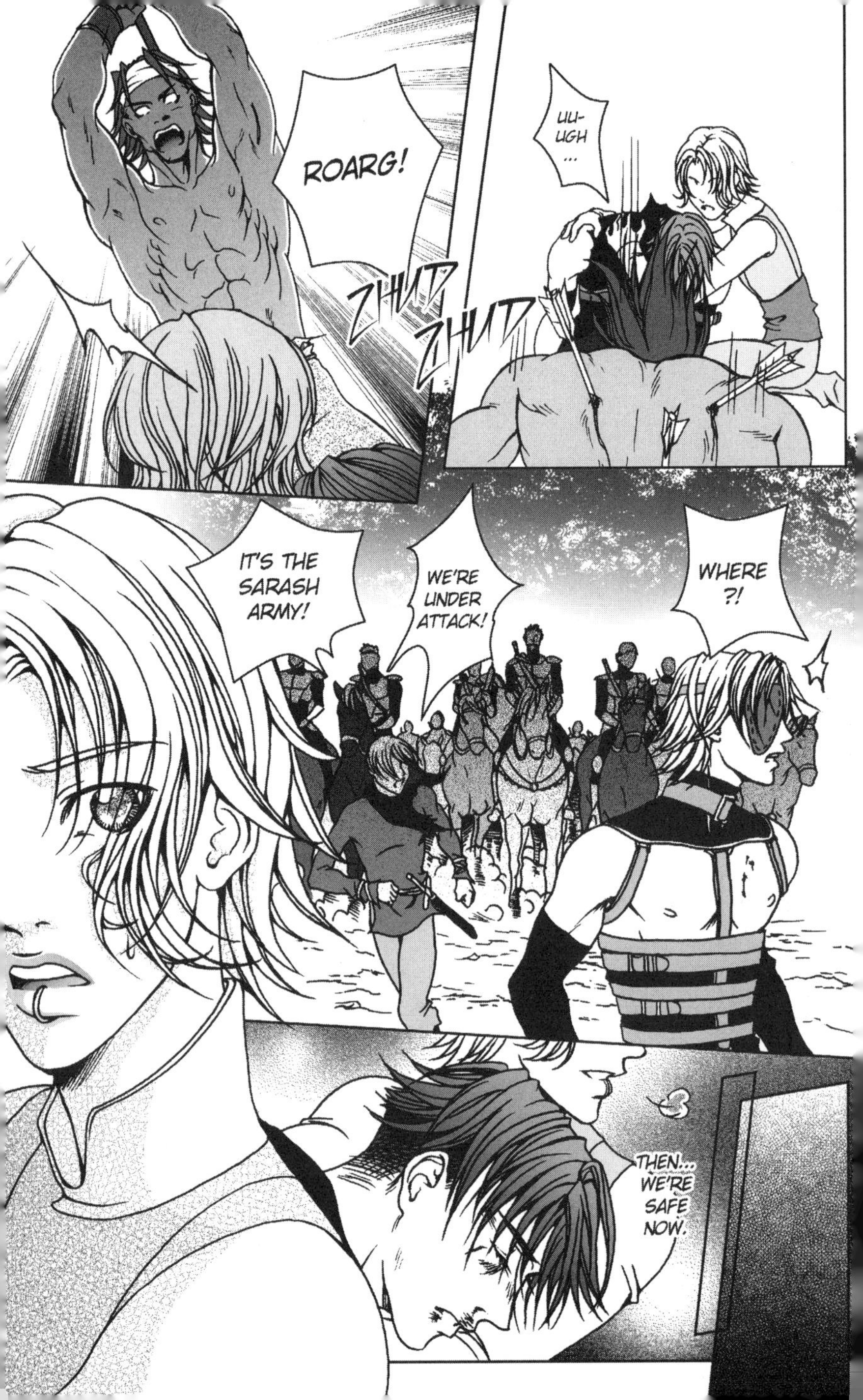
ROARG!
ZHUD ZHUD
UU-UGH...
IT'S THE SARASH ARMY!
WE'RE UNDER ATTACK!
WHERE ?!
THEN... WE'RE SAFE NOW.

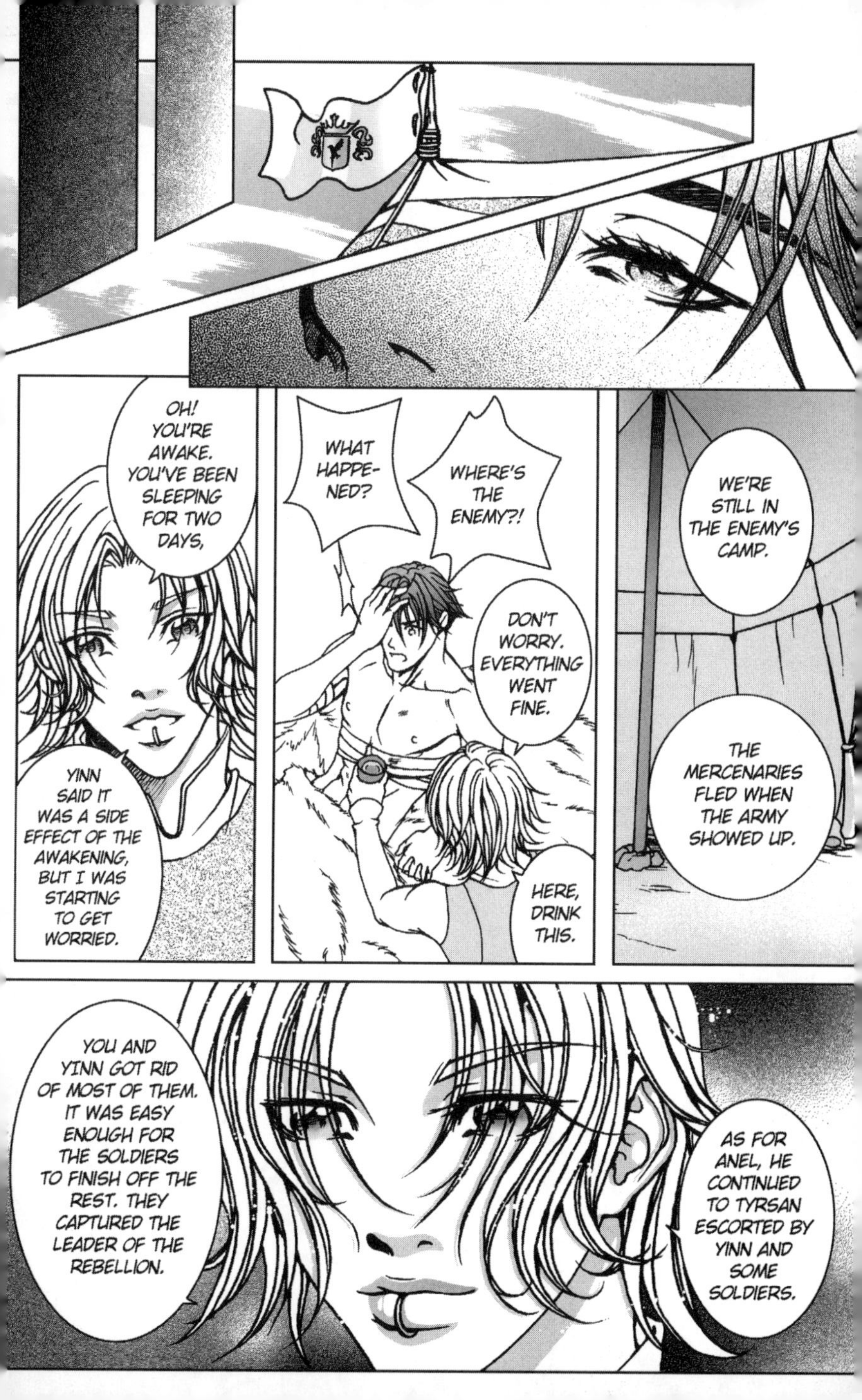
OH! YOU'RE AWAKE. YOU'VE BEEN SLEEPING FOR TWO DAYS,
YINN SAID IT WAS A SIDE EFFECT OF THE AWAKENING, BUT I WAS STARTING TO GET WORRIED.
WHAT HAPPENED?
WHERE'S THE ENEMY?!
DON'T WORRY. EVERYTHING WENT FINE.
HERE, DRINK THIS.
WE'RE STILL IN THE ENEMY'S CAMP.
THE MERCENARIES FLED WHEN THE ARMY SHOWED UP.
YOU AND YINN GOT RID OF MOST OF THEM. IT WAS EASY ENOUGH FOR THE SOLDIERS TO FINISH OFF THE REST. THEY CAPTURED THE LEADER OF THE REBELLION.
AS FOR ANEL, HE CONTINUED TO TYRSAN ESCORTED BY YINN AND SOME SOLDIERS.

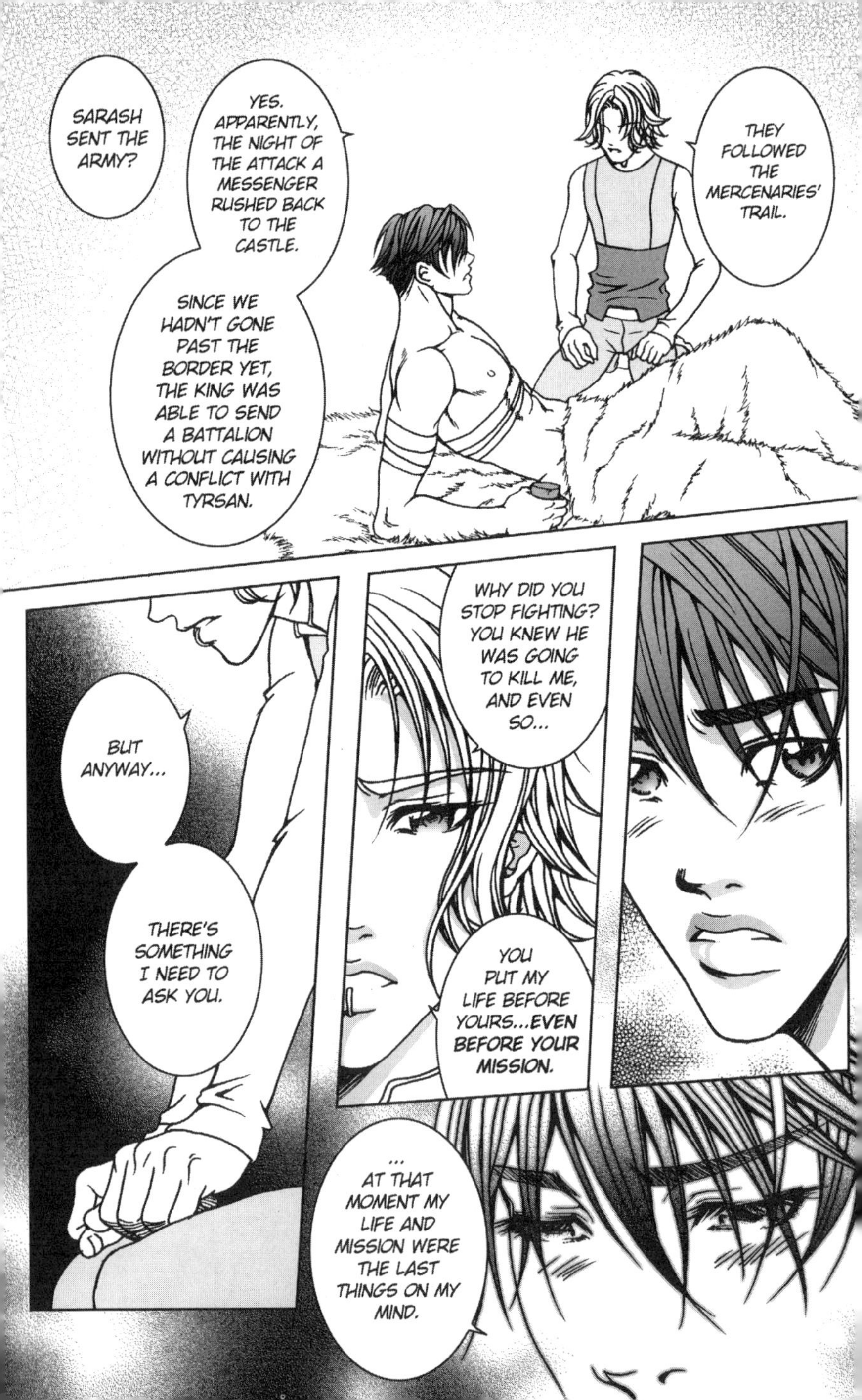

SARASH SENT THE ARMY?
YES. APPARENTLY, THE NIGHT OF THE ATTACK A MESSENGER RUSHED BACK TO THE CASTLE.
THEY FOLLOWED THE MERCENARIES' TRAIL.
SINCE WE HADN'T GONE PAST THE BORDER YET, THE KING WAS ABLE TO SEND A BATTALION WITHOUT CAUSING A CONFLICT WITH TYRSAN.
BUT ANYWAY...
THERE'S SOMETHING I NEED TO ASK YOU.
WHY DID YOU STOP FIGHTING? YOU KNEW HE WAS GOING TO KILL ME, AND EVEN SO...
YOU PUT MY LIFE BEFORE YOURS...EVEN BEFORE YOUR MISSION.
... AT THAT MOMENT MY LIFE AND MISSION WERE THE LAST THINGS ON MY MIND.

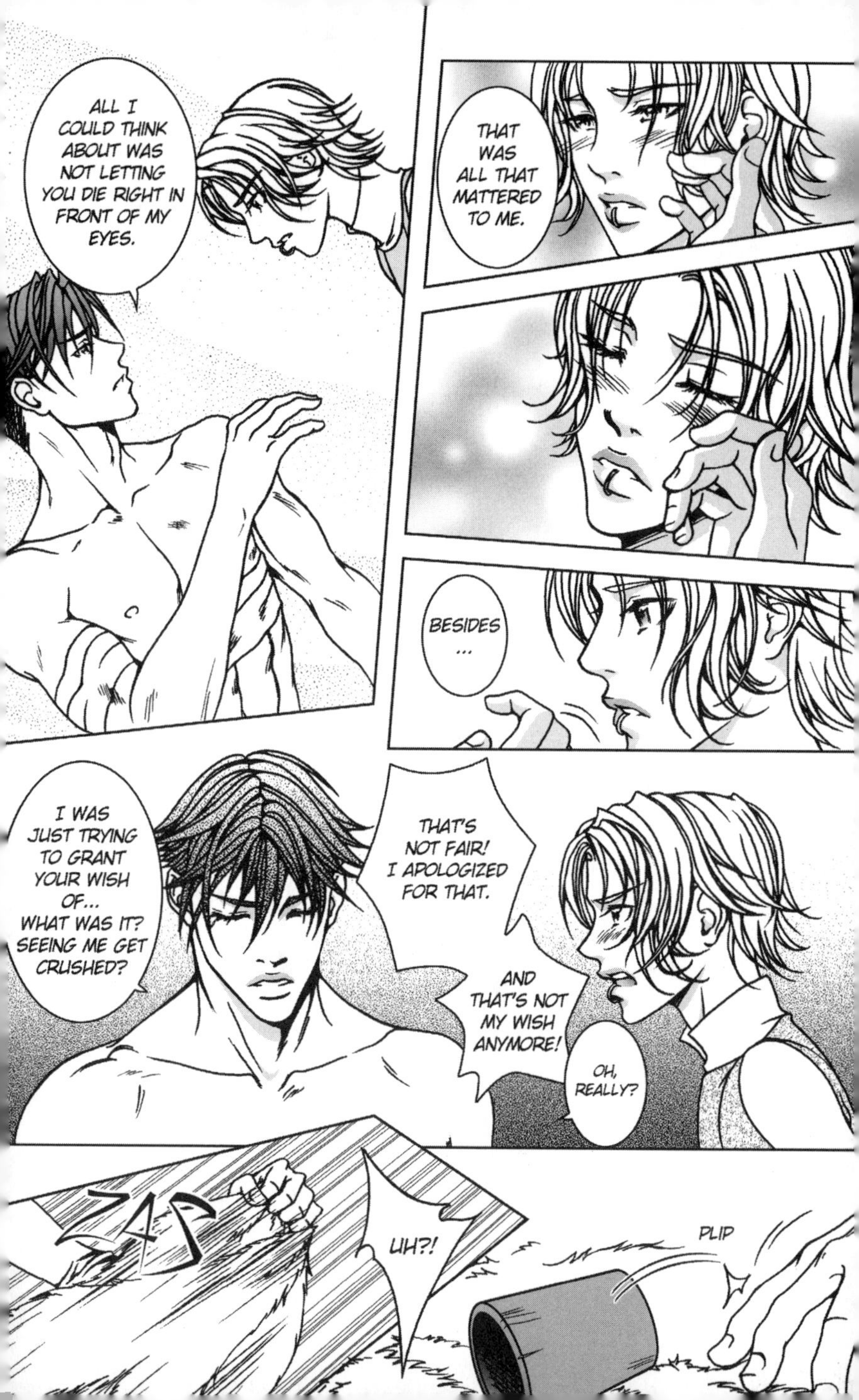
ALL I COULD THINK ABOUT WAS NOT LETTING YOU DIE RIGHT IN FRONT OF MY EYES.
THAT WAS ALL THAT MATTERED TO ME.
BESIDES ...
I WAS JUST TRYING TO GRANT YOUR WISH OF... WHAT WAS IT? SEEING ME GET CRUSHED?
THAT'S NOT FAIR! I APOLOGIZED FOR THAT.
AND THAT'S NOT MY WISH ANYMORE!
OH, REALLY?
ZAP
UH?!
PLIP

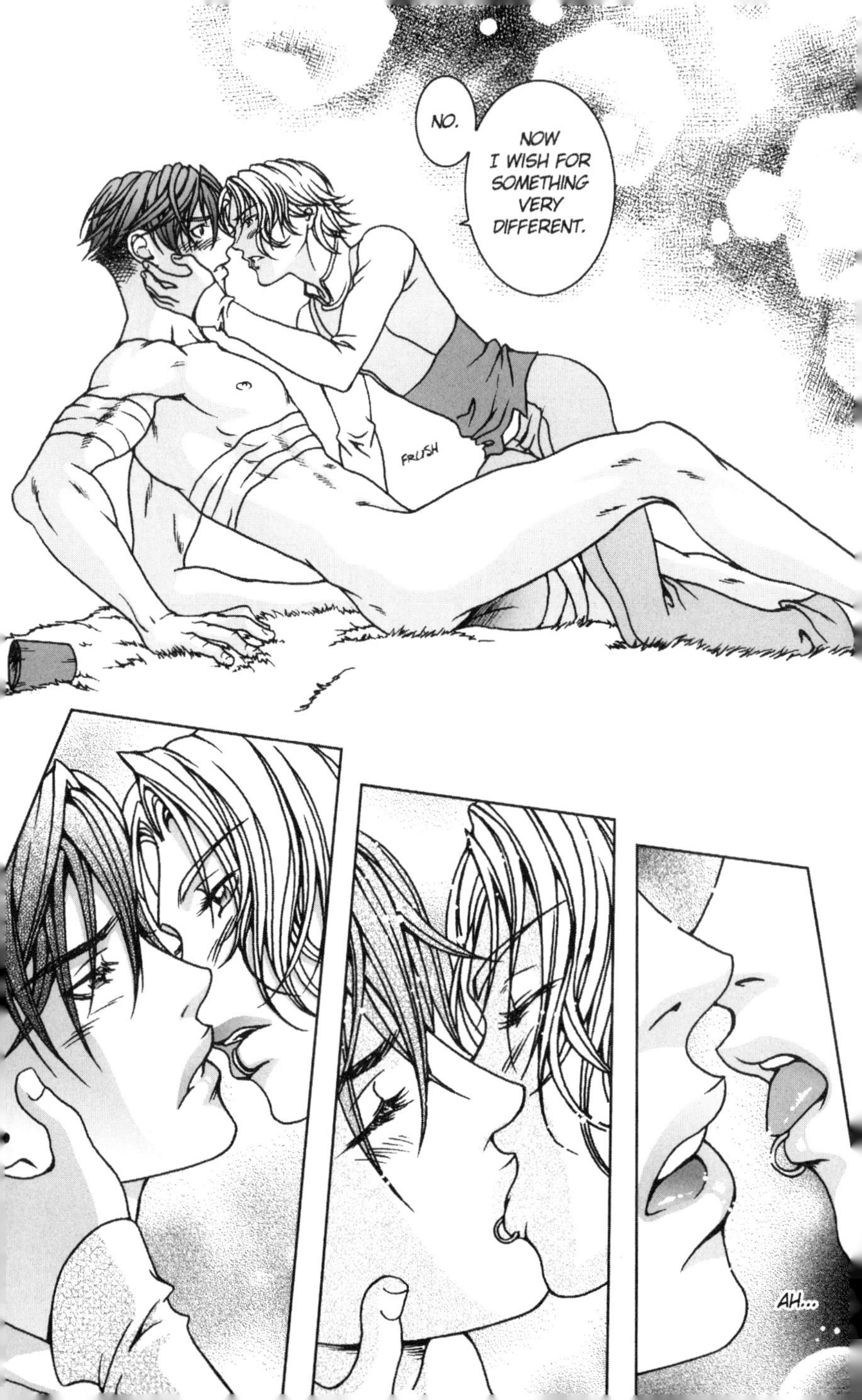
NO.
NOW I WISH FOR SOMETHING VERY DIFFERENT.
FRUSH
AH...

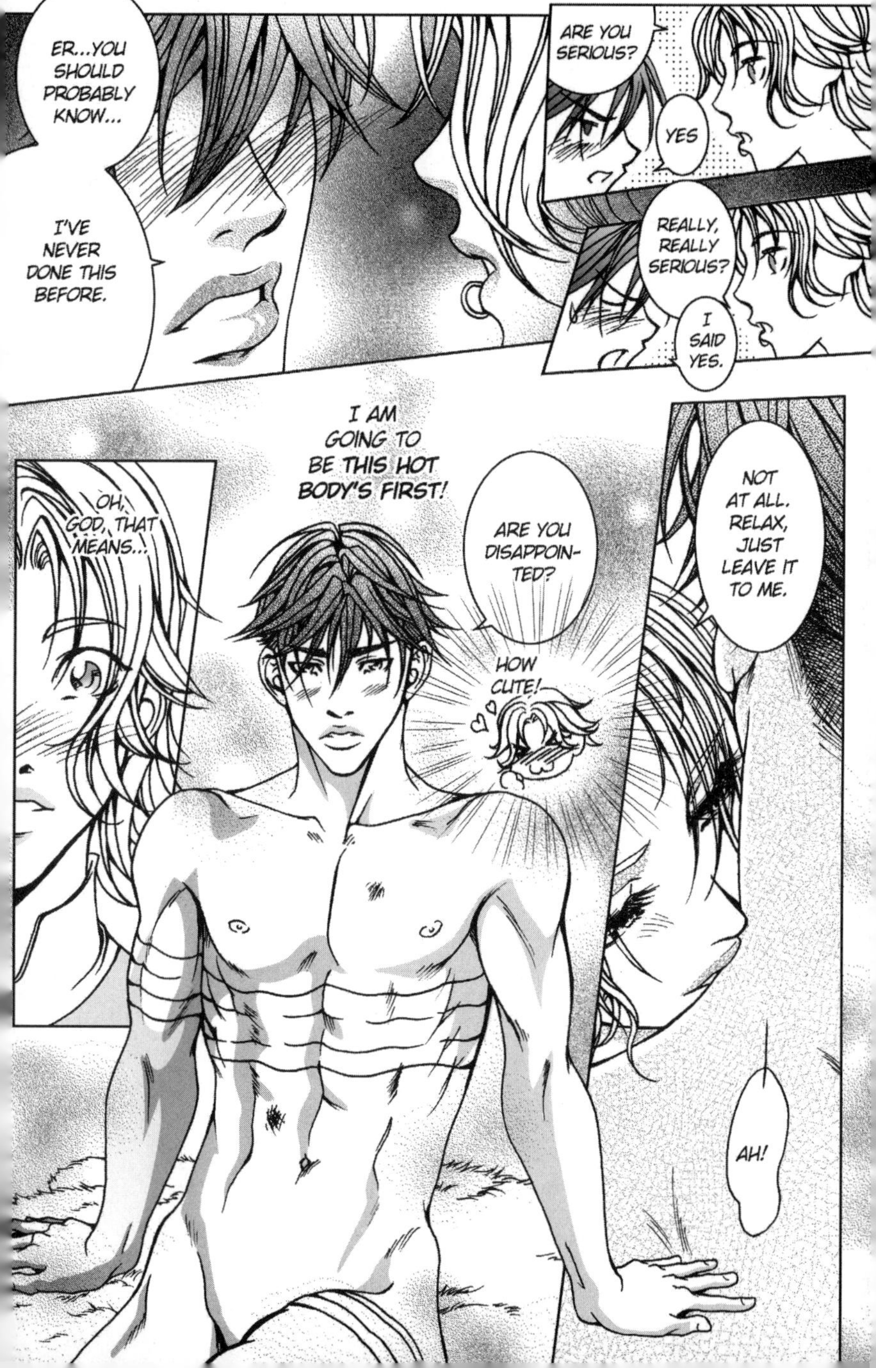
ARE YOU SERIOUS?
YES
REALLY, REALLY SERIOUS?
I SAID YES.
ER...YOU SHOULD PROBABLY KNOW...
I'VE NEVER DONE THIS BEFORE.
NOT AT ALL. RELAX, JUST LEAVE IT TO ME.
AH!
ARE YOU DISAPPOIN-TED?
HOW CUTE!
I AM GOING TO BE THIS HOT BODY'S FIRST!
OH, GOD, THAT MEANS...

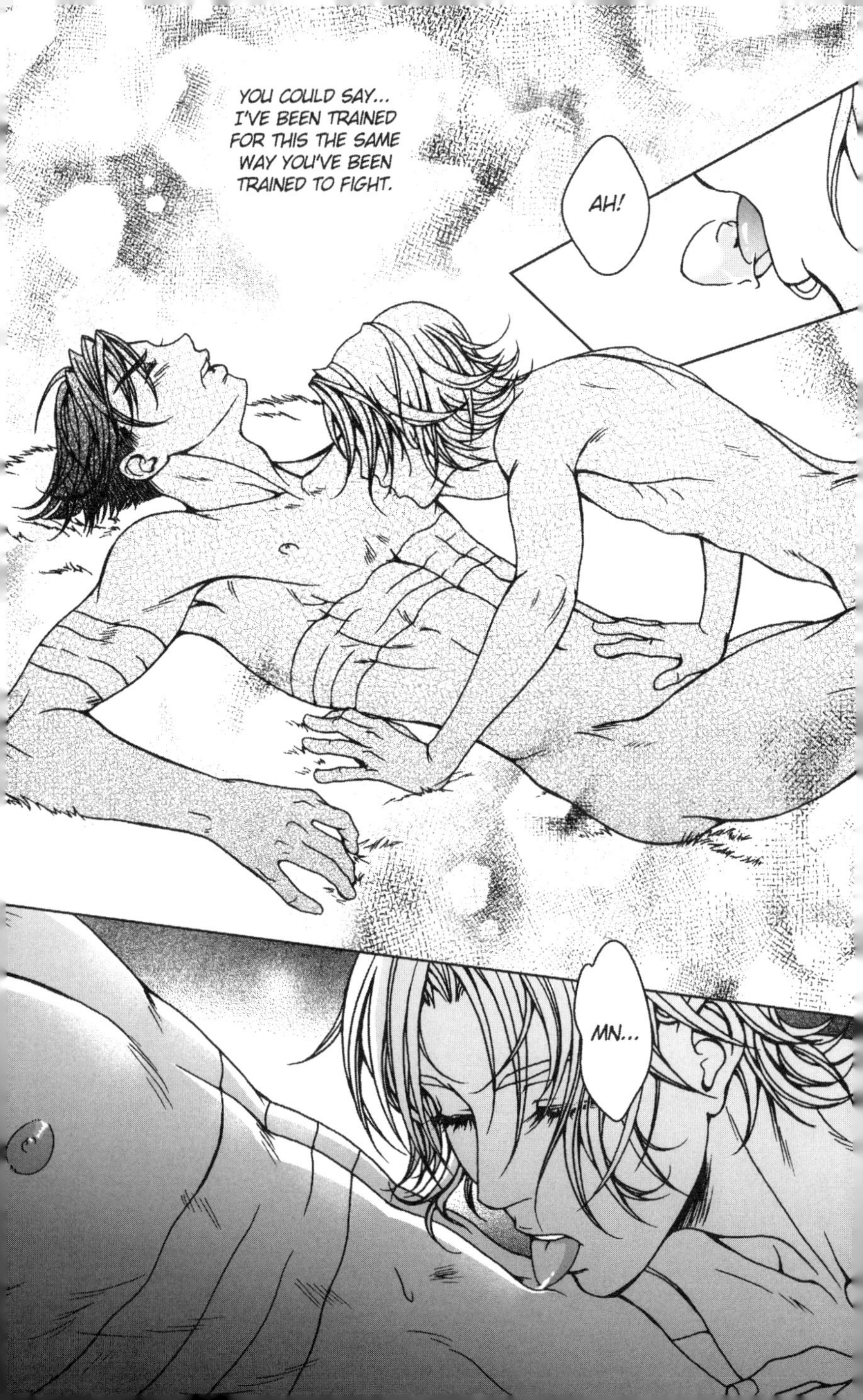
YOU COULD SAY... I'VE BEEN TRAINED FOR THIS THE SAME WAY YOU'VE BEEN TRAINED TO FIGHT.
AH!
MN...

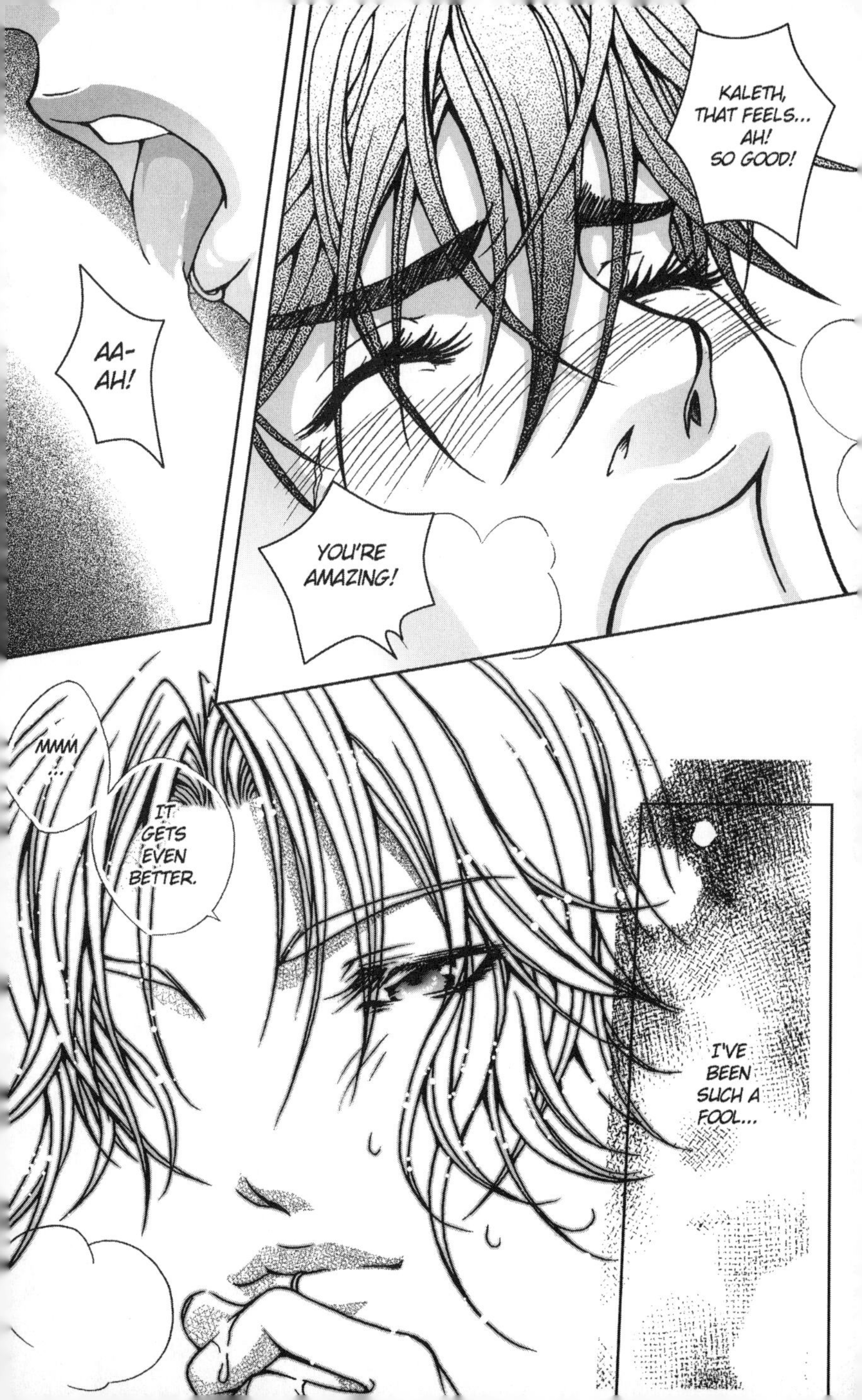
KALETH, THAT FEELS... AH! SO GOOD!
AA-AH!
YOU'RE AMAZING!
MMM ...
IT GETS EVEN BETTER.
I'VE BEEN SUCH A FOOL...

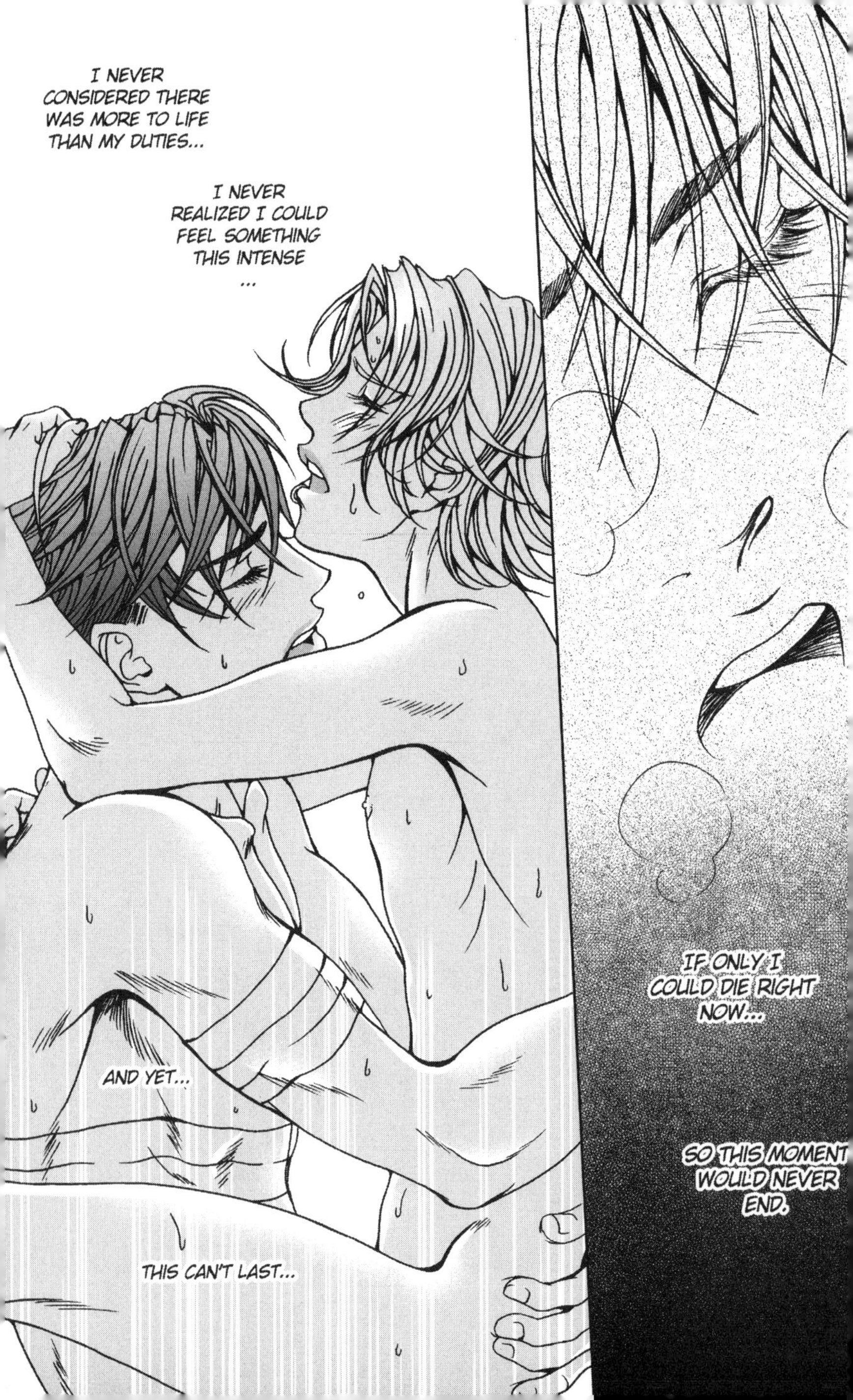
I NEVER CONSIDERED THERE WAS MORE TO LIFE THAN MY DUTIES...
I NEVER REALIZED I COULD FEEL SOMETHING THIS INTENSE ...
AND YET...
THIS CAN'T LAST...
IF ONLY I COULD DIE RIGHT NOW...
SO THIS MOMENT WOULD NEVER END.

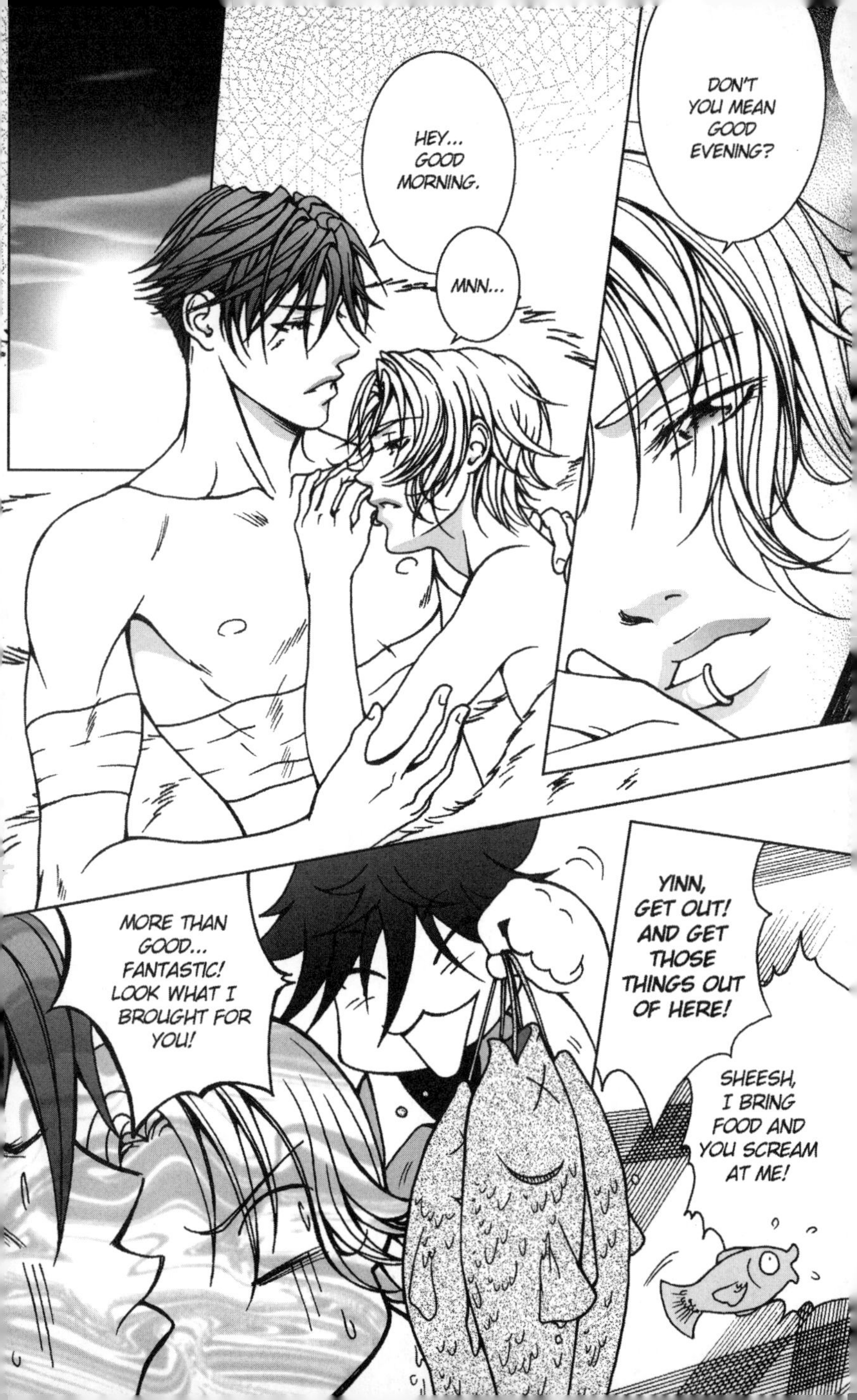
HEY... GOOD MORNING.
MNN...
DON'T YOU MEAN GOOD EVENING?
MORE THAN GOOD... FANTASTIC! LOOK WHAT I BROUGHT FOR YOU!
YINN, GET OUT! AND GET THOSE THINGS OUT OF HERE!
SHEESH, I BRING FOOD AND YOU SCREAM AT ME!

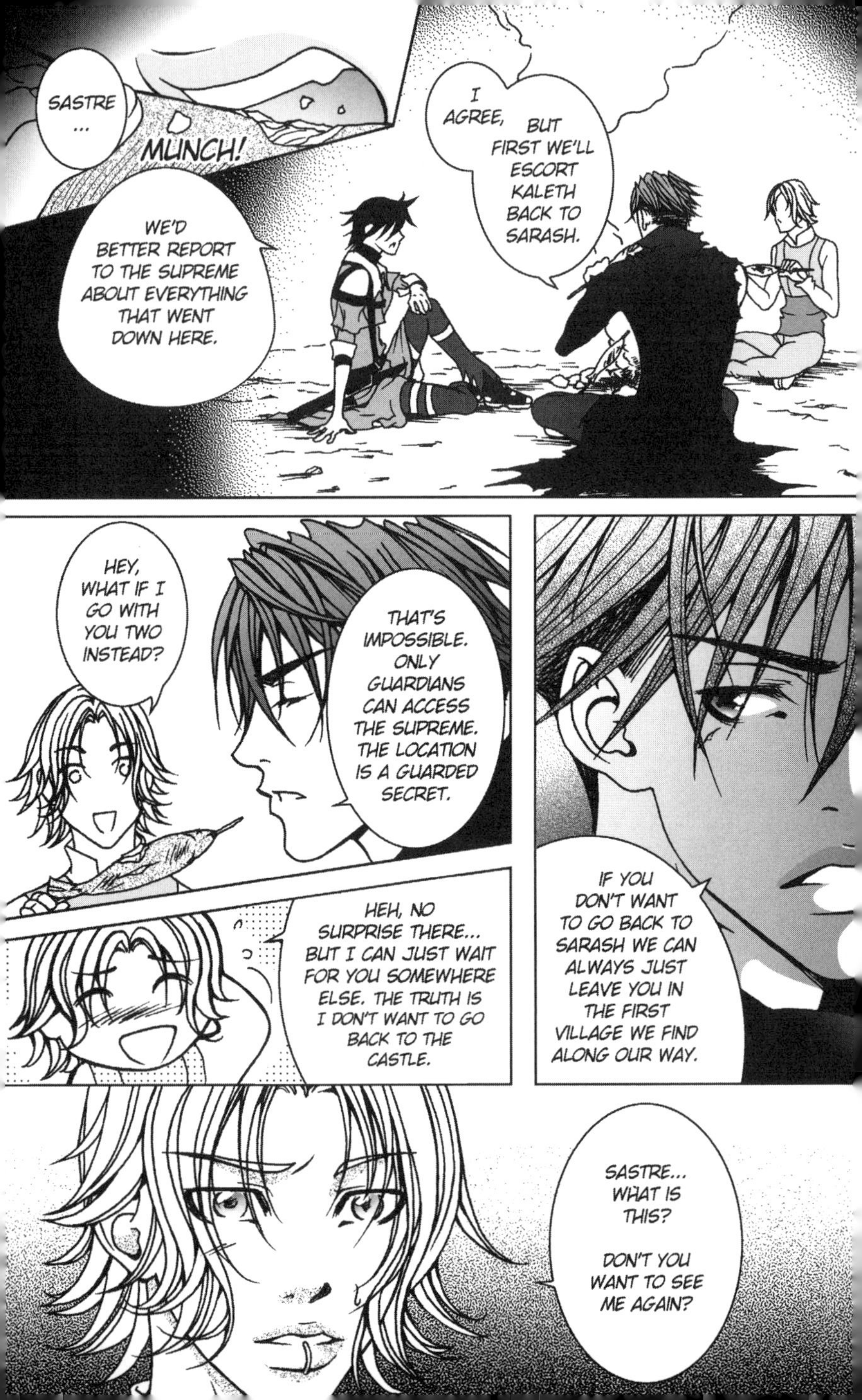
SASTRE ...
MUNCH!
WE'D BETTER REPORT TO THE SUPREME ABOUT EVERYTHING THAT WENT DOWN HERE.
I AGREE, BUT FIRST WE'LL ESCORT KALETH BACK TO SARASH.
HEY, WHAT IF I GO WITH YOU TWO INSTEAD?
THAT'S IMPOSSIBLE. ONLY GUARDIANS CAN ACCESS THE SUPREME. THE LOCATION IS A GUARDED SECRET.
HEH, NO SURPRISE THERE... BUT I CAN JUST WAIT FOR YOU SOMEWHERE ELSE. THE TRUTH IS I DON'T WANT TO GO BACK TO THE CASTLE.
IF YOU DON'T WANT TO GO BACK TO SARASH WE CAN ALWAYS JUST LEAVE YOU IN THE FIRST VILLAGE WE FIND ALONG OUR WAY.
SASTRE... WHAT IS THIS?
DON'T YOU WANT TO SEE ME AGAIN?

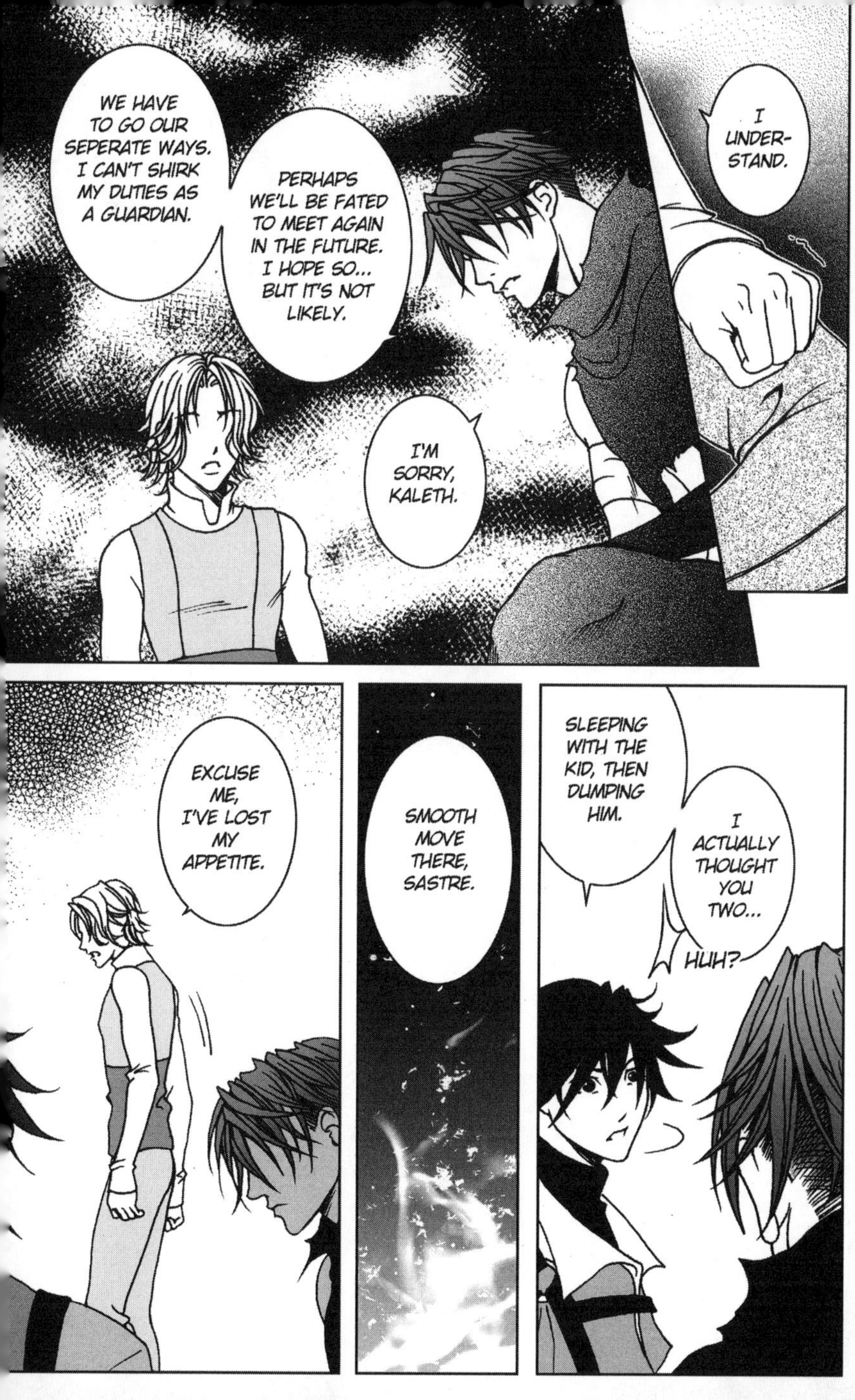
WE HAVE TO GO OUR SEPERATE WAYS. I CAN'T SHIRK MY DUTIES AS A GUARDIAN.
PERHAPS WE'LL BE FATED TO MEET AGAIN IN THE FUTURE. I HOPE SO... BUT IT'S NOT LIKELY.
I UNDER-STAND.
I'M SORRY, KALETH.
EXCUSE ME, I'VE LOST MY APPETITE.
SMOOTH MOVE THERE, SASTRE.
SLEEPING WITH THE KID, THEN DUMPING HIM.
I ACTUALLY THOUGHT YOU TWO...
HUH?

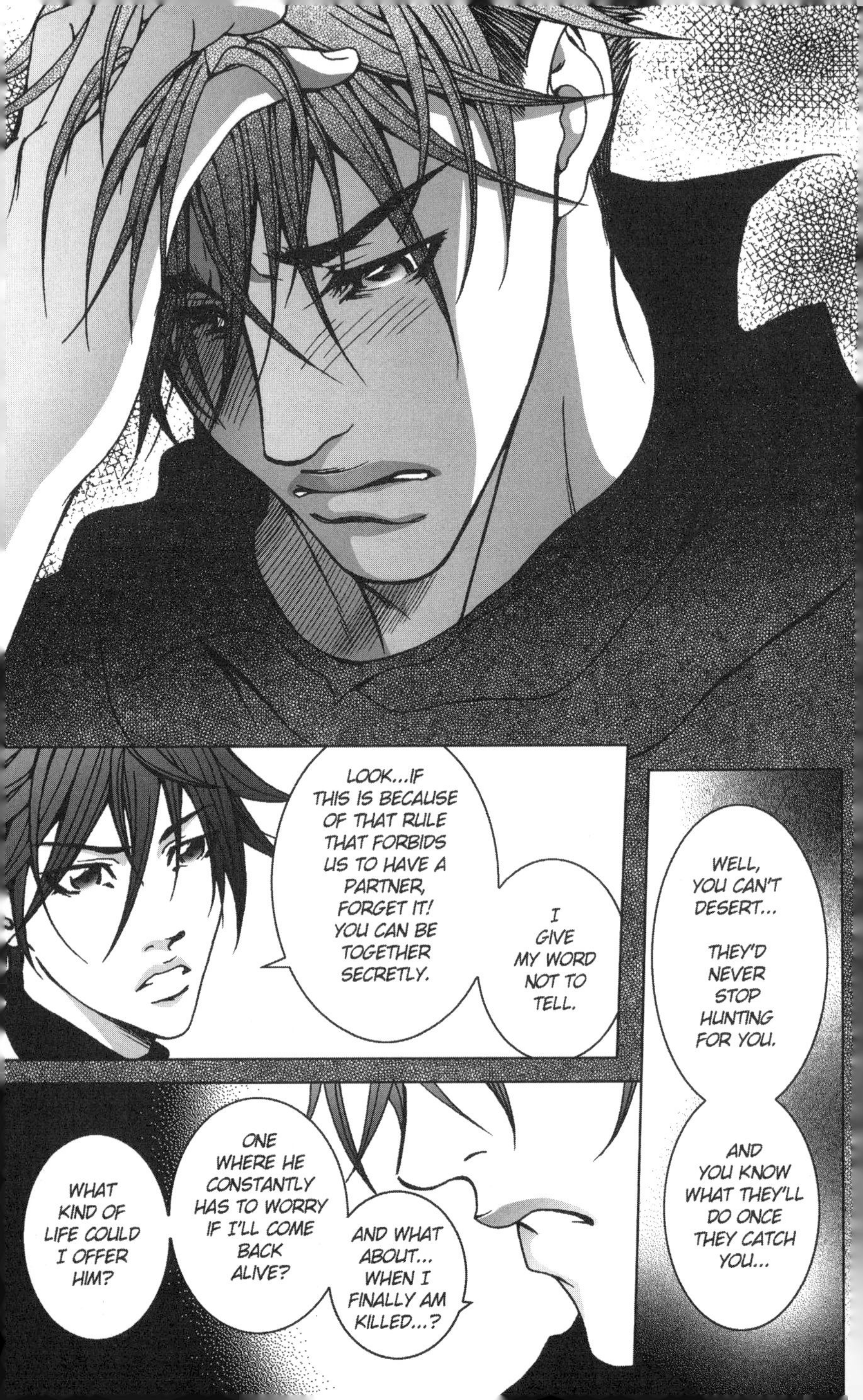
LOOK...IF THIS IS BECAUSE OF THAT RULE THAT FORBIDS US TO HAVE A PARTNER, FORGET IT! YOU CAN BE TOGETHER SECRETLY.
I GIVE MY WORD NOT TO TELL.
WELL, YOU CAN'T DESERT... THEY'D NEVER STOP HUNTING FOR YOU.
AND YOU KNOW WHAT THEY'LL DO ONCE THEY CATCH YOU...
WHAT KIND OF LIFE COULD I OFFER HIM?
ONE WHERE HE CONSTANTLY HAS TO WORRY IF I'LL COME BACK ALIVE?
AND WHAT ABOUT... WHEN I FINALLY AM KILLED...?

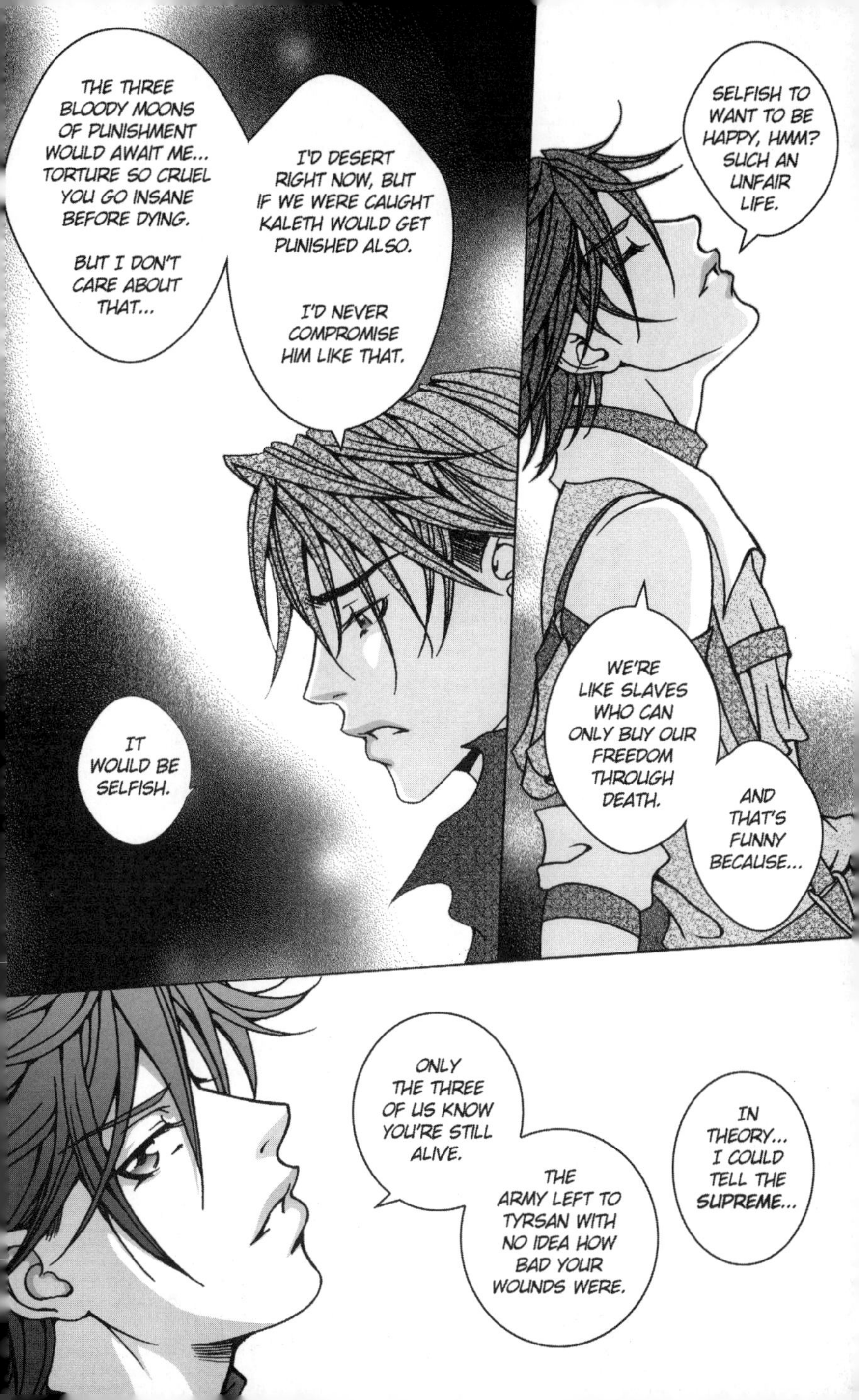
THE THREE BLOODY MOONS OF PUNISHMENT WOULD AWAIT ME... TORTURE SO CRUEL YOU GO INSANE BEFORE DYING.
BUT I DON'T CARE ABOUT THAT...
I'D DESERT RIGHT NOW, BUT IF WE WERE CAUGHT KALETH WOULD GET PUNISHED ALSO.
I'D NEVER COMPROMISE HIM LIKE THAT.
IT WOULD BE SELFISH.
SELFISH TO WANT TO BE HAPPY, HMM? SUCH AN UNFAIR LIFE.
WE'RE LIKE SLAVES WHO CAN ONLY BUY OUR FREEDOM THROUGH DEATH.
AND THAT'S FUNNY BECAUSE...
ONLY THE THREE OF US KNOW YOU'RE STILL ALIVE.
THE ARMY LEFT TO TYRSAN WITH NO IDEA HOW BAD YOUR WOUNDS WERE.
IN THEORY... I COULD TELL THE SUPREME...

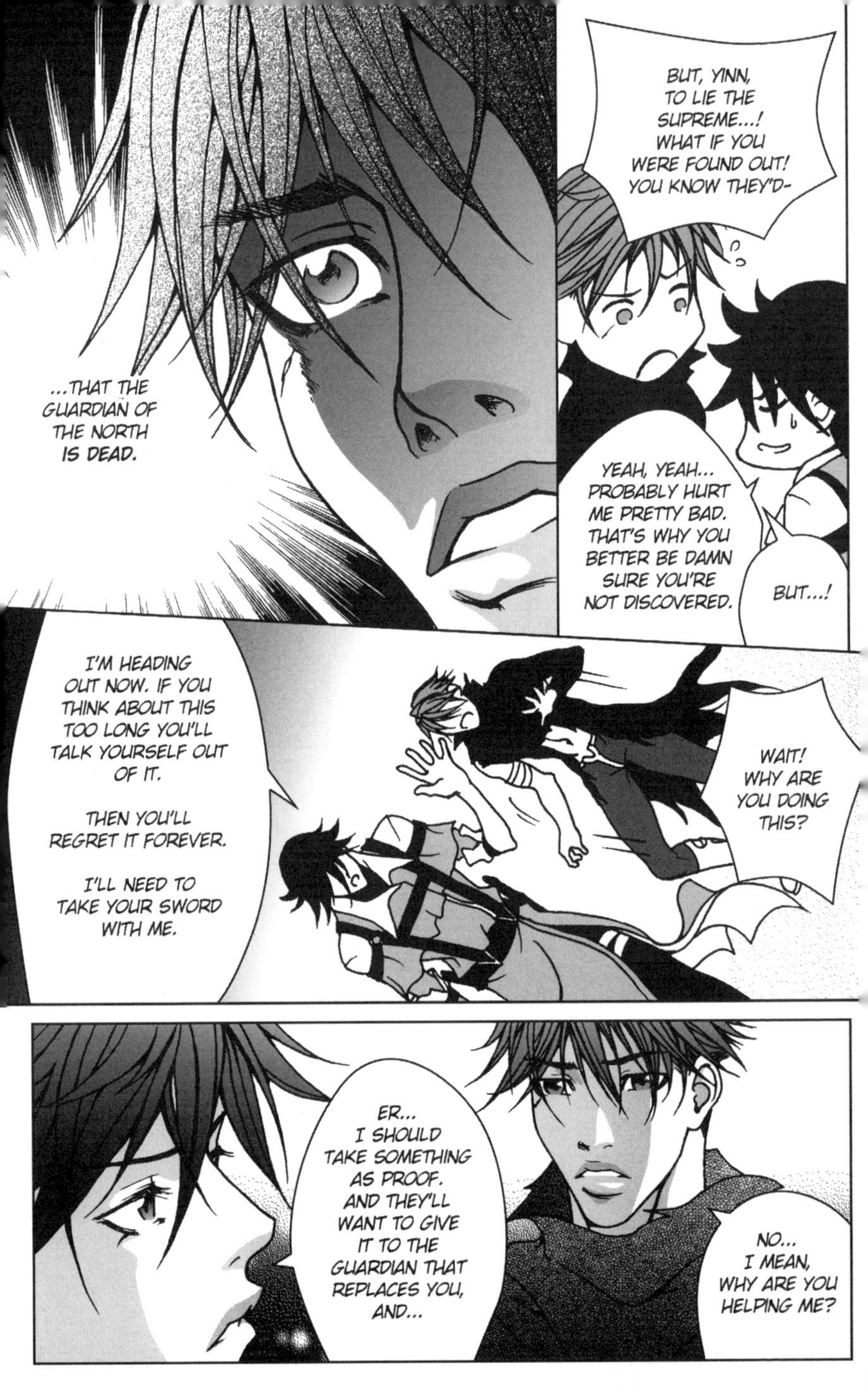
...THAT THE GUARDIAN OF THE NORTH IS DEAD.
BUT, YINN, TO LIE THE SUPREME...! WHAT IF YOU WERE FOUND OUT! YOU KNOW THEY'D-
YEAH, YEAH... PROBABLY HURT ME PRETTY BAD. THAT'S WHY YOU BETTER BE DAMN SURE YOU'RE NOT DISCOVERED.
BUT...!
I'M HEADING OUT NOW. IF YOU THINK ABOUT THIS TOO LONG YOU'LL TALK YOURSELF OUT OF IT.
THEN YOU'LL REGRET IT FOREVER.
I'LL NEED TO TAKE YOUR SWORD WITH ME.
WAIT! WHY ARE YOU DOING THIS?
ER... I SHOULD TAKE SOMETHING AS PROOF. AND THEY'LL WANT TO GIVE IT TO THE GUARDIAN THAT REPLACES YOU, AND...
NO... I MEAN, WHY ARE YOU HELPING ME?

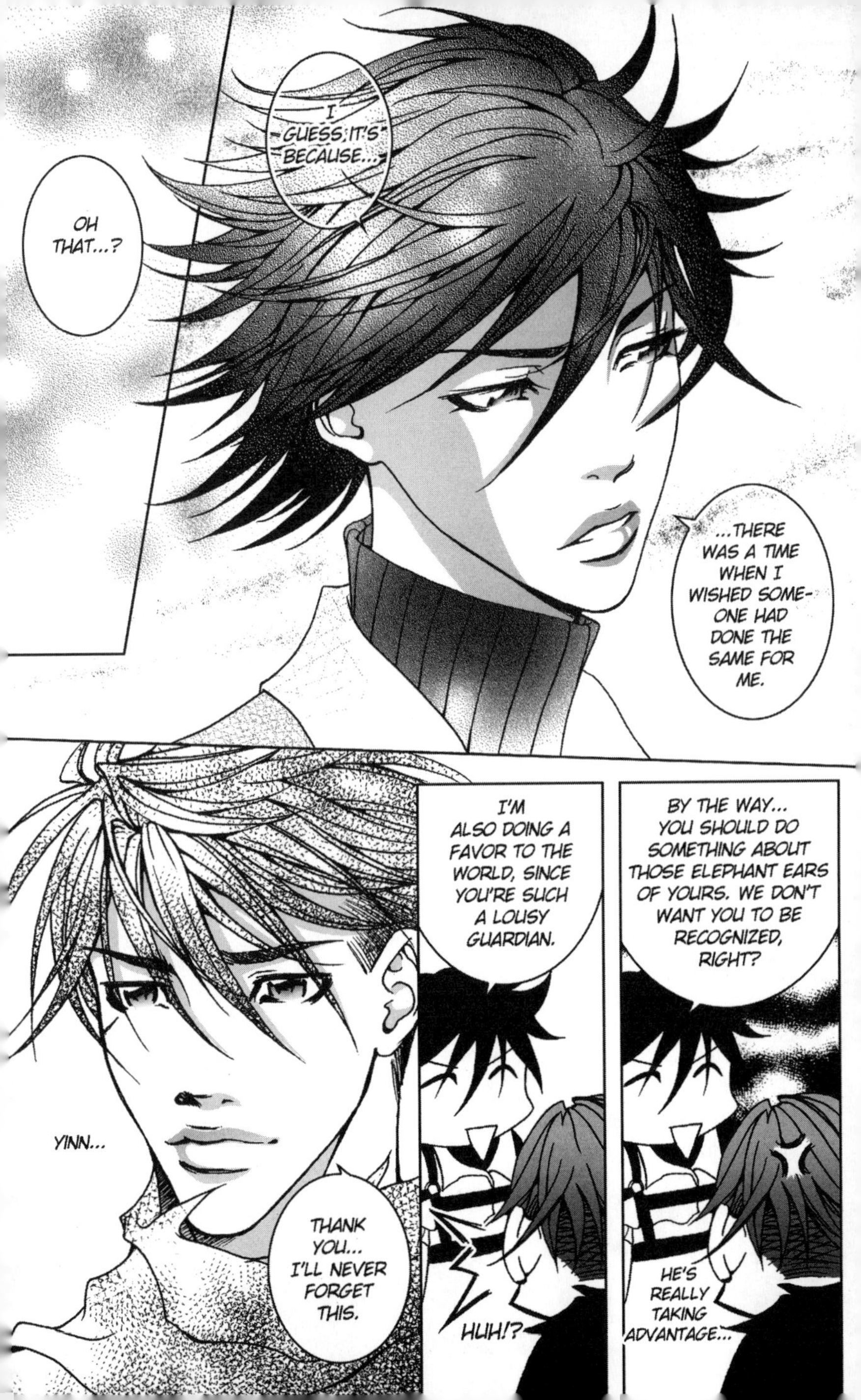

OH THAT...?
I GUESS IT'S BECAUSE...
...THERE WAS A TIME WHEN I WISHED SOME-ONE HAD DONE THE SAME FOR ME.
YINN...
THANK YOU... I'LL NEVER FORGET THIS.
I'M ALSO DOING A FAVOR TO THE WORLD, SINCE YOU'RE SUCH A LOUSY GUARDIAN.
HUH!?
BY THE WAY... YOU SHOULD DO SOMETHING ABOUT THOSE ELEPHANT EARS OF YOURS. WE DON'T WANT YOU TO BE RECOGNIZED, RIGHT?
HE'S REALLY TAKING ADVANTAGE...

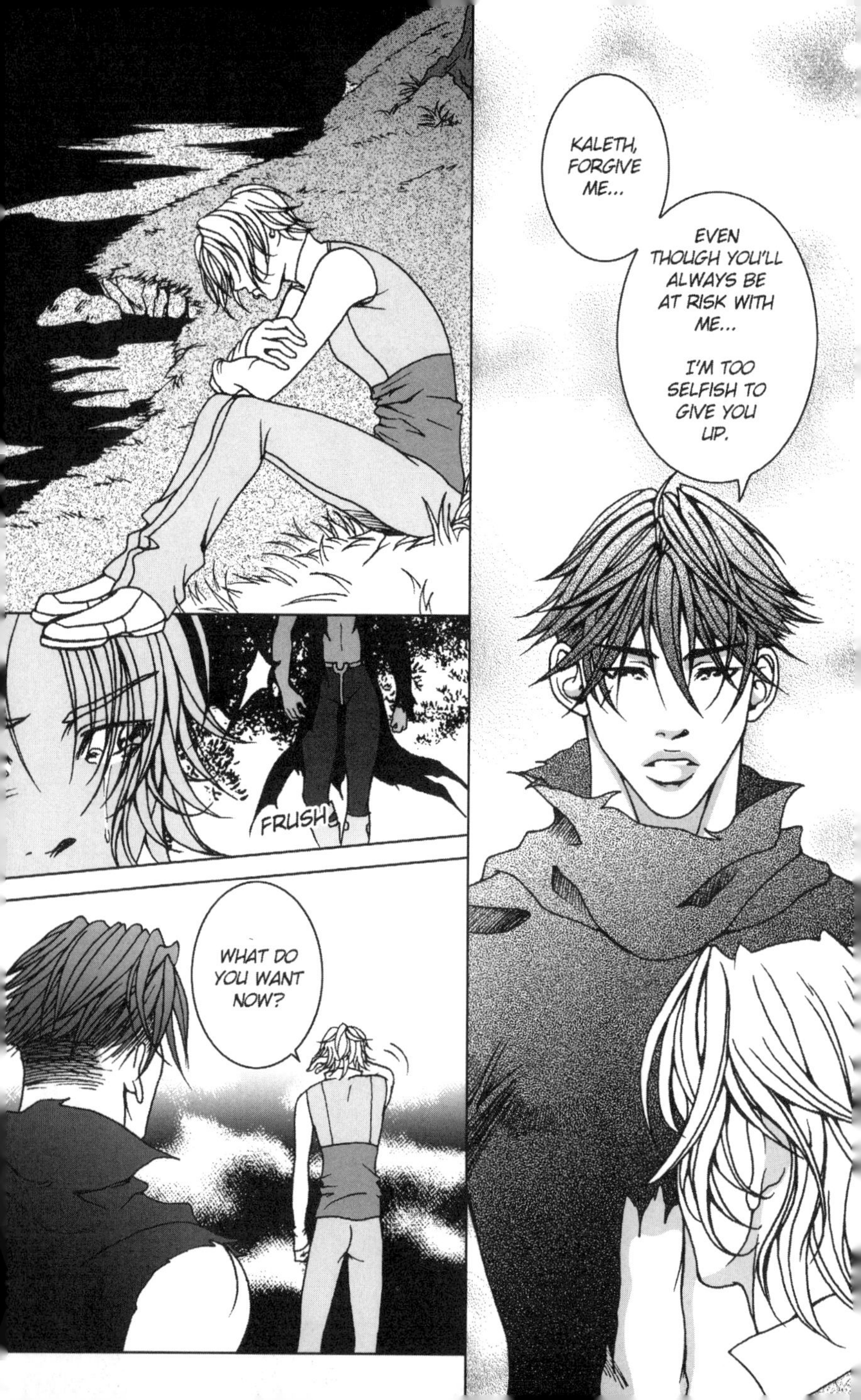
KALETH, FORGIVE ME...
EVEN THOUGH YOU'LL ALWAYS BE AT RISK WITH ME...
I'M TOO SELFISH TO GIVE YOU UP.
FRUSH
WHAT DO YOU WANT NOW?

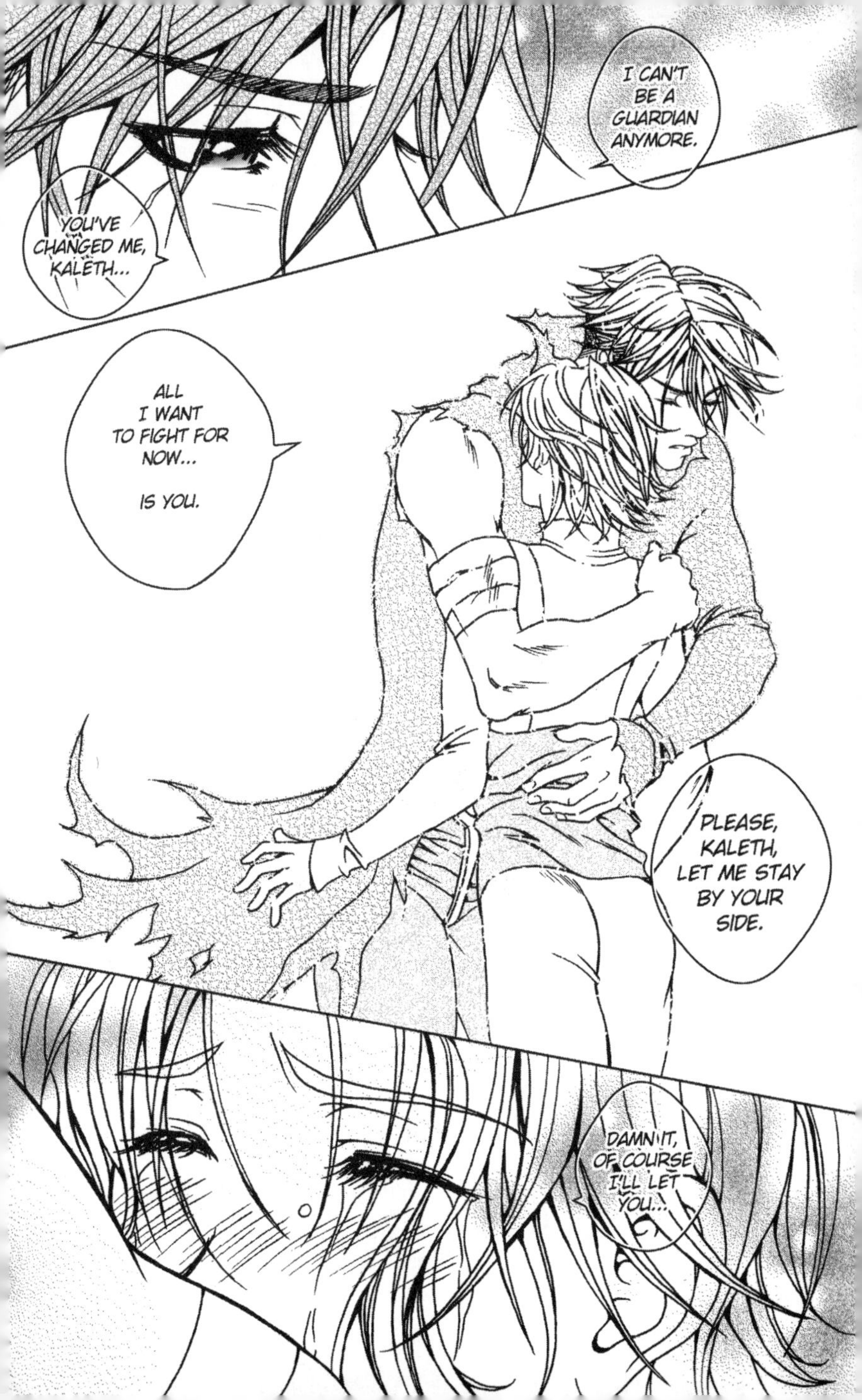
I CAN'T BE A GUARDIAN ANYMORE.
YOU'VE CHANGED ME, KALETH...
ALL I WANT TO FIGHT FOR NOW...
IS YOU.
PLEASE, KALETH, LET ME STAY BY YOUR SIDE.
DAMN IT, OF COURSE I'LL LET YOU...

SAIHŌSHI, THE GUARDIAN. THE END.

Saihôshi The SD

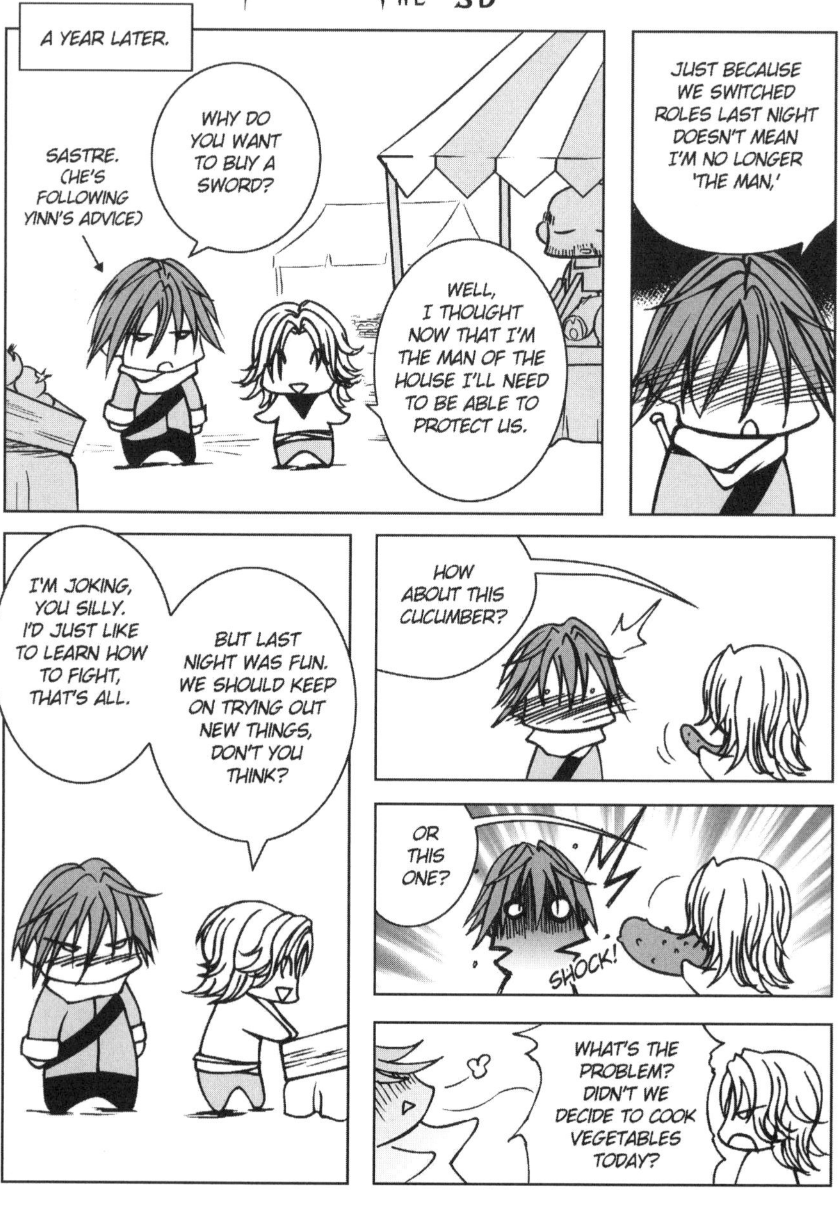
A YEAR LATER.
SASTRE. (HE'S FOLLOWING YINN'S ADVICE)
WHY DO YOU WANT TO BUY A SWORD?
WELL, I THOUGHT NOW THAT I'M THE MAN OF THE HOUSE I'LL NEED TO BE ABLE TO PROTECT US.
JUST BECAUSE WE SWITCHED ROLES LAST NIGHT DOESN'T MEAN I'M NO LONGER 'THE MAN,'
I'M JOKING, YOU SILLY. I'D JUST LIKE TO LEARN HOW TO FIGHT, THAT'S ALL.
BUT LAST NIGHT WAS FUN. WE SHOULD KEEP ON TRYING OUT NEW THINGS, DON'T YOU THINK?
HOW ABOUT THIS CUCUMBER?
OR THIS ONE?
SHOCK!
WHAT'S THE PROBLEM? DIDN'T WE DECIDE TO COOK VEGETABLES TODAY?

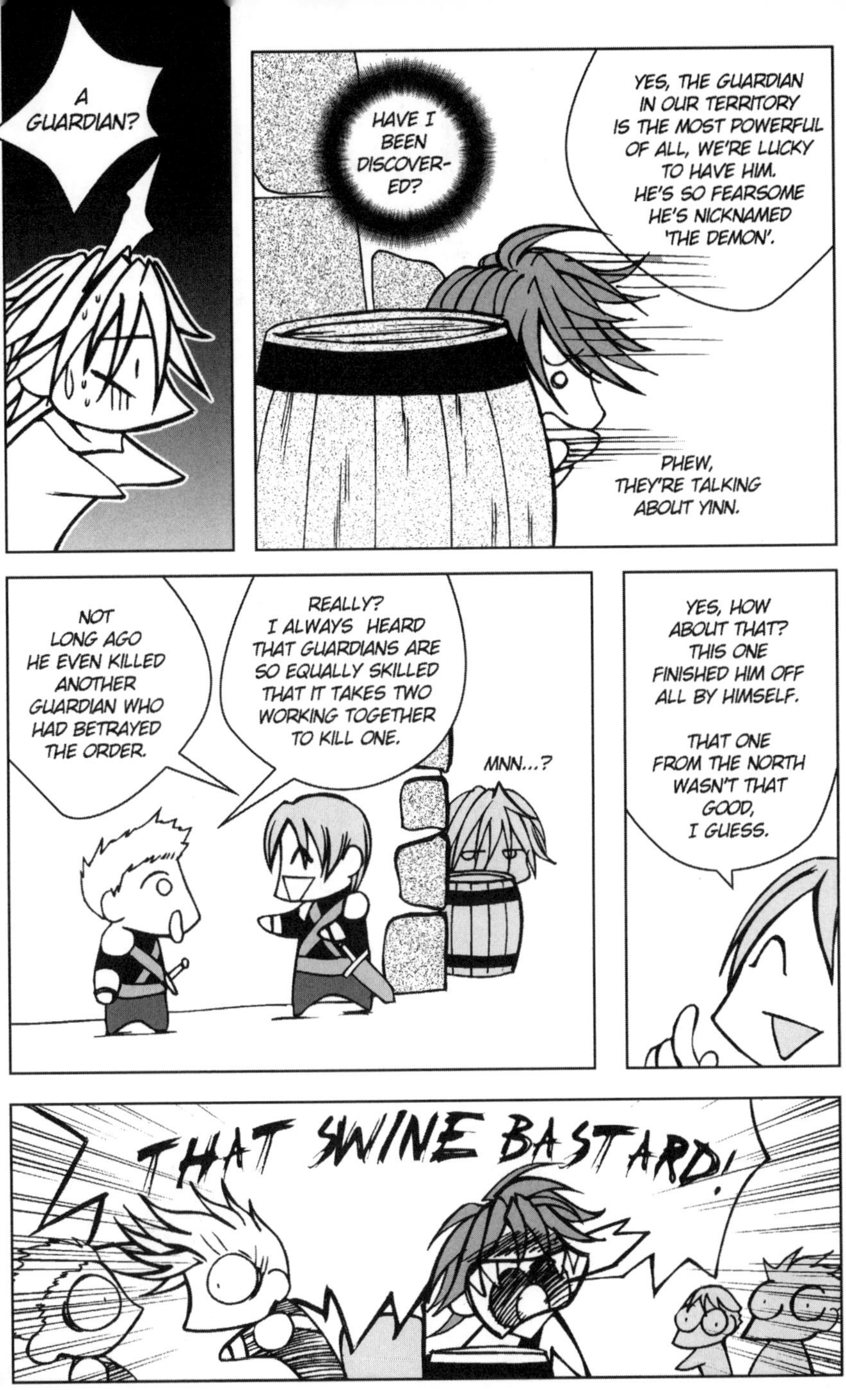
A GUARDIAN?
HAVE I BEEN DISCOVER-ED?
YES, THE GUARDIAN IN OUR TERRITORY IS THE MOST POWERFUL OF ALL, WE'RE LUCKY TO HAVE HIM. HE'S SO FEARSOME HE'S NICKNAMED 'THE DEMON'.
PHEW, THEY'RE TALKING ABOUT YINN.
NOT LONG AGO HE EVEN KILLED ANOTHER GUARDIAN WHO HAD BETRAYED THE ORDER.
REALLY? I ALWAYS HEARD THAT GUARDIANS ARE SO EQUALLY SKILLED THAT IT TAKES TWO WORKING TOGETHER TO KILL ONE.
MNN...?
YES, HOW ABOUT THAT? THIS ONE FINISHED HIM OFF ALL BY HIMSELF.
THAT ONE FROM THE NORTH WASN'T THAT GOOD, I GUESS.
THAT SWINE BASTARD!

Saihôshi THE SD

REGARDING THE REST OF THEM:

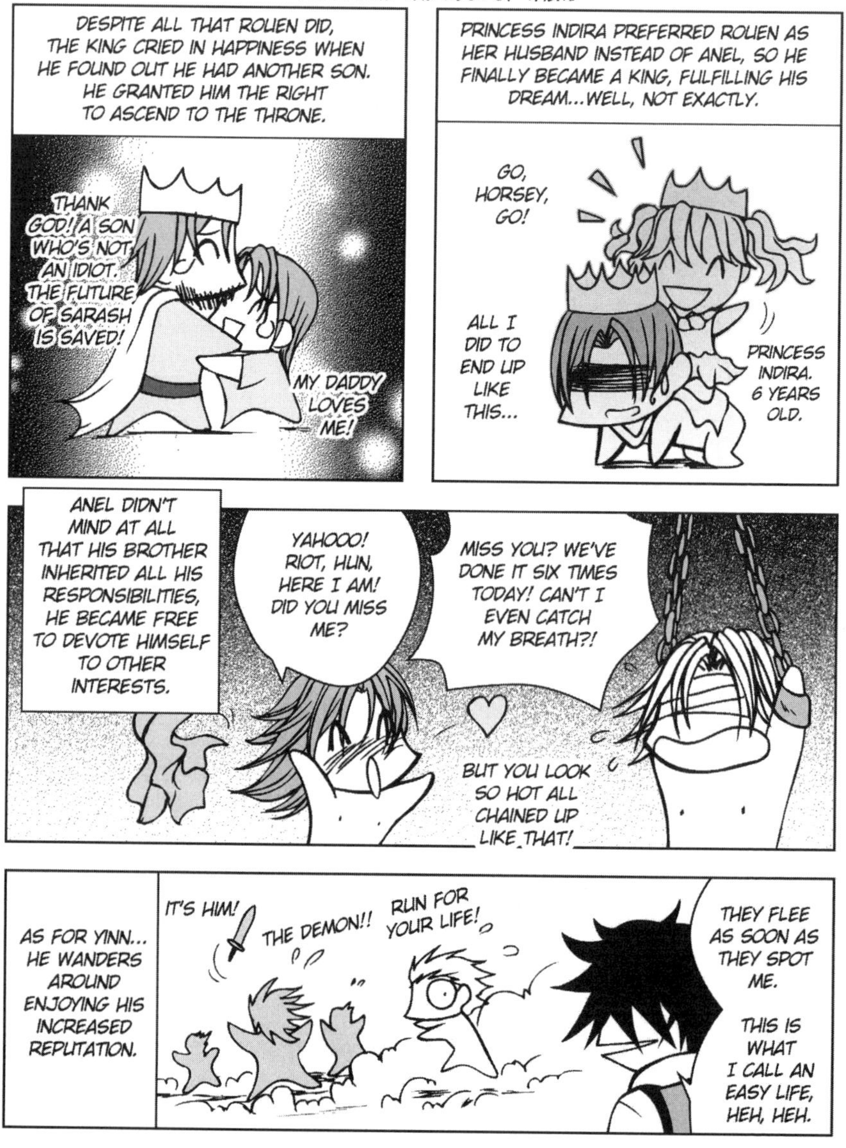
DESPITE ALL THAT ROUEN DID, THE KING CRIED IN HAPPINESS WHEN HE FOUND OUT HE HAD ANOTHER SON. HE GRANTED HIM THE RIGHT TO ASCEND TO THE THRONE.
THANK GOD! A SON WHO'S NOT AN IDIOT. THE FUTURE OF SARASH IS SAVED!
MY DADDY LOVES ME!
PRINCESS INDIRA PREFERRED ROUEN AS HER HUSBAND INSTEAD OF ANEL, SO HE FINALLY BECAME A KING, FULFILLING HIS DREAM...WELL, NOT EXACTLY.
GO, HORSEY, GO!
ALL I DID TO END UP LIKE THIS...
PRINCESS INDIRA. 6 YEARS OLD.
ANEL DIDN'T MIND AT ALL THAT HIS BROTHER INHERITED ALL HIS RESPONSIBILITIES, HE BECAME FREE TO DEVOTE HIMSELF TO OTHER INTERESTS.
YAHOOO! RIOT, HUN, HERE I AM! DID YOU MISS ME?
MISS YOU? WE'VE DONE IT SIX TIMES TODAY! CAN'T I EVEN CATCH MY BREATH?!
BUT YOU LOOK SO HOT ALL CHAINED UP LIKE THAT!
AS FOR YINN... HE WANDERS AROUND ENJOYING HIS INCREASED REPUTATION.
IT'S HIM!
THE DEMON!!
RUN FOR YOUR LIFE!
THEY FLEE AS SOON AS THEY SPOT ME.
THIS IS WHAT I CALL AN EASY LIFE, HEH, HEH.

SAIHÔSHI
THE GUARDIAN
⊱ BONUS ⊰

HI, WE'RE KÔSEN!

SAIHÔSHI, THE GUARDIAN IS
FINALLY COMPLETED!
THANK YOU VERY MUCH FOR
READING THIS STORY, WE
REALLY HOPE YOU HAVE
ENJOYED IT.
WE ALSO WISH YOU'LL
CONTINUE READING OUR NEXT
PROJECTS FROM NOW ON.

TO BE INFORMED, CHECK OUR
PUBLISHER'S SITE:
HTTP://WWW.YAOIPRESS.COM

OR OUR OWN:
HTTP://WWW.STKOSEN.COM

IN THE FOLLOWING SECTION
YOU'LL SEE SOME EARLY
CONCEPT DESIGNS AND COVERS
FOR THE STORY.

KÔSEN

Sastre

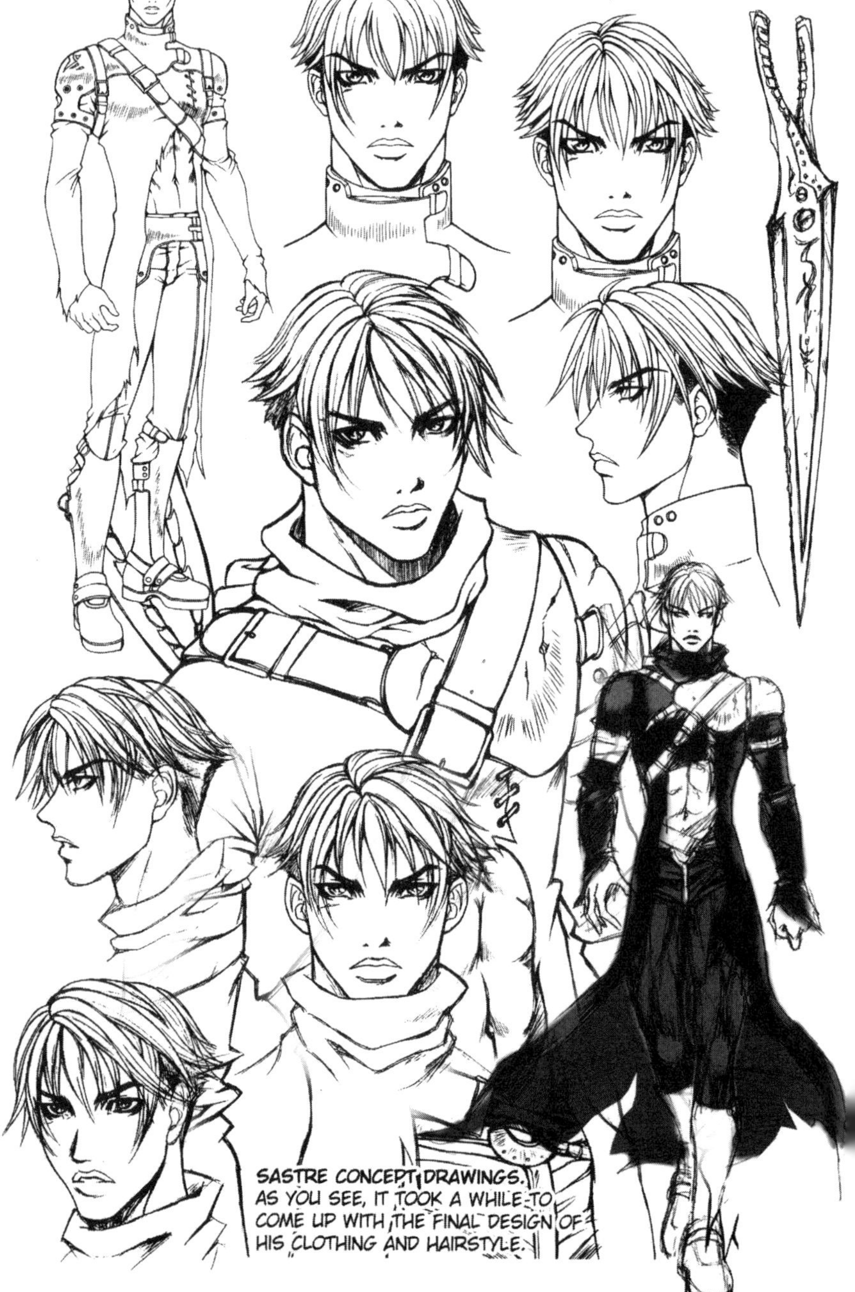
SASTRE CONCEPT DRAWINGS. AS YOU SEE, IT TOOK A WHILE TO COME UP WITH THE FINAL DESIGN OF HIS CLOTHING AND HAIRSTYLE.

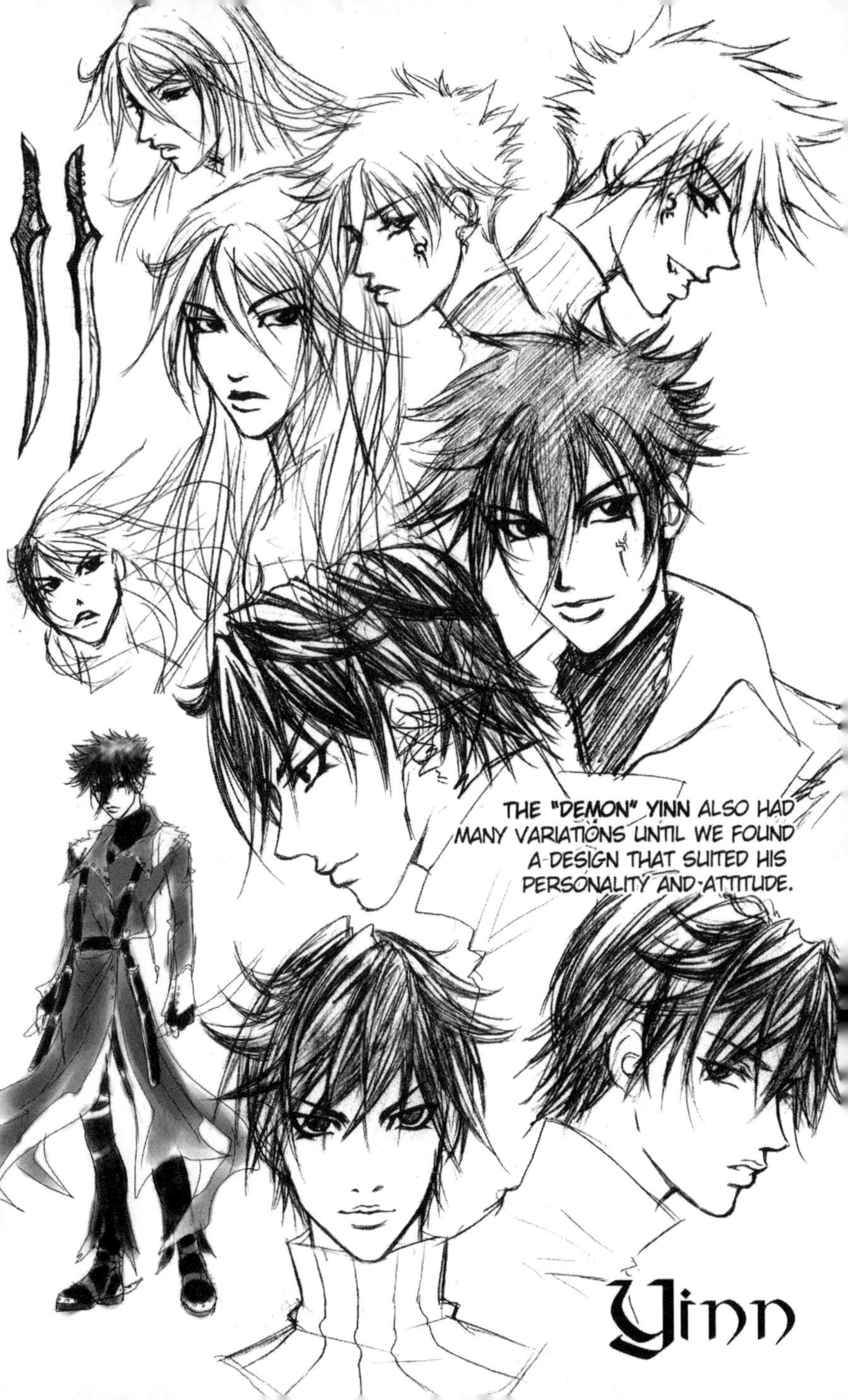
THE "DEMON" YINN ALSO HAD MANY VARIATIONS UNTIL WE FOUND A DESIGN THAT SUITED HIS PERSONALITY AND ATTITUDE.
Yinn

REJECTED COVER.
THIS ROUGH WAS ONE OF THE ALTERNATE COVERS WE DESIGNED, BUT WE DECIDED IT WAS TOO REVEALING TO SUIT THE STORY, WHICH WAS CENTERED IN THE PLOT AND NOT IN THE CHARACTERS SEXUAL RELATIONSHIPS.

WE STILL LIKE IT, THOUGH, SO WE DECIDED TO SHARE IT WITH YOU ALL.

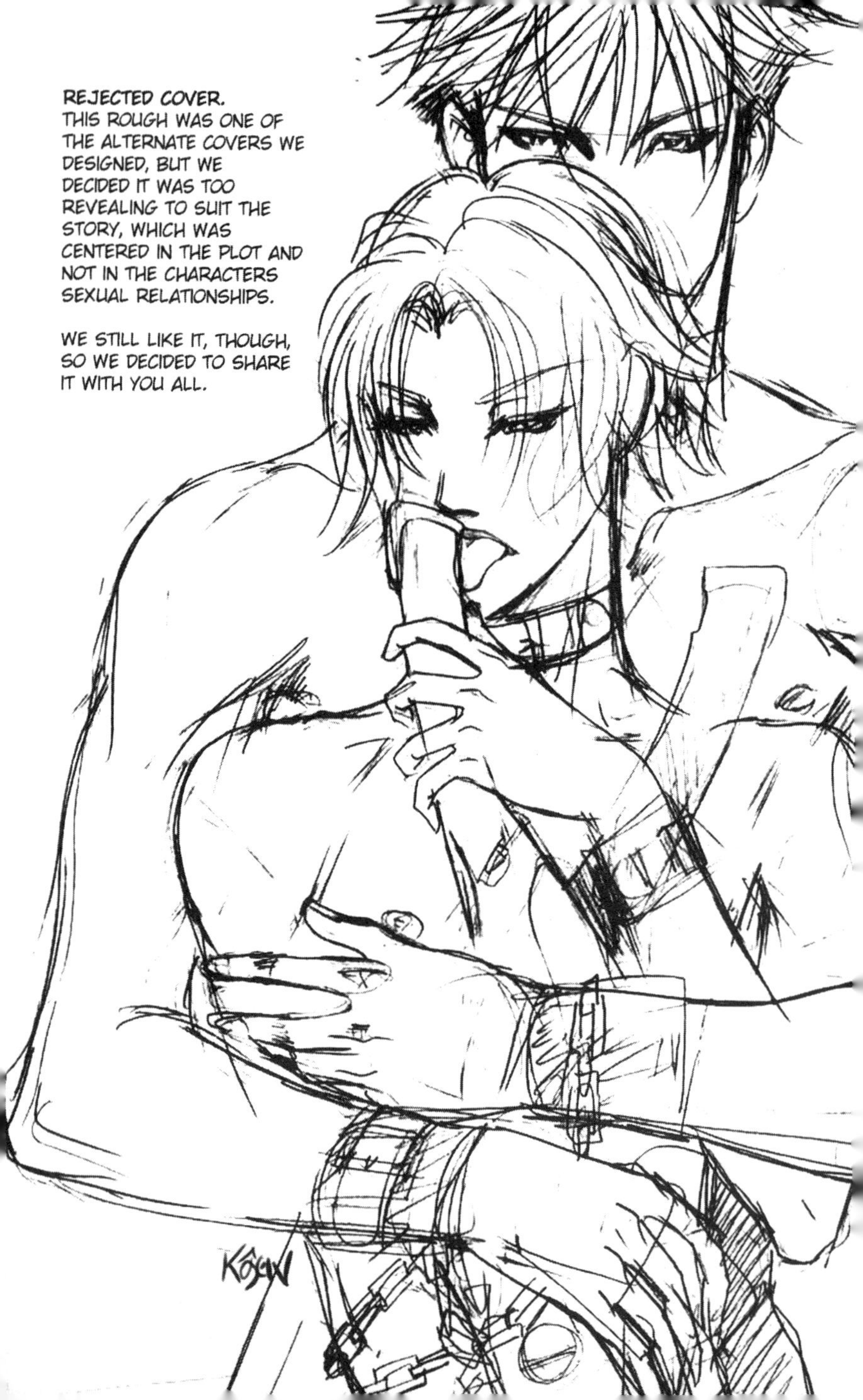

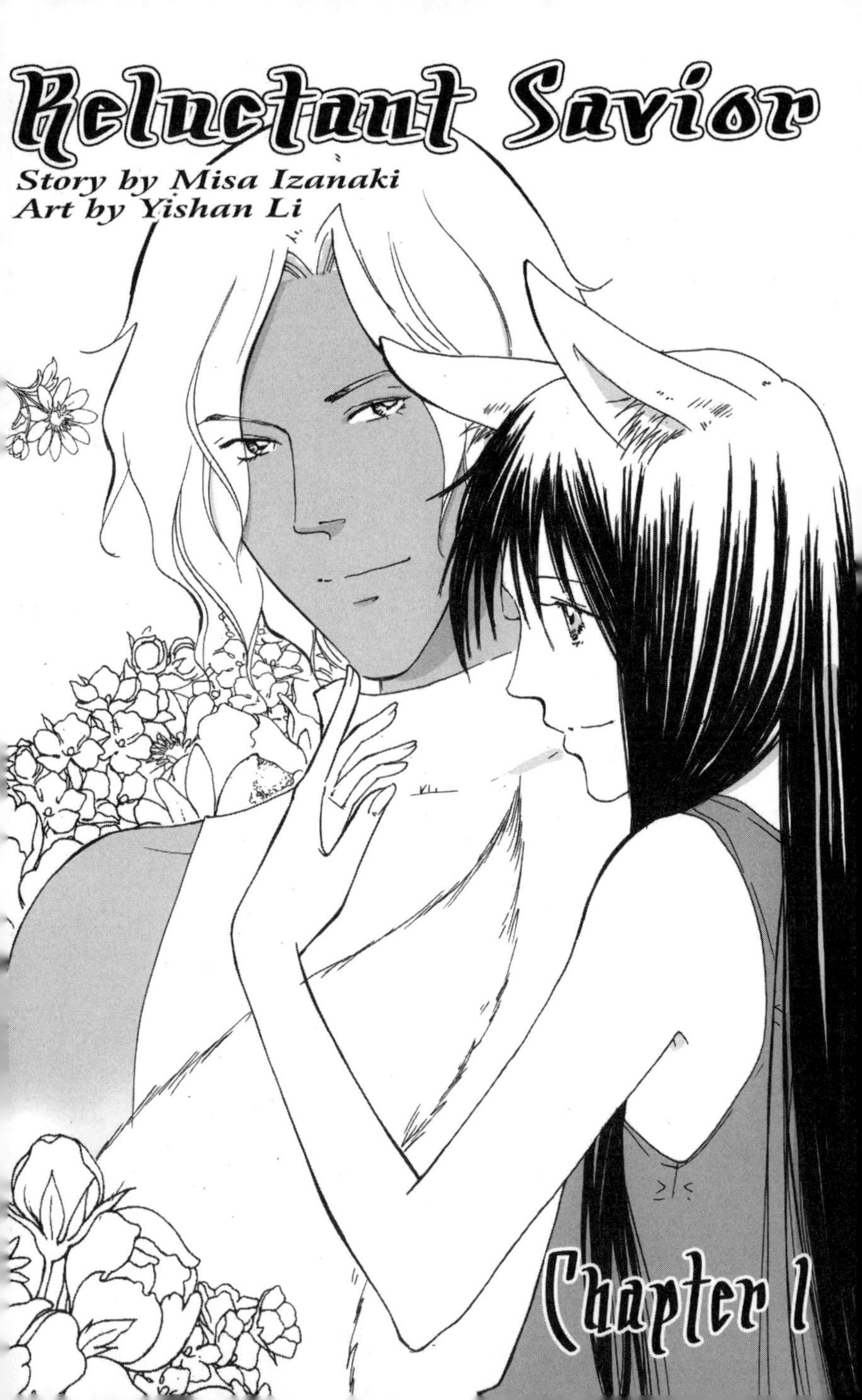
Reluctant Savior
Story by Misa Izanaki
Art by Yishan Li
Chapter 1

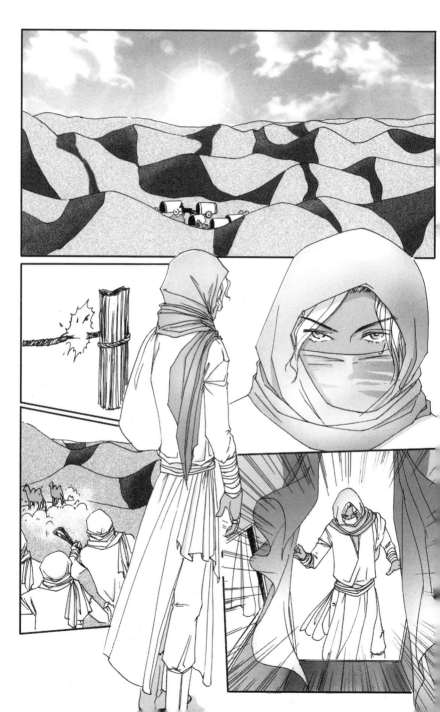

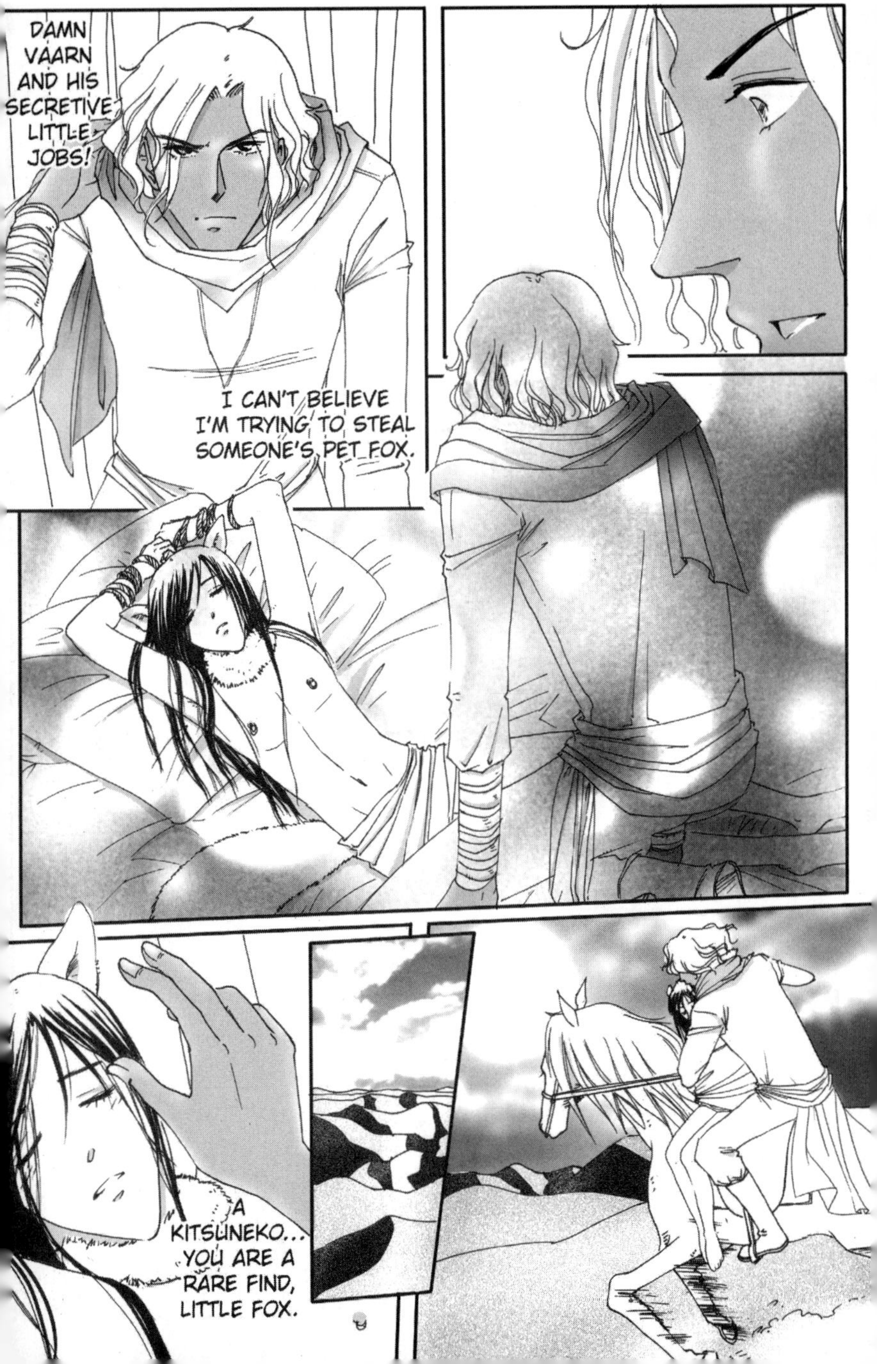
DAMN VAARN AND HIS SECRETIVE LITTLE JOBS!
I CAN'T BELIEVE I'M TRYING TO STEAL SOMEONE'S PET FOX.
A KITSUNEKO... YOU ARE A RARE FIND, LITTLE FOX.

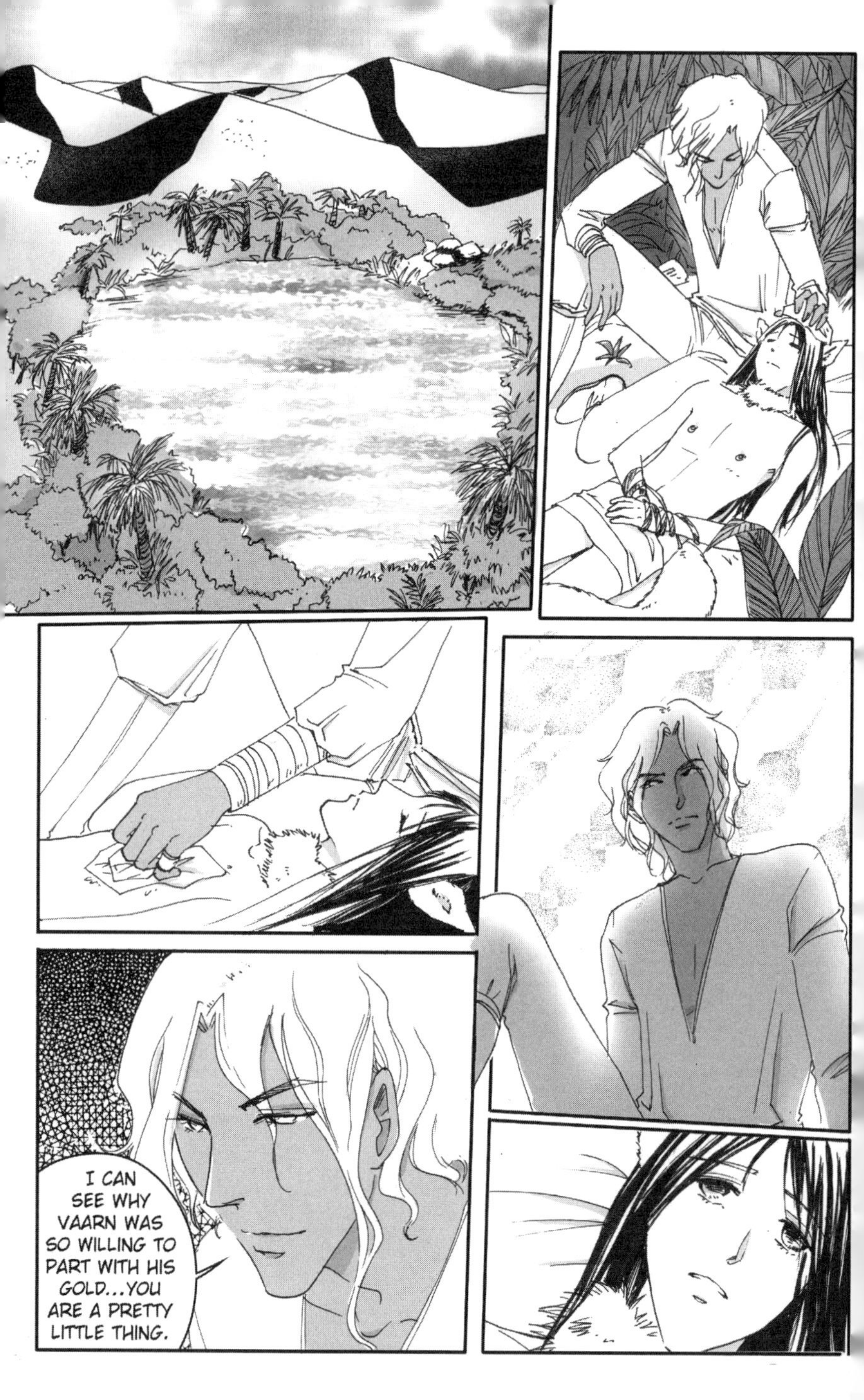
I CAN SEE WHY VAARN WAS SO WILLING TO PART WITH HIS GOLD...YOU ARE A PRETTY LITTLE THING.

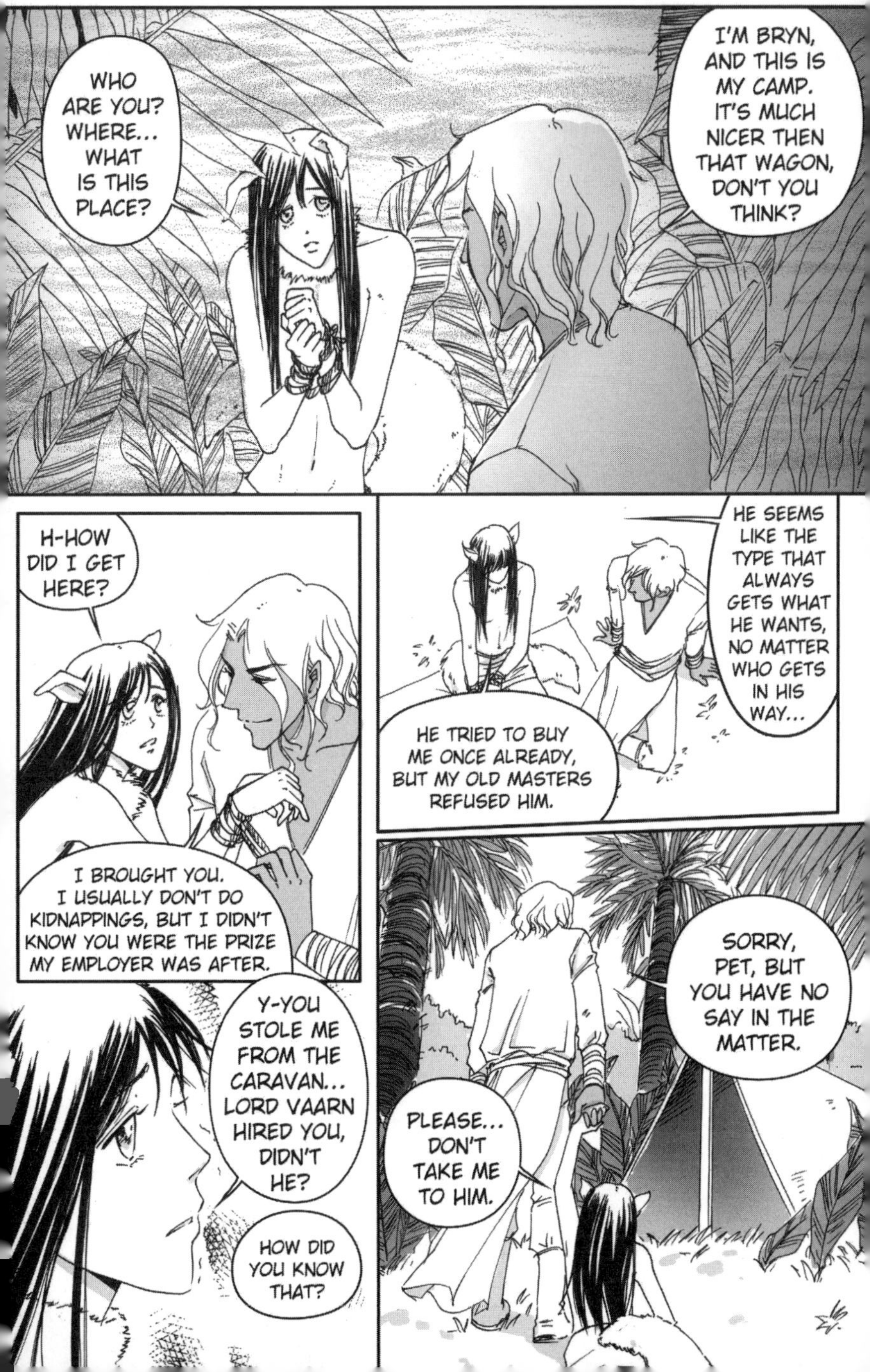
WHO ARE YOU? WHERE... WHAT IS THIS PLACE?
I'M BRYN, AND THIS IS MY CAMP. IT'S MUCH NICER THEN THAT WAGON, DON'T YOU THINK?
H-HOW DID I GET HERE?
I BROUGHT YOU. I USUALLY DON'T DO KIDNAPPINGS, BUT I DIDN'T KNOW YOU WERE THE PRIZE MY EMPLOYER WAS AFTER.
HE SEEMS LIKE THE TYPE THAT ALWAYS GETS WHAT HE WANTS, NO MATTER WHO GETS IN HIS WAY...
HE TRIED TO BUY ME ONCE ALREADY, BUT MY OLD MASTERS REFUSED HIM.
Y-YOU STOLE ME FROM THE CARAVAN... LORD VAARN HIRED YOU, DIDN'T HE?
HOW DID YOU KNOW THAT?
SORRY, PET, BUT YOU HAVE NO SAY IN THE MATTER.
PLEASE... DON'T TAKE ME TO HIM.

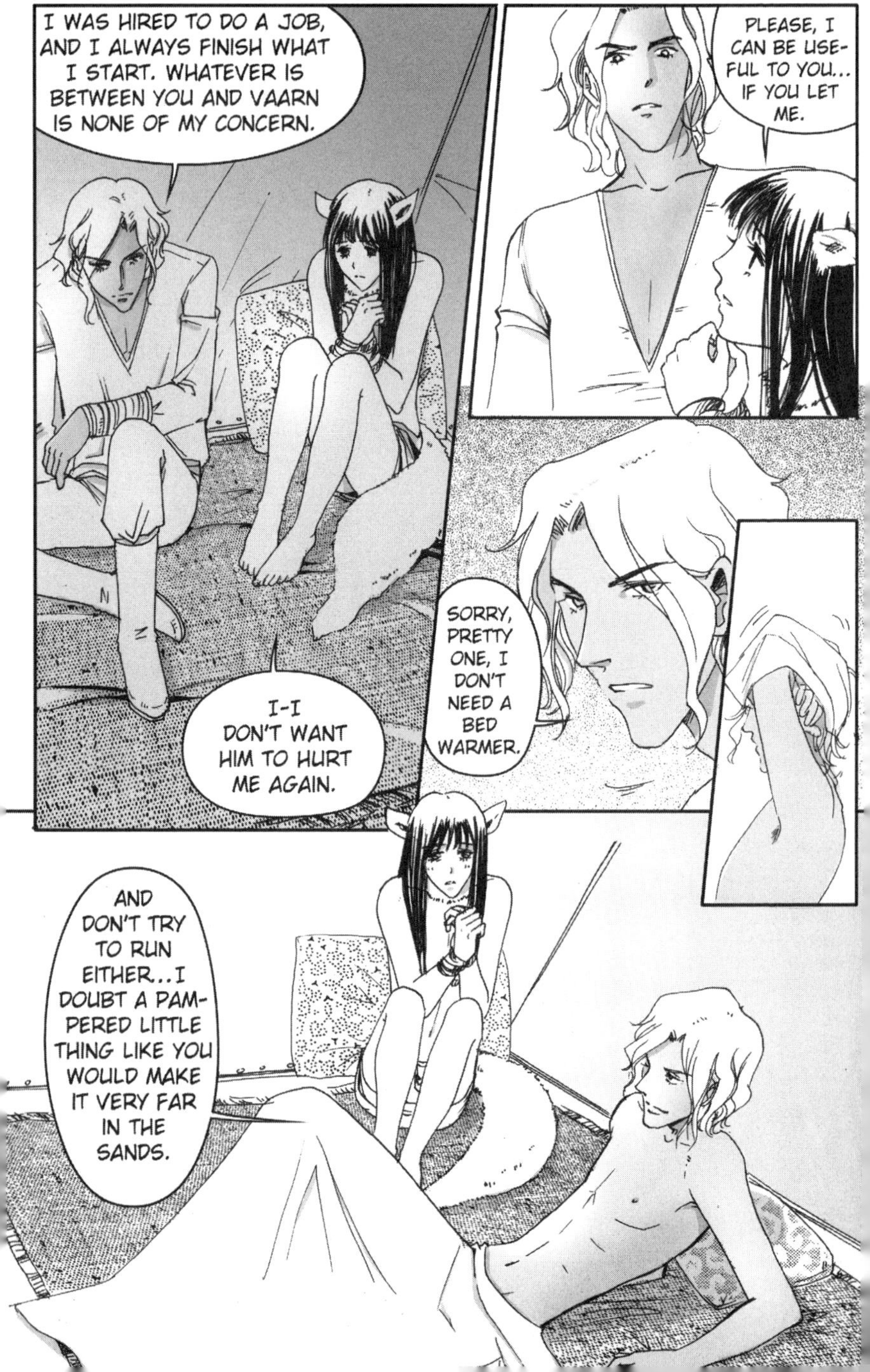
I WAS HIRED TO DO A JOB, AND I ALWAYS FINISH WHAT I START. WHATEVER IS BETWEEN YOU AND VAARN IS NONE OF MY CONCERN.
I-I DON'T WANT HIM TO HURT ME AGAIN.
PLEASE, I CAN BE USE-FUL TO YOU... IF YOU LET ME.
SORRY, PRETTY ONE, I DON'T NEED A BED WARMER.
AND DON'T TRY TO RUN EITHER...I DOUBT A PAM-PERED LITTLE THING LIKE YOU WOULD MAKE IT VERY FAR IN THE SANDS.

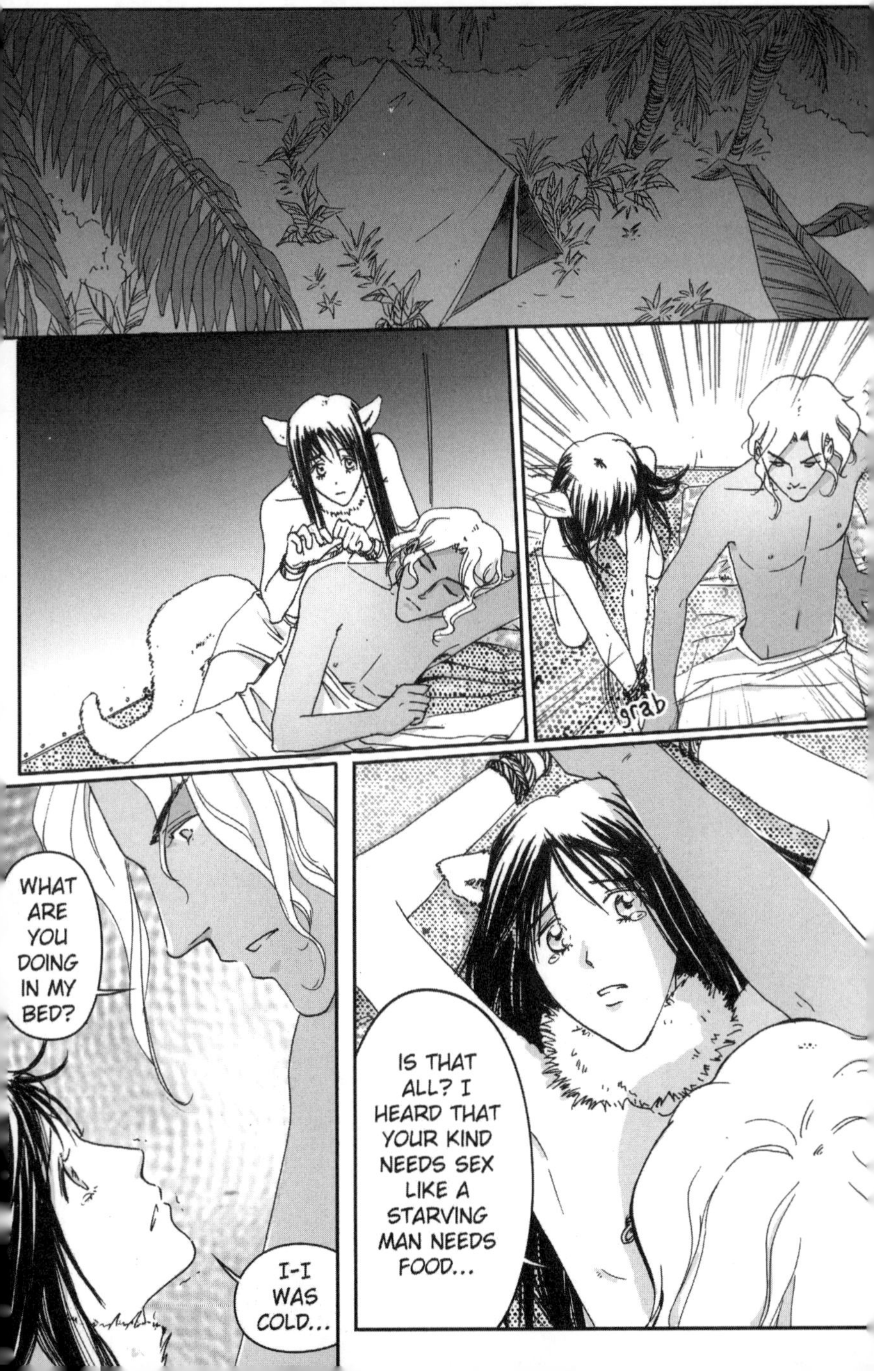
grab
WHAT ARE YOU DOING IN MY BED?
I-I WAS COLD...
IS THAT ALL? I HEARD THAT YOUR KIND NEEDS SEX LIKE A STARVING MAN NEEDS FOOD...

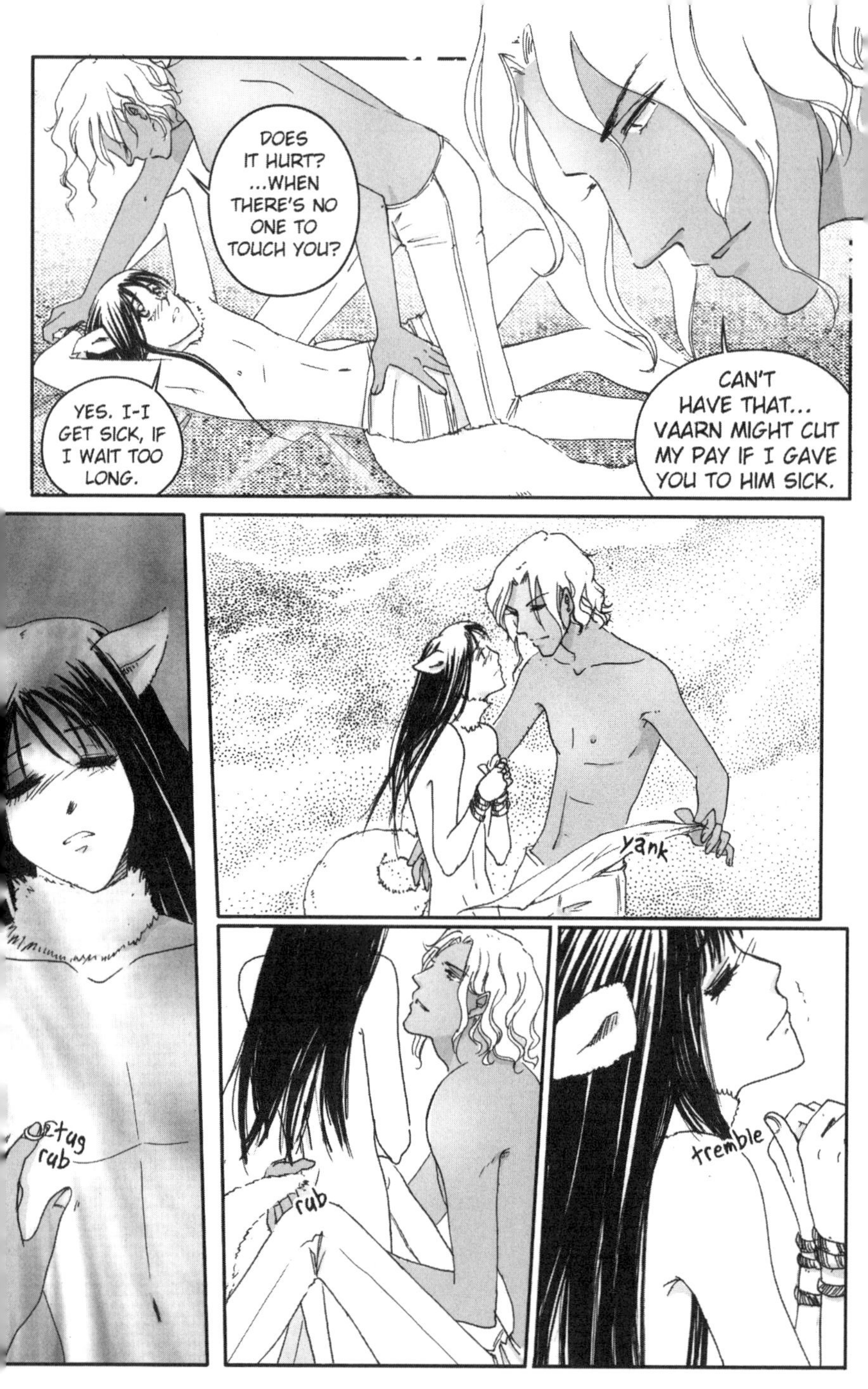
DOES IT HURT? ...WHEN THERE'S NO ONE TO TOUCH YOU?
YES. I-I GET SICK, IF I WAIT TOO LONG.
CAN'T HAVE THAT... VAARN MIGHT CUT MY PAY IF I GAVE YOU TO HIM SICK.
yank
tug
rub
rub
tremble

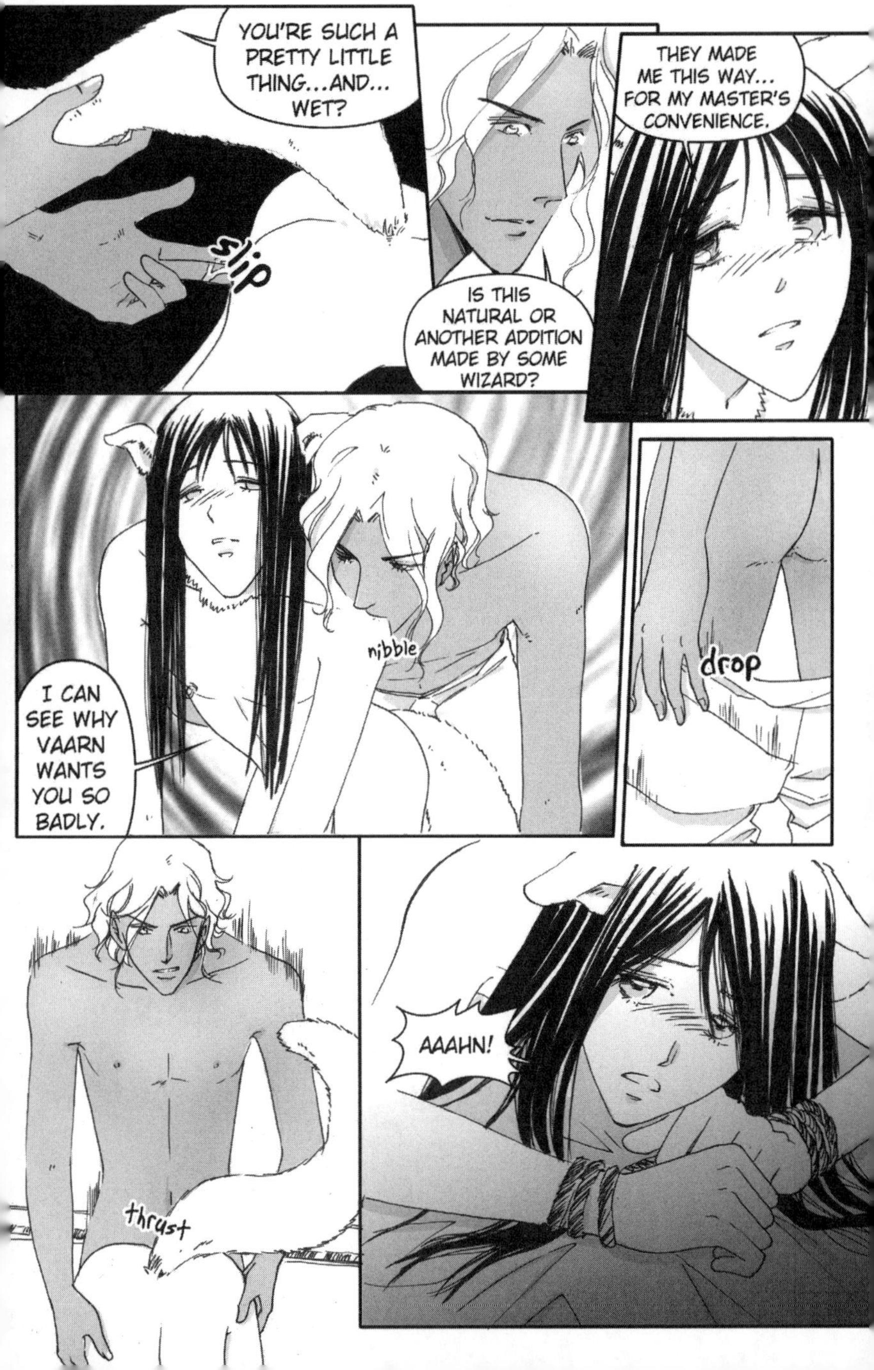
YOU'RE SUCH A PRETTY LITTLE THING...AND... WET?
slip
IS THIS NATURAL OR ANOTHER ADDITION MADE BY SOME WIZARD?
THEY MADE ME THIS WAY... FOR MY MASTER'S CONVENIENCE.
nibble
I CAN SEE WHY VAARN WANTS YOU SO BADLY.
drop
thrust
AAAHN!

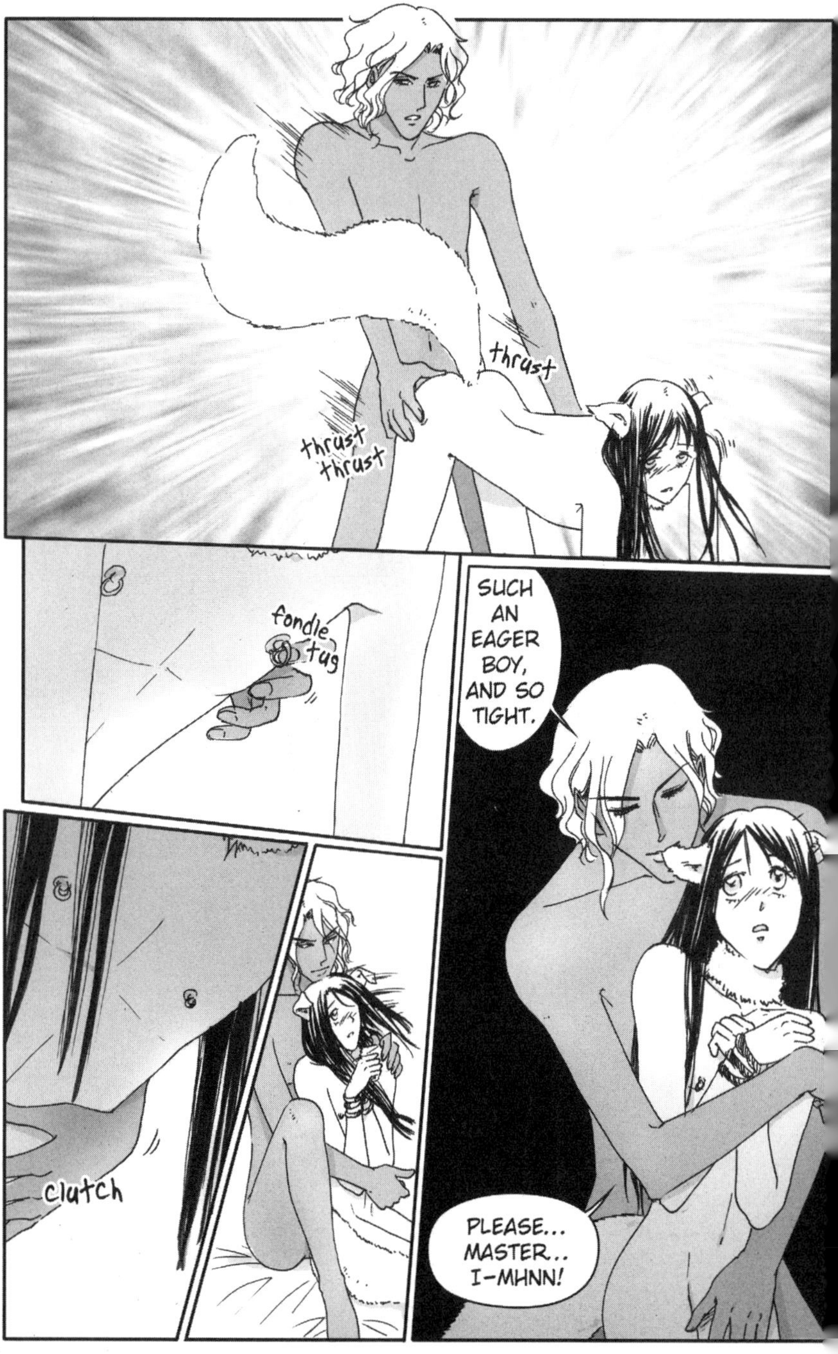
thrust
thrust
thrust
fondle
tug
SUCH AN EAGER BOY, AND SO TIGHT.
clutch
PLEASE... MASTER.. I-MHNN!

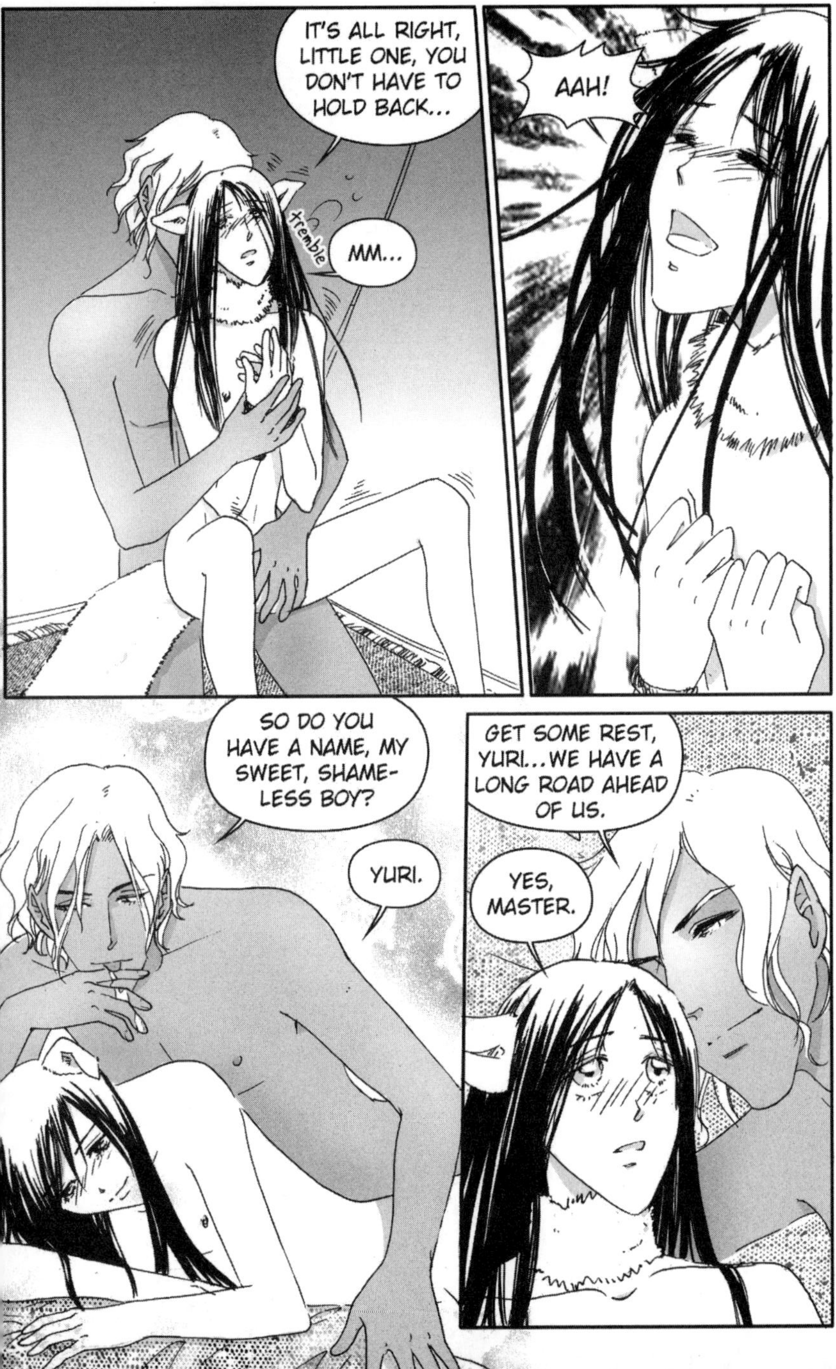
IT'S ALL RIGHT, LITTLE ONE, YOU DON'T HAVE TO HOLD BACK...
tremble
MM...
AAH!
SO DO YOU HAVE A NAME, MY SWEET, SHAME-LESS BOY?
YURI.
GET SOME REST, YURI...WE HAVE A LONG ROAD AHEAD OF US.
YES, MASTER.

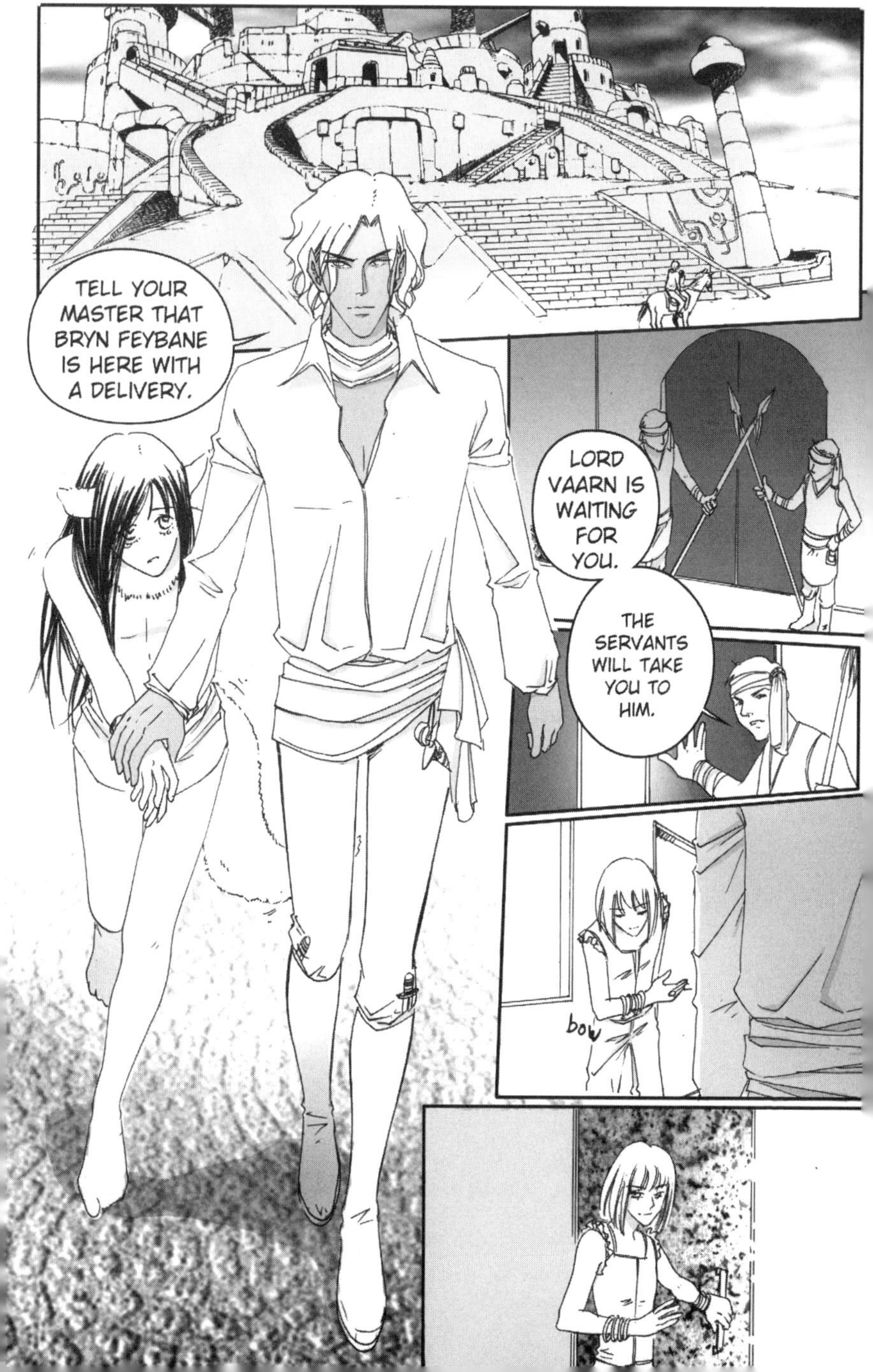
TELL YOUR MASTER THAT BRYN FEYBANE IS HERE WITH A DELIVERY.
LORD VAARN IS WAITING FOR YOU.
THE SERVANTS WILL TAKE YOU TO HIM.
bow

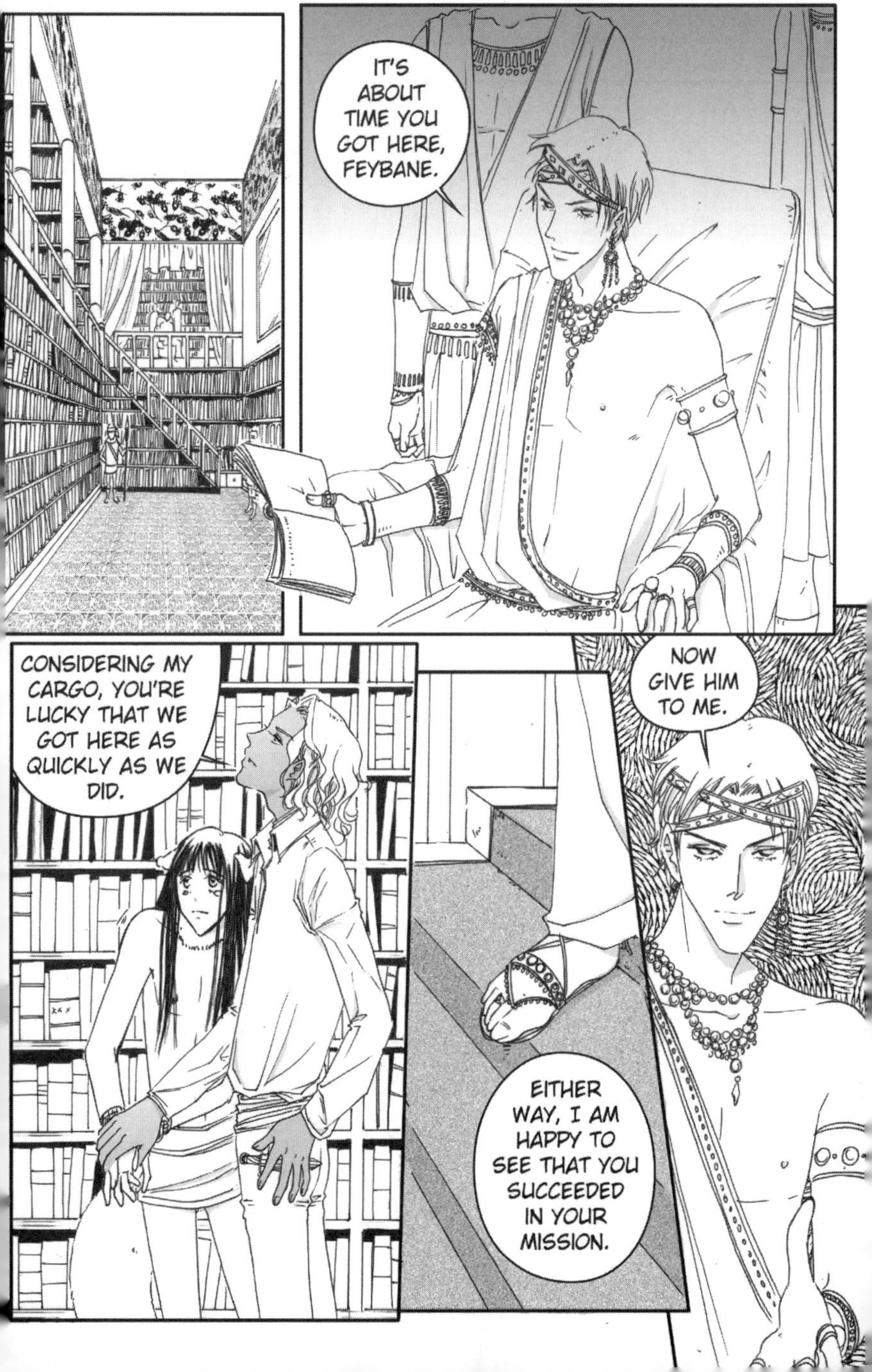
IT'S ABOUT TIME YOU GOT HERE, FEYBANE.
CONSIDERING MY CARGO, YOU'RE LUCKY THAT WE GOT HERE AS QUICKLY AS WE DID.
NOW GIVE HIM TO ME.
EITHER WAY, I AM HAPPY TO SEE THAT YOU SUCCEEDED IN YOUR MISSION.

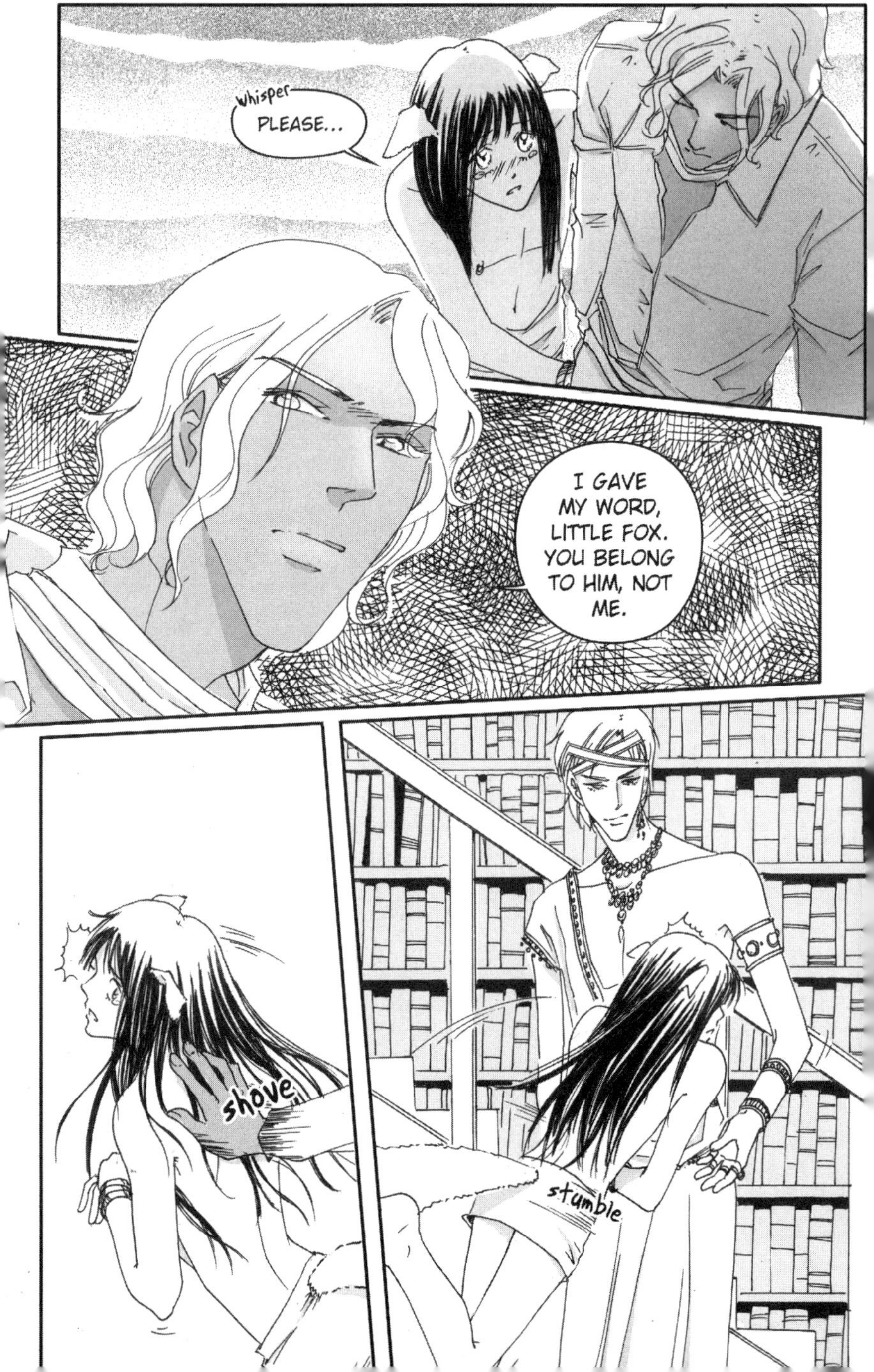

whisper
PLEASE...
I GAVE MY WORD, LITTLE FOX. YOU BELONG TO HIM, NOT ME.
shove
stumble

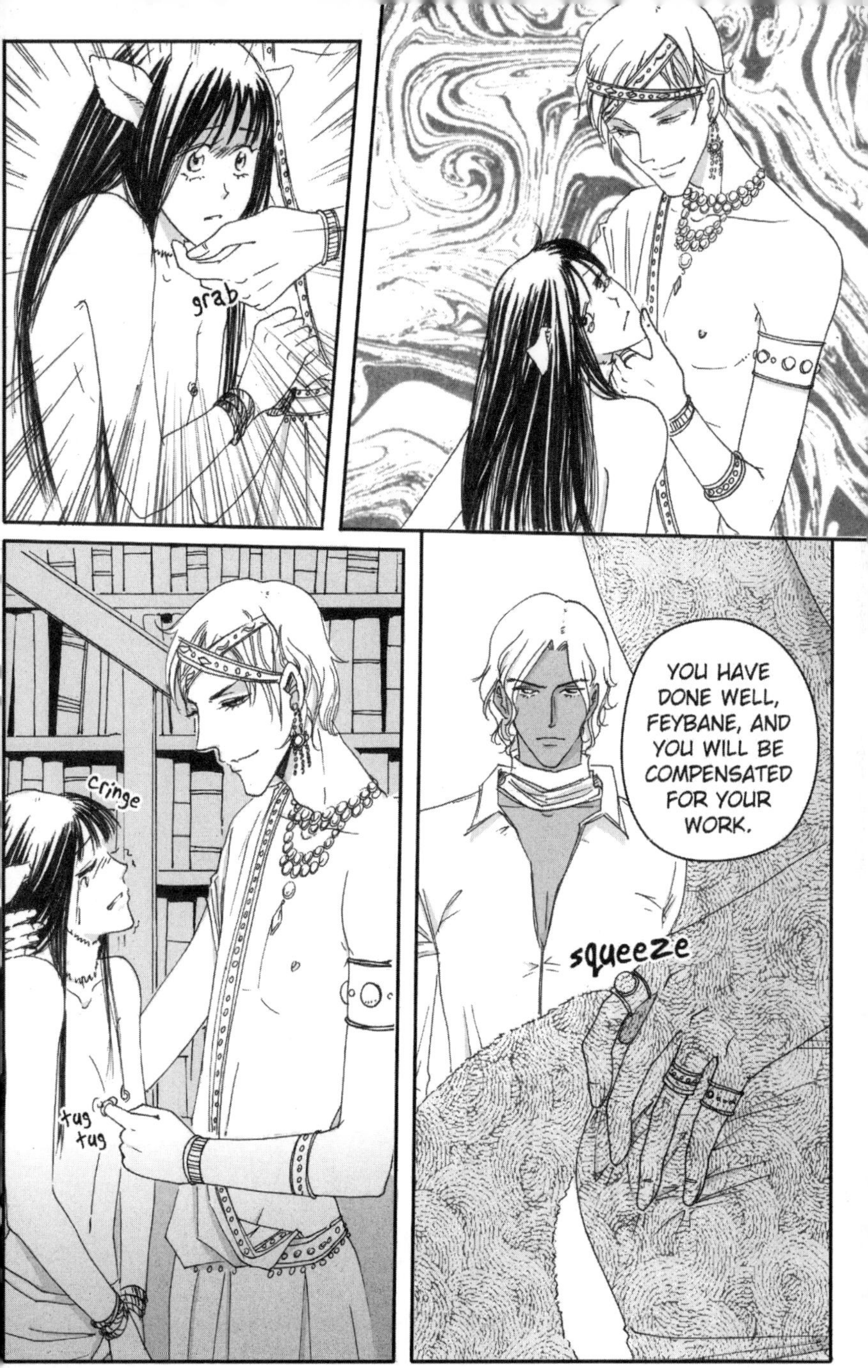
grab
cringe
tug tug
YOU HAVE DONE WELL, FEYBANE, AND YOU WILL BE COMPENSATED FOR YOUR WORK.
squeeze

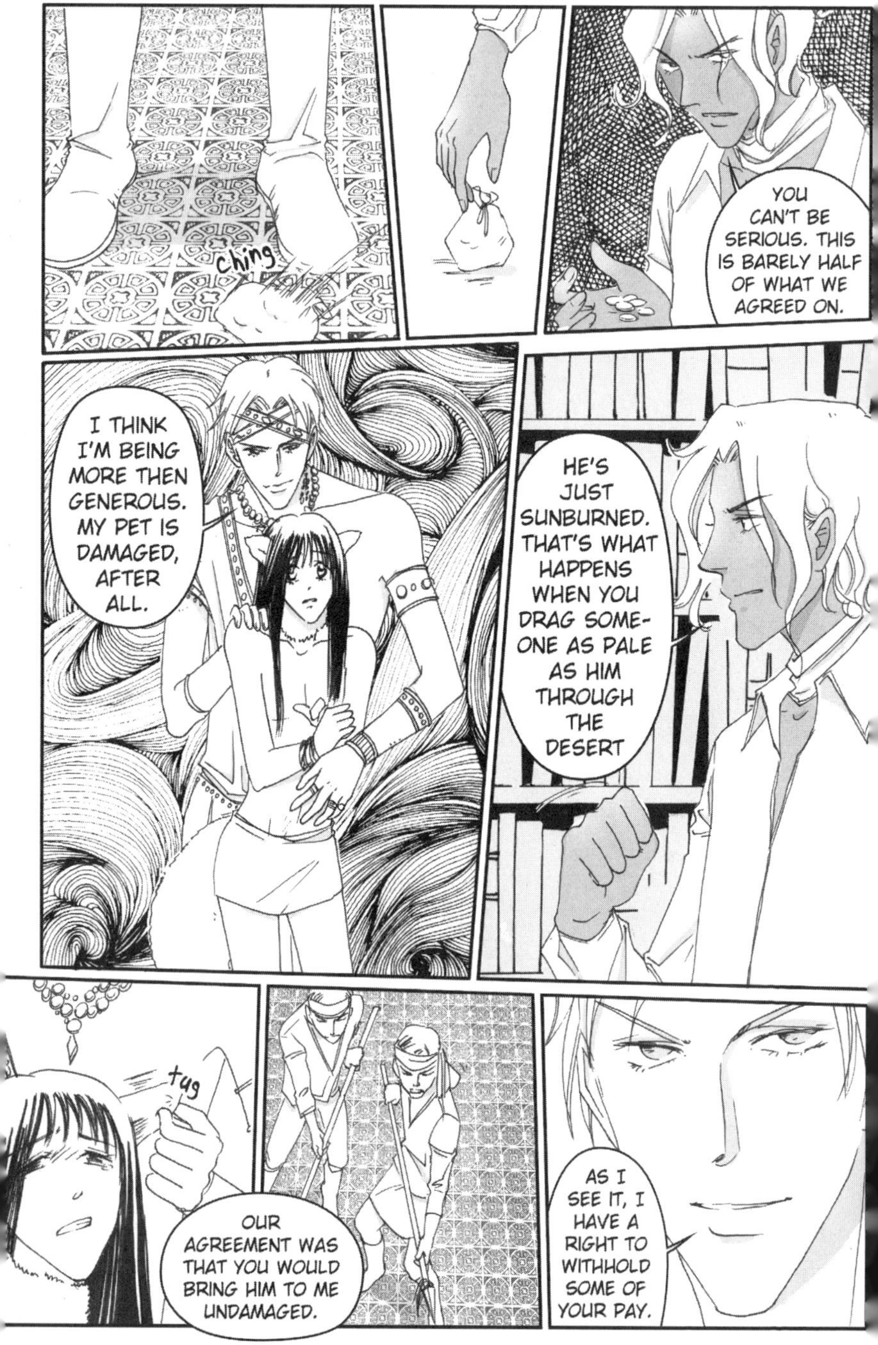
Ching
YOU CAN'T BE SERIOUS. THIS IS BARELY HALF OF WHAT WE AGREED ON.
I THINK I'M BEING MORE THEN GENEROUS. MY PET IS DAMAGED, AFTER ALL.
HE'S JUST SUNBURNED. THAT'S WHAT HAPPENS WHEN YOU DRAG SOME-ONE AS PALE AS HIM THROUGH THE DESERT
tug
OUR AGREEMENT WAS THAT YOU WOULD BRING HIM TO ME UNDAMAGED.
AS I SEE IT, I HAVE A RIGHT TO WITHHOLD SOME OF YOUR PAY.

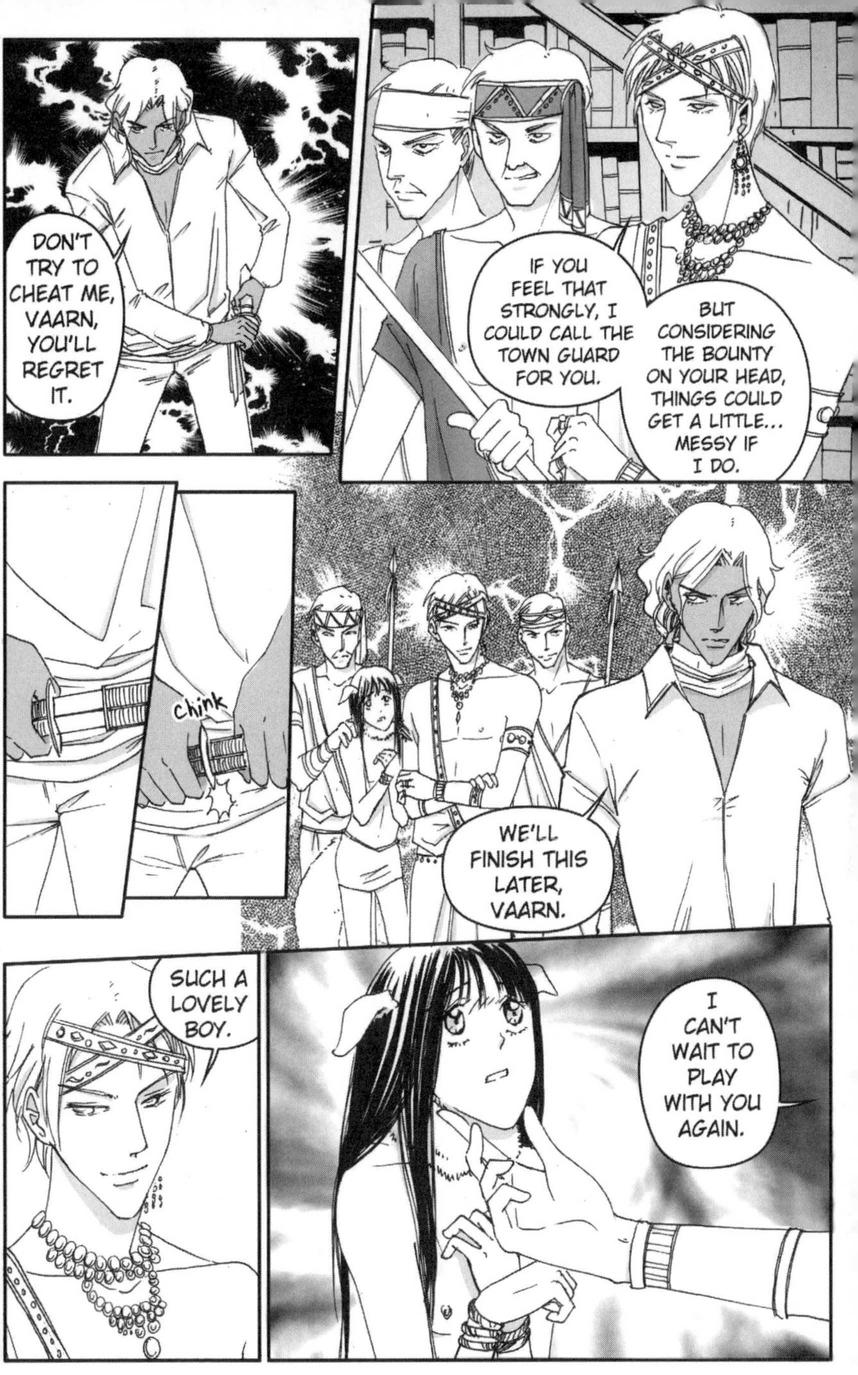
DON'T TRY TO CHEAT ME, VAARN, YOU'LL REGRET IT.
IF YOU FEEL THAT STRONGLY, I COULD CALL THE TOWN GUARD FOR YOU.
BUT CONSIDERING THE BOUNTY ON YOUR HEAD, THINGS COULD GET A LITTLE... MESSY IF I DO.
chink
WE'LL FINISH THIS LATER, VAARN.
SUCH A LOVELY BOY.
I CAN'T WAIT TO PLAY WITH YOU AGAIN.

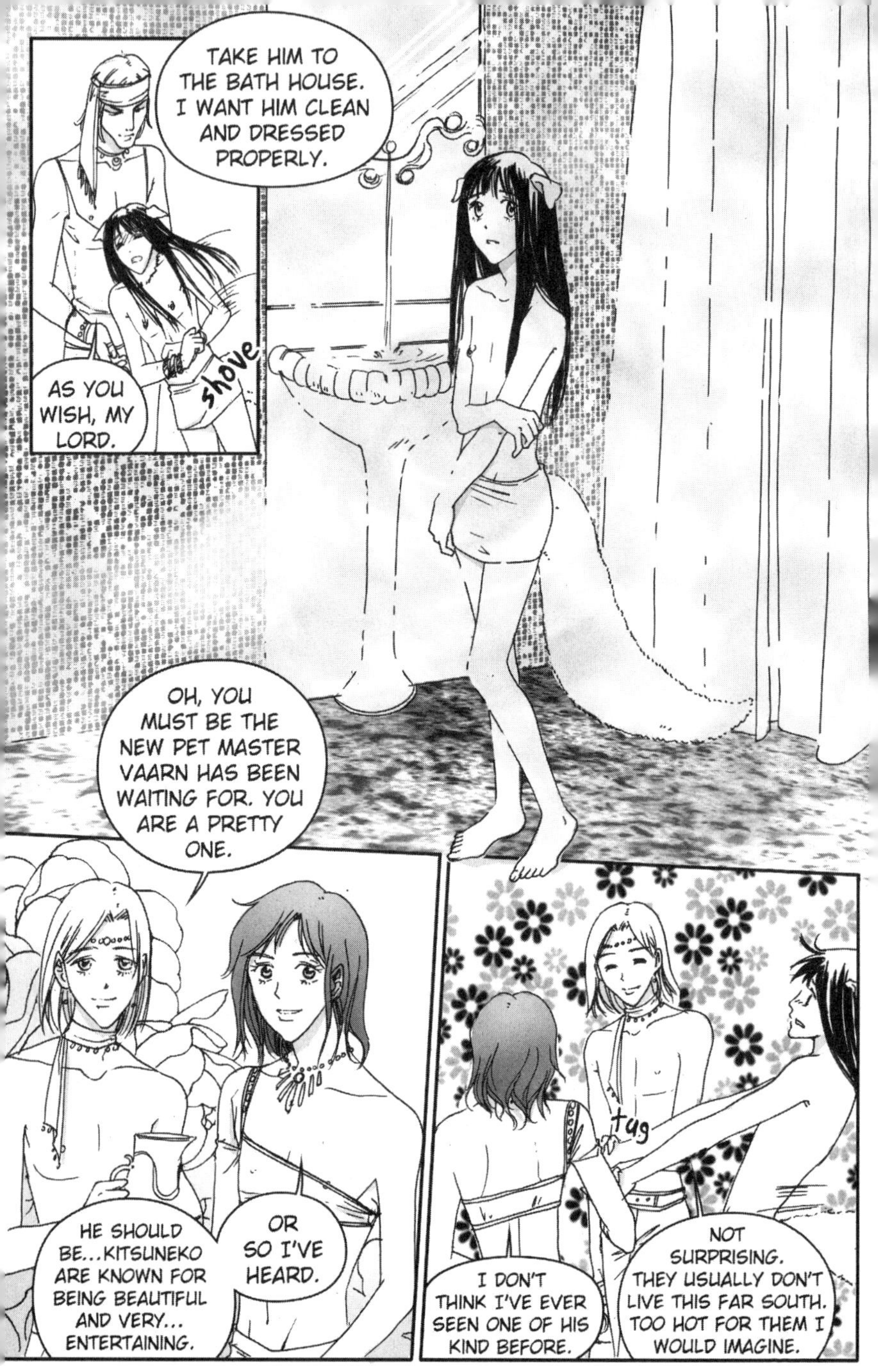
TAKE HIM TO THE BATH HOUSE. I WANT HIM CLEAN AND DRESSED PROPERLY.
AS YOU WISH, MY LORD.
shove
OH, YOU MUST BE THE NEW PET MASTER VAARN HAS BEEN WAITING FOR. YOU ARE A PRETTY ONE.
HE SHOULD BE...KITSUNEKO ARE KNOWN FOR BEING BEAUTIFUL AND VERY... ENTERTAINING.
OR SO I'VE HEARD.
tug
I DON'T THINK I'VE EVER SEEN ONE OF HIS KIND BEFORE.
NOT SURPRISING. THEY USUALLY DON'T LIVE THIS FAR SOUTH. TOO HOT FOR THEM I WOULD IMAGINE.

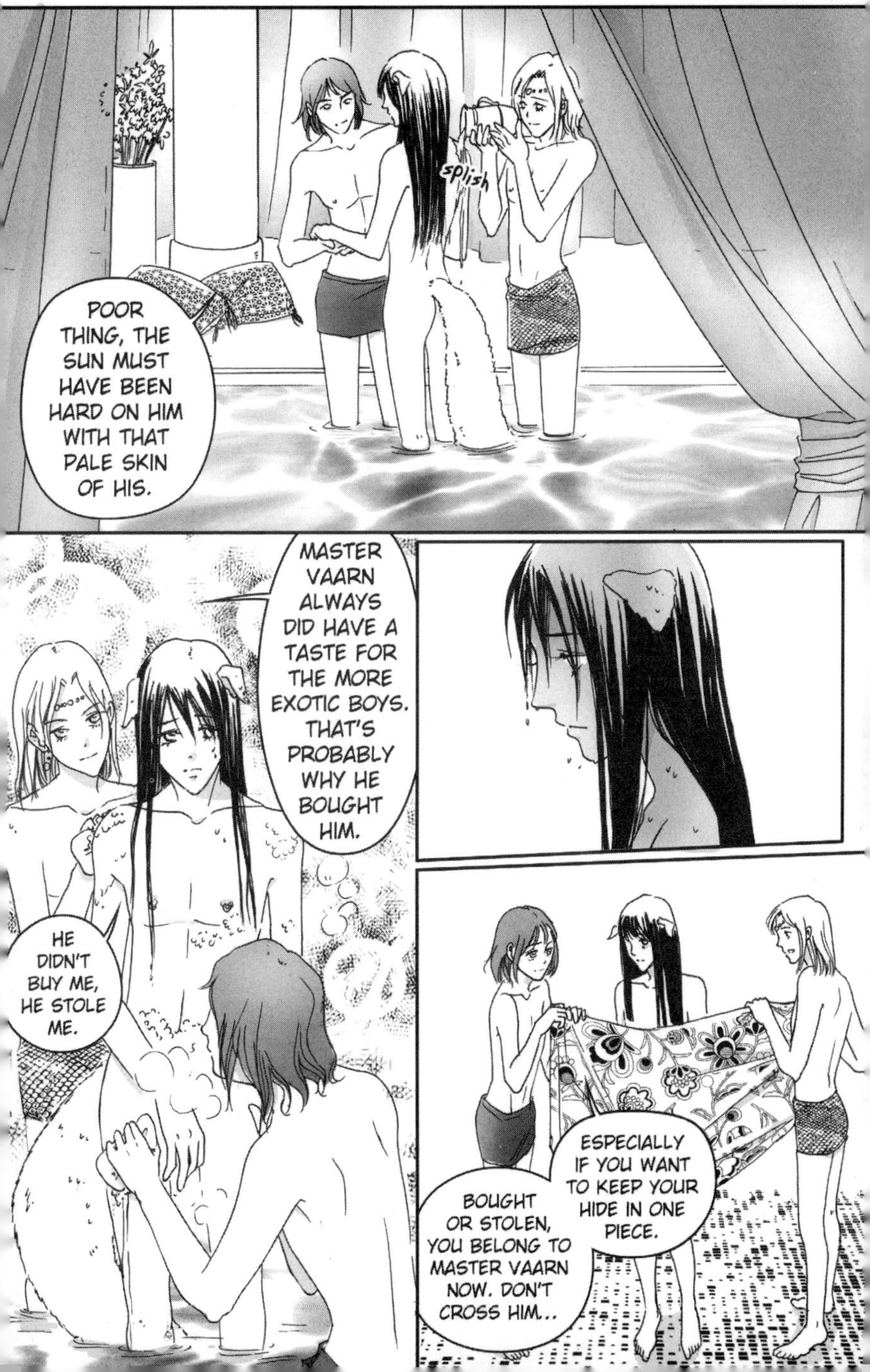
splish
POOR THING, THE SUN MUST HAVE BEEN HARD ON HIM WITH THAT PALE SKIN OF HIS.
MASTER VAARN ALWAYS DID HAVE A TASTE FOR THE MORE EXOTIC BOYS. THAT'S PROBABLY WHY HE BOUGHT HIM.
HE DIDN'T BUY ME, HE STOLE ME.
BOUGHT OR STOLEN, YOU BELONG TO MASTER VAARN NOW. DON'T CROSS HIM...
ESPECIALLY IF YOU WANT TO KEEP YOUR HIDE IN ONE PIECE.

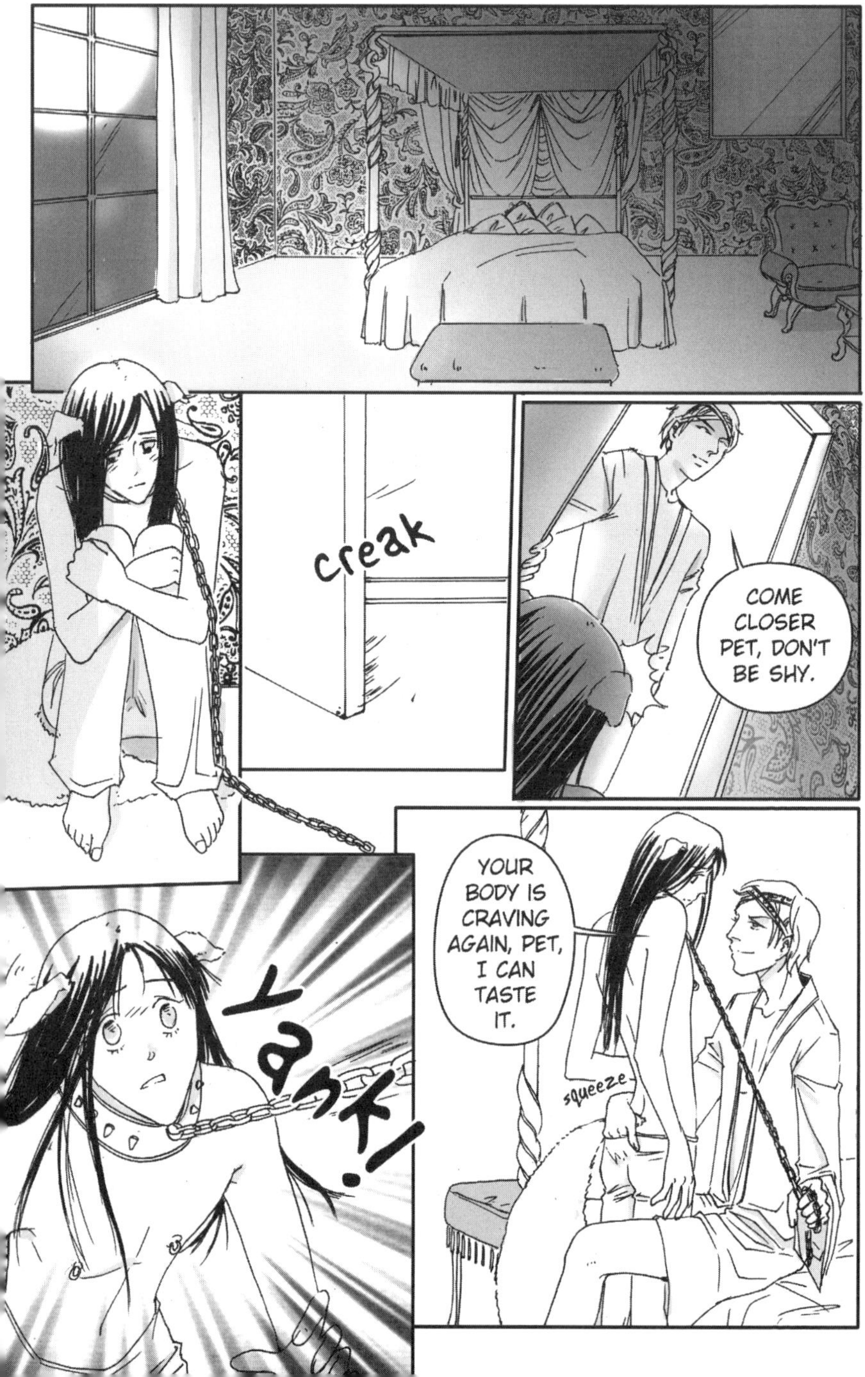
creak
COME CLOSER PET, DON'T BE SHY.
Yank!
YOUR BODY IS CRAVING AGAIN, PET, I CAN TASTE IT.
squeeze

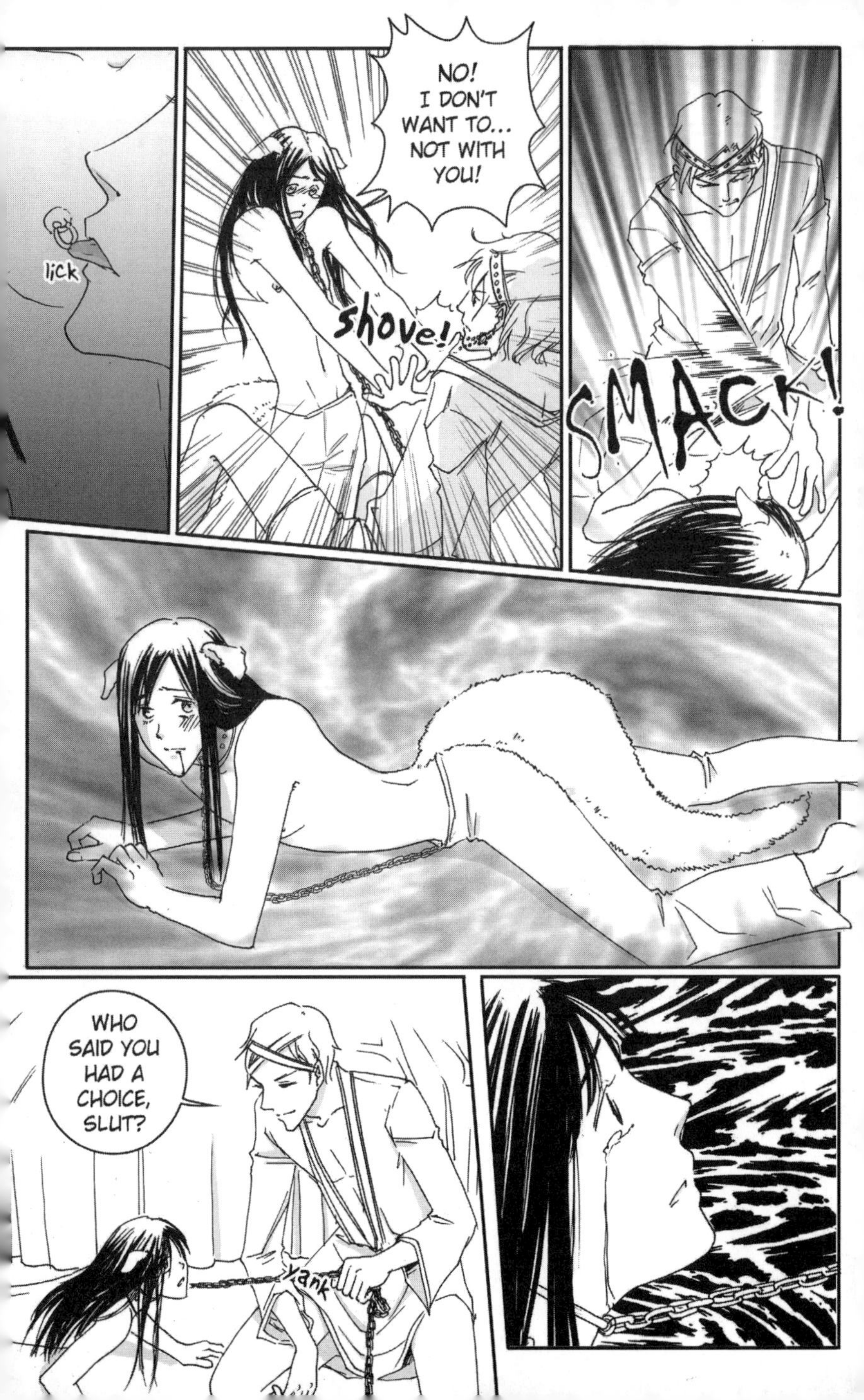
lick
NO! I DON'T WANT TO... NOT WITH YOU!
shove!
SMACK!
WHO SAID YOU HAD A CHOICE, SLUT?
yank

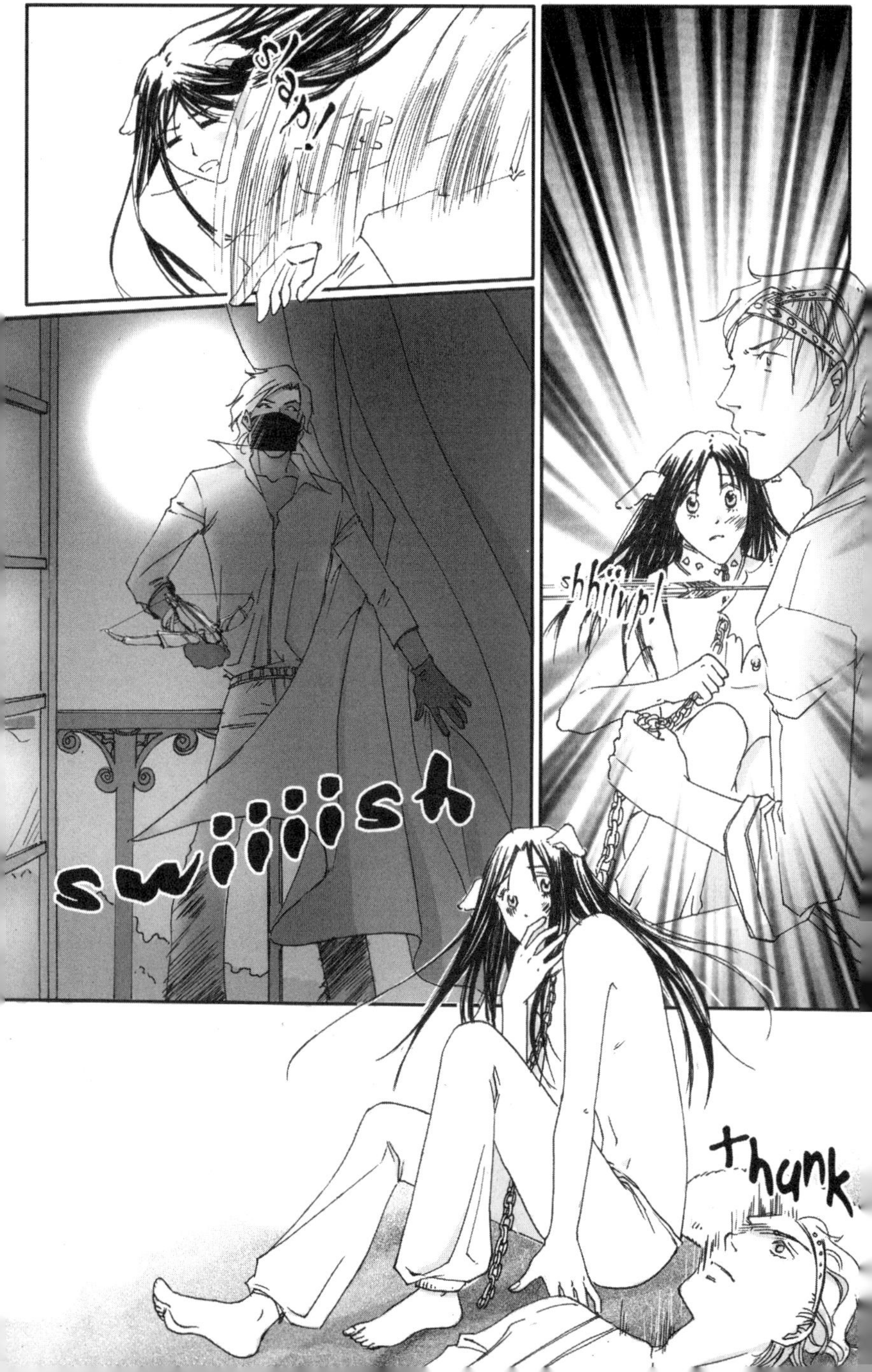
slap!
shhiiwp!
swiiiish
thunk

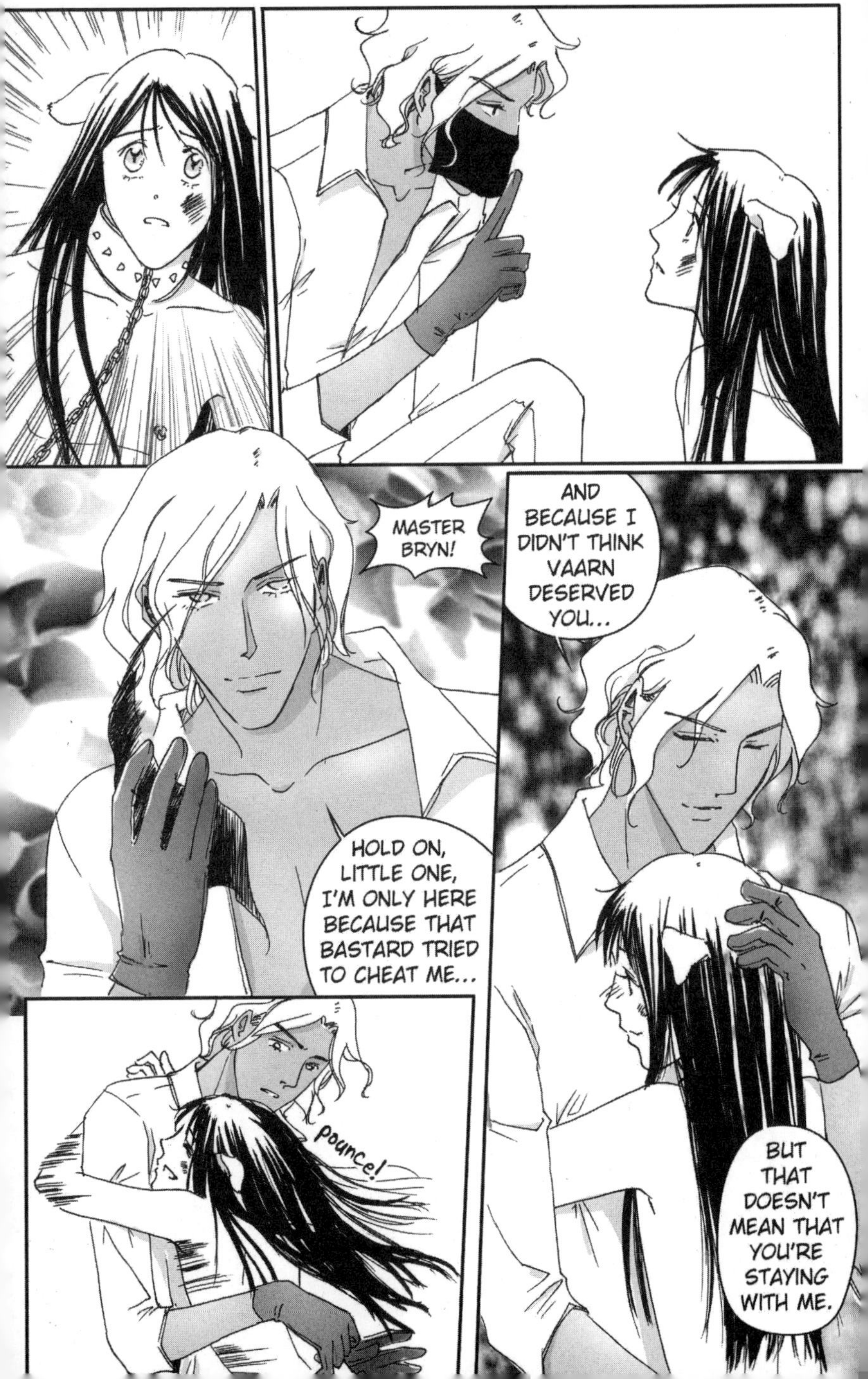
MASTER BRYN!
HOLD ON, LITTLE ONE, I'M ONLY HERE BECAUSE THAT BASTARD TRIED TO CHEAT ME...
AND BECAUSE I DIDN'T THINK VAARN DESERVED YOU...
pounce!
BUT THAT DOESN'T MEAN THAT YOU'RE STAYING WITH ME.

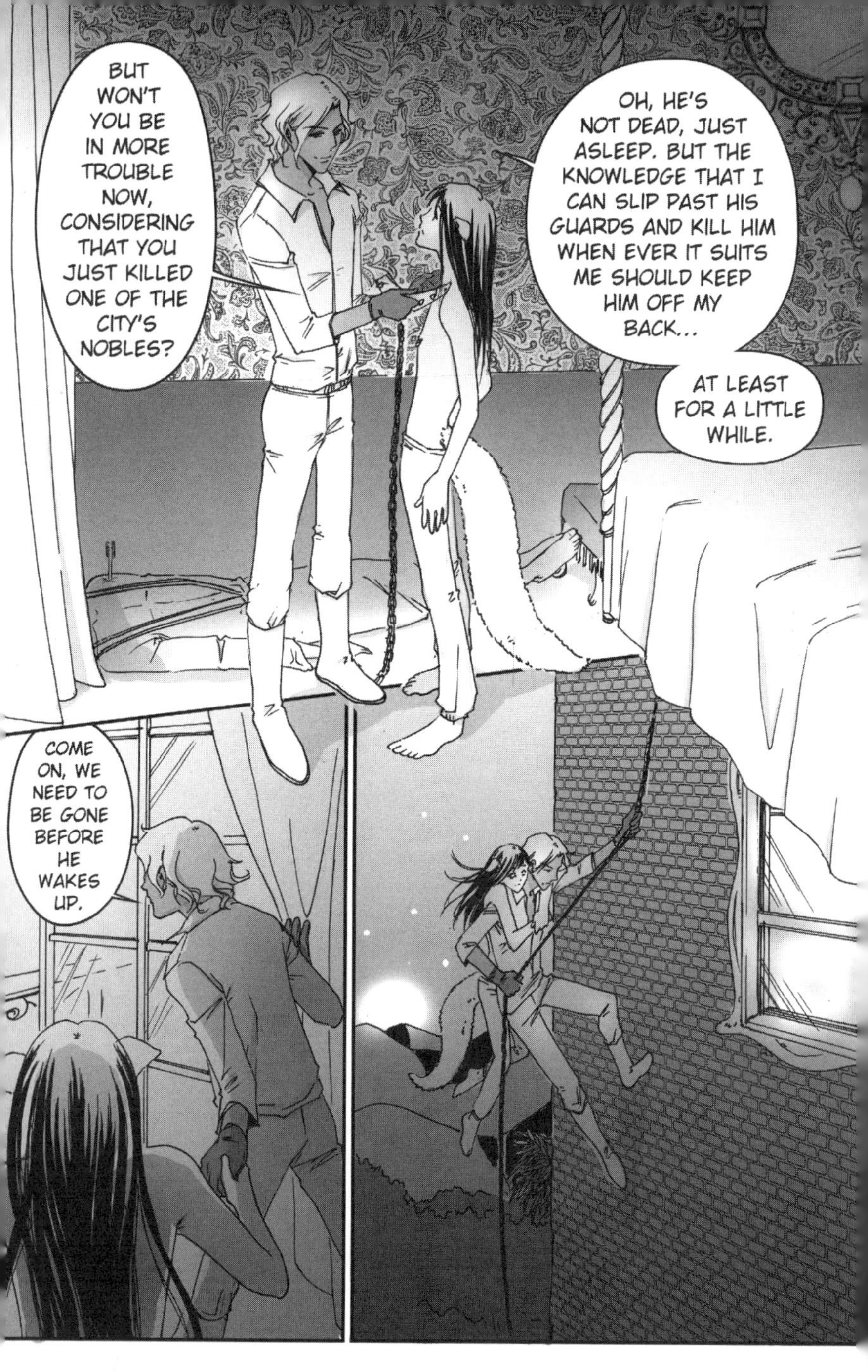

BUT WON'T YOU BE IN MORE TROUBLE NOW, CONSIDERING THAT YOU JUST KILLED ONE OF THE CITY'S NOBLES?
OH, HE'S NOT DEAD, JUST ASLEEP. BUT THE KNOWLEDGE THAT I CAN SLIP PAST HIS GUARDS AND KILL HIM WHEN EVER IT SUITS ME SHOULD KEEP HIM OFF MY BACK...
AT LEAST FOR A LITTLE WHILE.
COME ON, WE NEED TO BE GONE BEFORE HE WAKES UP.

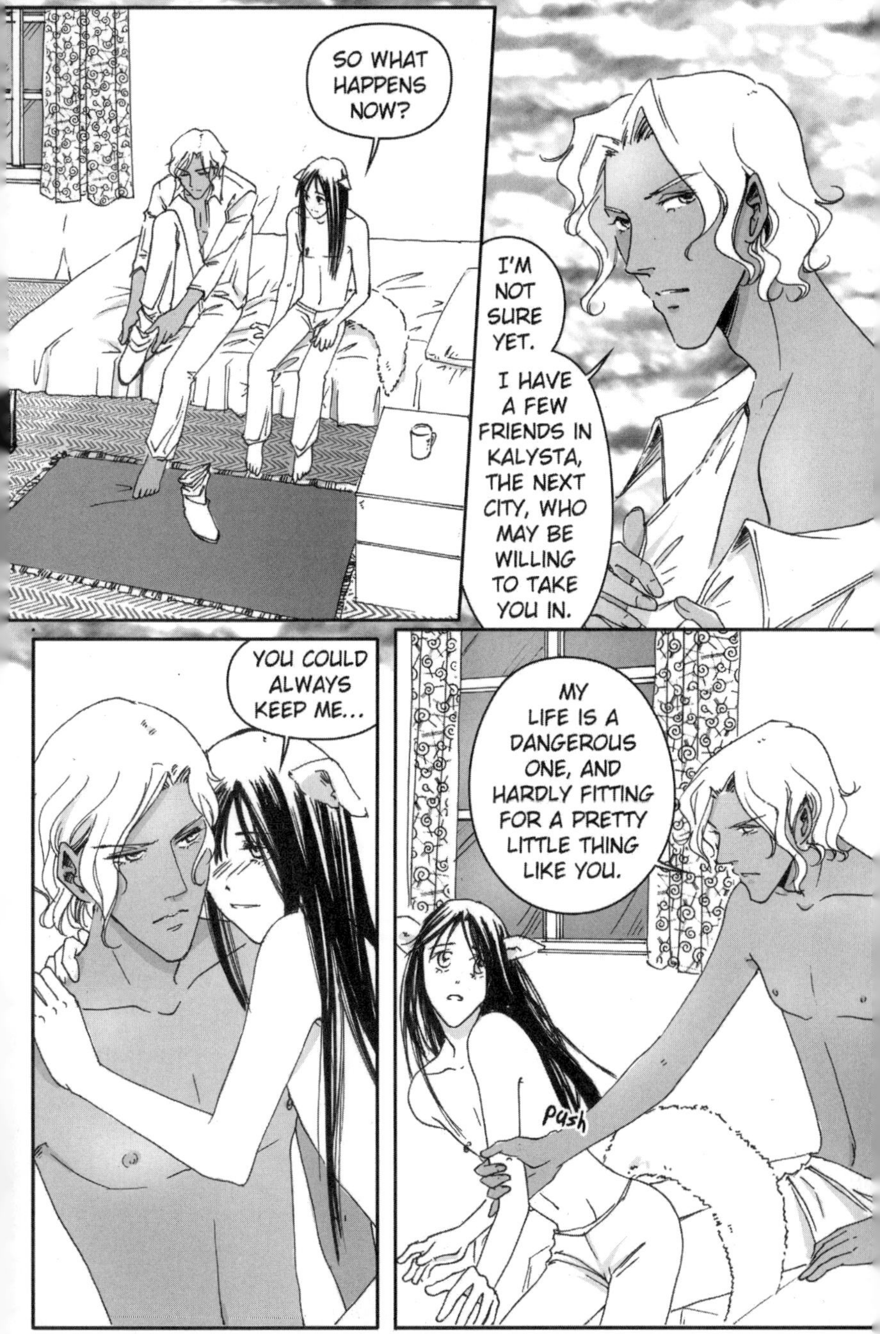
SO WHAT HAPPENS NOW?
I'M NOT SURE YET.
I HAVE A FEW FRIENDS IN KALYSTA, THE NEXT CITY, WHO MAY BE WILLING TO TAKE YOU IN.
YOU COULD ALWAYS KEEP ME...
MY LIFE IS A DANGEROUS ONE, AND HARDLY FITTING FOR A PRETTY LITTLE THING LIKE YOU.
PUSH

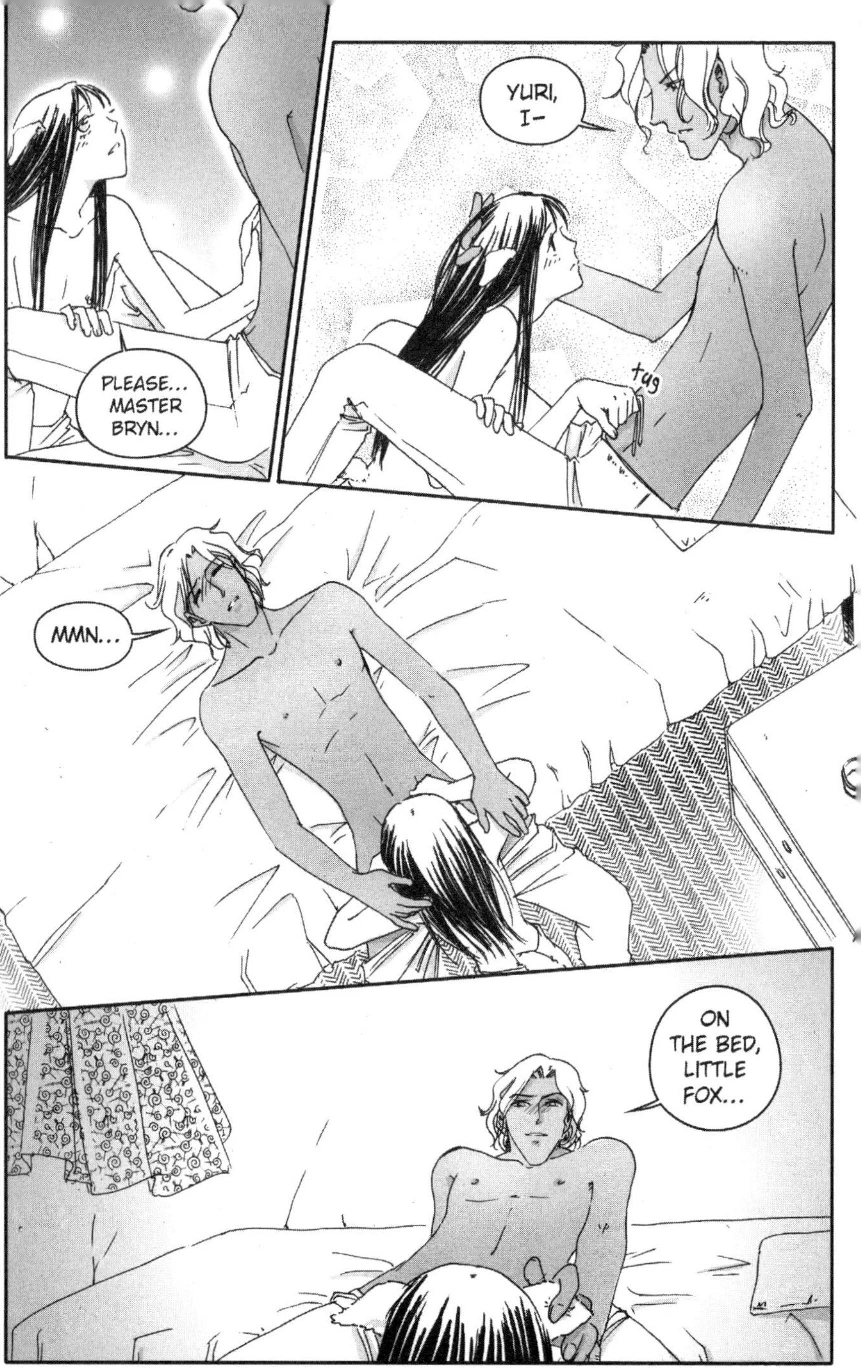
PLEASE... MASTER BRYN...
YURI, I—
tug
MMN...
ON THE BED, LITTLE FOX...

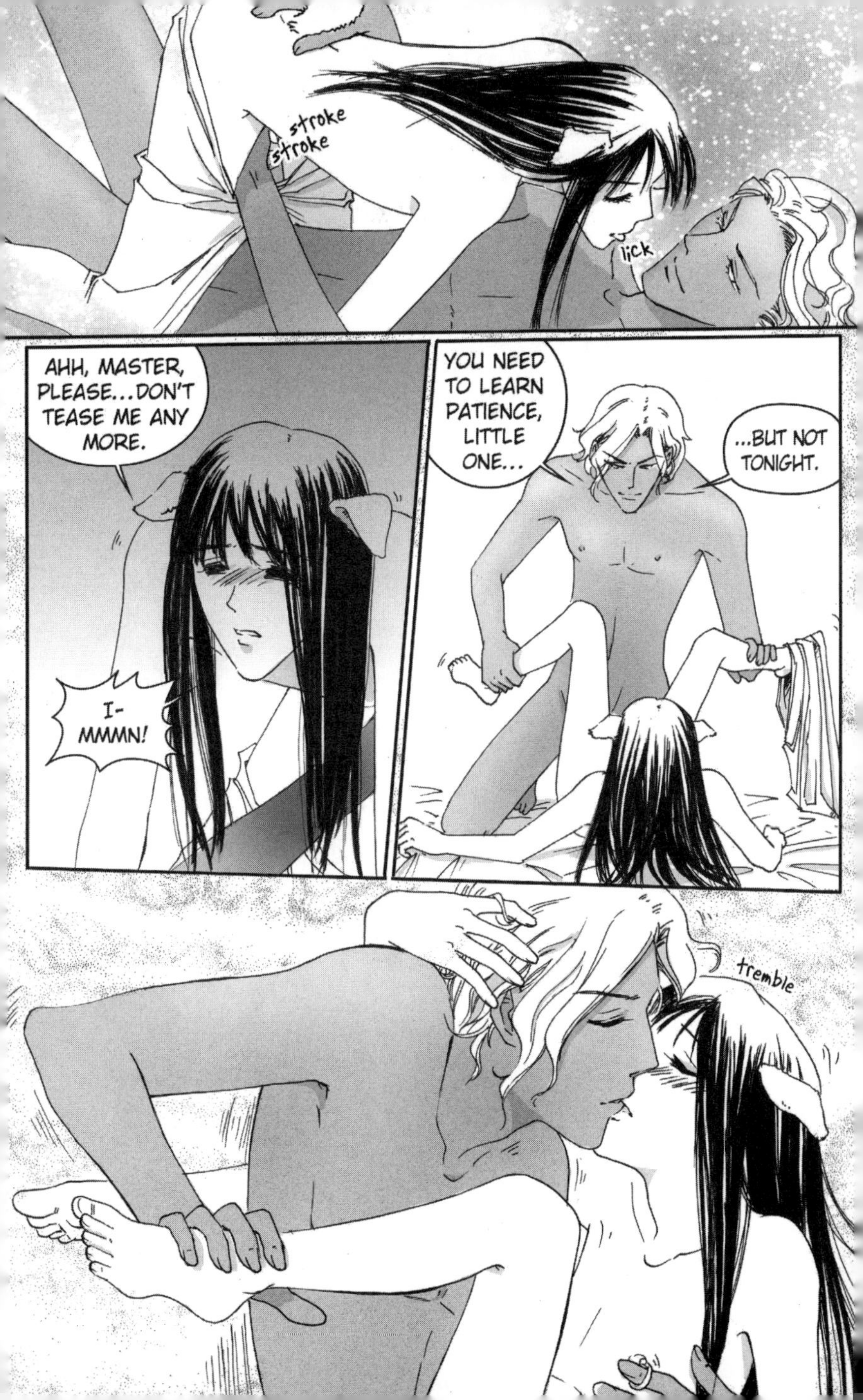
stroke
stroke
lick
AHH, MASTER, PLEASE...DON'T TEASE ME ANY MORE.
I- MMMN!
YOU NEED TO LEARN PATIENCE, LITTLE ONE...
...BUT NOT TONIGHT.
tremble

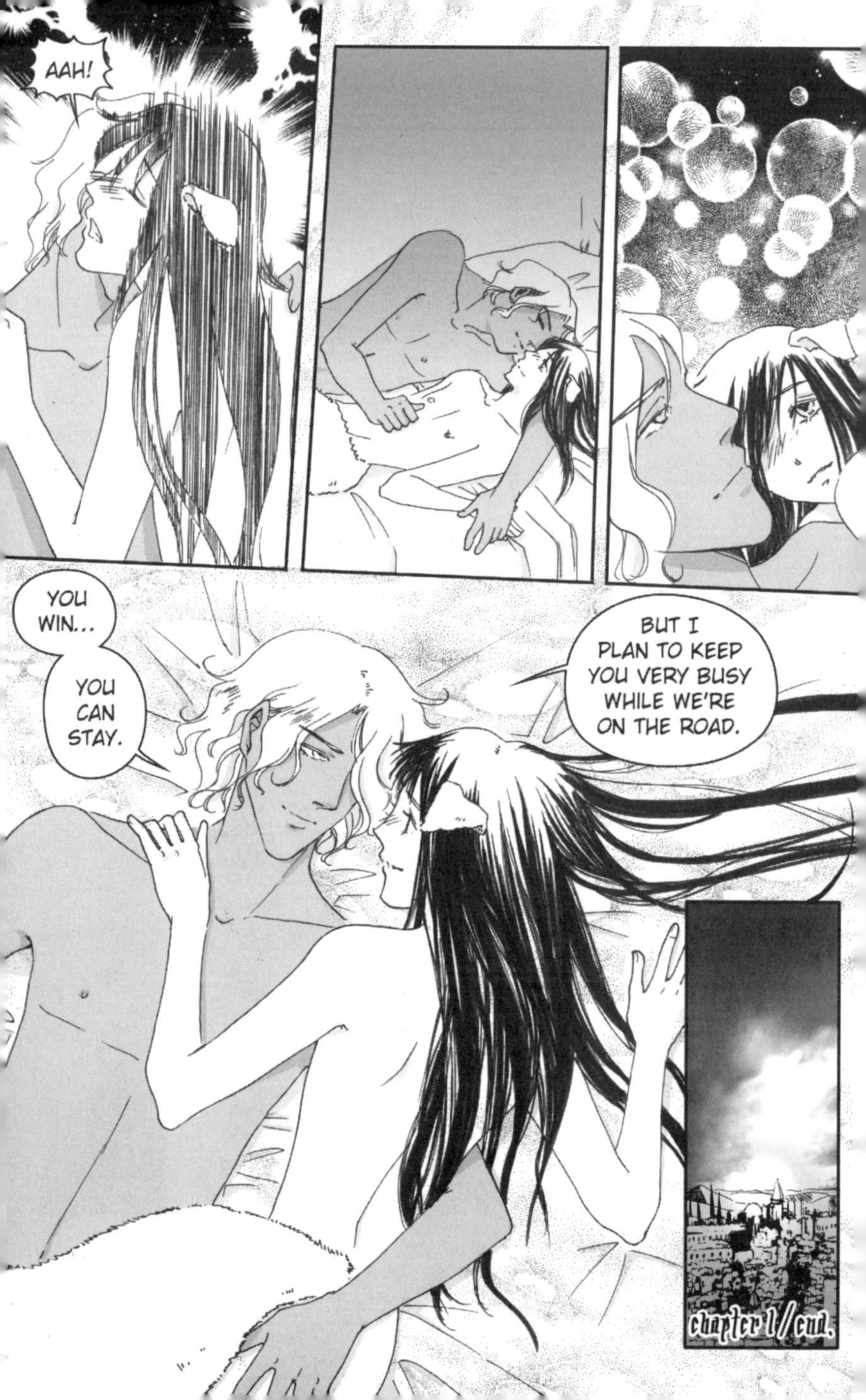
AAH!
YOU WIN...
YOU CAN STAY.
BUT I PLAN TO KEEP YOU VERY BUSY WHILE WE'RE ON THE ROAD.
chapter 1//end.

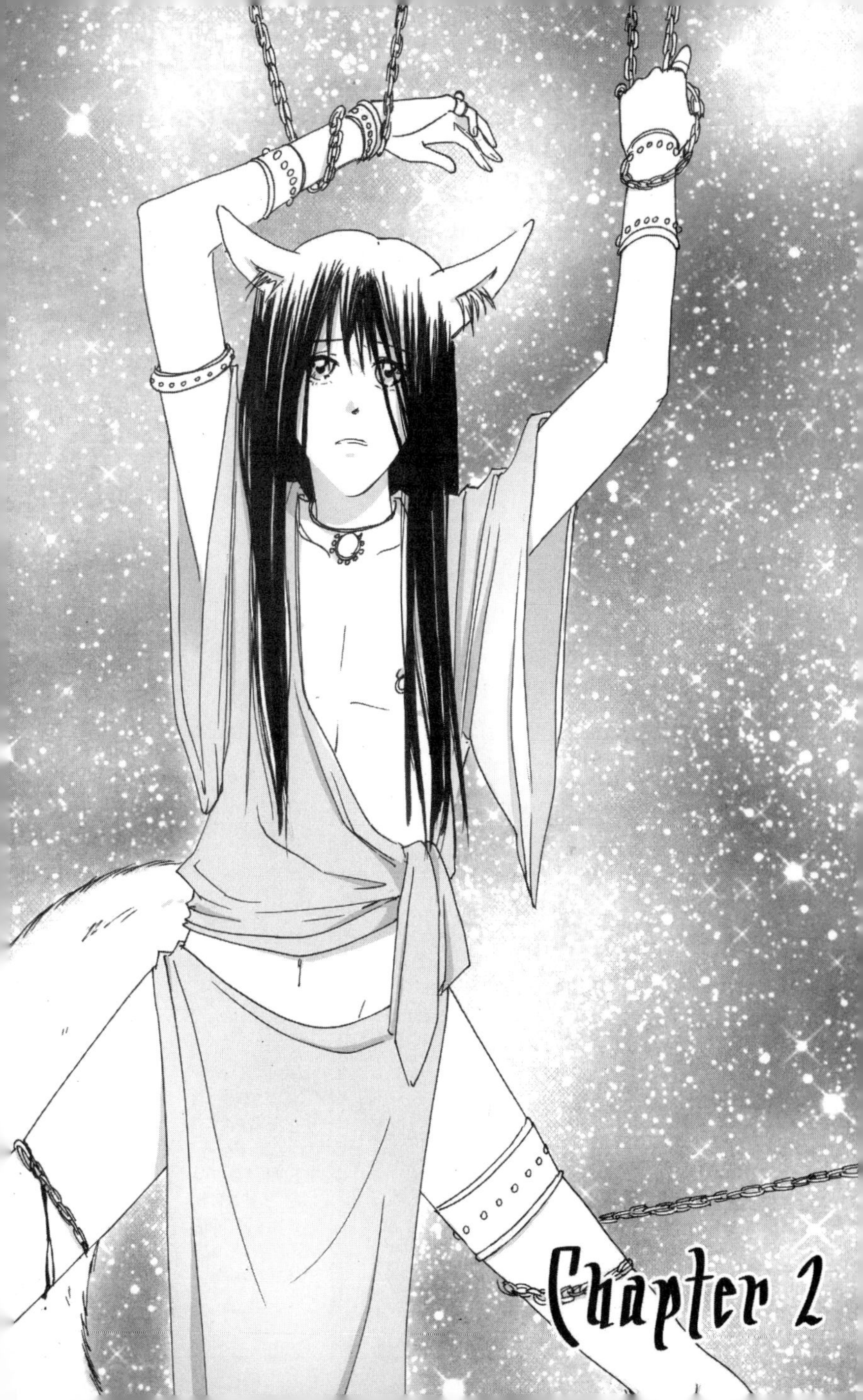
Chapter 2

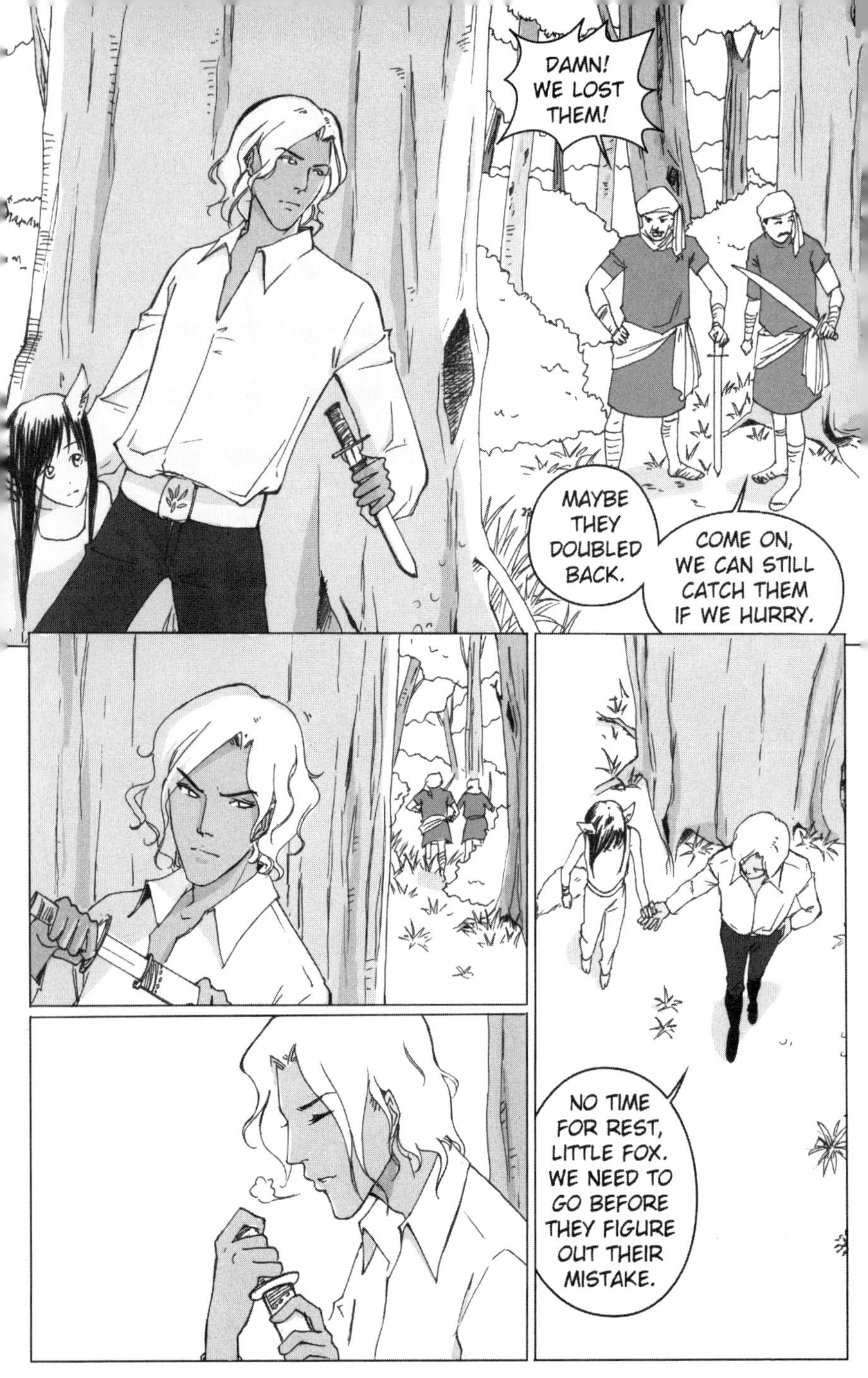
DAMN! WE LOST THEM!
MAYBE THEY DOUBLED BACK.
COME ON, WE CAN STILL CATCH THEM IF WE HURRY.
NO TIME FOR REST, LITTLE FOX. WE NEED TO GO BEFORE THEY FIGURE OUT THEIR MISTAKE.

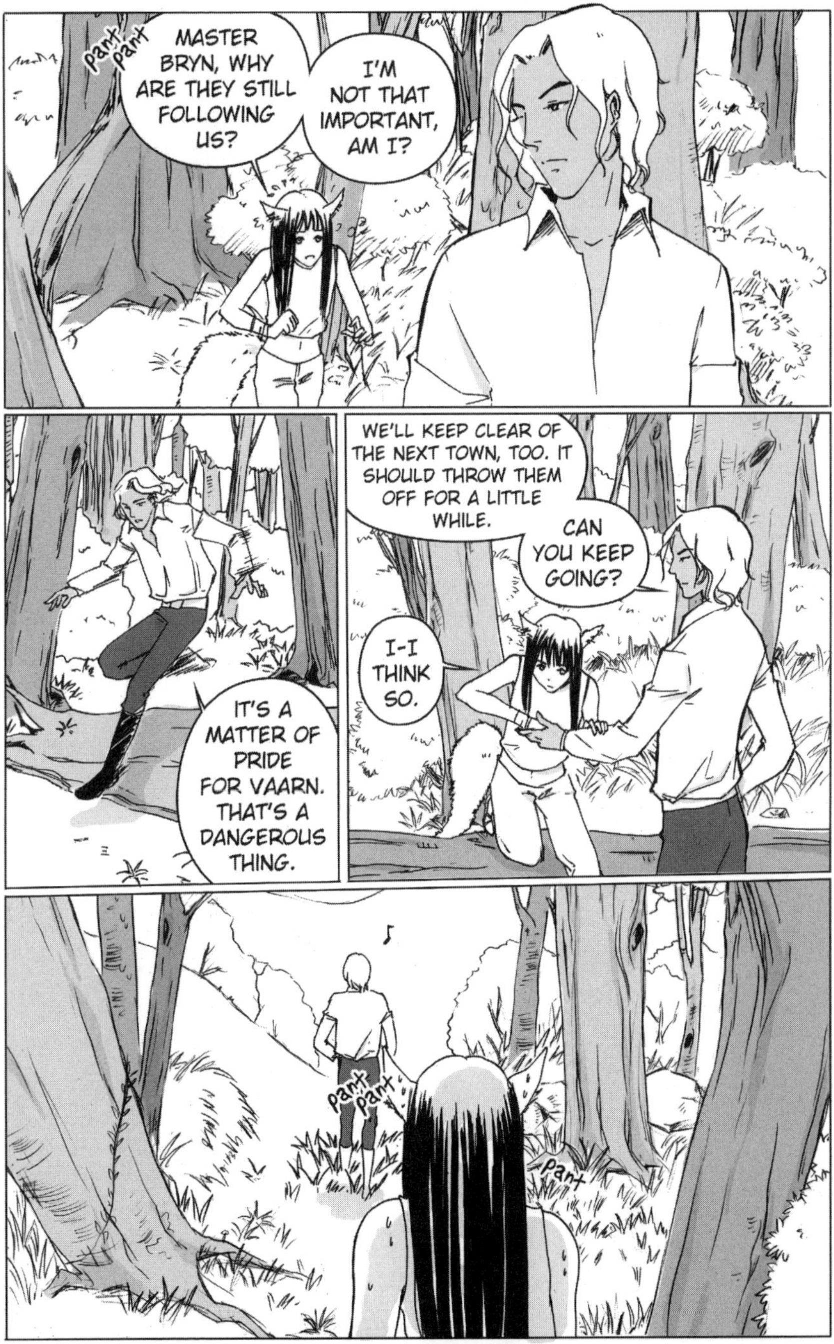
pant pant
MASTER BRYN, WHY ARE THEY STILL FOLLOWING US?
I'M NOT THAT IMPORTANT, AM I?
IT'S A MATTER OF PRIDE FOR VAARN. THAT'S A DANGEROUS THING.
WE'LL KEEP CLEAR OF THE NEXT TOWN, TOO. IT SHOULD THROW THEM OFF FOR A LITTLE WHILE.
CAN YOU KEEP GOING?
I-I THINK SO.
pant pant
pant

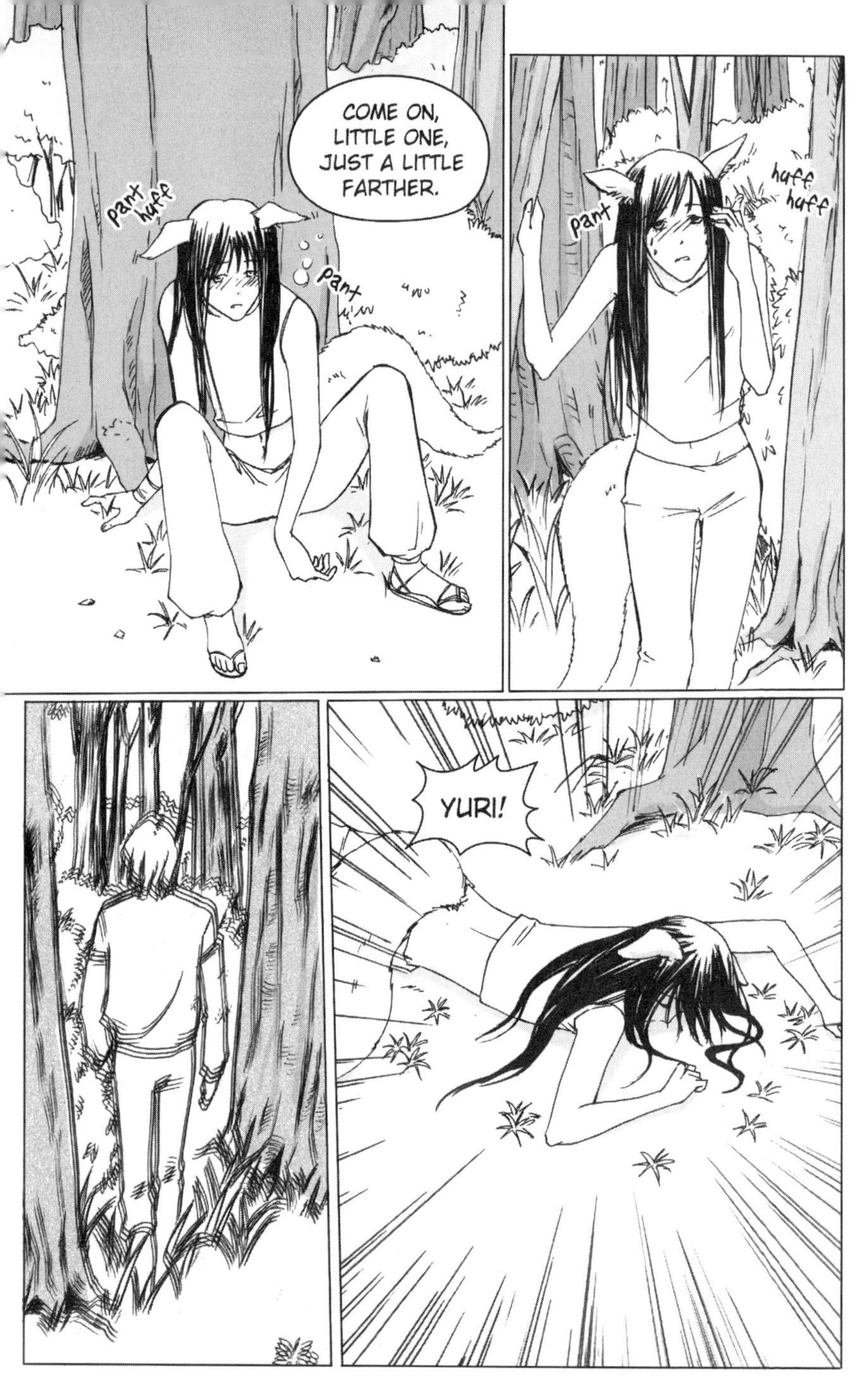
COME ON, LITTLE ONE, JUST A LITTLE FARTHER.
pant huff
pant
pant
huff huff
YURI!

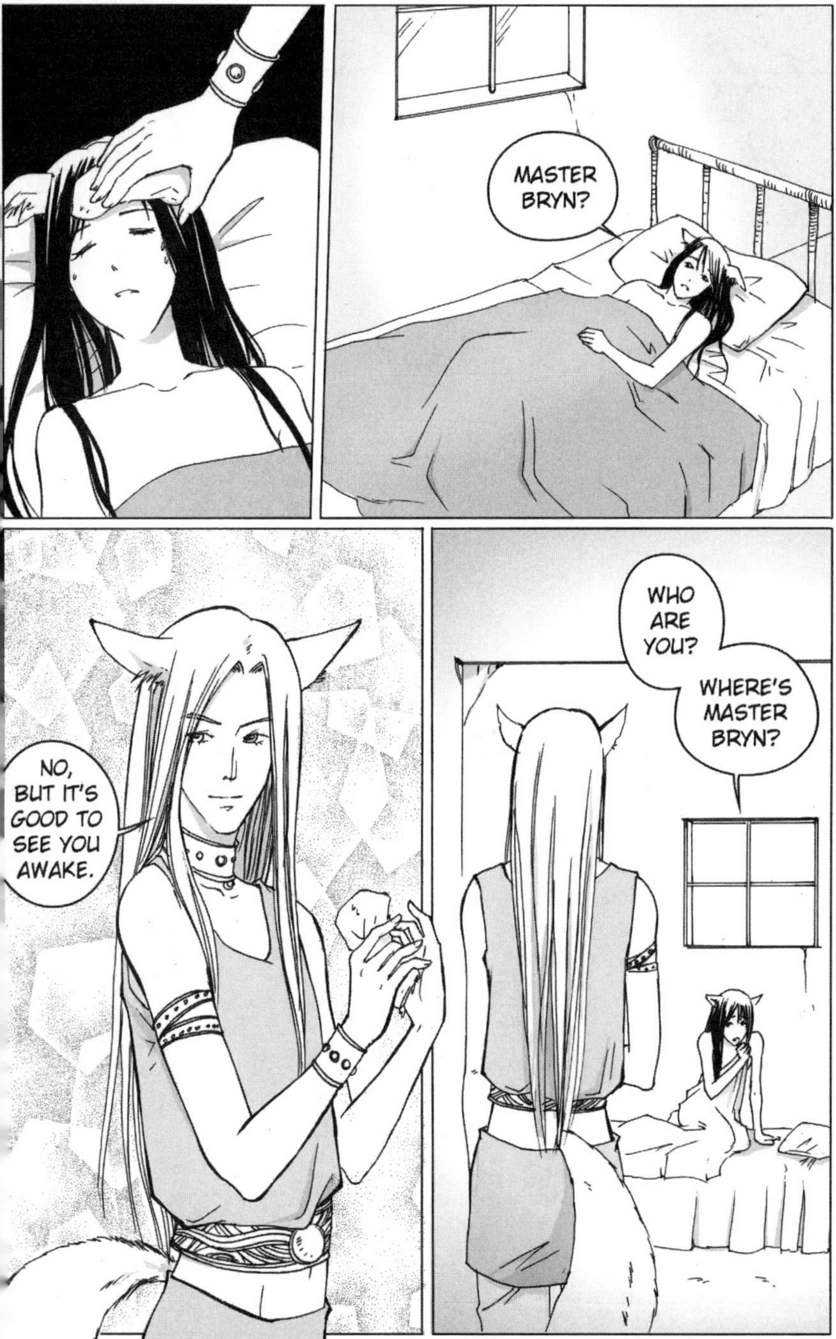
MASTER BRYN?
NO, BUT IT'S GOOD TO SEE YOU AWAKE.
WHO ARE YOU?
WHERE'S MASTER BRYN?

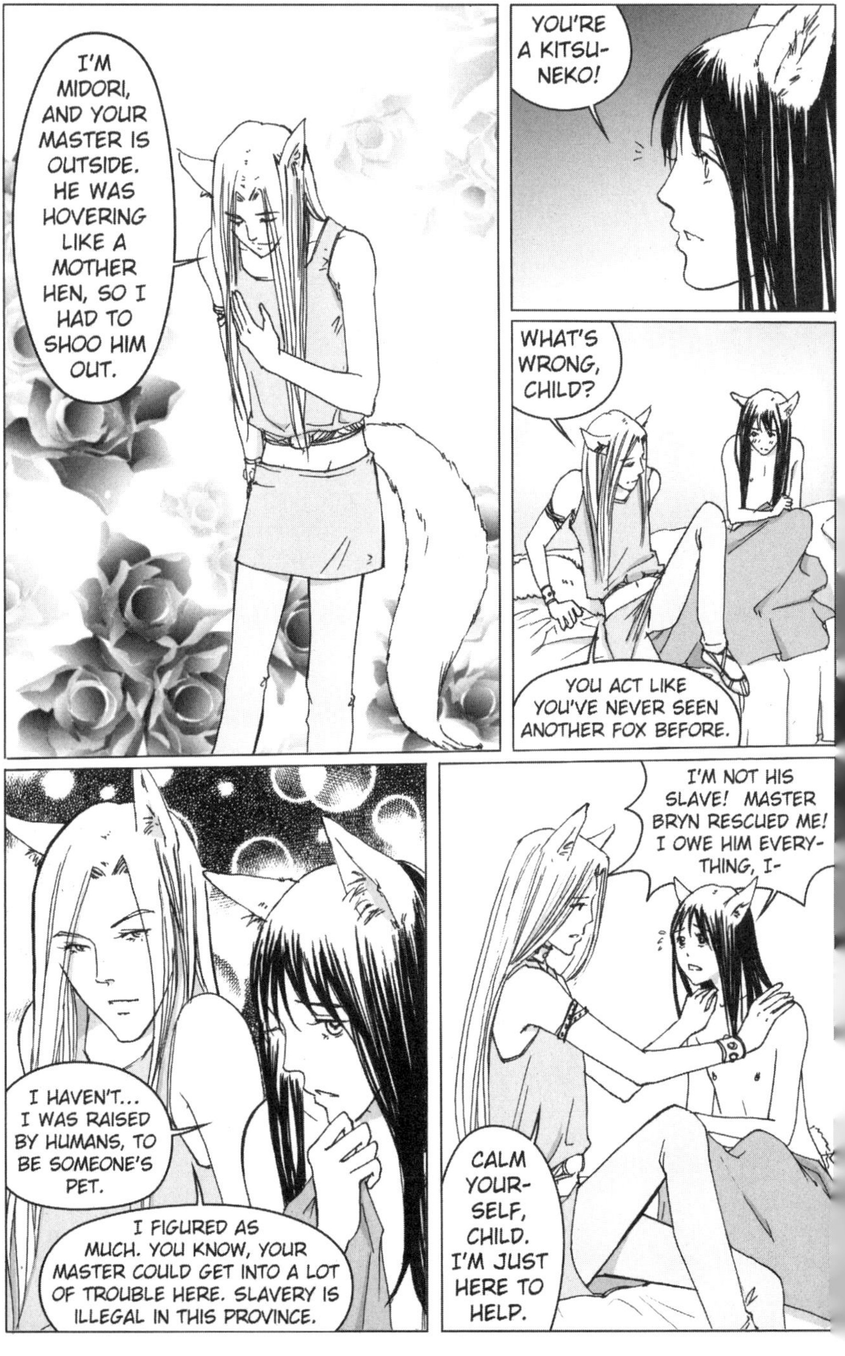
I'M MIDORI, AND YOUR MASTER IS OUTSIDE. HE WAS HOVERING LIKE A MOTHER HEN, SO I HAD TO SHOO HIM OUT.
YOU'RE A KITSU-NEKO!
WHAT'S WRONG, CHILD?
YOU ACT LIKE YOU'VE NEVER SEEN ANOTHER FOX BEFORE.
I HAVEN'T... I WAS RAISED BY HUMANS, TO BE SOMEONE'S PET.
I FIGURED AS MUCH. YOU KNOW, YOUR MASTER COULD GET INTO A LOT OF TROUBLE HERE. SLAVERY IS ILLEGAL IN THIS PROVINCE.
I'M NOT HIS SLAVE! MASTER BRYN RESCUED ME! I OWE HIM EVERY-THING, I-
CALM YOUR-SELF, CHILD. I'M JUST HERE TO HELP.

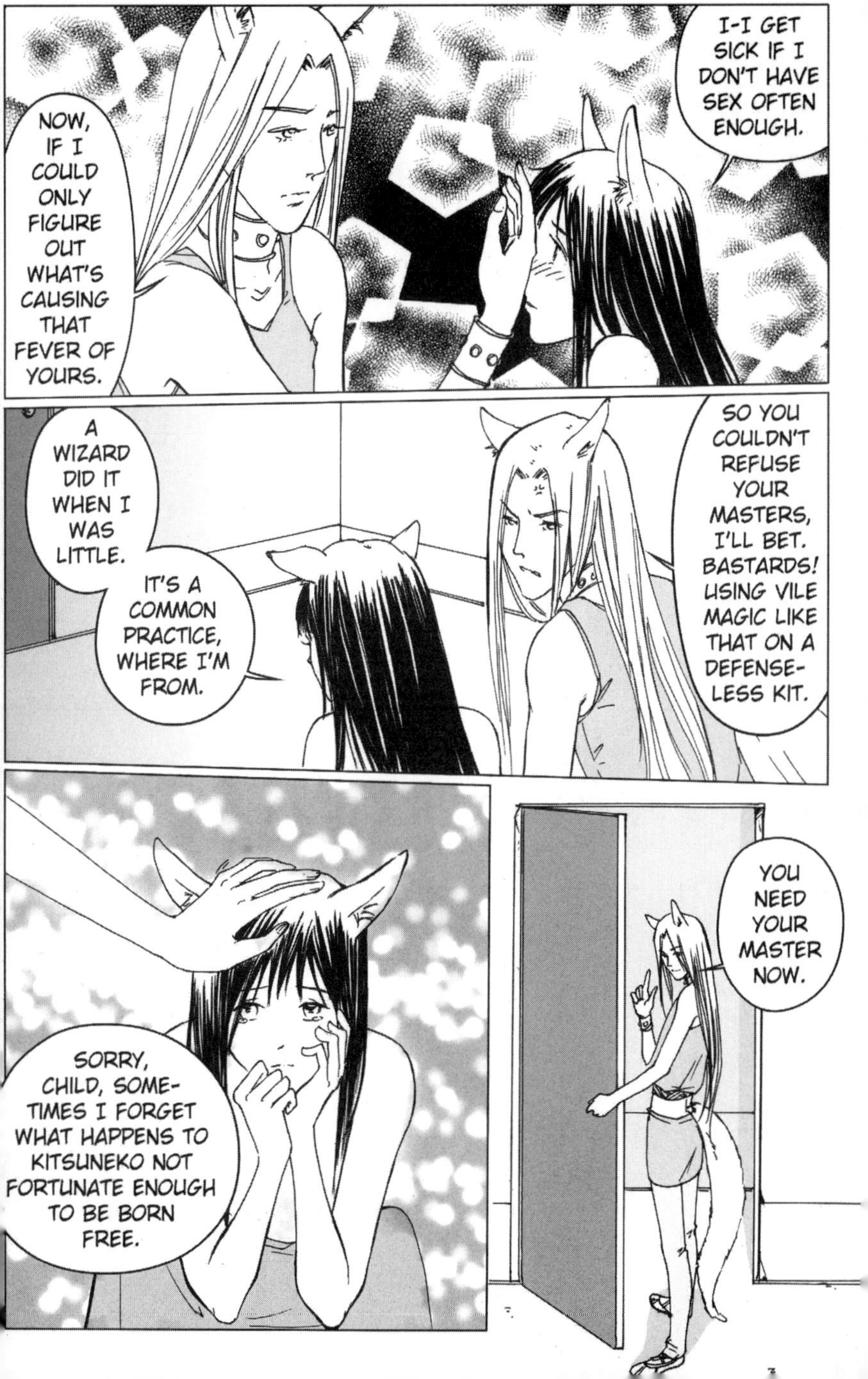
NOW, IF I COULD ONLY FIGURE OUT WHAT'S CAUSING THAT FEVER OF YOURS.
I-I GET SICK IF I DON'T HAVE SEX OFTEN ENOUGH.
SO YOU COULDN'T REFUSE YOUR MASTERS, I'LL BET. BASTARDS! USING VILE MAGIC LIKE THAT ON A DEFENSE-LESS KIT.
A WIZARD DID IT WHEN I WAS LITTLE.
IT'S A COMMON PRACTICE, WHERE I'M FROM.
SORRY, CHILD, SOME-TIMES I FORGET WHAT HAPPENS TO KITSUNEKO NOT FORTUNATE ENOUGH TO BE BORN FREE.
YOU NEED YOUR MASTER NOW.

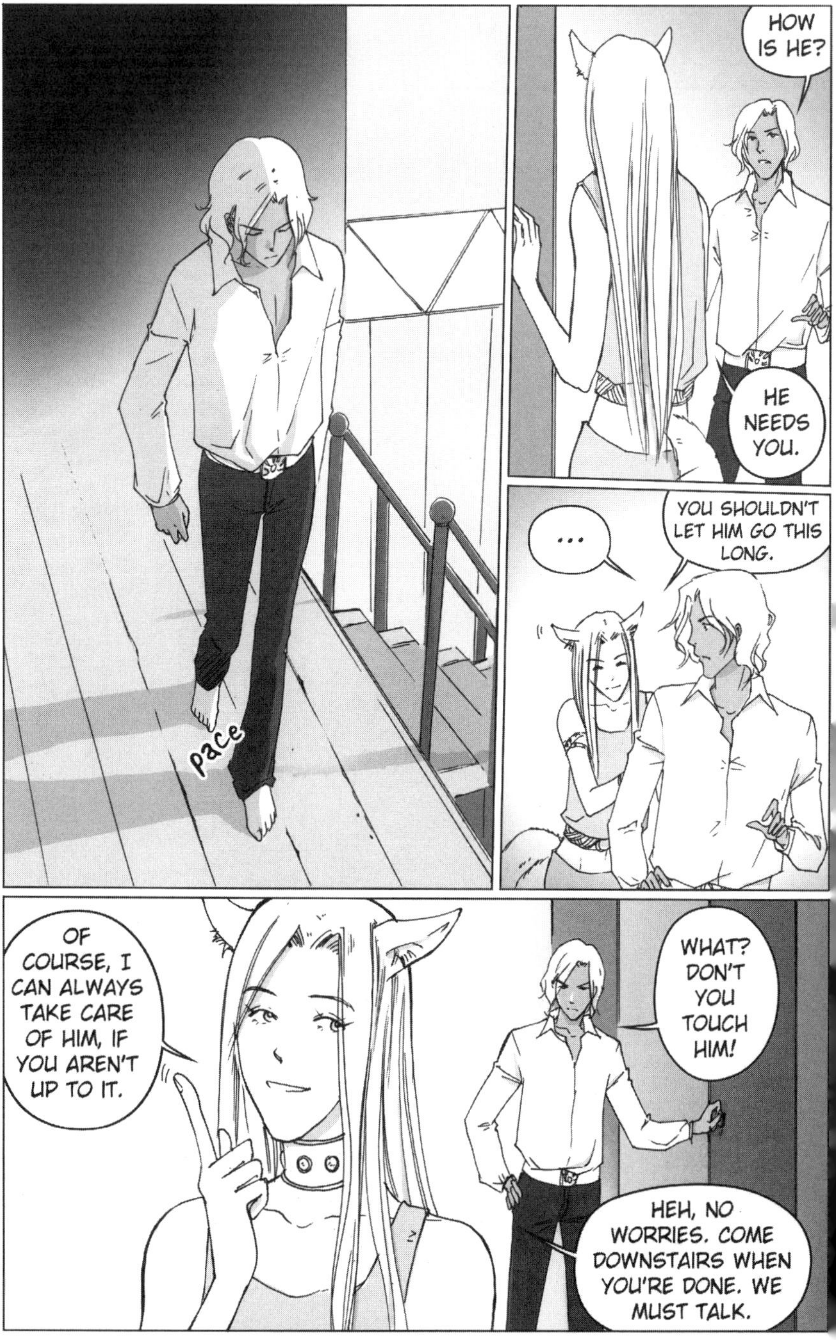
pace
HOW IS HE?
HE NEEDS YOU.
YOU SHOULDN'T LET HIM GO THIS LONG.
...
OF COURSE, I CAN ALWAYS TAKE CARE OF HIM, IF YOU AREN'T UP TO IT.
WHAT? DON'T YOU TOUCH HIM!
HEH, NO WORRIES. COME DOWNSTAIRS WHEN YOU'RE DONE. WE MUST TALK.

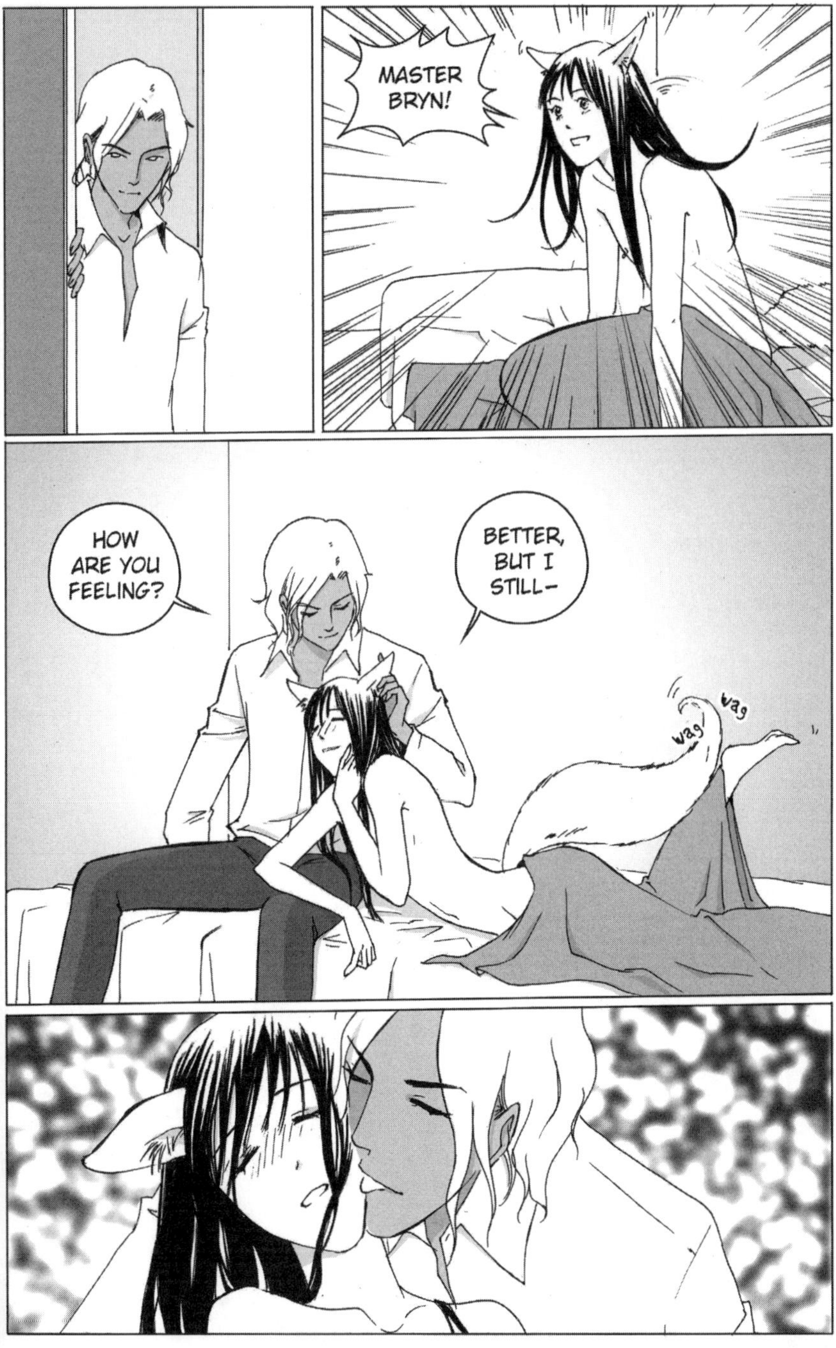
MASTER BRYN!
HOW ARE YOU FEELING?
BETTER, BUT I STILL-
wag
wag

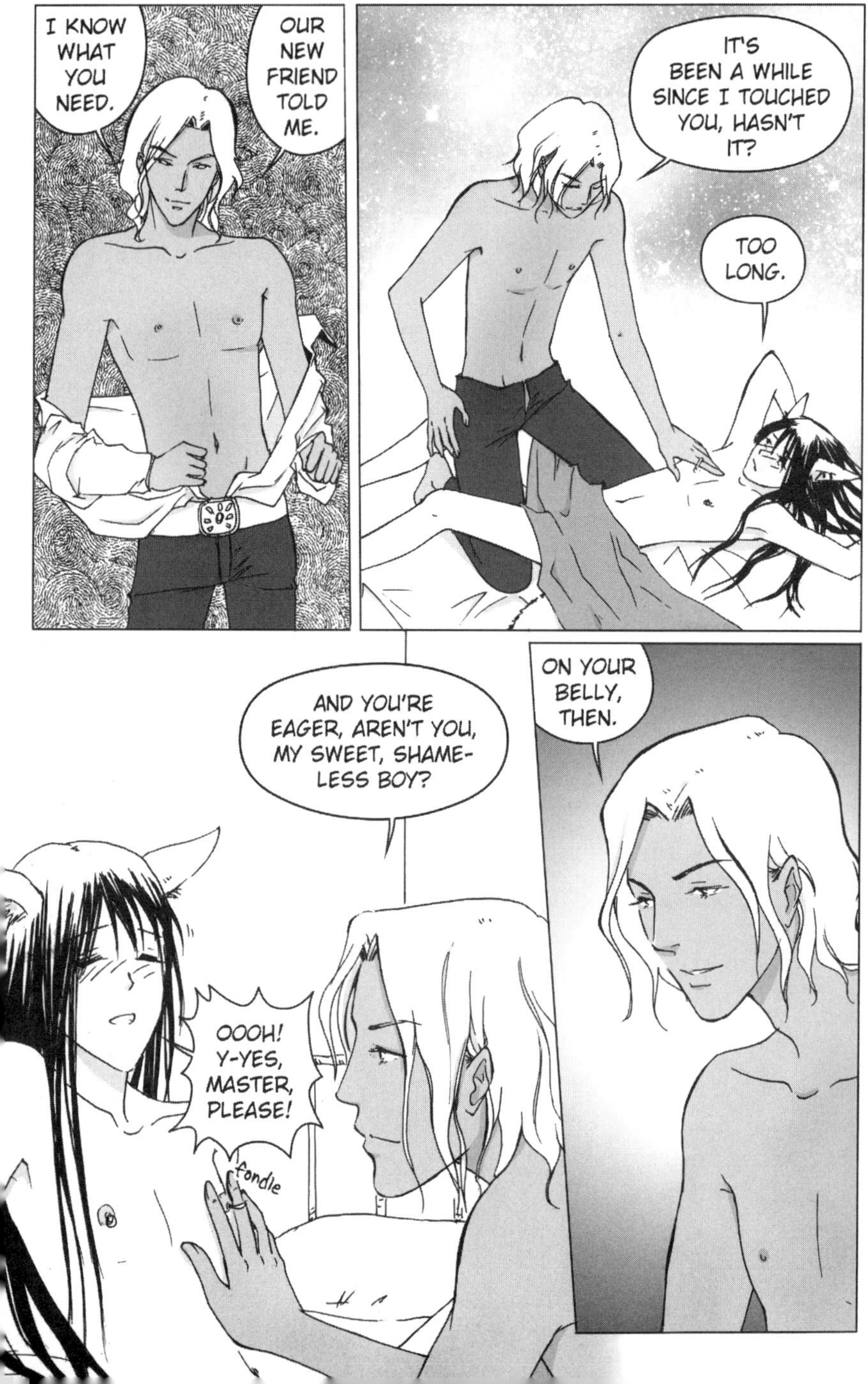
I KNOW WHAT YOU NEED.
OUR NEW FRIEND TOLD ME.
IT'S BEEN A WHILE SINCE I TOUCHED YOU, HASN'T IT?
TOO LONG.
AND YOU'RE EAGER, AREN'T YOU, MY SWEET, SHAME-LESS BOY?
OOOH! Y-YES, MASTER, PLEASE!
fondle
ON YOUR BELLY, THEN.

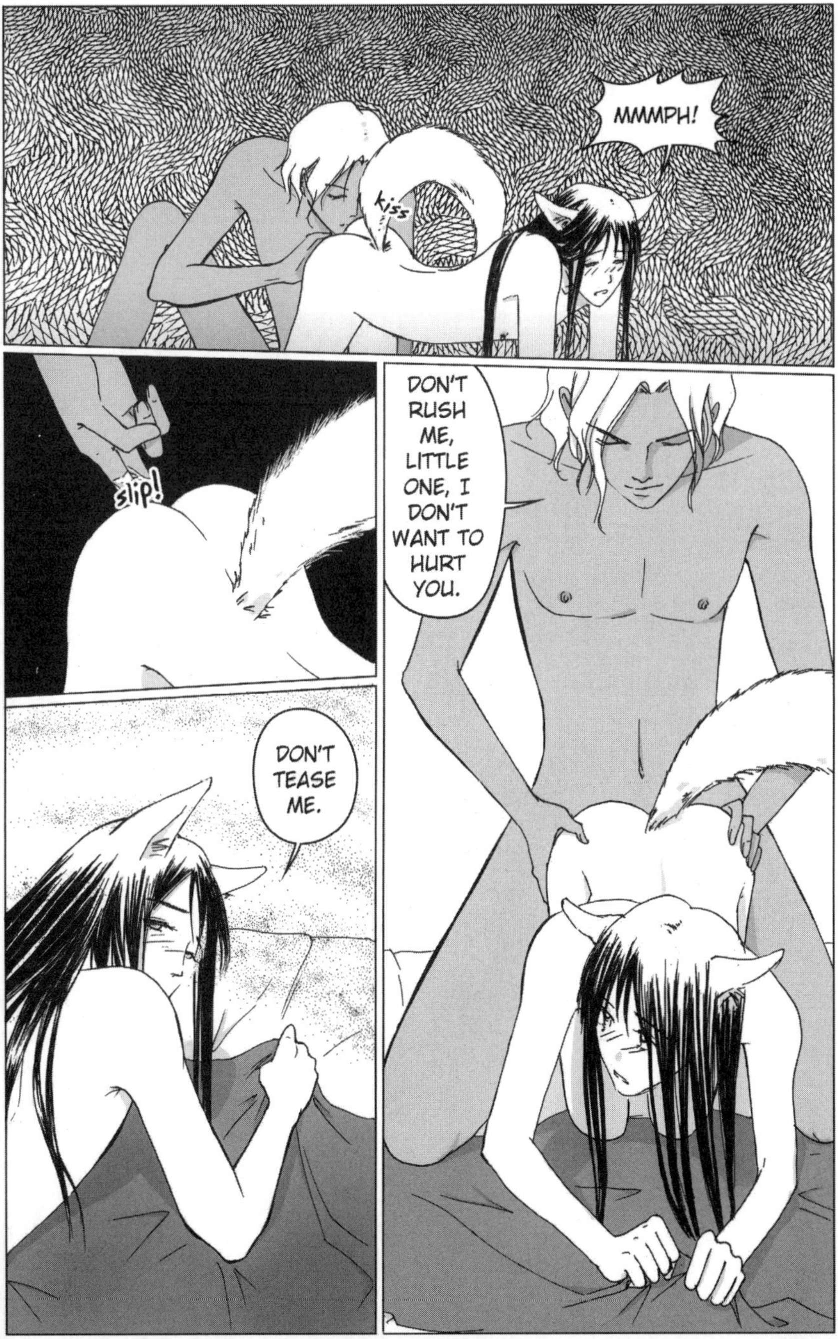
kiss
MMMPH!
slip!
DON'T TEASE ME.
DON'T RUSH ME, LITTLE ONE, I DON'T WANT TO HURT YOU.

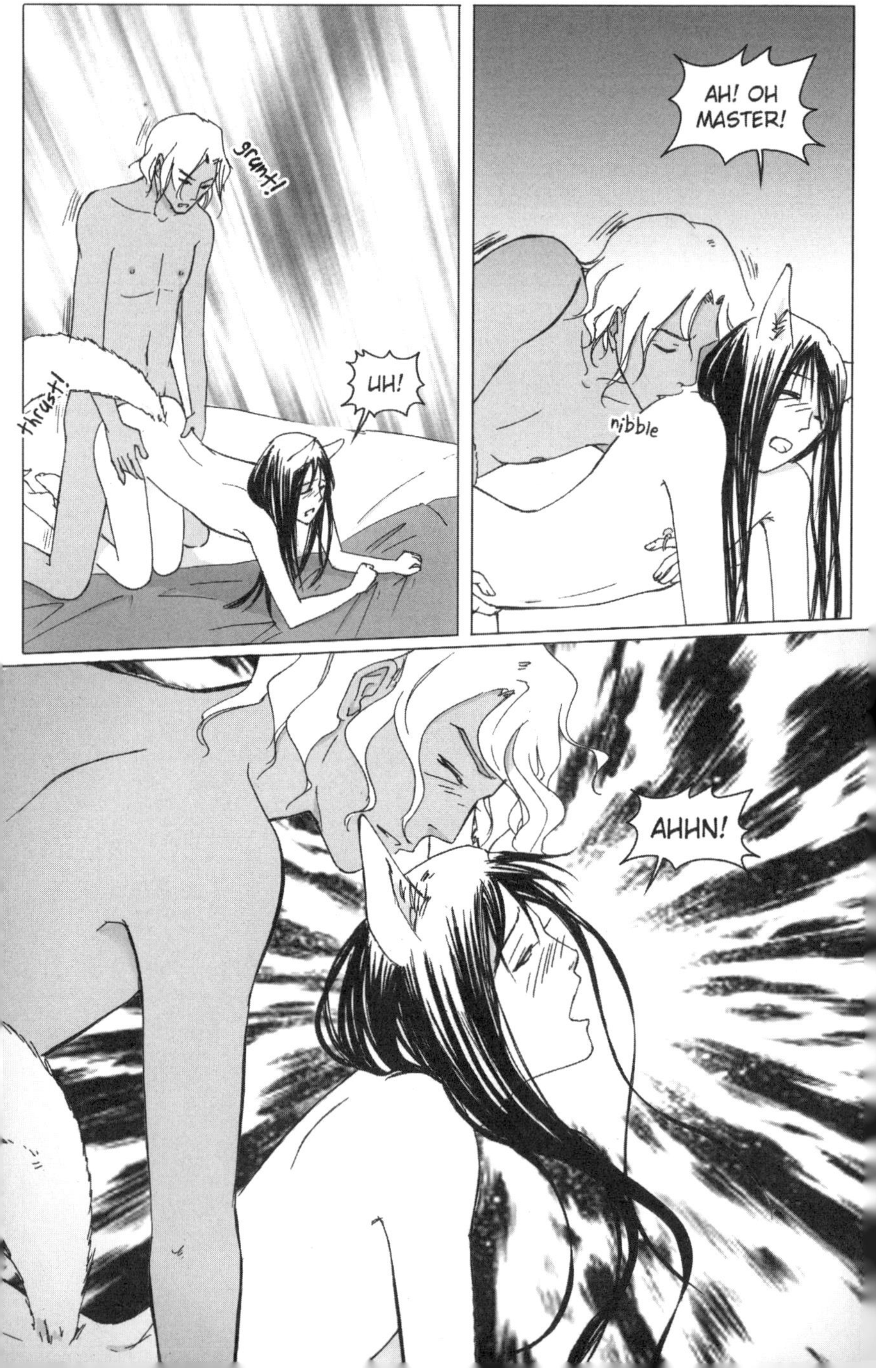
grunt!
thrust!
UH!
AH! OH MASTER!
nibble
AHHN!

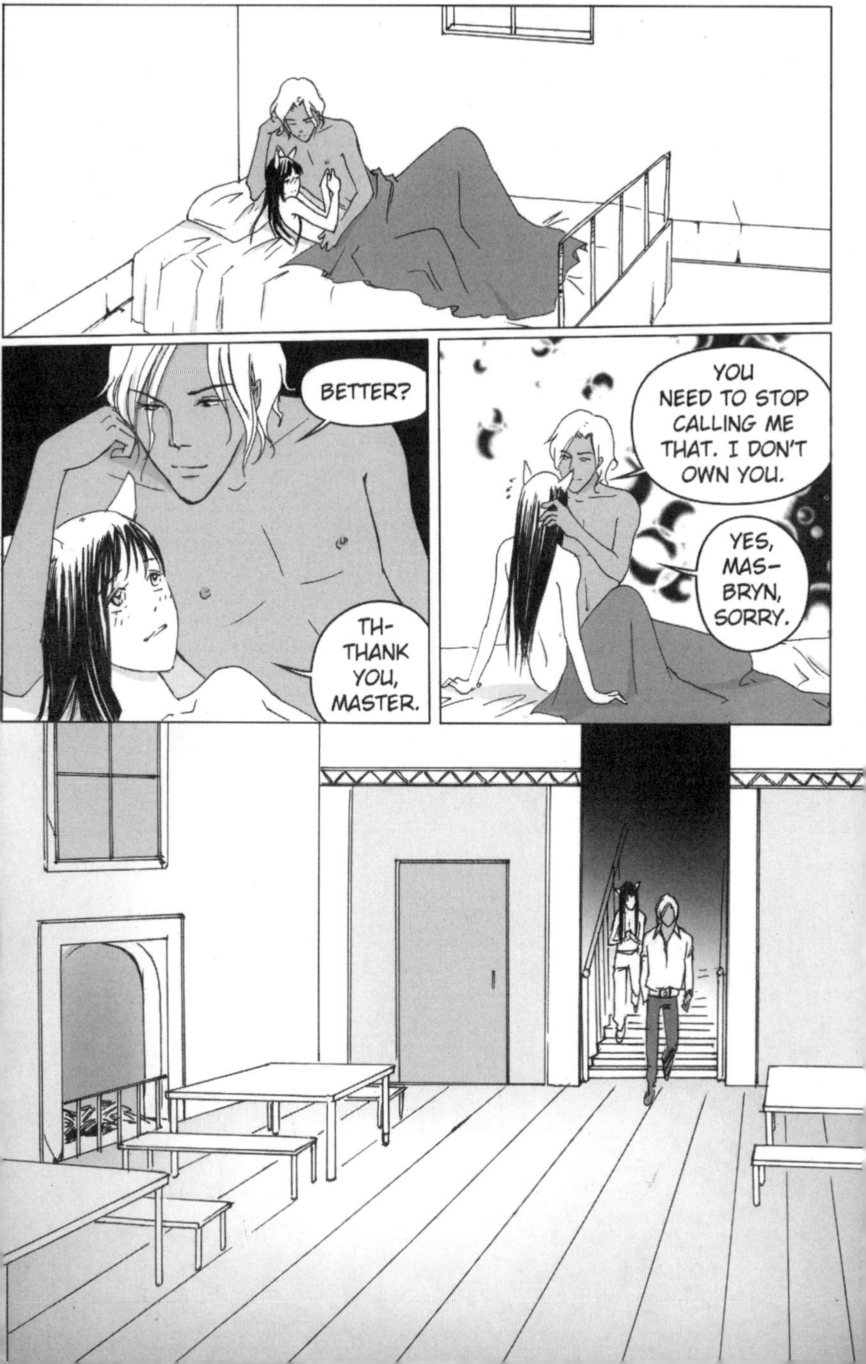
BETTER?
TH-THANK YOU, MASTER.
YOU NEED TO STOP CALLING ME THAT. I DON'T OWN YOU.
YES, MAS-BRYN, SORRY.

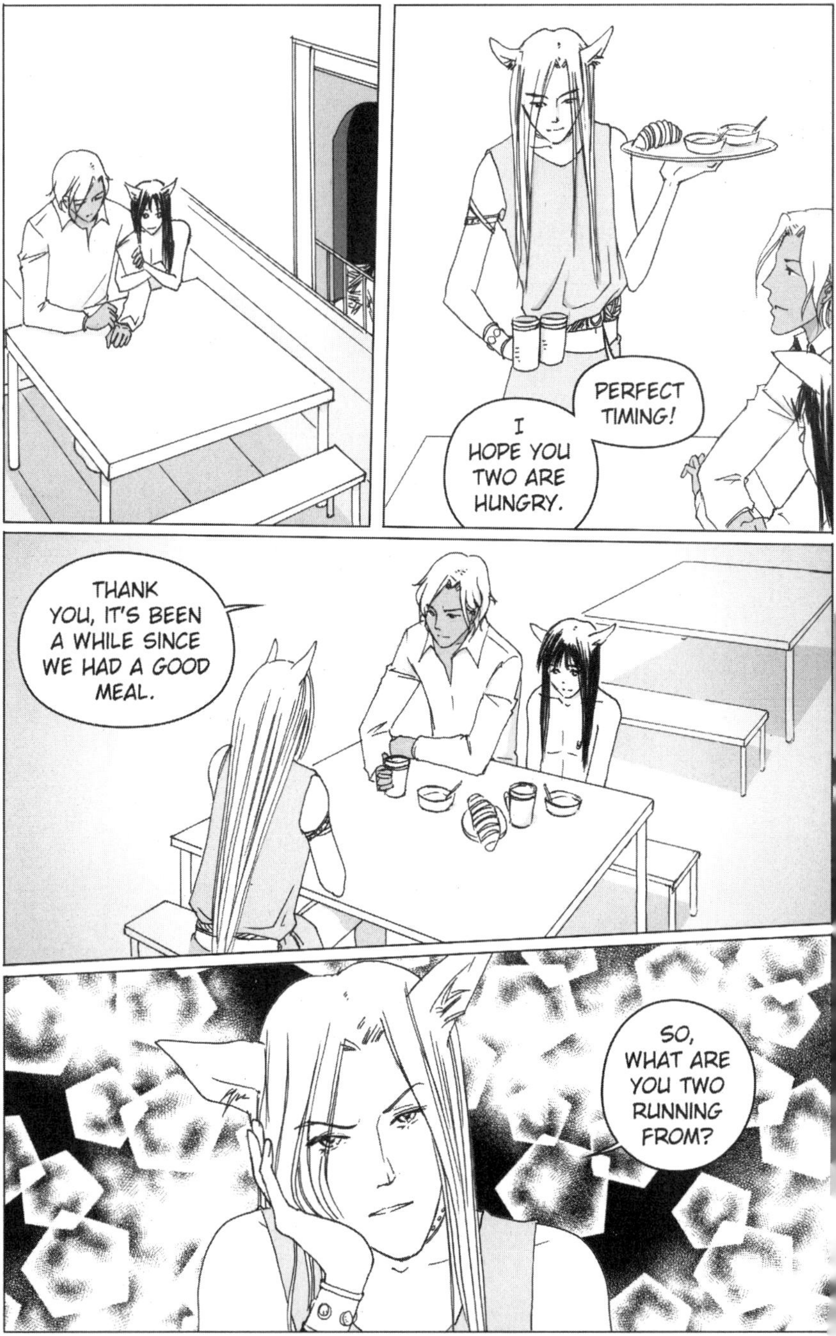
PERFECT TIMING!
I HOPE YOU TWO ARE HUNGRY.
THANK YOU, IT'S BEEN A WHILE SINCE WE HAD A GOOD MEAL.
SO, WHAT ARE YOU TWO RUNNING FROM?

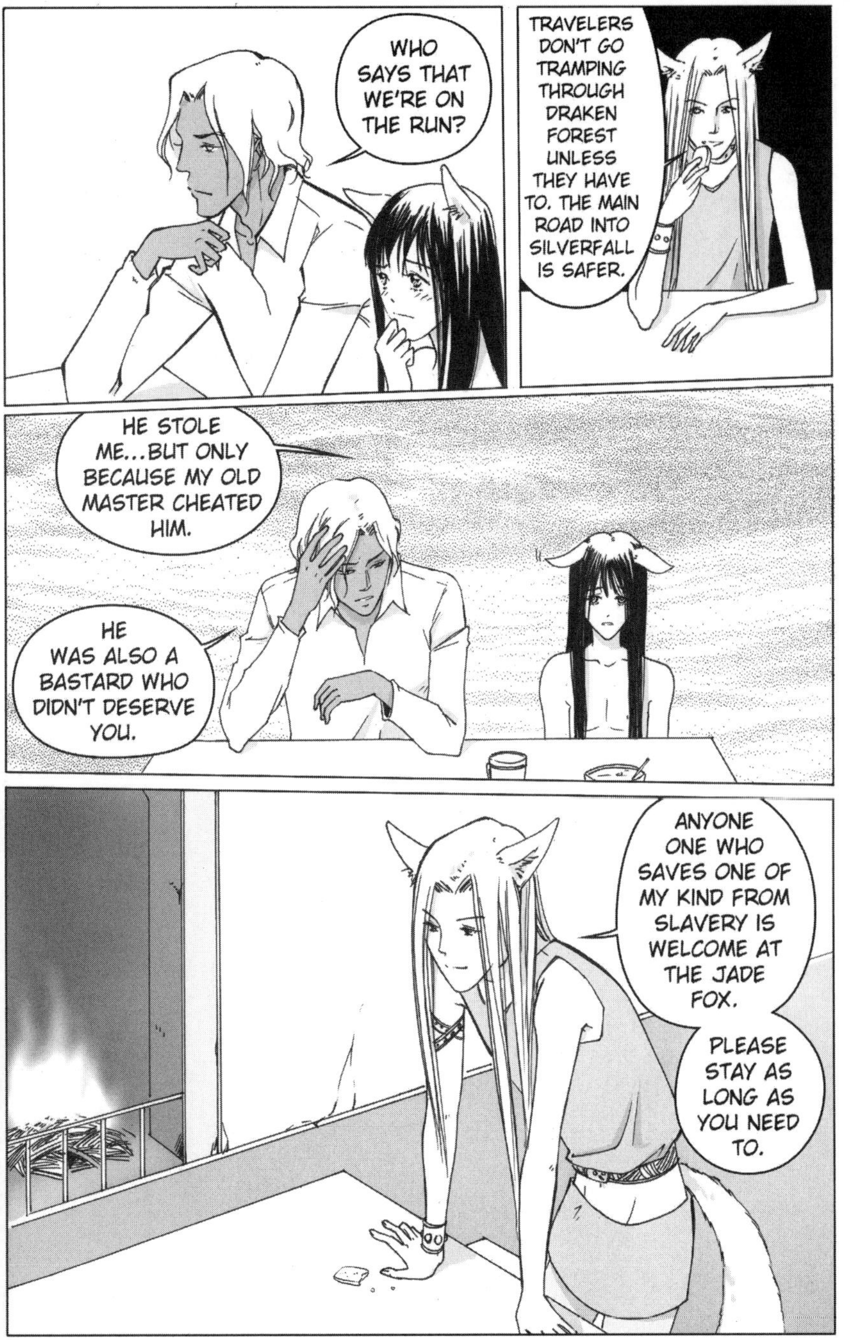
WHO SAYS THAT WE'RE ON THE RUN?
TRAVELERS DON'T GO TRAMPING THROUGH DRAKEN FOREST UNLESS THEY HAVE TO. THE MAIN ROAD INTO SILVERFALL IS SAFER.
HE STOLE ME...BUT ONLY BECAUSE MY OLD MASTER CHEATED HIM.
HE WAS ALSO A BASTARD WHO DIDN'T DESERVE YOU.
ANYONE ONE WHO SAVES ONE OF MY KIND FROM SLAVERY IS WELCOME AT THE JADE FOX.
PLEASE STAY AS LONG AS YOU NEED TO.

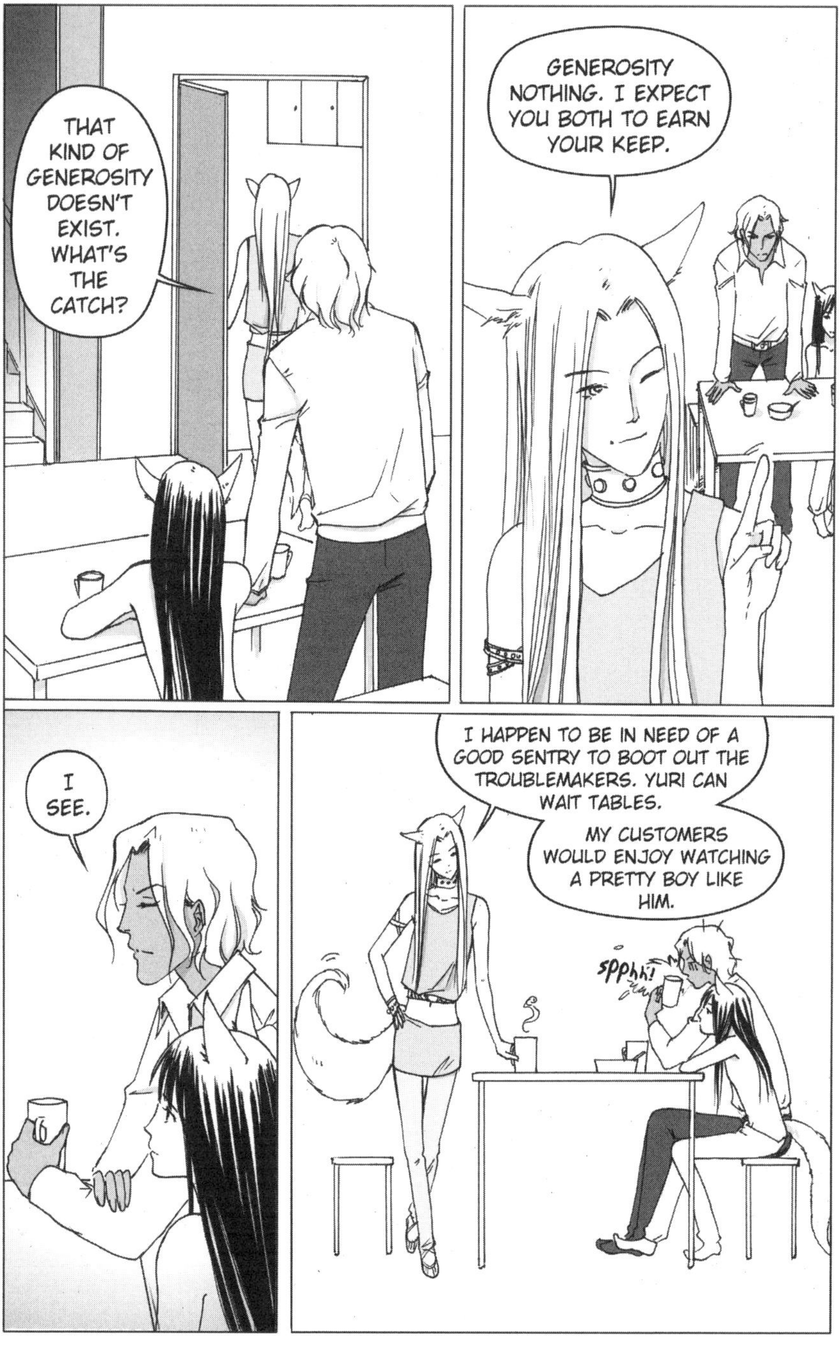
THAT KIND OF GENEROSITY DOESN'T EXIST. WHAT'S THE CATCH?
GENEROSITY NOTHING. I EXPECT YOU BOTH TO EARN YOUR KEEP.
I SEE.
I HAPPEN TO BE IN NEED OF A GOOD SENTRY TO BOOT OUT THE TROUBLEMAKERS. YURI CAN WAIT TABLES.
MY CUSTOMERS WOULD ENJOY WATCHING A PRETTY BOY LIKE HIM.
SPPHH!

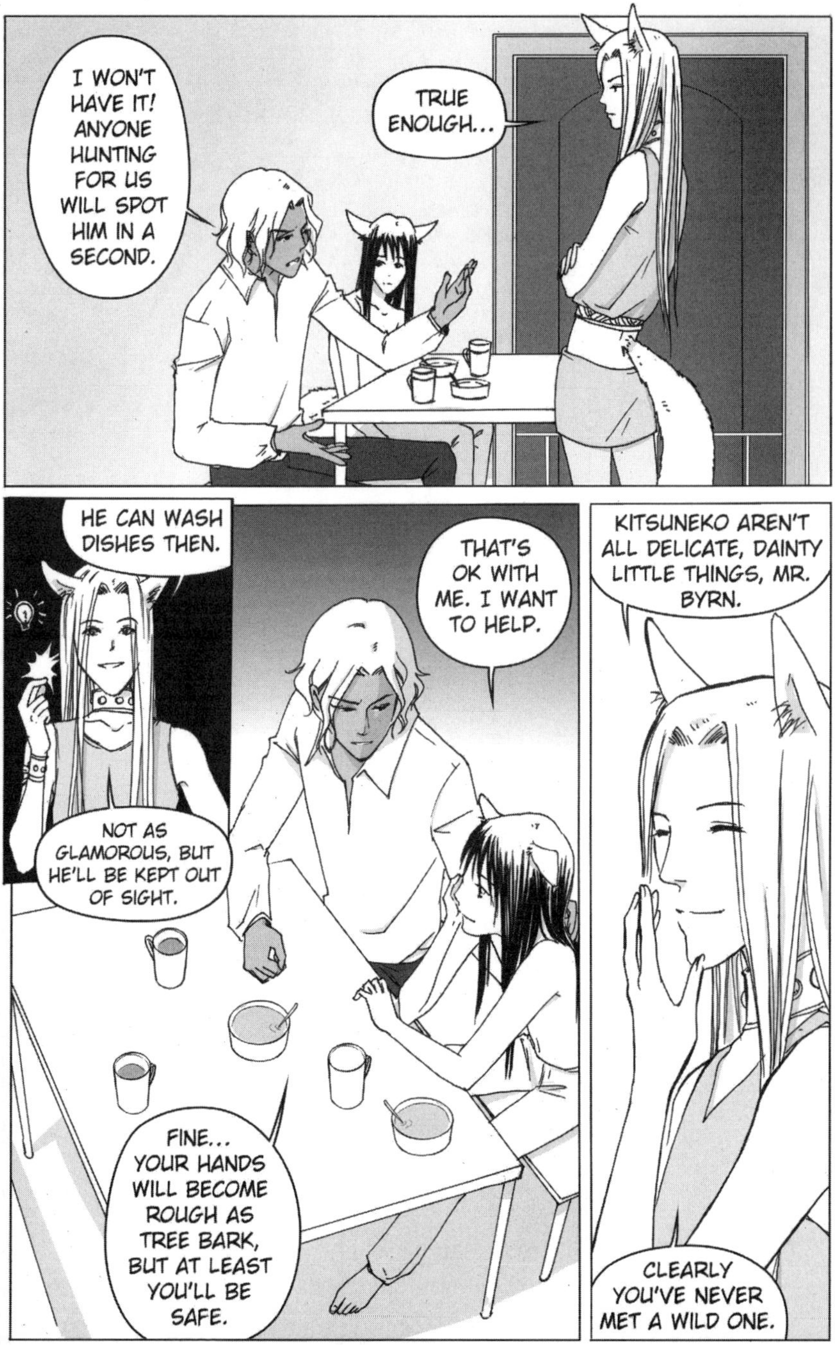
I WON'T HAVE IT! ANYONE HUNTING FOR US WILL SPOT HIM IN A SECOND.
TRUE ENOUGH...
HE CAN WASH DISHES THEN.
NOT AS GLAMOROUS, BUT HE'LL BE KEPT OUT OF SIGHT.
THAT'S OK WITH ME. I WANT TO HELP.
FINE... YOUR HANDS WILL BECOME ROUGH AS TREE BARK, BUT AT LEAST YOU'LL BE SAFE.
KITSUNEKO AREN'T ALL DELICATE, DAINTY LITTLE THINGS, MR. BYRN.
CLEARLY YOU'VE NEVER MET A WILD ONE.

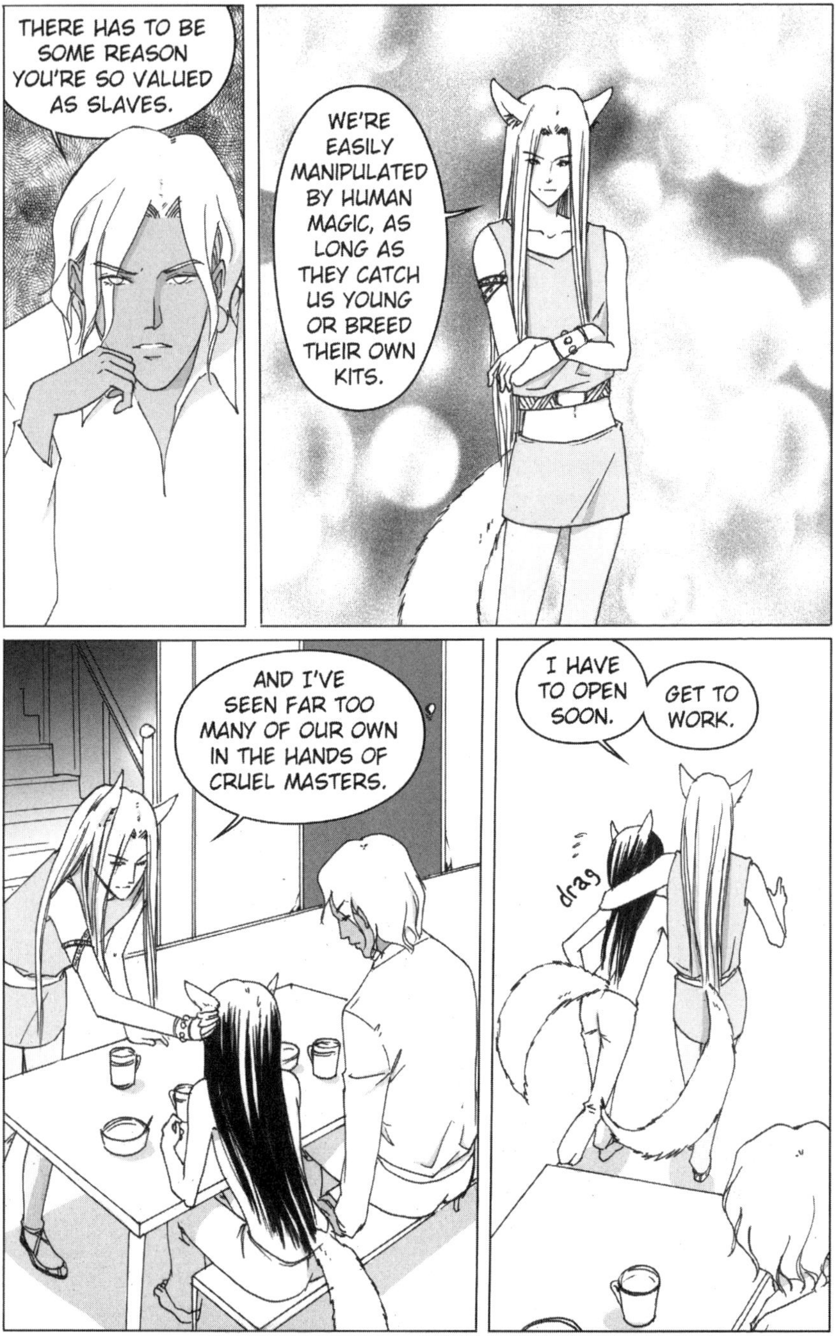
THERE HAS TO BE SOME REASON YOU'RE SO VALUED AS SLAVES.
WE'RE EASILY MANIPULATED BY HUMAN MAGIC, AS LONG AS THEY CATCH US YOUNG OR BREED THEIR OWN KITS.
AND I'VE SEEN FAR TOO MANY OF OUR OWN IN THE HANDS OF CRUEL MASTERS.
I HAVE TO OPEN SOON.
GET TO WORK.
drag

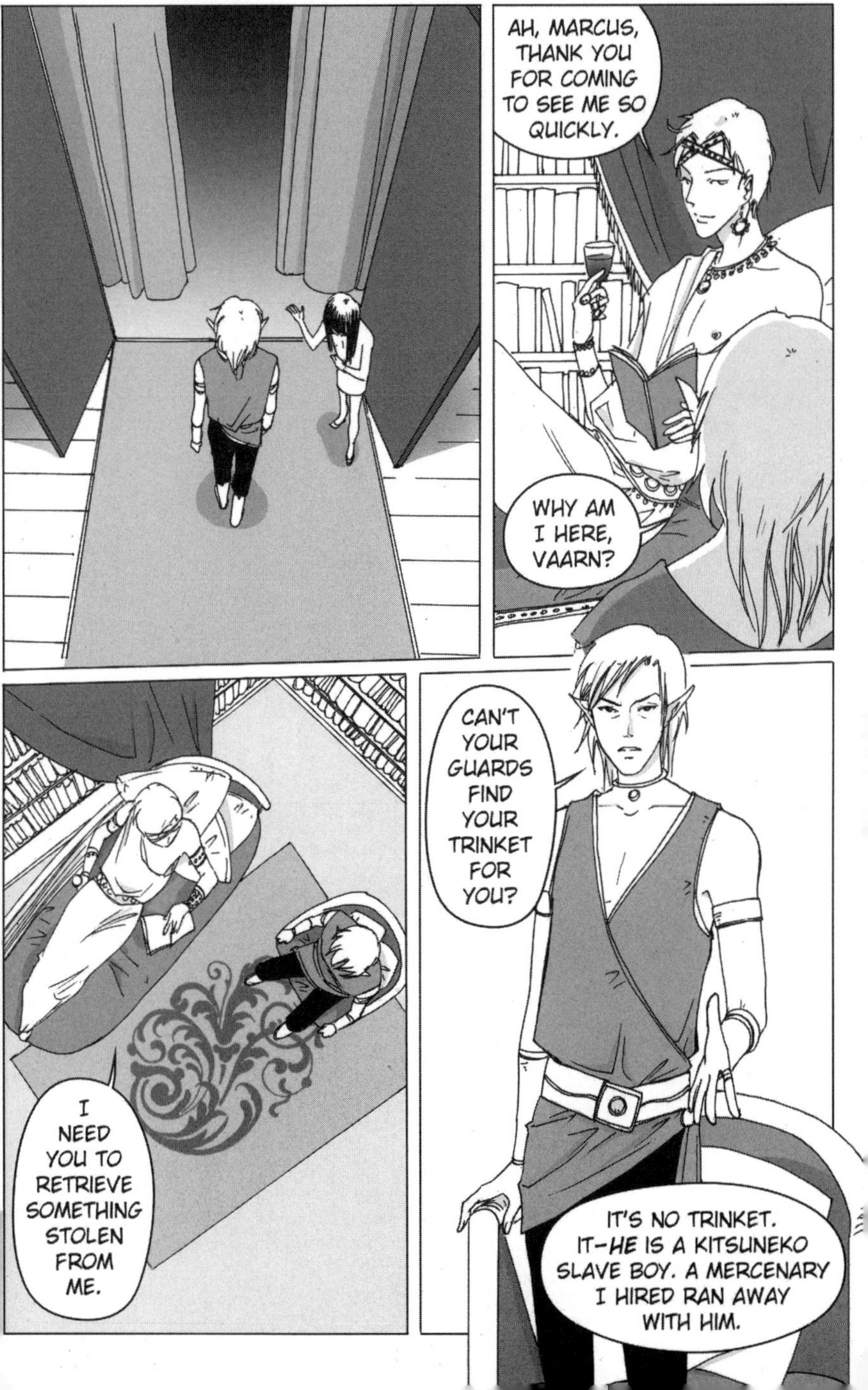
AH, MARCUS, THANK YOU FOR COMING TO SEE ME SO QUICKLY.
WHY AM I HERE, VAARN?
I NEED YOU TO RETRIEVE SOMETHING STOLEN FROM ME.
CAN'T YOUR GUARDS FIND YOUR TRINKET FOR YOU?
IT'S NO TRINKET. IT—*HE* IS A KITSUNEKO SLAVE BOY. A MERCENARY I HIRED RAN AWAY WITH HIM.

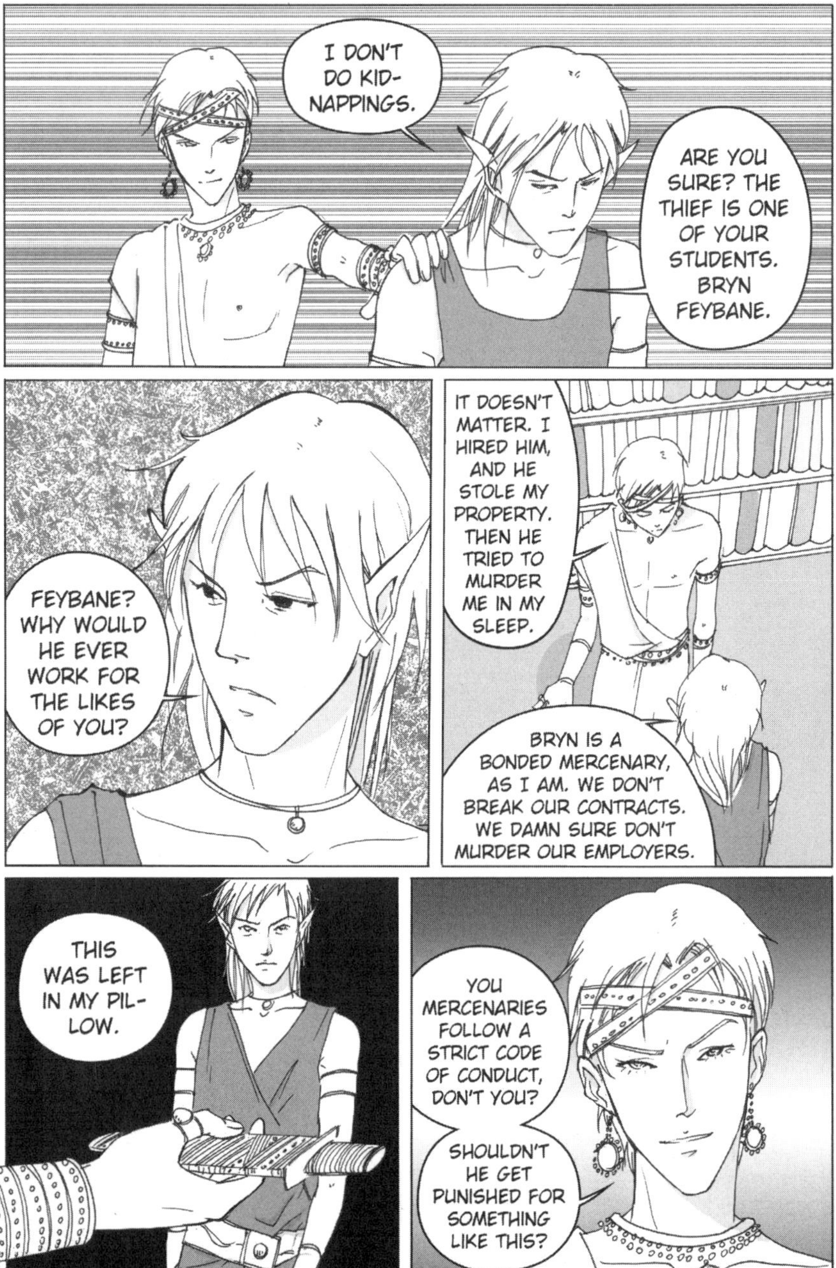
I DON'T DO KID-NAPPINGS.
ARE YOU SURE? THE THIEF IS ONE OF YOUR STUDENTS. BRYN FEYBANE.
FEYBANE? WHY WOULD HE EVER WORK FOR THE LIKES OF YOU?
IT DOESN'T MATTER. I HIRED HIM, AND HE STOLE MY PROPERTY. THEN HE TRIED TO MURDER ME IN MY SLEEP.
BRYN IS A BONDED MERCENARY, AS I AM. WE DON'T BREAK OUR CONTRACTS. WE DAMN SURE DON'T MURDER OUR EMPLOYERS.
THIS WAS LEFT IN MY PIL-LOW.
YOU MERCENARIES FOLLOW A STRICT CODE OF CONDUCT, DON'T YOU?
SHOULDN'T HE GET PUNISHED FOR SOMETHING LIKE THIS?

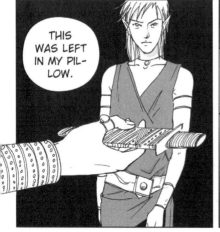

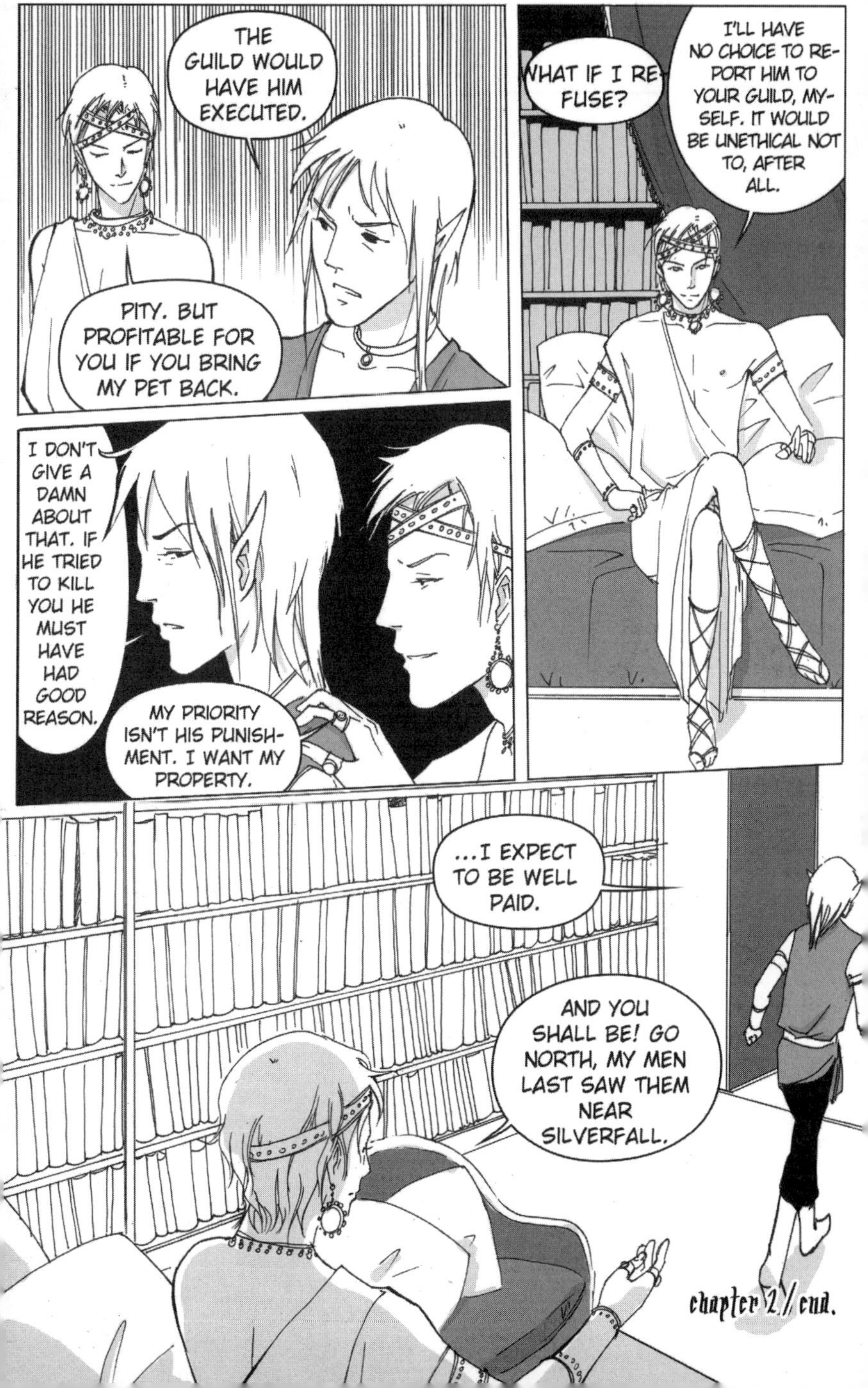
THE GUILD WOULD HAVE HIM EXECUTED.
PITY. BUT PROFITABLE FOR YOU IF YOU BRING MY PET BACK.
WHAT IF I REFUSE?
I'LL HAVE NO CHOICE TO REPORT HIM TO YOUR GUILD, MYSELF. IT WOULD BE UNETHICAL NOT TO, AFTER ALL.
I DON'T GIVE A DAMN ABOUT THAT. IF HE TRIED TO KILL YOU HE MUST HAVE HAD GOOD REASON.
MY PRIORITY ISN'T HIS PUNISHMENT. I WANT MY PROPERTY.
...I EXPECT TO BE WELL PAID.
AND YOU SHALL BE! GO NORTH, MY MEN LAST SAW THEM NEAR SILVERFALL.
chapter 2 / end.

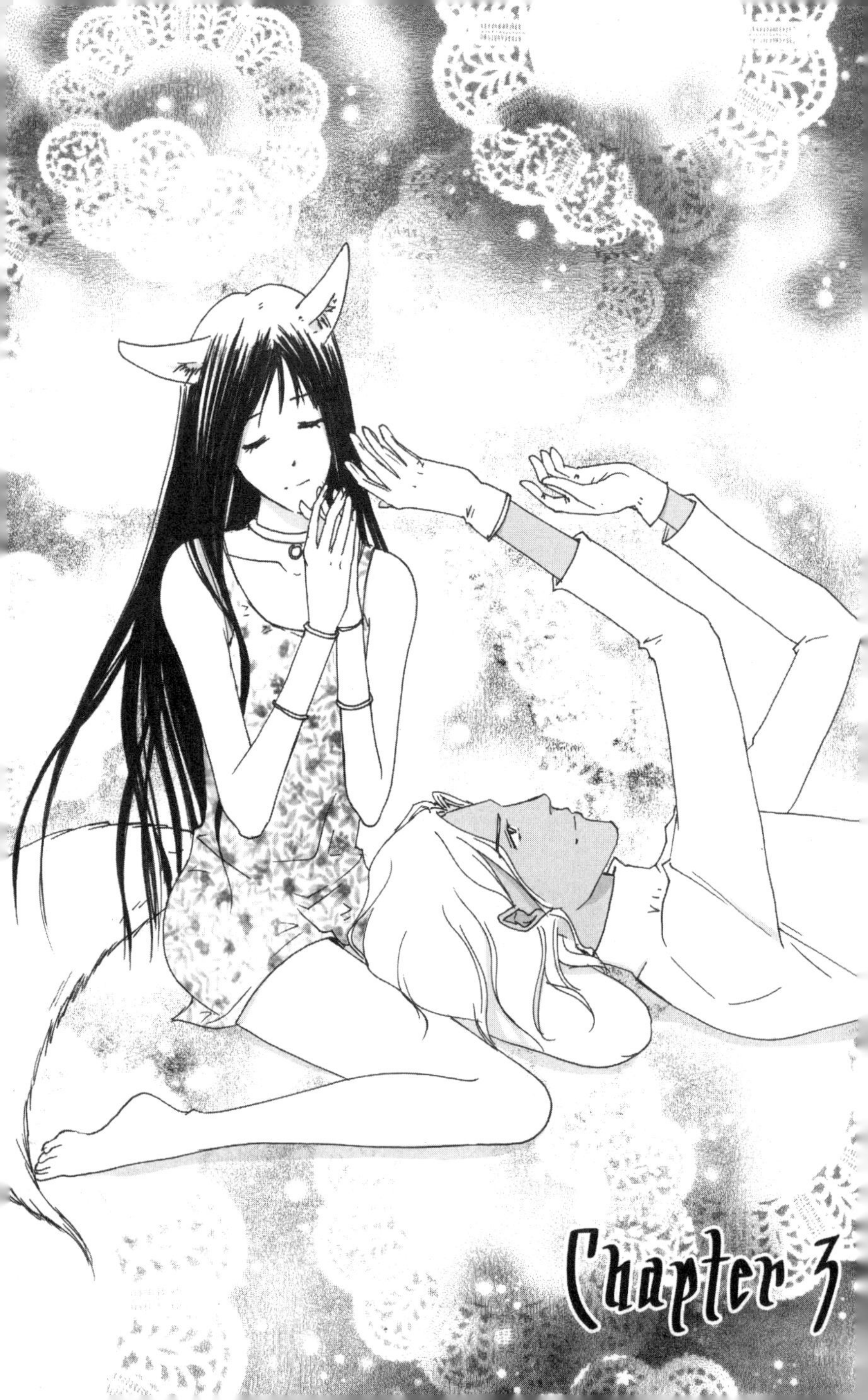
Chapter 3

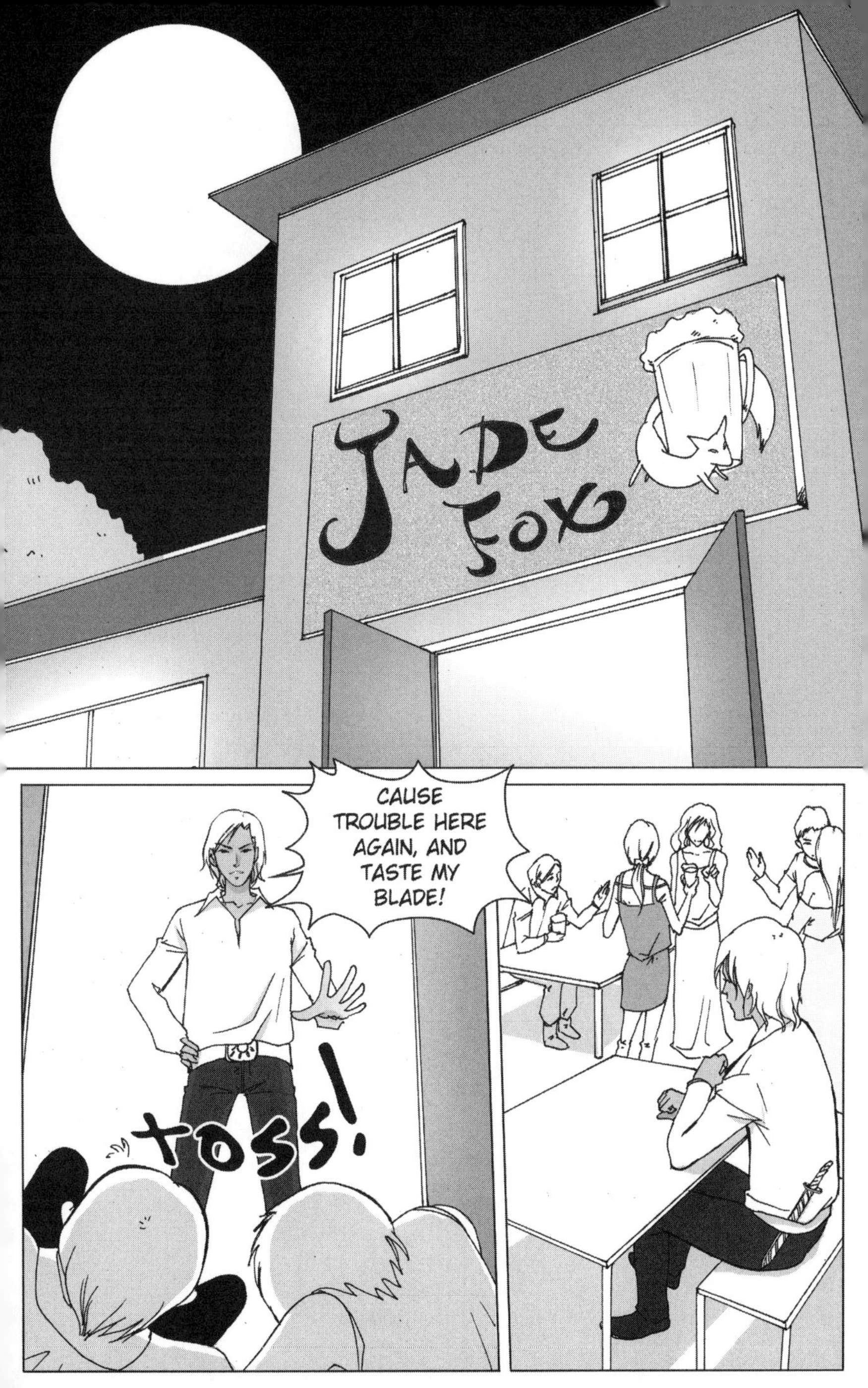
JADE FOX
CAUSE TROUBLE HERE AGAIN, AND TASTE MY BLADE!
TOSS!

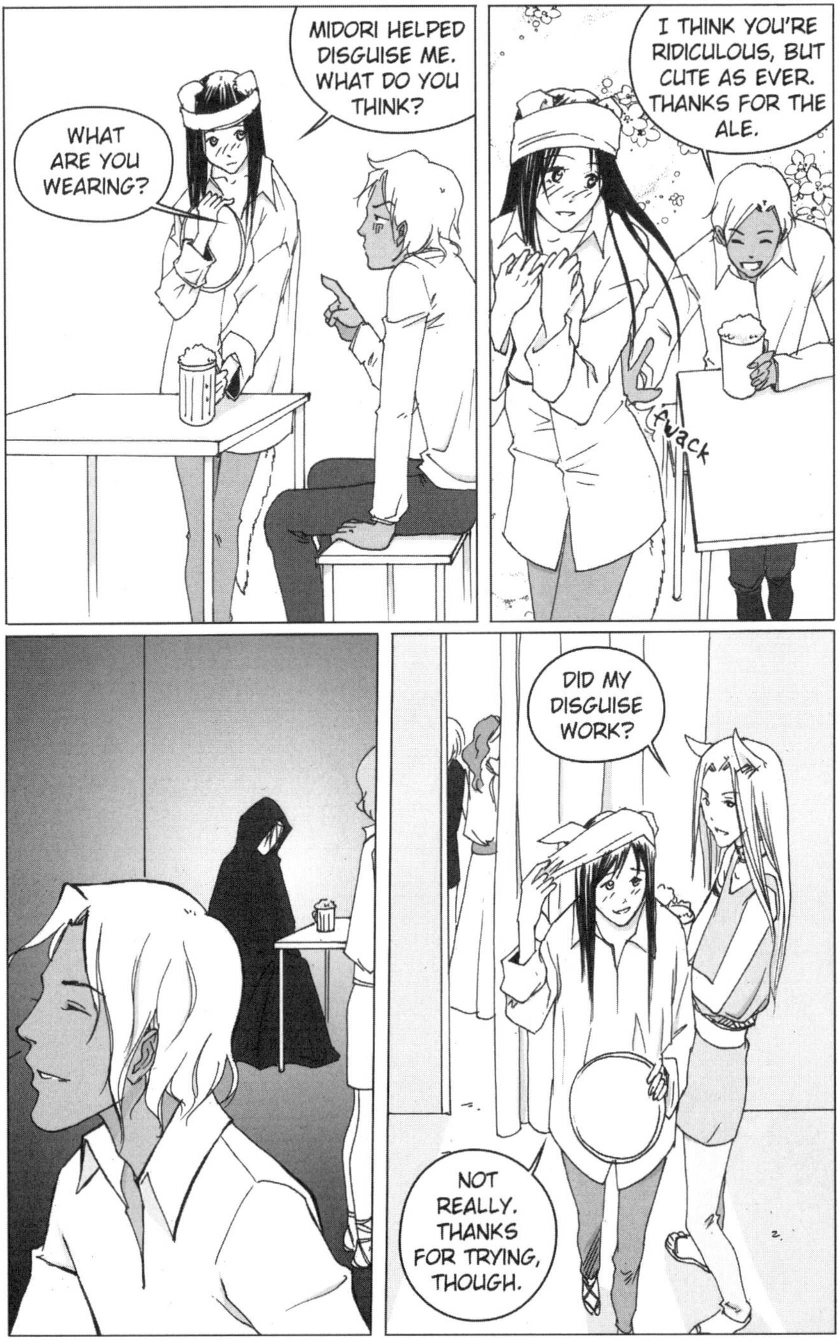
MIDORI HELPED DISGUISE ME. WHAT DO YOU THINK?
WHAT ARE YOU WEARING?
I THINK YOU'RE RIDICULOUS, BUT CUTE AS EVER. THANKS FOR THE ALE.
Awack
DID MY DISGUISE WORK?
NOT REALLY. THANKS FOR TRYING, THOUGH.

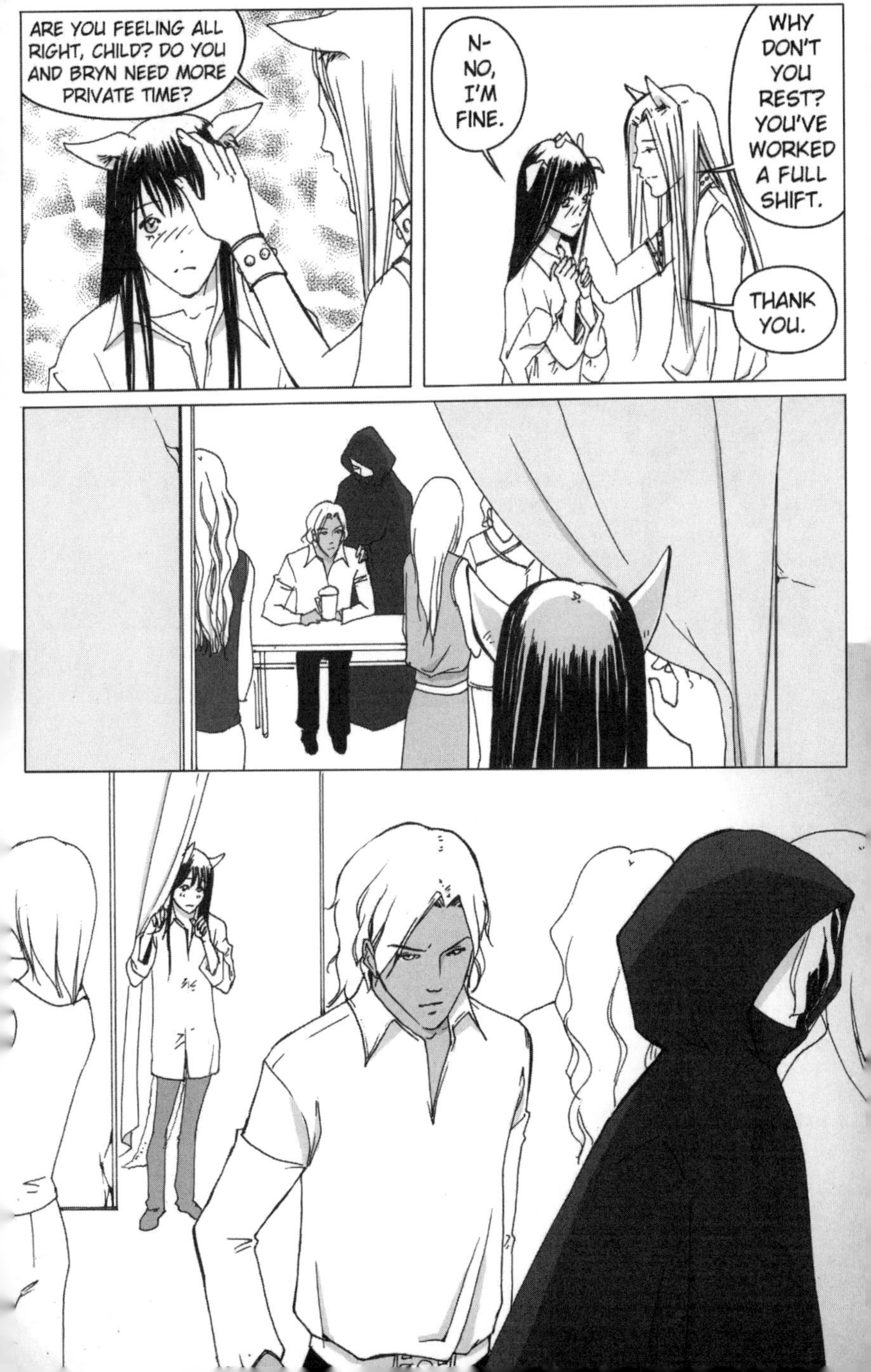
ARE YOU FEELING ALL RIGHT, CHILD? DO YOU AND BRYN NEED MORE PRIVATE TIME?
N-NO, I'M FINE.
WHY DON'T YOU REST? YOU'VE WORKED A FULL SHIFT.
THANK YOU.

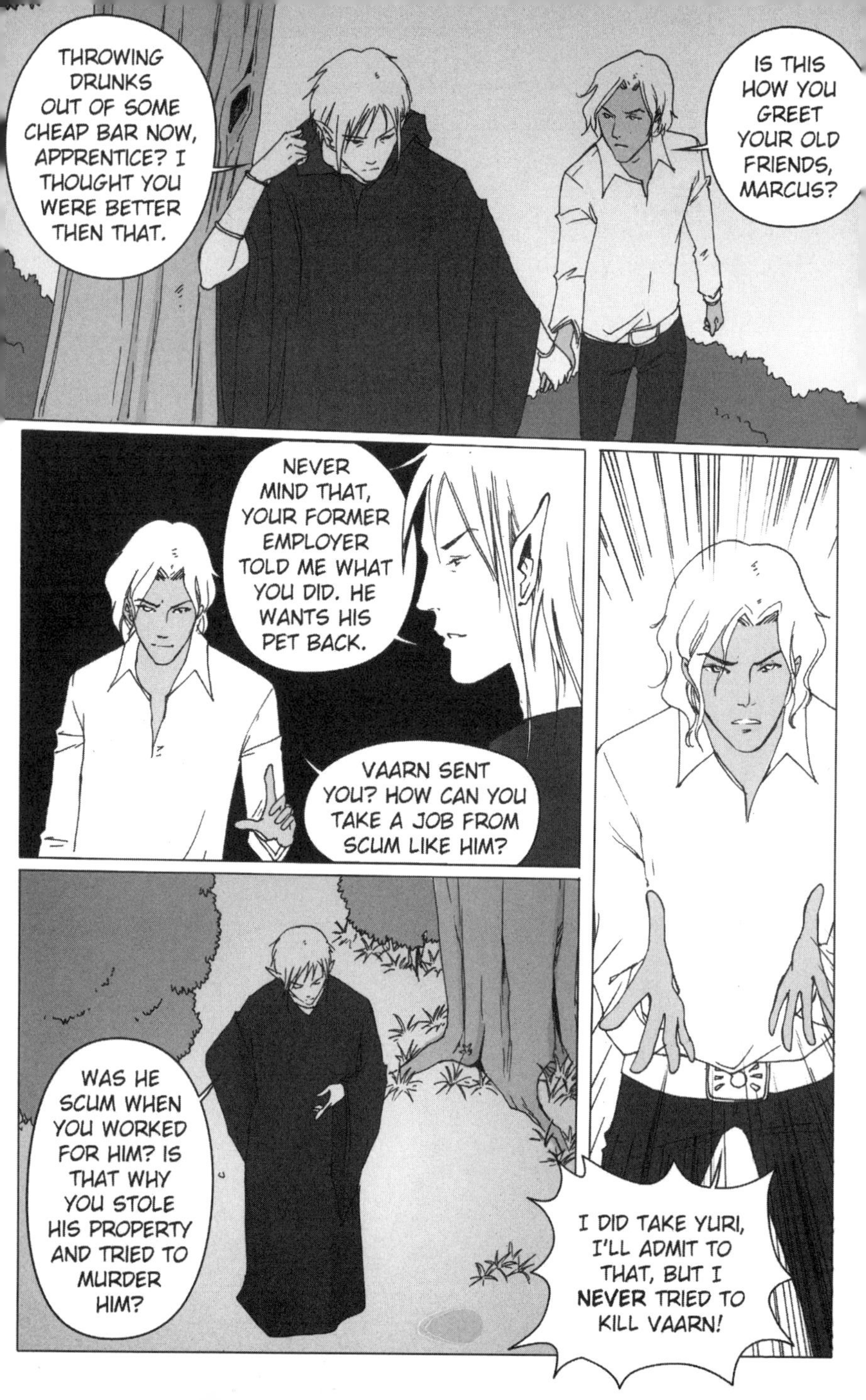
THROWING DRUNKS OUT OF SOME CHEAP BAR NOW, APPRENTICE? I THOUGHT YOU WERE BETTER THEN THAT.
IS THIS HOW YOU GREET YOUR OLD FRIENDS, MARCUS?
NEVER MIND THAT, YOUR FORMER EMPLOYER TOLD ME WHAT YOU DID. HE WANTS HIS PET BACK.
VAARN SENT YOU? HOW CAN YOU TAKE A JOB FROM SCUM LIKE HIM?
WAS HE SCUM WHEN YOU WORKED FOR HIM? IS THAT WHY YOU STOLE HIS PROPERTY AND TRIED TO MURDER HIM?
I DID TAKE YURI, I'LL ADMIT TO THAT, BUT I **NEVER** TRIED TO KILL VAARN!

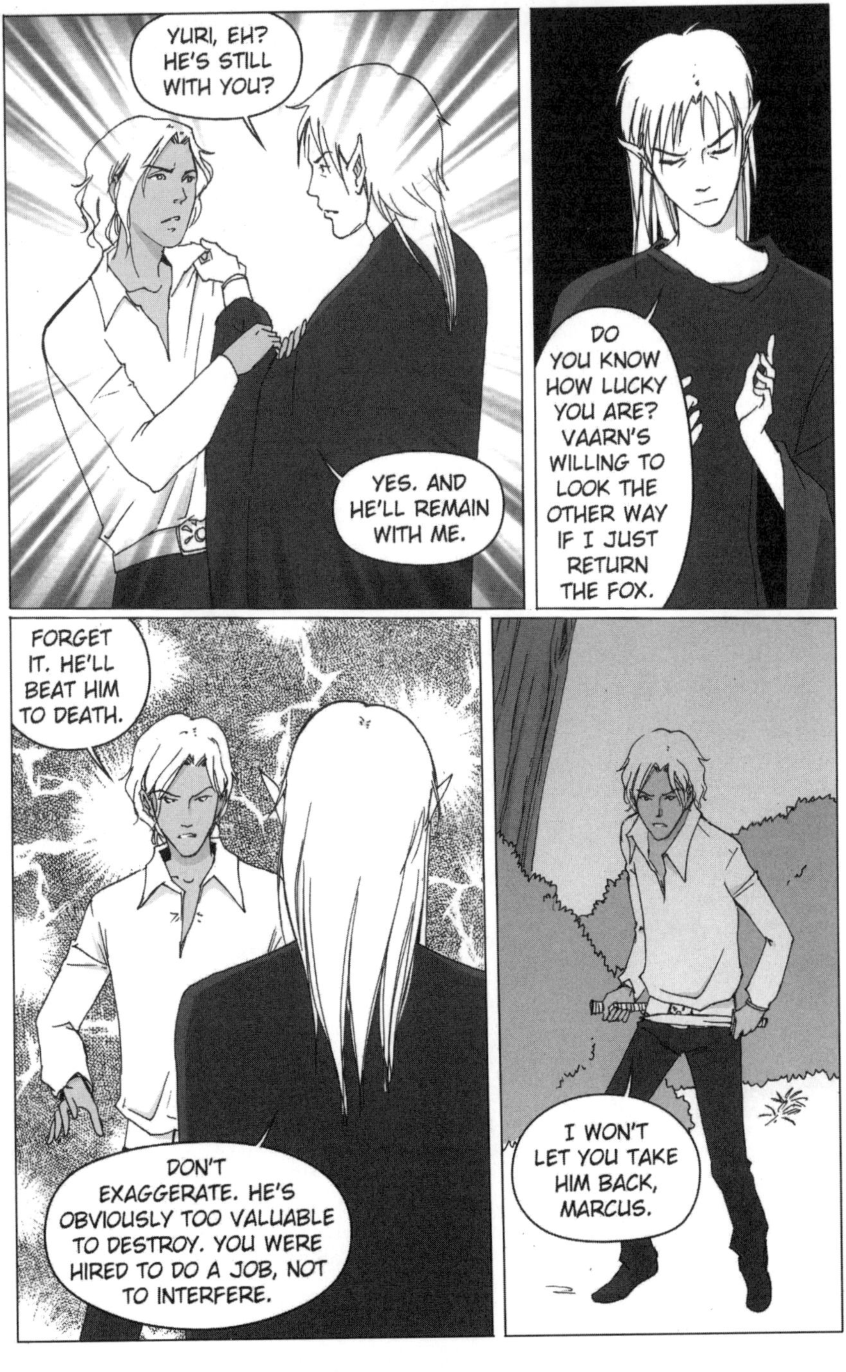
YURI, EH? HE'S STILL WITH YOU?
YES. AND HE'LL REMAIN WITH ME.
DO YOU KNOW HOW LUCKY YOU ARE? VAARN'S WILLING TO LOOK THE OTHER WAY IF I JUST RETURN THE FOX.
FORGET IT. HE'LL BEAT HIM TO DEATH.
DON'T EXAGGERATE. HE'S OBVIOUSLY TOO VALUABLE TO DESTROY. YOU WERE HIRED TO DO A JOB, NOT TO INTERFERE.
I WON'T LET YOU TAKE HIM BACK, MARCUS.

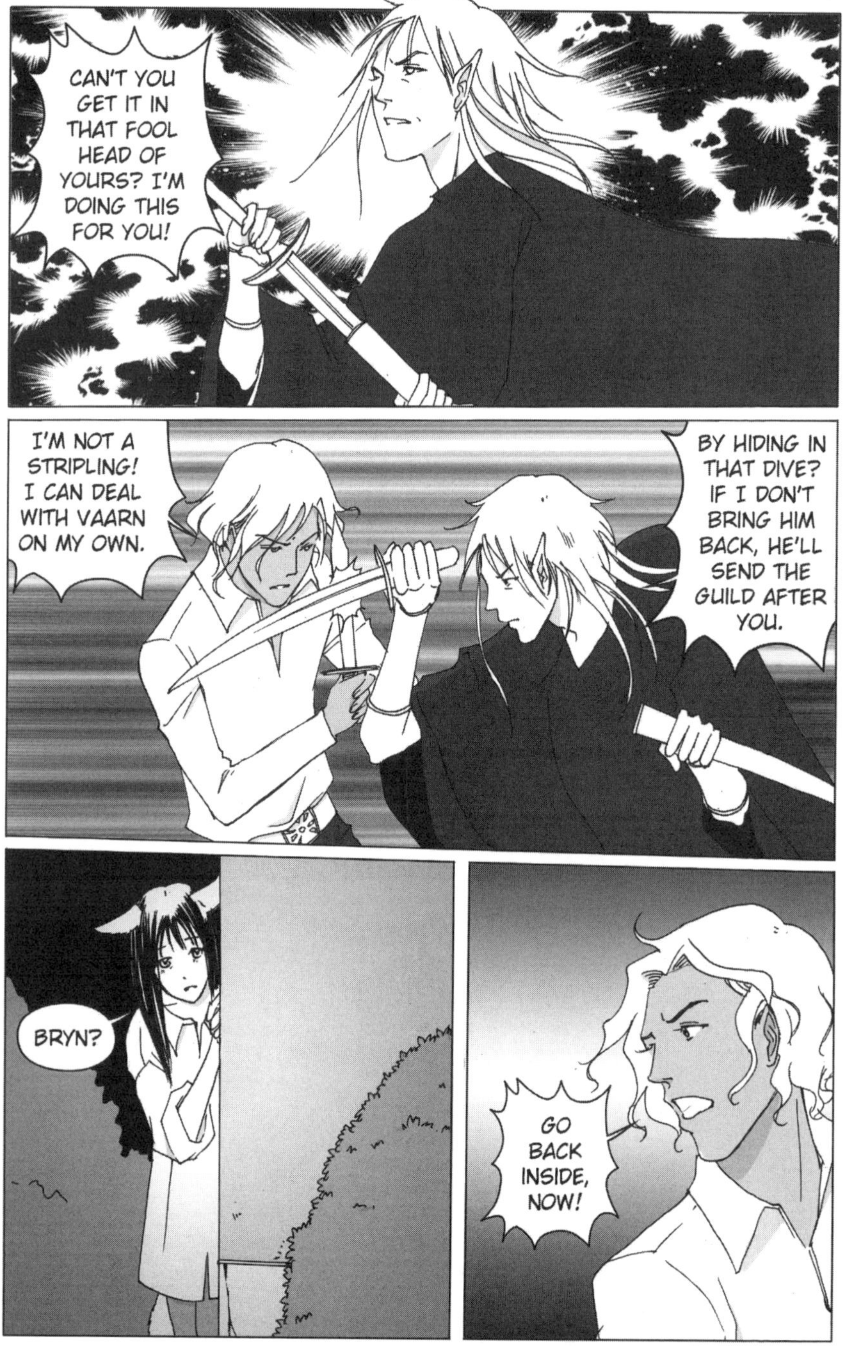
CAN'T YOU GET IT IN THAT FOOL HEAD OF YOURS? I'M DOING THIS FOR YOU!
I'M NOT A STRIPLING! I CAN DEAL WITH VAARN ON MY OWN.
BY HIDING IN THAT DIVE? IF I DON'T BRING HIM BACK, HE'LL SEND THE GUILD AFTER YOU.
BRYN?
GO BACK INSIDE, NOW!

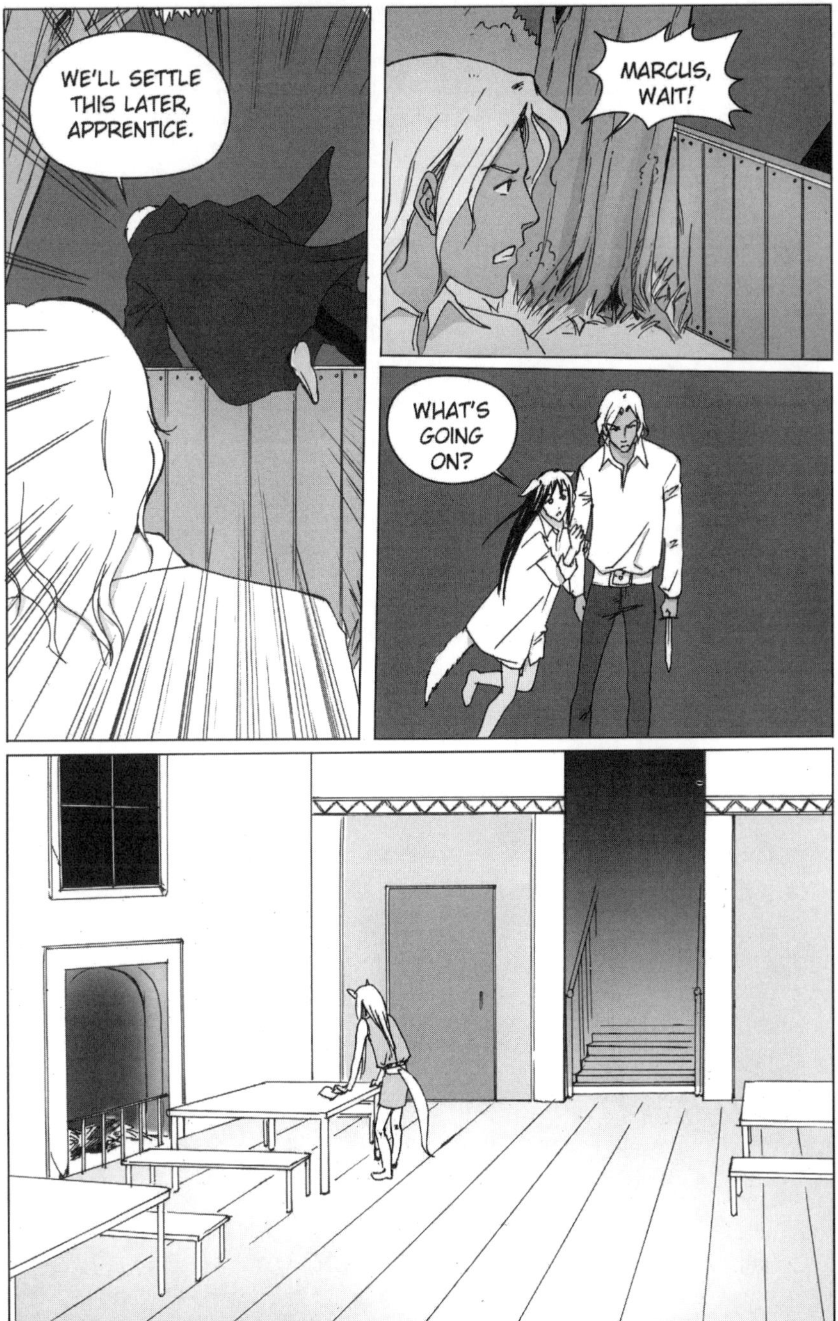
WE'LL SETTLE THIS LATER, APPRENTICE.
MARCUS, WAIT!
WHAT'S GOING ON?

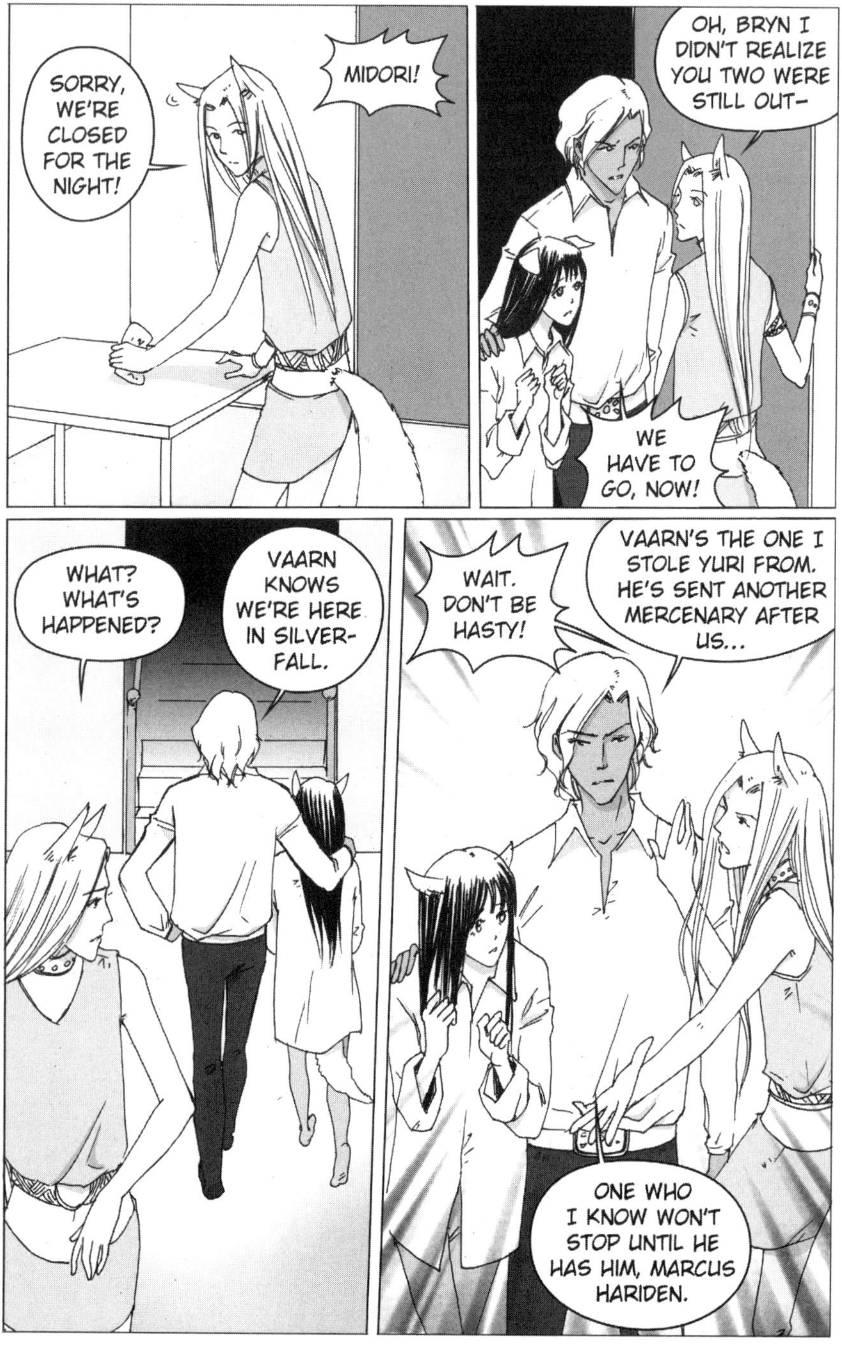
SORRY, WE'RE CLOSED FOR THE NIGHT!
MIDORI!
OH, BRYN I DIDN'T REALIZE YOU TWO WERE STILL OUT–
WE HAVE TO GO, NOW!
WHAT? WHAT'S HAPPENED?
VAARN KNOWS WE'RE HERE IN SILVER-FALL.
VAARN'S THE ONE I STOLE YURI FROM. HE'S SENT ANOTHER MERCENARY AFTER US...
WAIT. DON'T BE HASTY!
ONE WHO I KNOW WON'T STOP UNTIL HE HAS HIM, MARCUS HARIDEN.

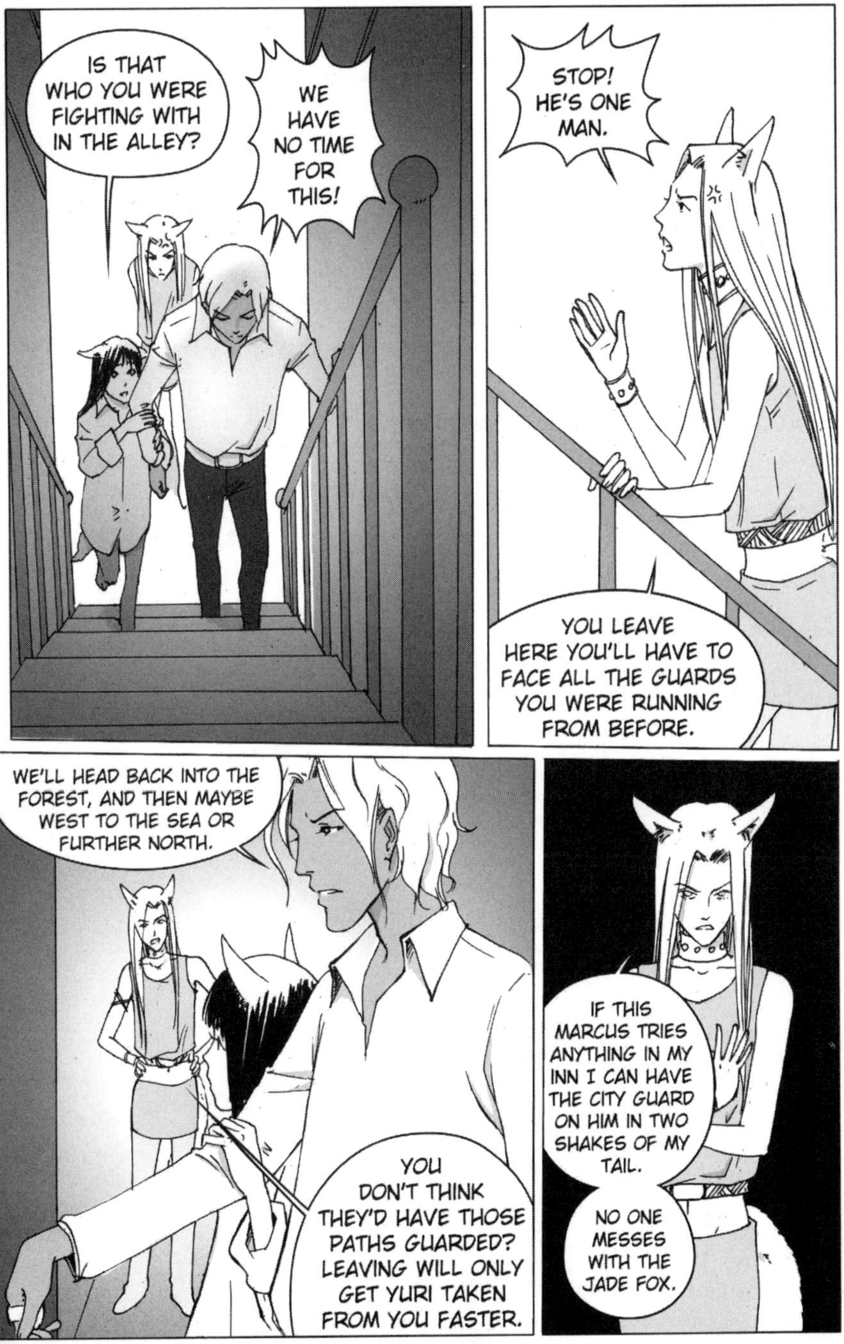
IS THAT WHO YOU WERE FIGHTING WITH IN THE ALLEY?
WE HAVE NO TIME FOR THIS!
STOP! HE'S ONE MAN.
YOU LEAVE HERE YOU'LL HAVE TO FACE ALL THE GUARDS YOU WERE RUNNING FROM BEFORE.
WE'LL HEAD BACK INTO THE FOREST, AND THEN MAYBE WEST TO THE SEA OR FURTHER NORTH.
YOU DON'T THINK THEY'D HAVE THOSE PATHS GUARDED? LEAVING WILL ONLY GET YURI TAKEN FROM YOU FASTER.
IF THIS MARCUS TRIES ANYTHING IN MY INN I CAN HAVE THE CITY GUARD ON HIM IN TWO SHAKES OF MY TAIL.
NO ONE MESSES WITH THE JADE FOX.

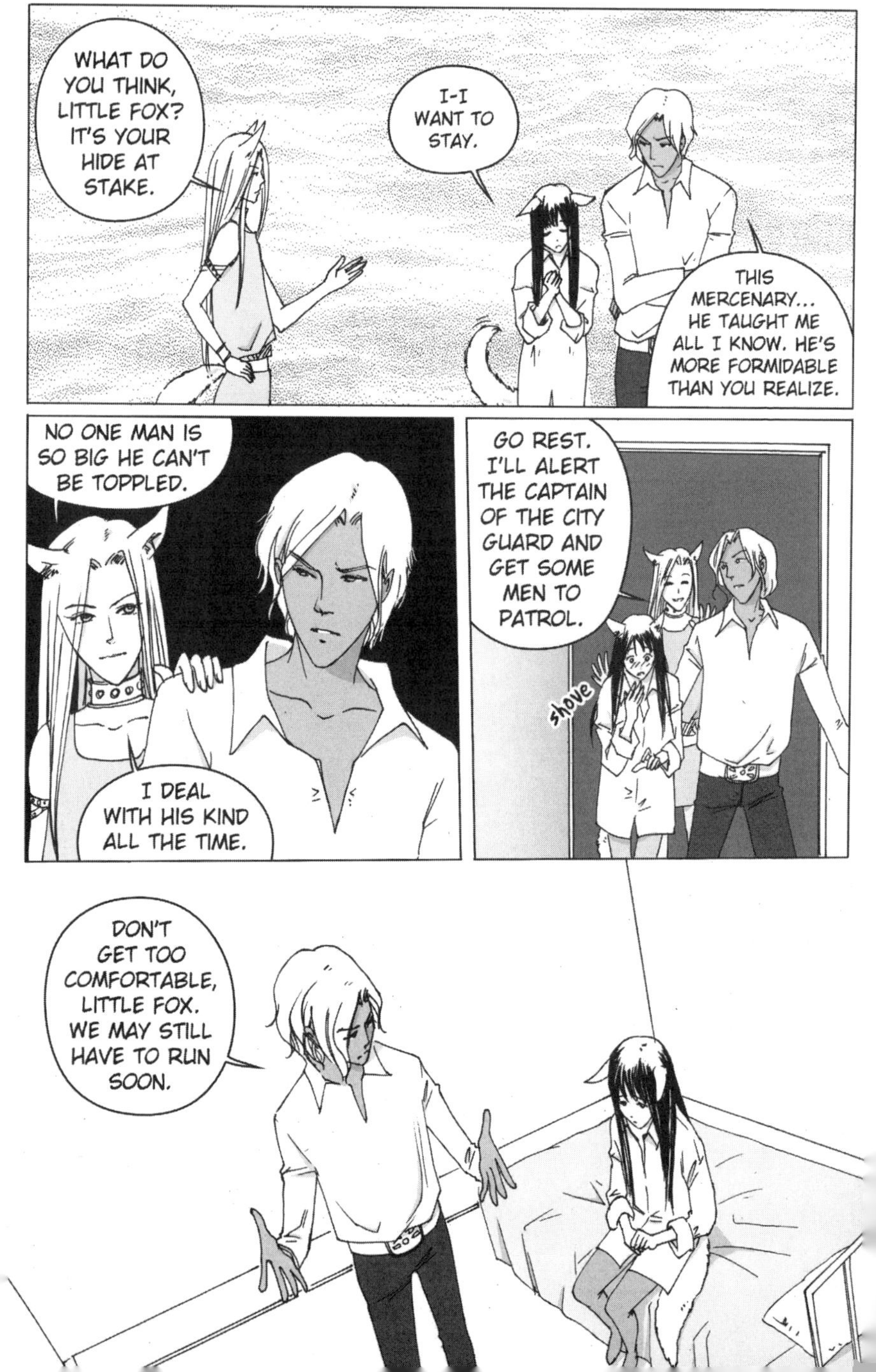
WHAT DO YOU THINK, LITTLE FOX? IT'S YOUR HIDE AT STAKE.
I-I WANT TO STAY.
THIS MERCENARY... HE TAUGHT ME ALL I KNOW. HE'S MORE FORMIDABLE THAN YOU REALIZE.
NO ONE MAN IS SO BIG HE CAN'T BE TOPPLED.
I DEAL WITH HIS KIND ALL THE TIME.
GO REST. I'LL ALERT THE CAPTAIN OF THE CITY GUARD AND GET SOME MEN TO PATROL.
shove
DON'T GET TOO COMFORTABLE, LITTLE FOX. WE MAY STILL HAVE TO RUN SOON.

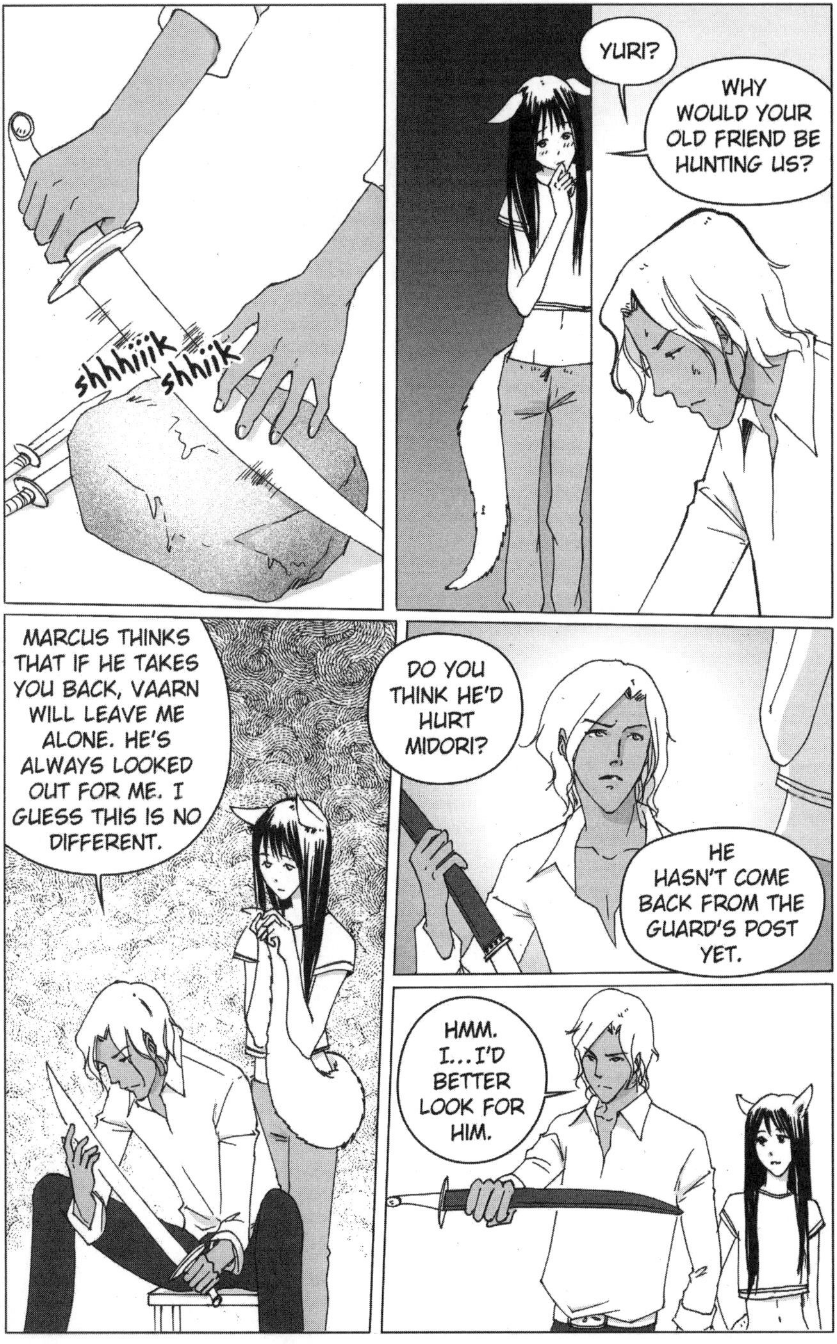
shhhiiik
shhiik
YURI?
WHY WOULD YOUR OLD FRIEND BE HUNTING US?
MARCUS THINKS THAT IF HE TAKES YOU BACK, VAARN WILL LEAVE ME ALONE. HE'S ALWAYS LOOKED OUT FOR ME. I GUESS THIS IS NO DIFFERENT.
DO YOU THINK HE'D HURT MIDORI?
HE HASN'T COME BACK FROM THE GUARD'S POST YET.
HMM. I...I'D BETTER LOOK FOR HIM.

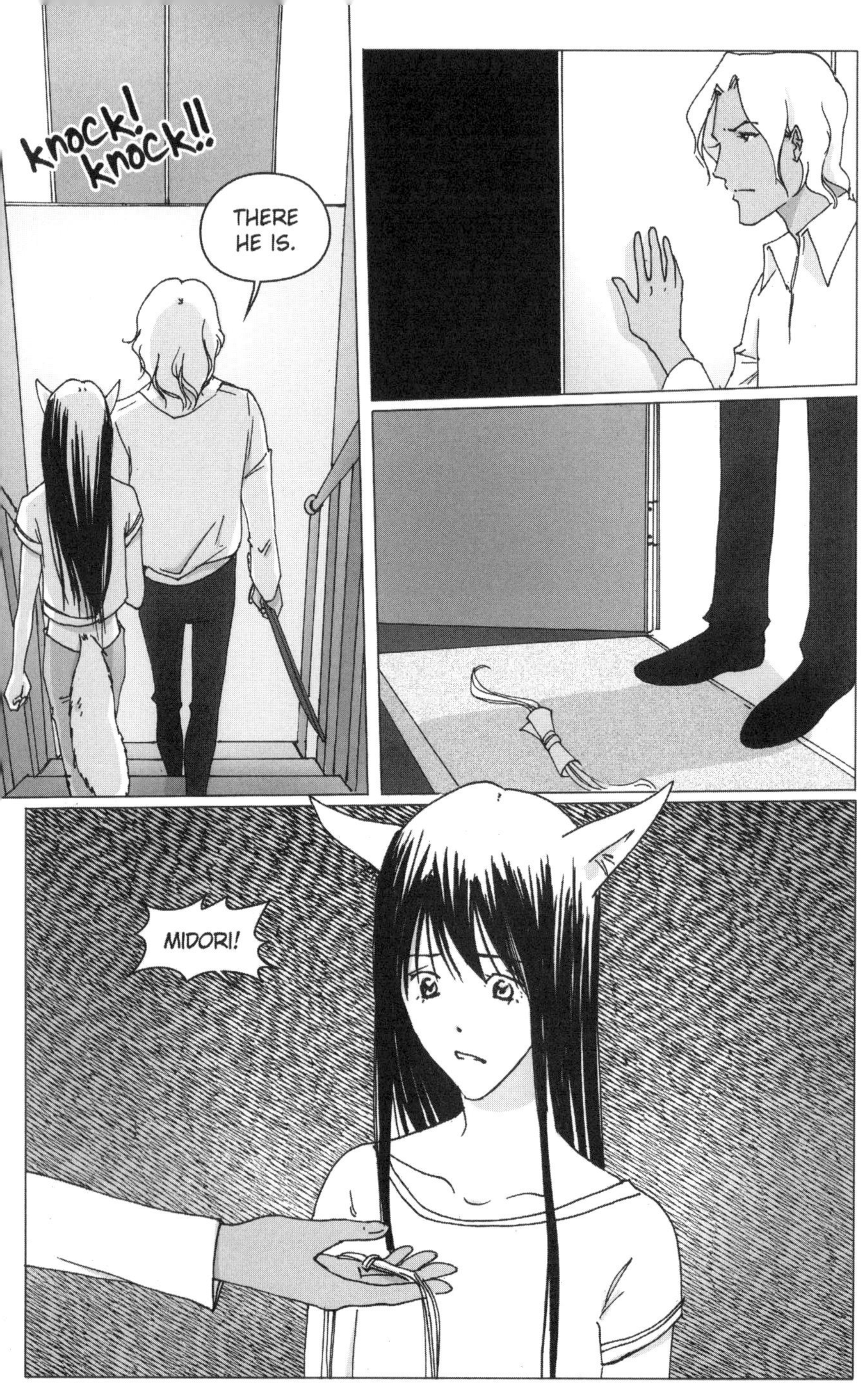
knock! knock!!
THERE HE IS.
MIDORI!

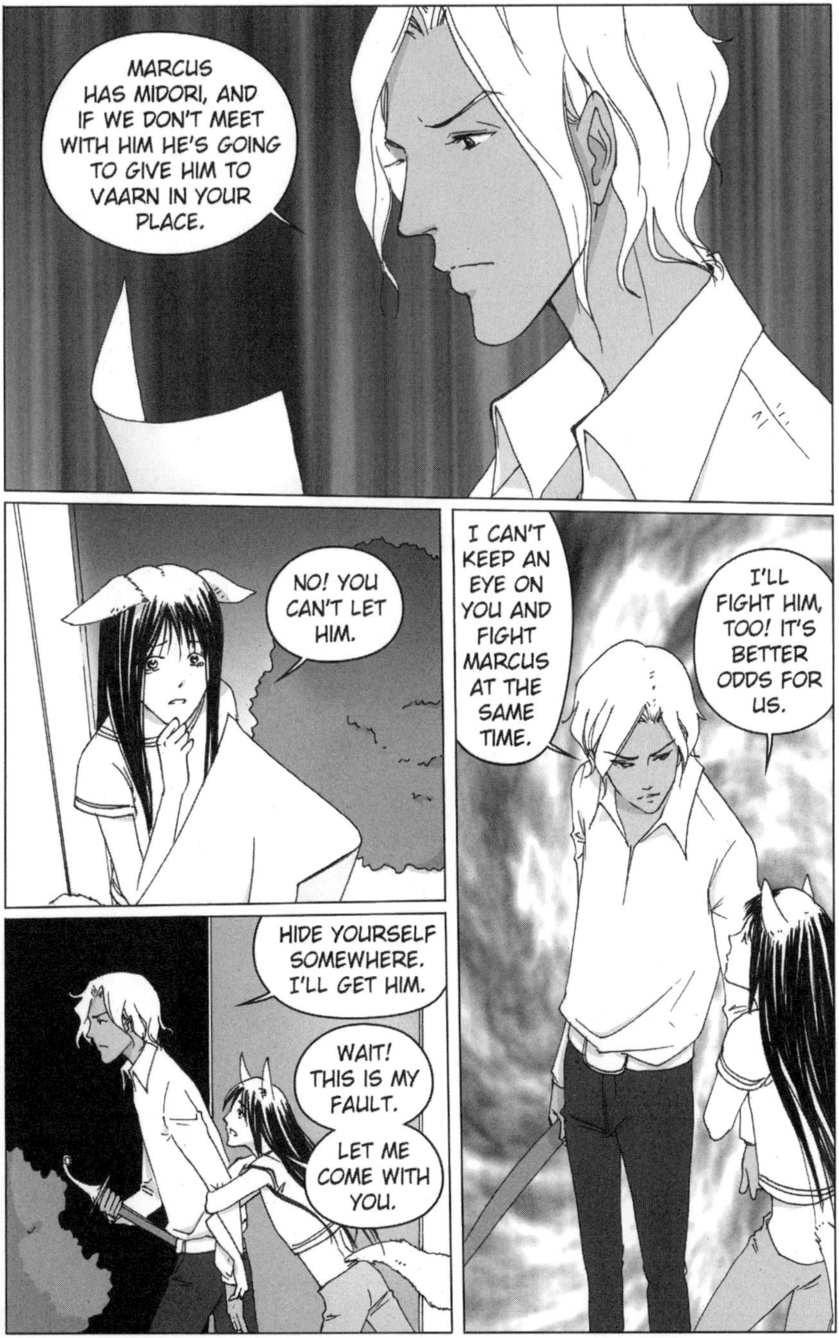
MARCUS HAS MIDORI, AND IF WE DON'T MEET WITH HIM HE'S GOING TO GIVE HIM TO VAARN IN YOUR PLACE.
NO! YOU CAN'T LET HIM.
HIDE YOURSELF SOMEWHERE. I'LL GET HIM.
WAIT! THIS IS MY FAULT.
LET ME COME WITH YOU.
I CAN'T KEEP AN EYE ON YOU AND FIGHT MARCUS AT THE SAME TIME.
I'LL FIGHT HIM, TOO! IT'S BETTER ODDS FOR US.

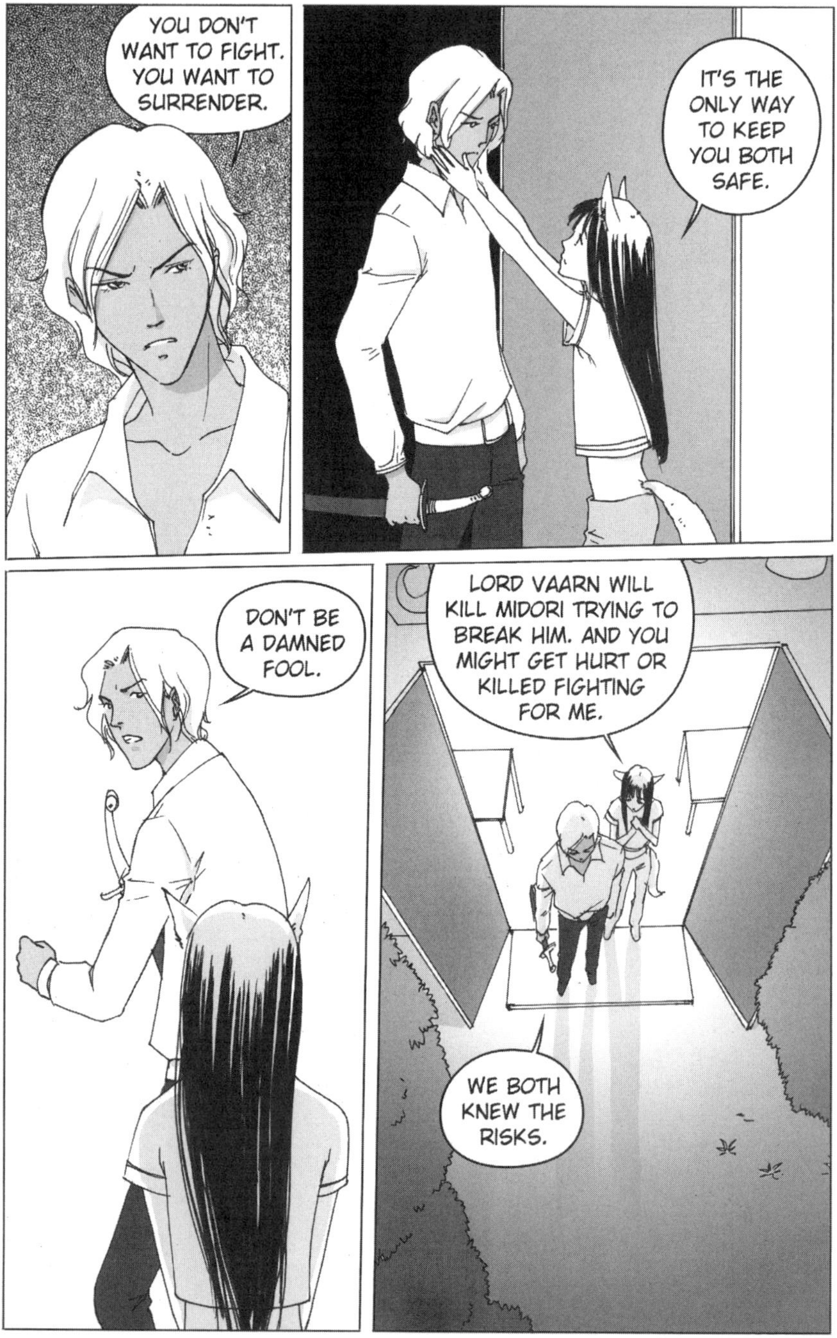
YOU DON'T WANT TO FIGHT. YOU WANT TO SURRENDER.
IT'S THE ONLY WAY TO KEEP YOU BOTH SAFE.
DON'T BE A DAMNED FOOL.
LORD VAARN WILL KILL MIDORI TRYING TO BREAK HIM. AND YOU MIGHT GET HURT OR KILLED FIGHTING FOR ME.
WE BOTH KNEW THE RISKS.

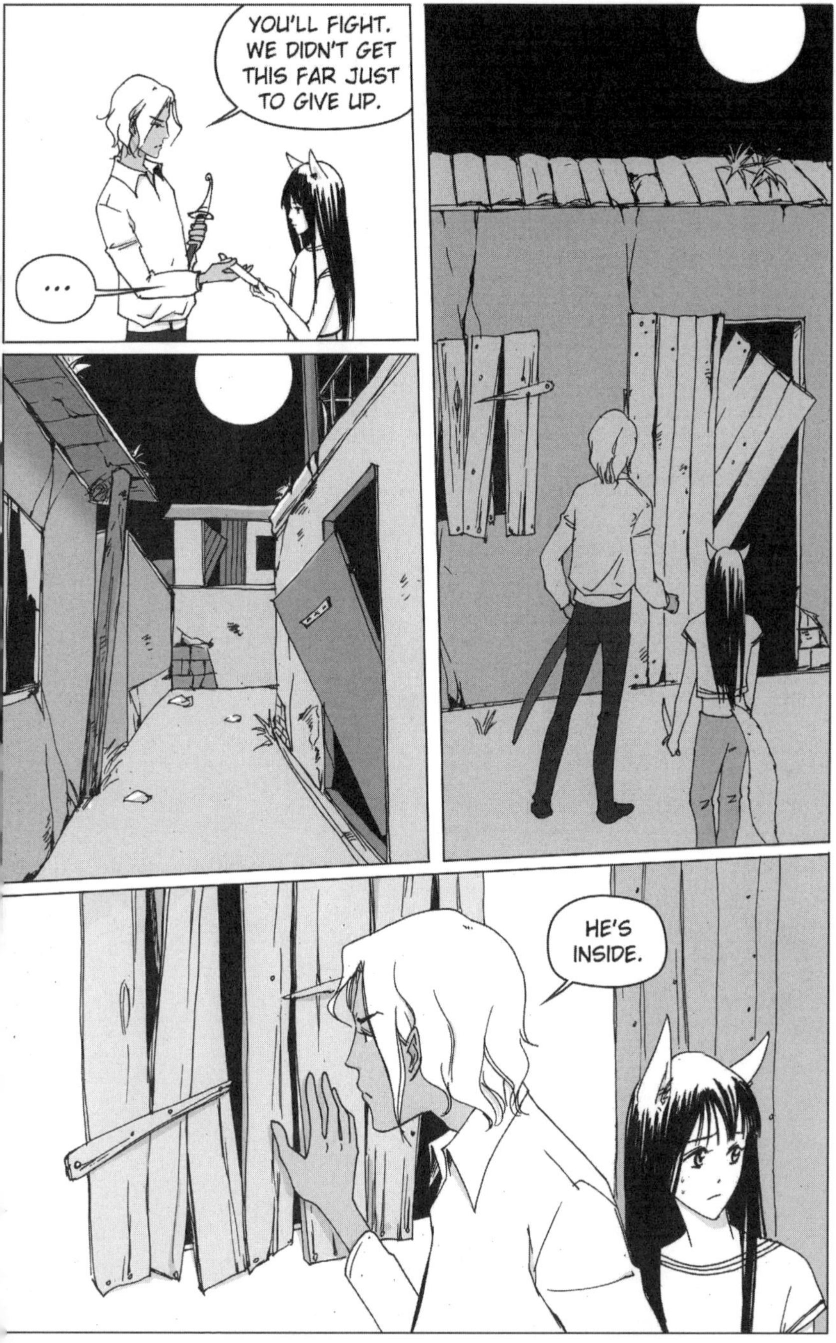
YOU'LL FIGHT. WE DIDN'T GET THIS FAR JUST TO GIVE UP.
...
HE'S INSIDE.

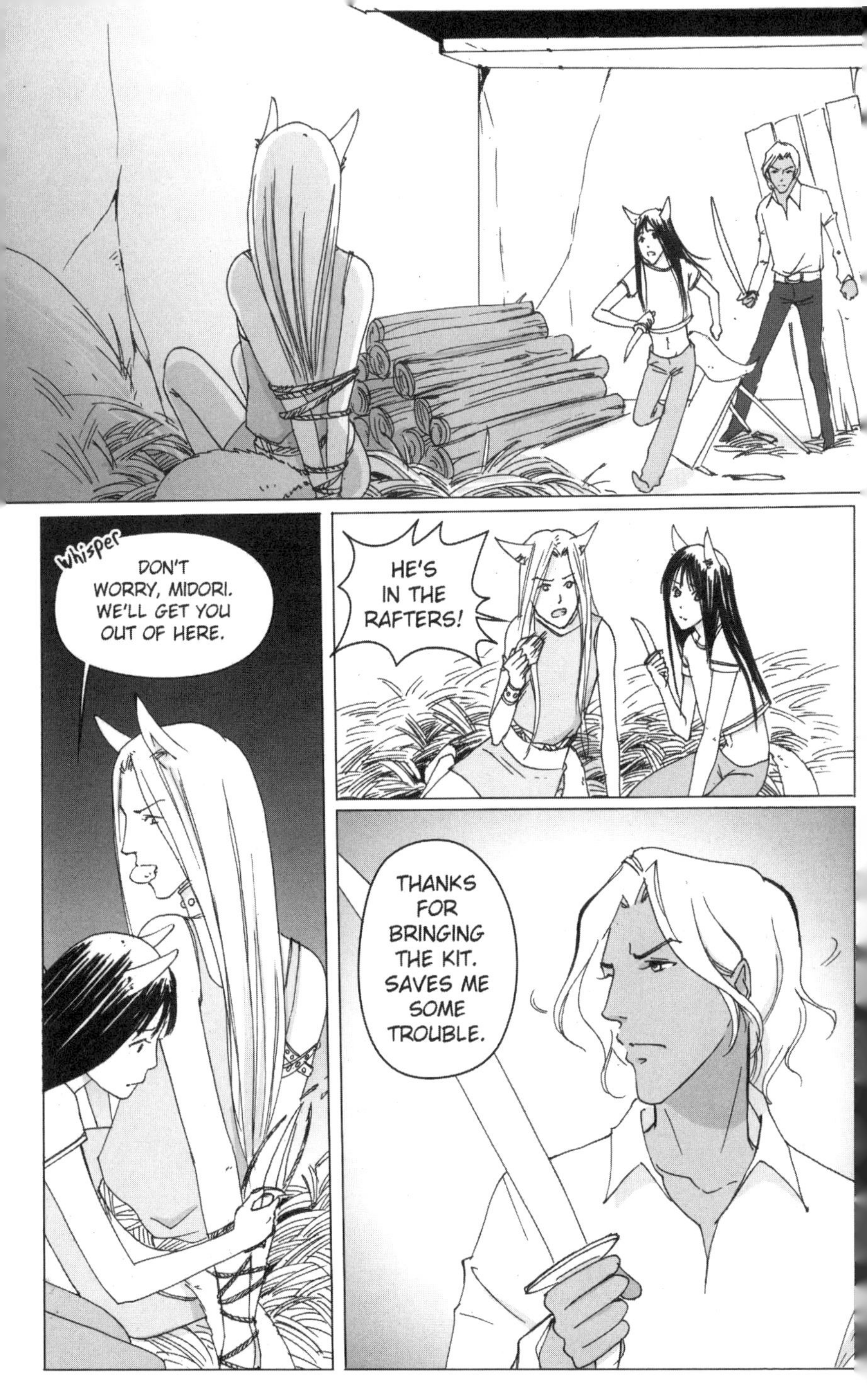

WHISPER
DON'T WORRY, MIDORI. WE'LL GET YOU OUT OF HERE.
HE'S IN THE RAFTERS!
THANKS FOR BRINGING THE KIT. SAVES ME SOME TROUBLE.

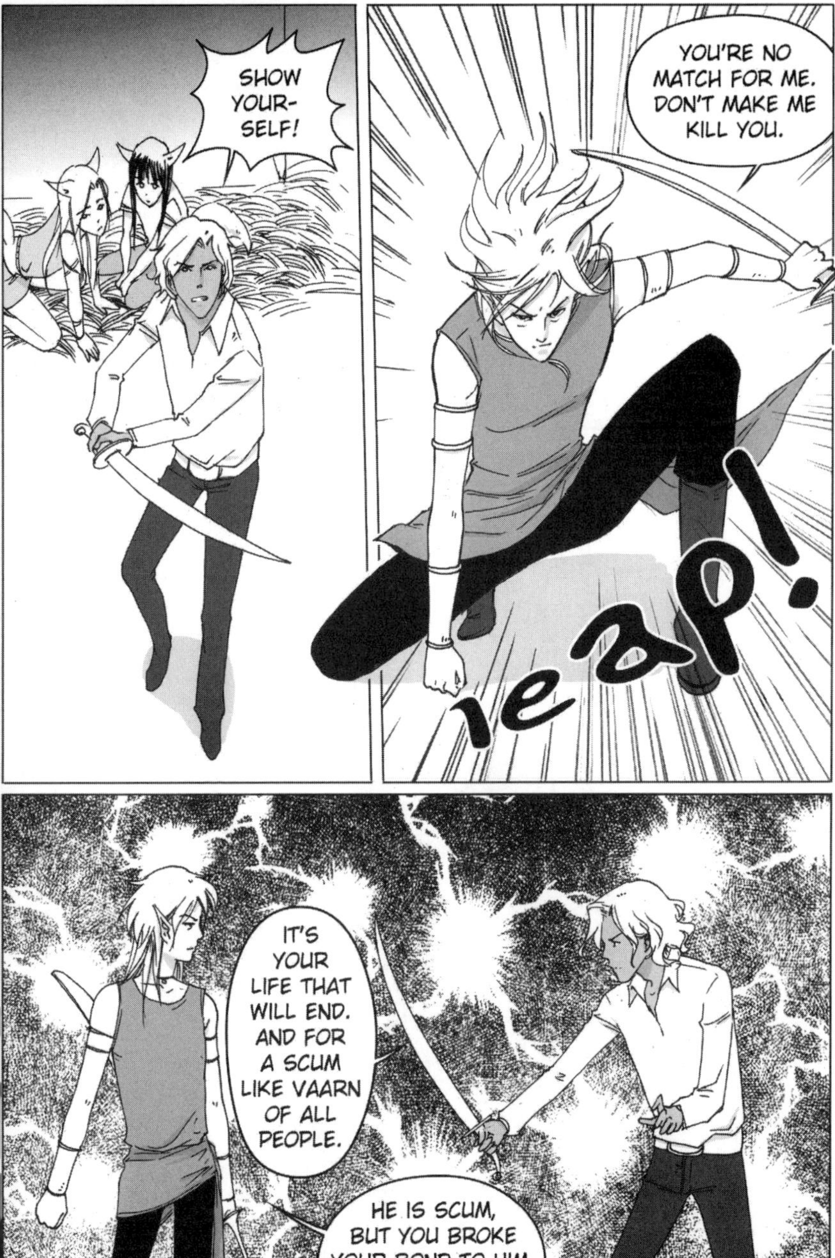
SHOW YOUR-SELF!
YOU'RE NO MATCH FOR ME. DON'T MAKE ME KILL YOU.
leap!
IT'S YOUR LIFE THAT WILL END. AND FOR A SCUM LIKE VAARN OF ALL PEOPLE.
HE IS SCUM, BUT YOU BROKE YOUR BOND TO HIM. I TAUGHT YOU BETTER, BRYN.

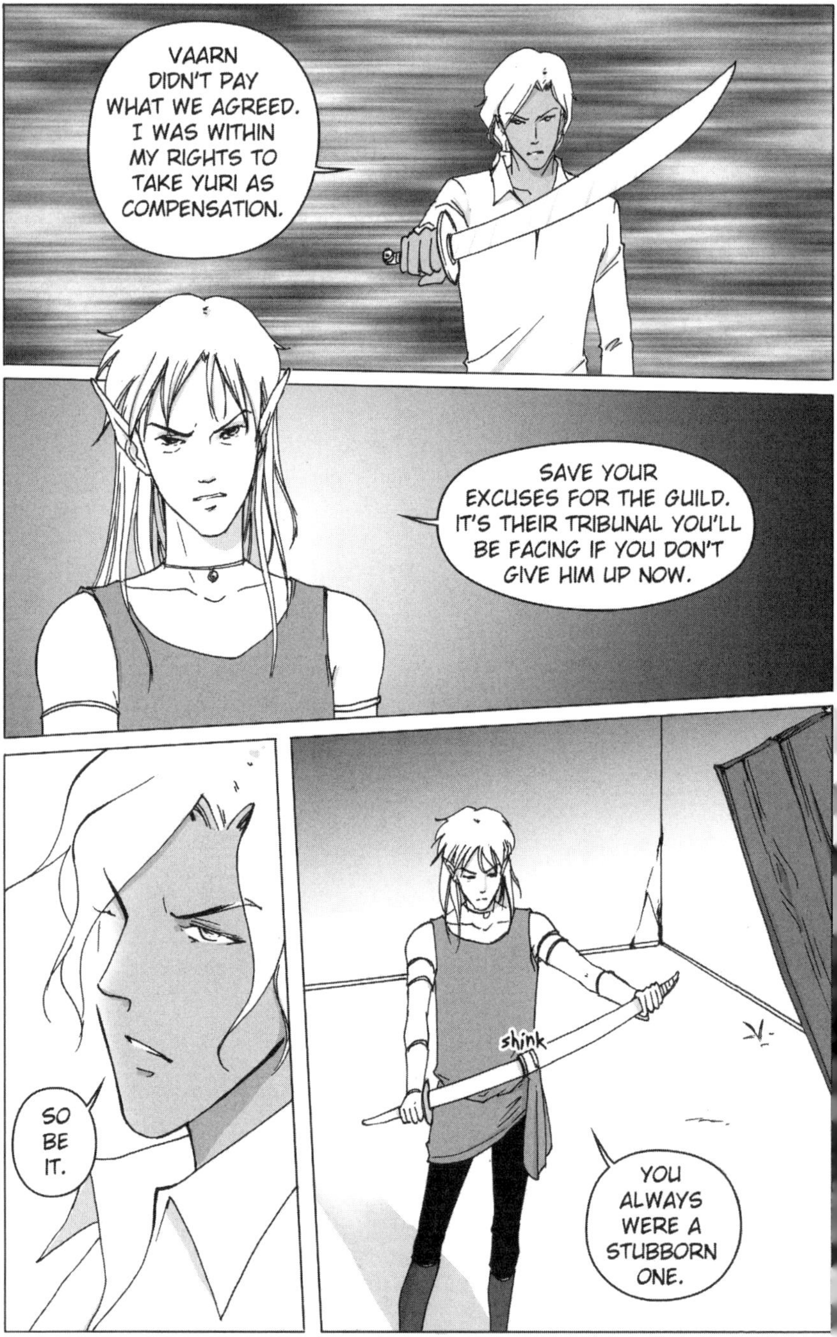
VAARN DIDN'T PAY WHAT WE AGREED. I WAS WITHIN MY RIGHTS TO TAKE YURI AS COMPENSATION.
SAVE YOUR EXCUSES FOR THE GUILD. IT'S THEIR TRIBUNAL YOU'LL BE FACING IF YOU DON'T GIVE HIM UP NOW.
SO BE IT.
shink
YOU ALWAYS WERE A STUBBORN ONE.

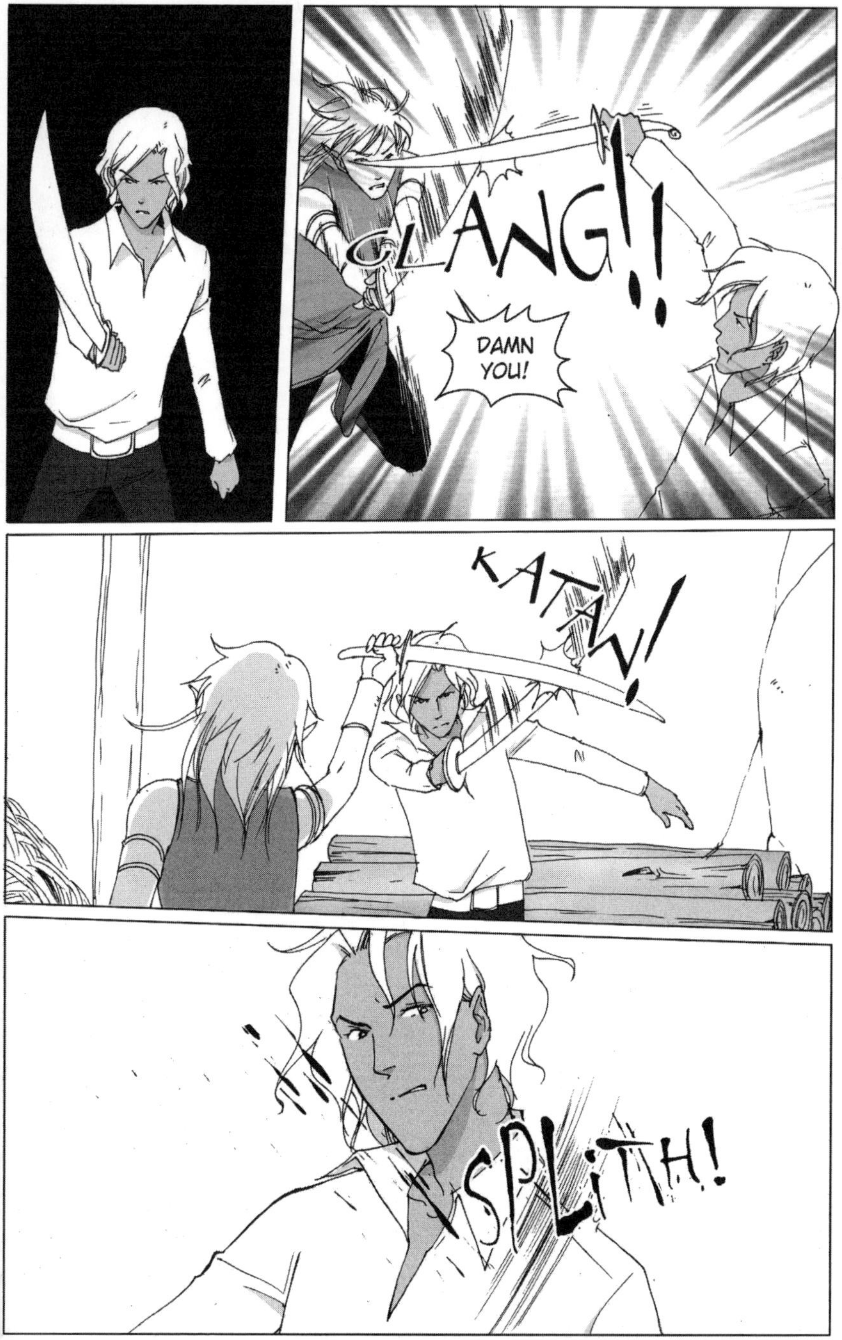
CLANG!!
DAMN YOU!
KATAW!
SPLITH!

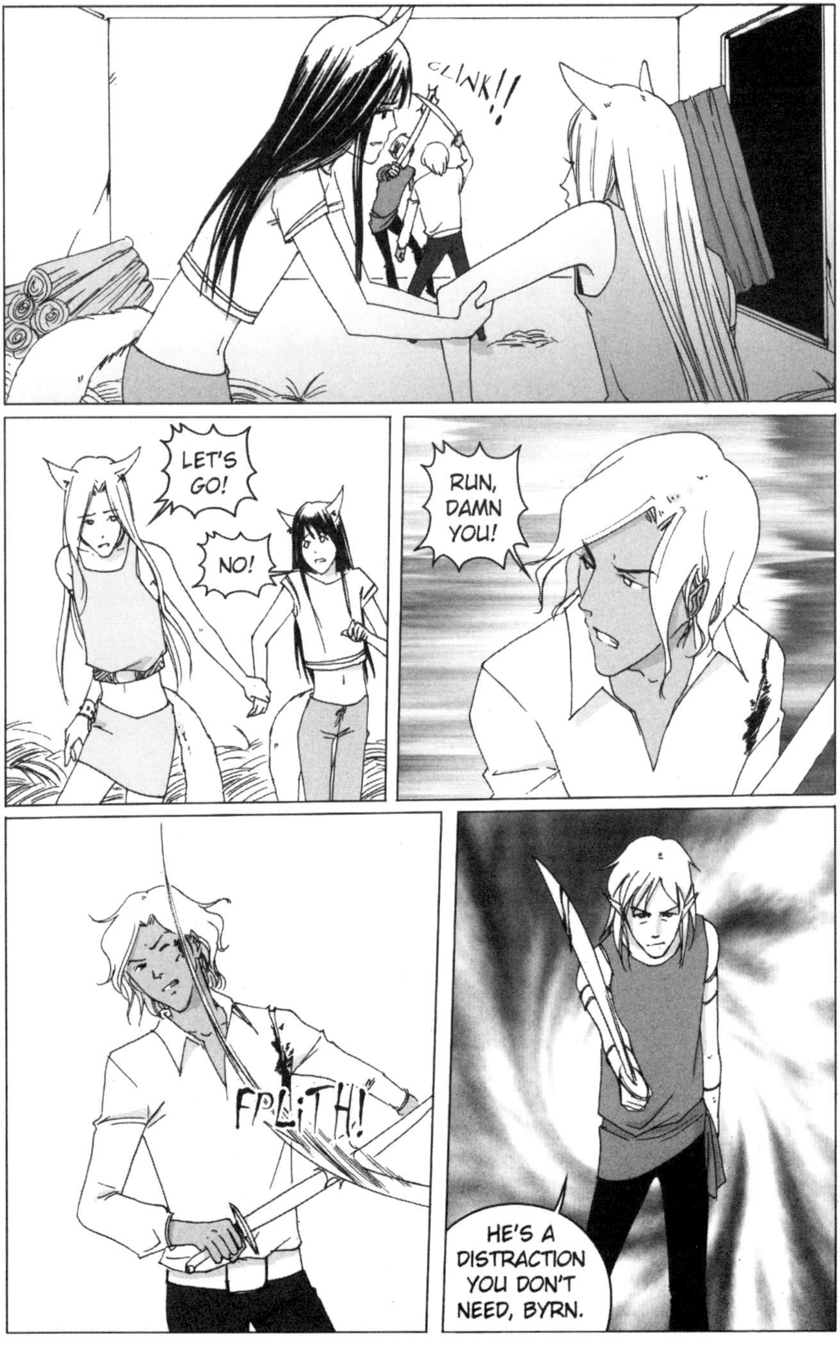
CLINK!!
LET'S GO!
NO!
RUN, DAMN YOU!
FPLiTH!
HE'S A DISTRACTION YOU DON'T NEED, BYRN.

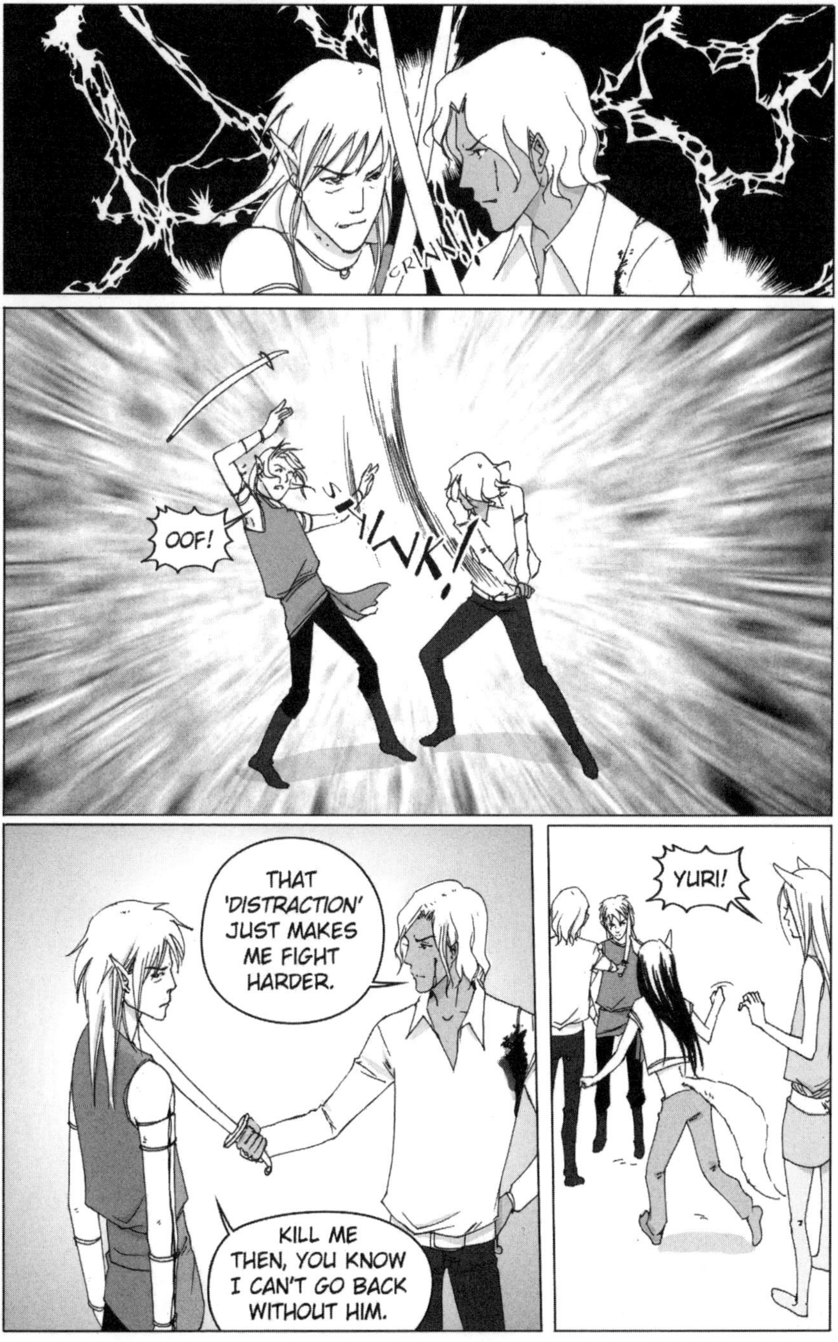
CRINK!!
OOF!
TINK!
THAT 'DISTRACTION' JUST MAKES ME FIGHT HARDER.
KILL ME THEN, YOU KNOW I CAN'T GO BACK WITHOUT HIM.
YURI!

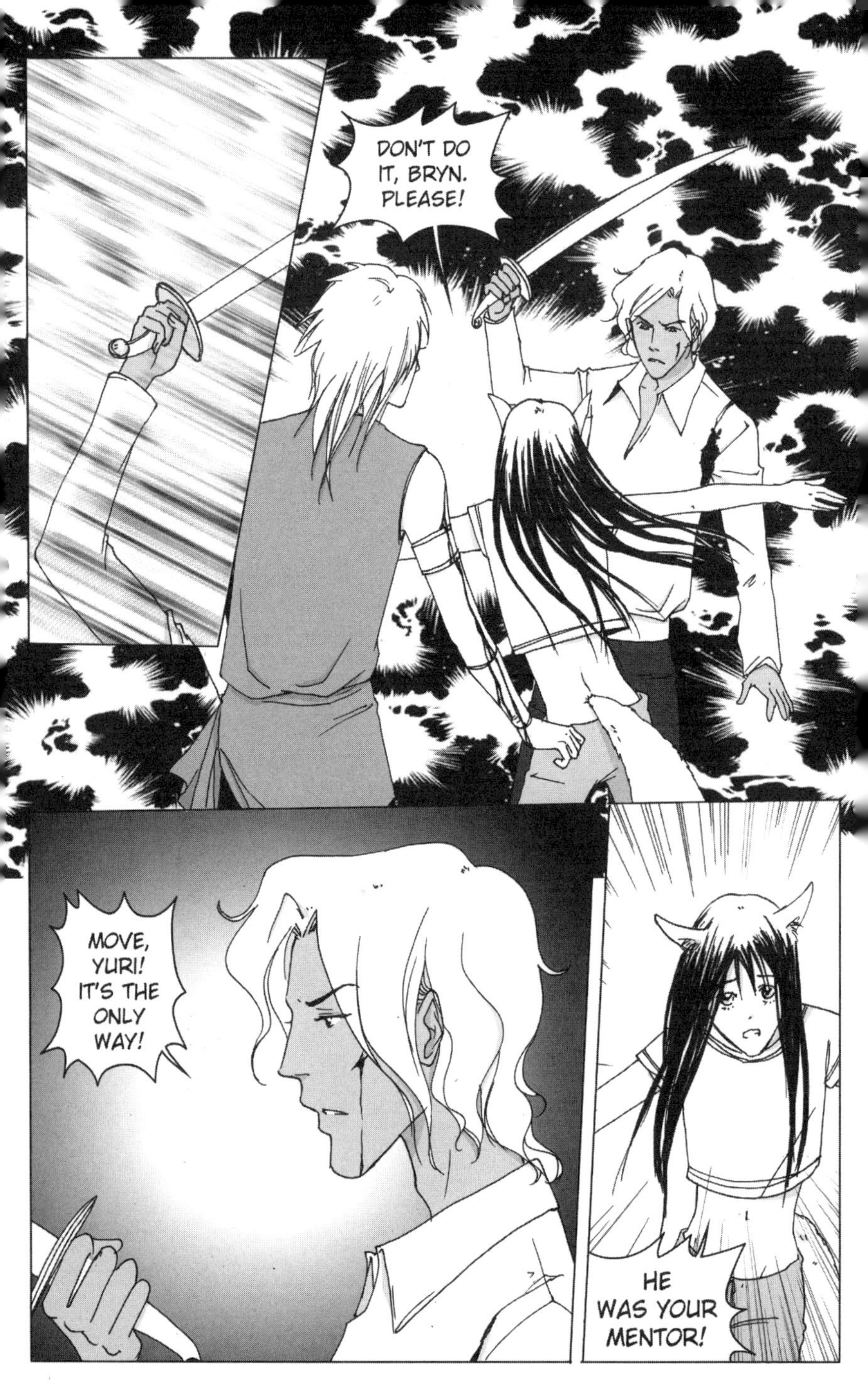
DON'T DO IT, BRYN. PLEASE!
MOVE, YURI! IT'S THE ONLY WAY!
HE WAS YOUR MENTOR!

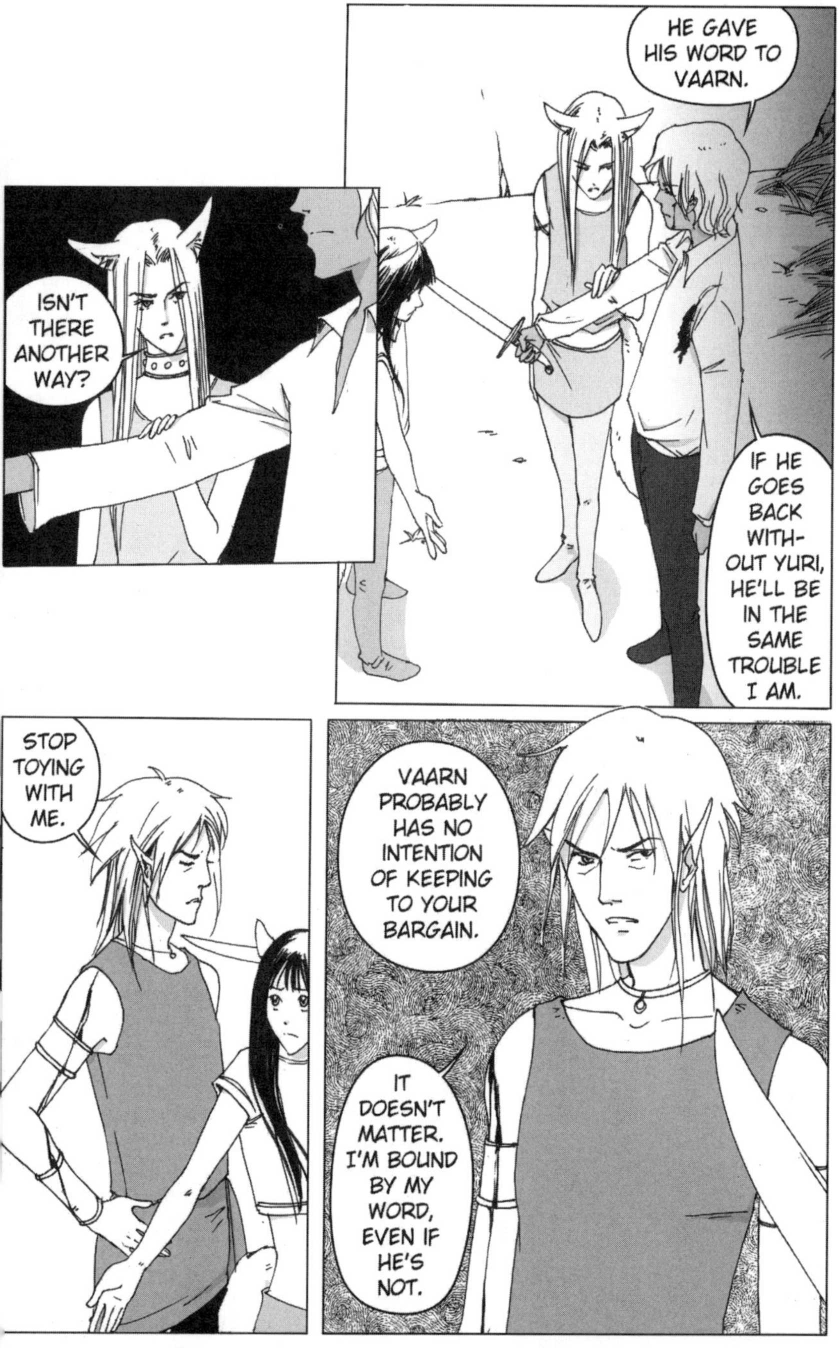
HE GAVE HIS WORD TO VAARN.
ISN'T THERE ANOTHER WAY?
IF HE GOES BACK WITH-OUT YURI, HE'LL BE IN THE SAME TROUBLE I AM.
STOP TOYING WITH ME.
VAARN PROBABLY HAS NO INTENTION OF KEEPING TO YOUR BARGAIN.
IT DOESN'T MATTER. I'M BOUND BY MY WORD, EVEN IF HE'S NOT.

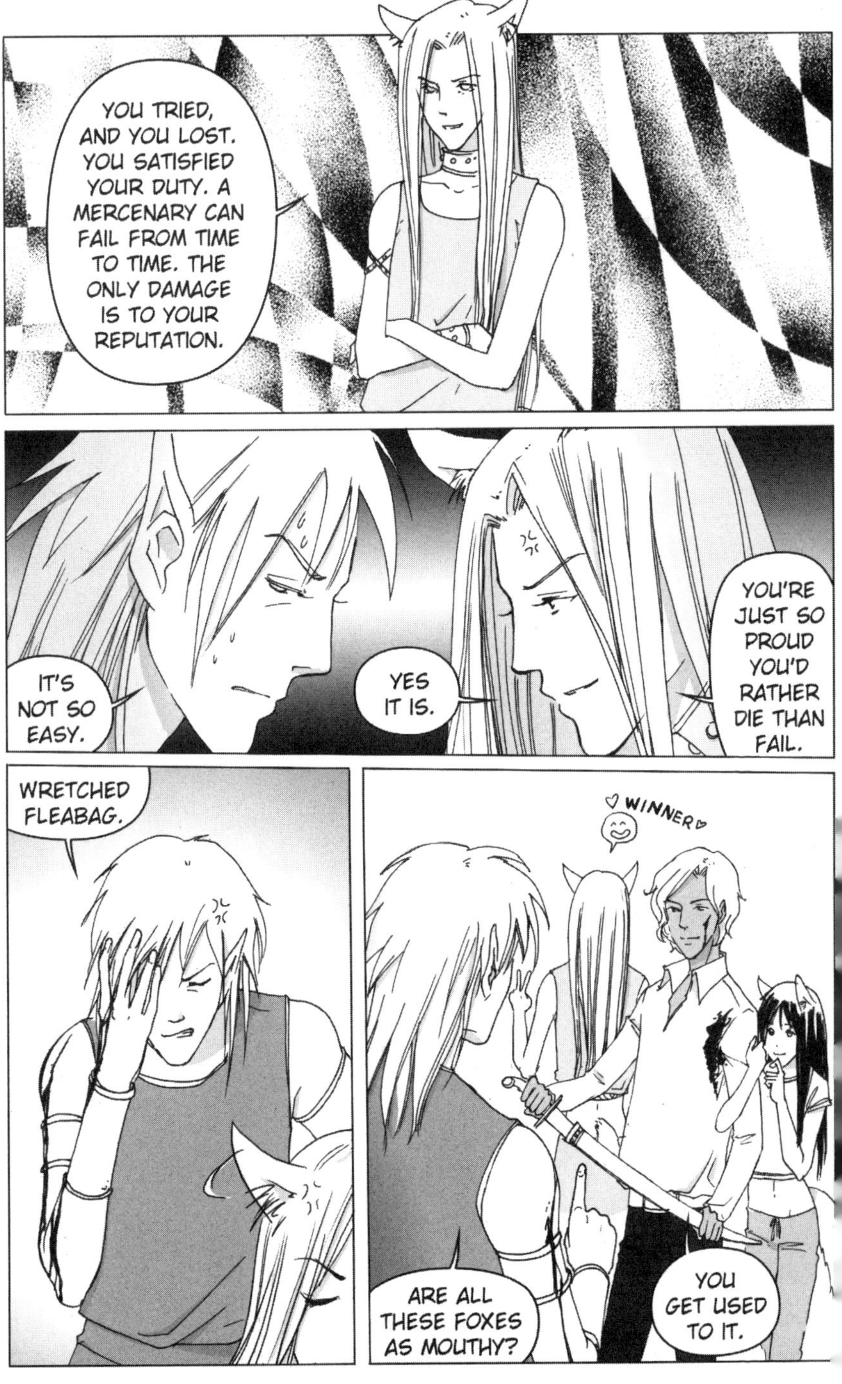
YOU TRIED, AND YOU LOST. YOU SATISFIED YOUR DUTY. A MERCENARY CAN FAIL FROM TIME TO TIME. THE ONLY DAMAGE IS TO YOUR REPUTATION.
IT'S NOT SO EASY.
YES IT IS.
YOU'RE JUST SO PROUD YOU'D RATHER DIE THAN FAIL.
WRETCHED FLEABAG.
WINNER
ARE ALL THESE FOXES AS MOUTHY?
YOU GET USED TO IT.

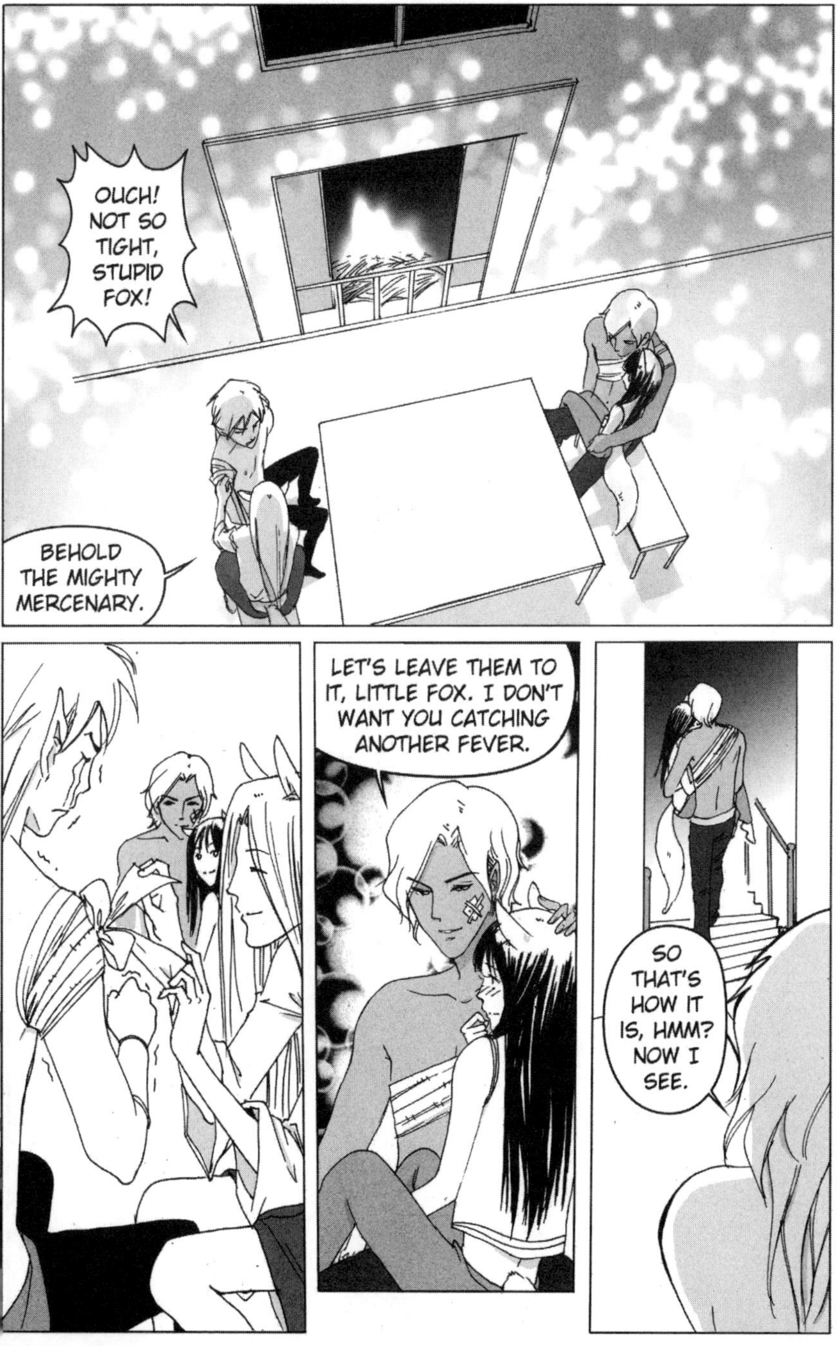
OUCH! NOT SO TIGHT, STUPID FOX!
BEHOLD THE MIGHTY MERCENARY.
LET'S LEAVE THEM TO IT, LITTLE FOX. I DON'T WANT YOU CATCHING ANOTHER FEVER.
SO THAT'S HOW IT IS, HMM? NOW I SEE.

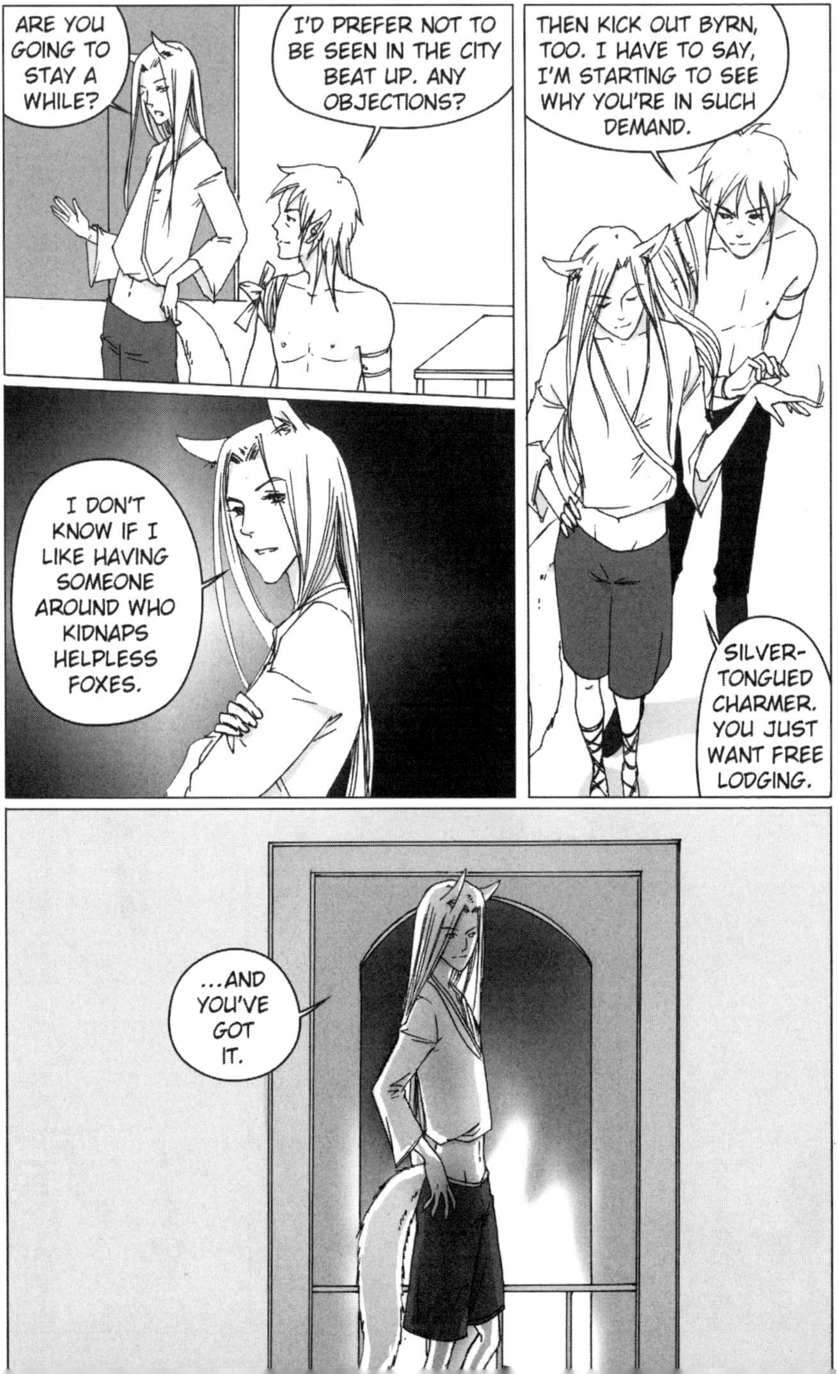
ARE YOU GOING TO STAY A WHILE?
I'D PREFER NOT TO BE SEEN IN THE CITY BEAT UP. ANY OBJECTIONS?
I DON'T KNOW IF I LIKE HAVING SOMEONE AROUND WHO KIDNAPS HELPLESS FOXES.
THEN KICK OUT BYRN, TOO. I HAVE TO SAY, I'M STARTING TO SEE WHY YOU'RE IN SUCH DEMAND.
SILVER-TONGUED CHARMER. YOU JUST WANT FREE LODGING.
...AND YOU'VE GOT IT.

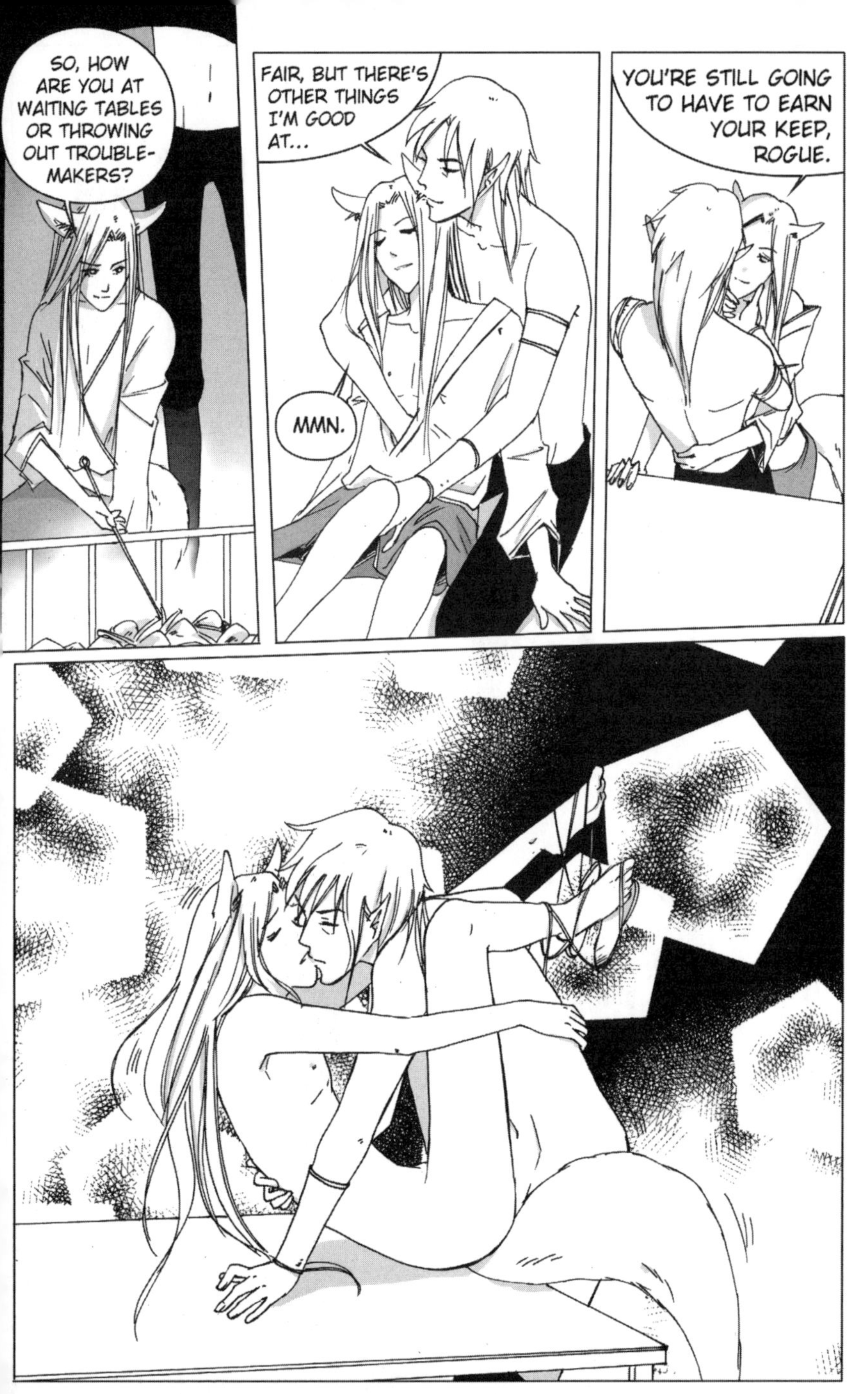
SO, HOW ARE YOU AT WAITING TABLES OR THROWING OUT TROUBLE-MAKERS?
FAIR, BUT THERE'S OTHER THINGS I'M GOOD AT...
MMN.
YOU'RE STILL GOING TO HAVE TO EARN YOUR KEEP, ROGUE.

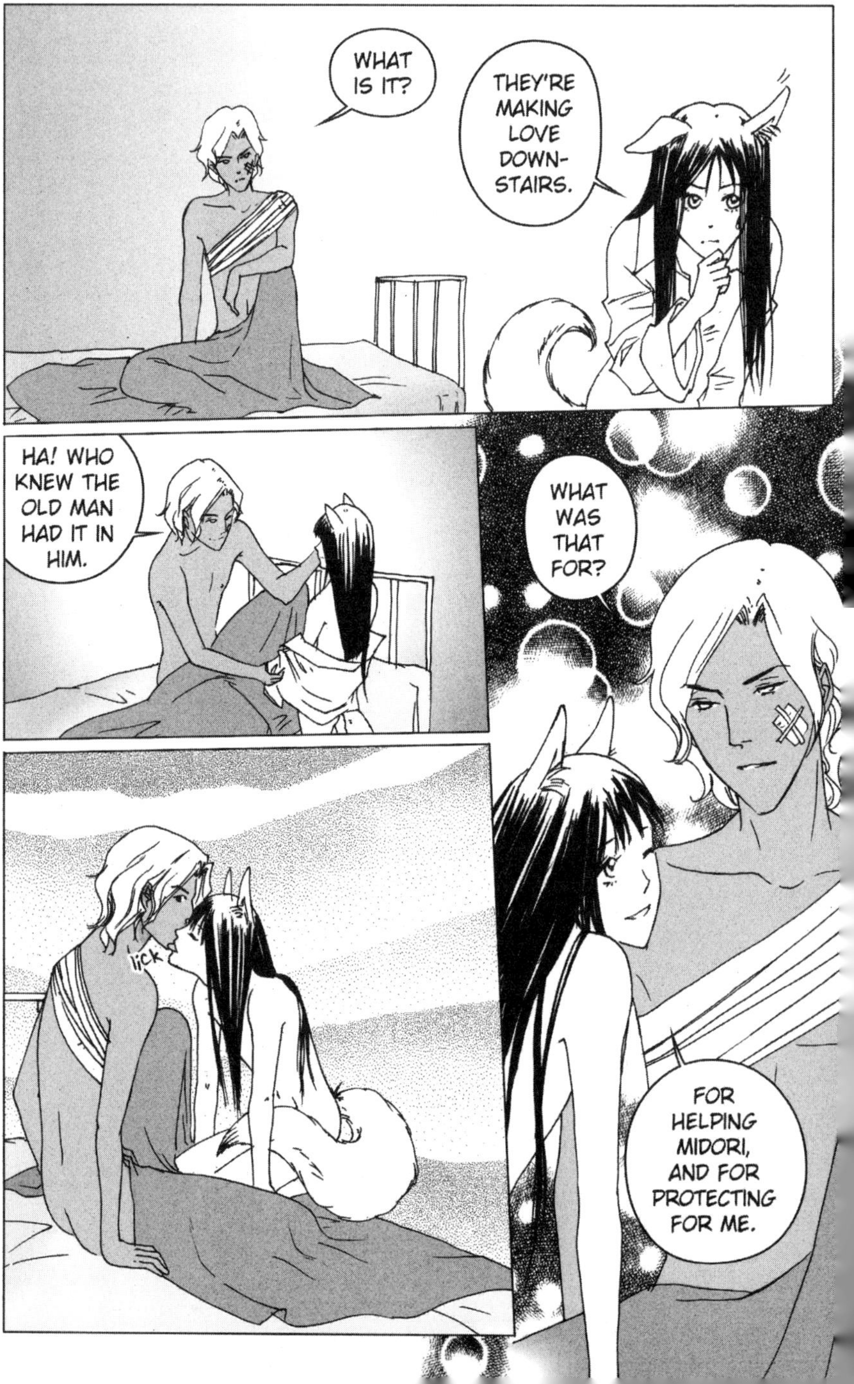
WHAT IS IT?
THEY'RE MAKING LOVE DOWN-STAIRS.
HA! WHO KNEW THE OLD MAN HAD IT IN HIM.
lick
WHAT WAS THAT FOR?
FOR HELPING MIDORI, AND FOR PROTECTING FOR ME.

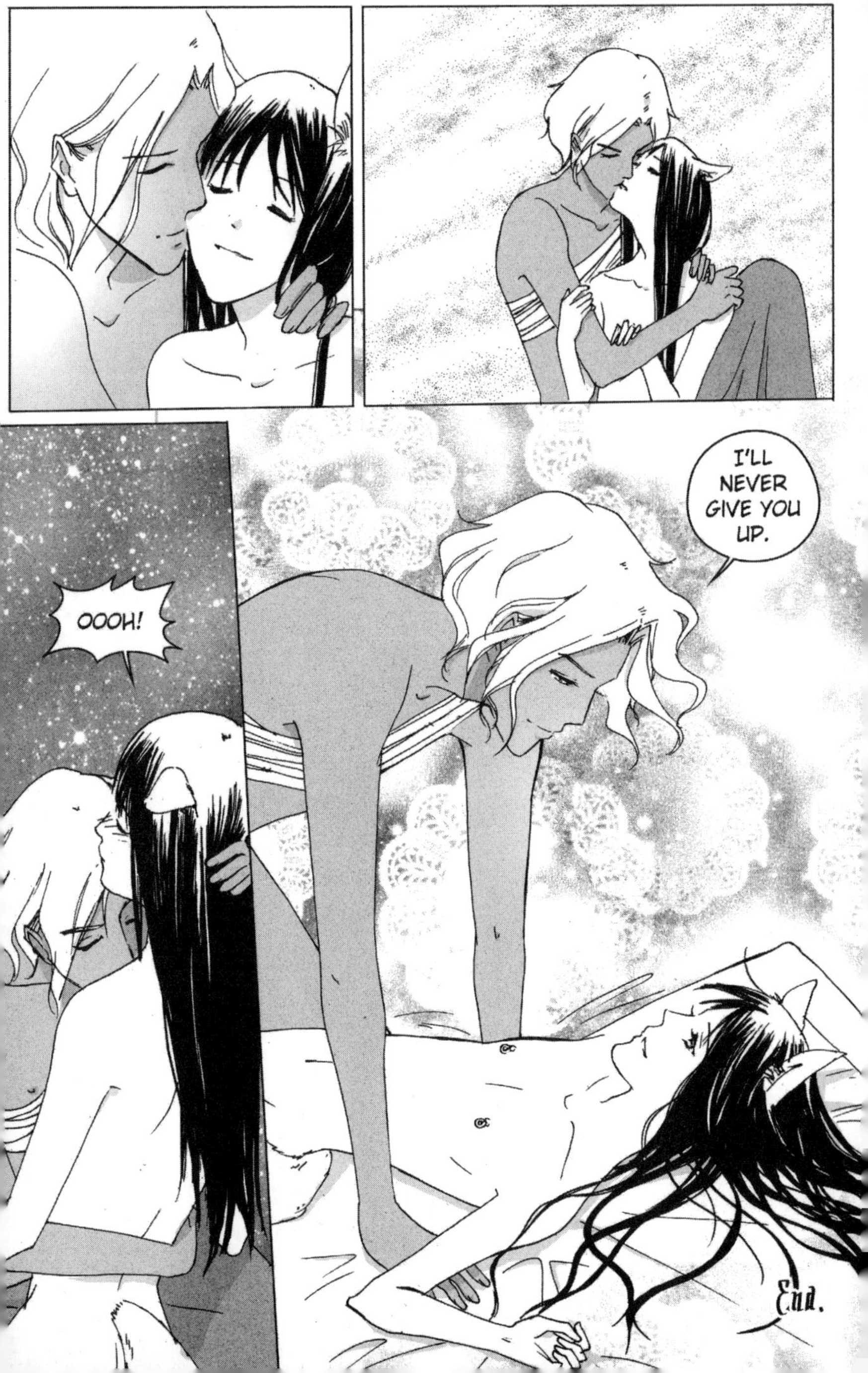
I'LL NEVER GIVE YOU UP.
OOOH!
End.

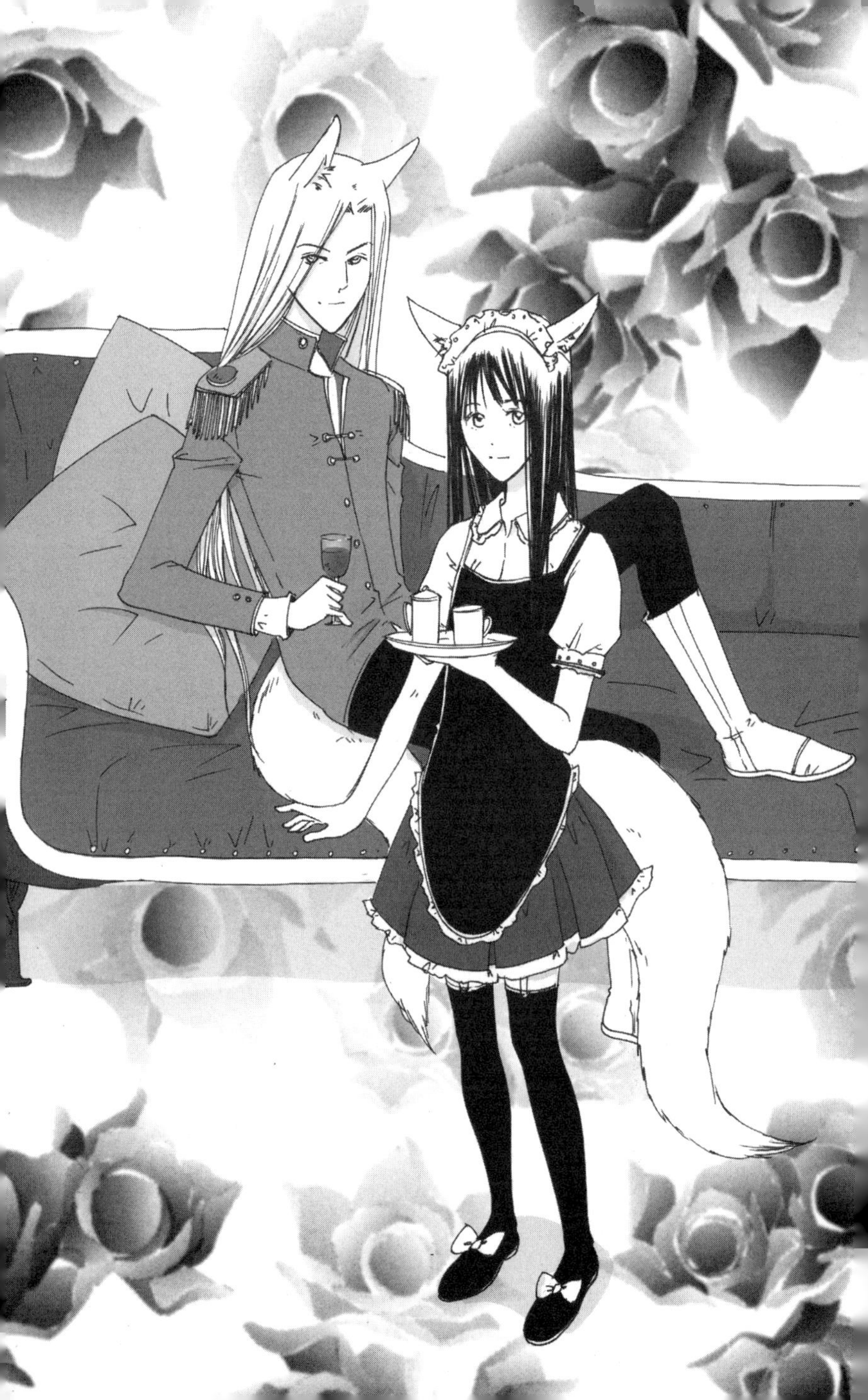

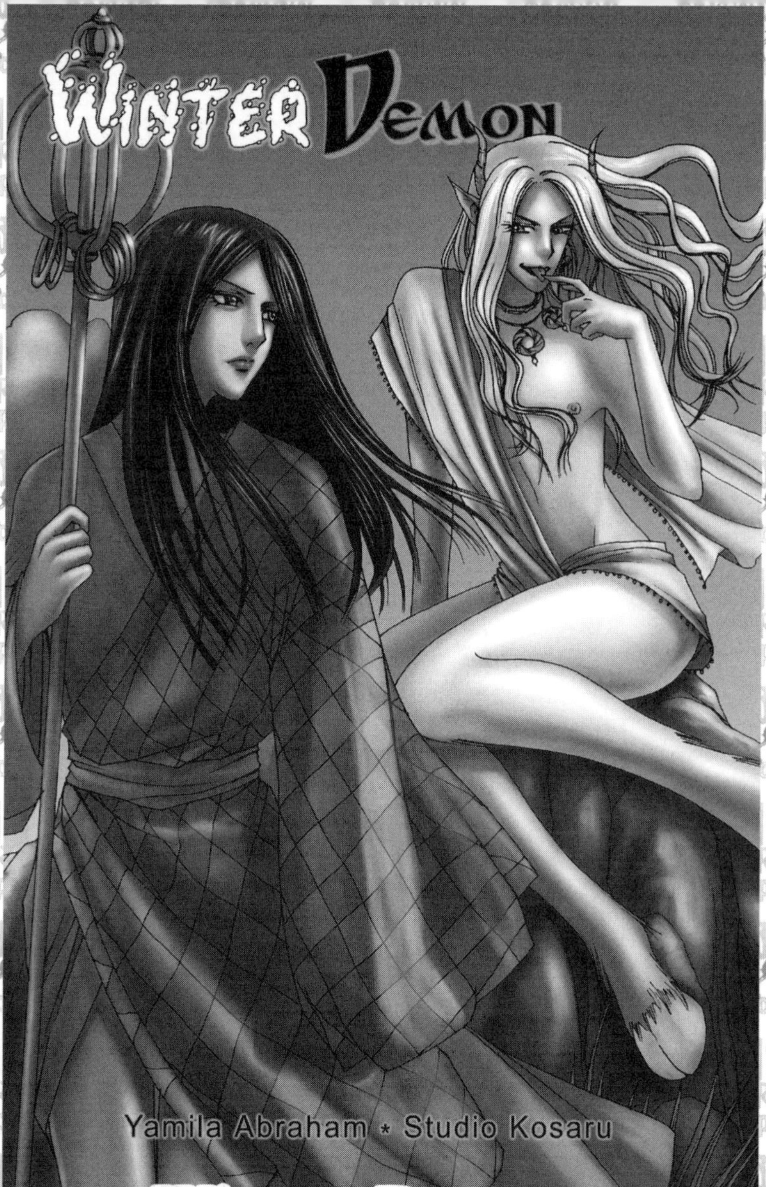

Winter Demon
Yamila Abraham * Studio Kosaru

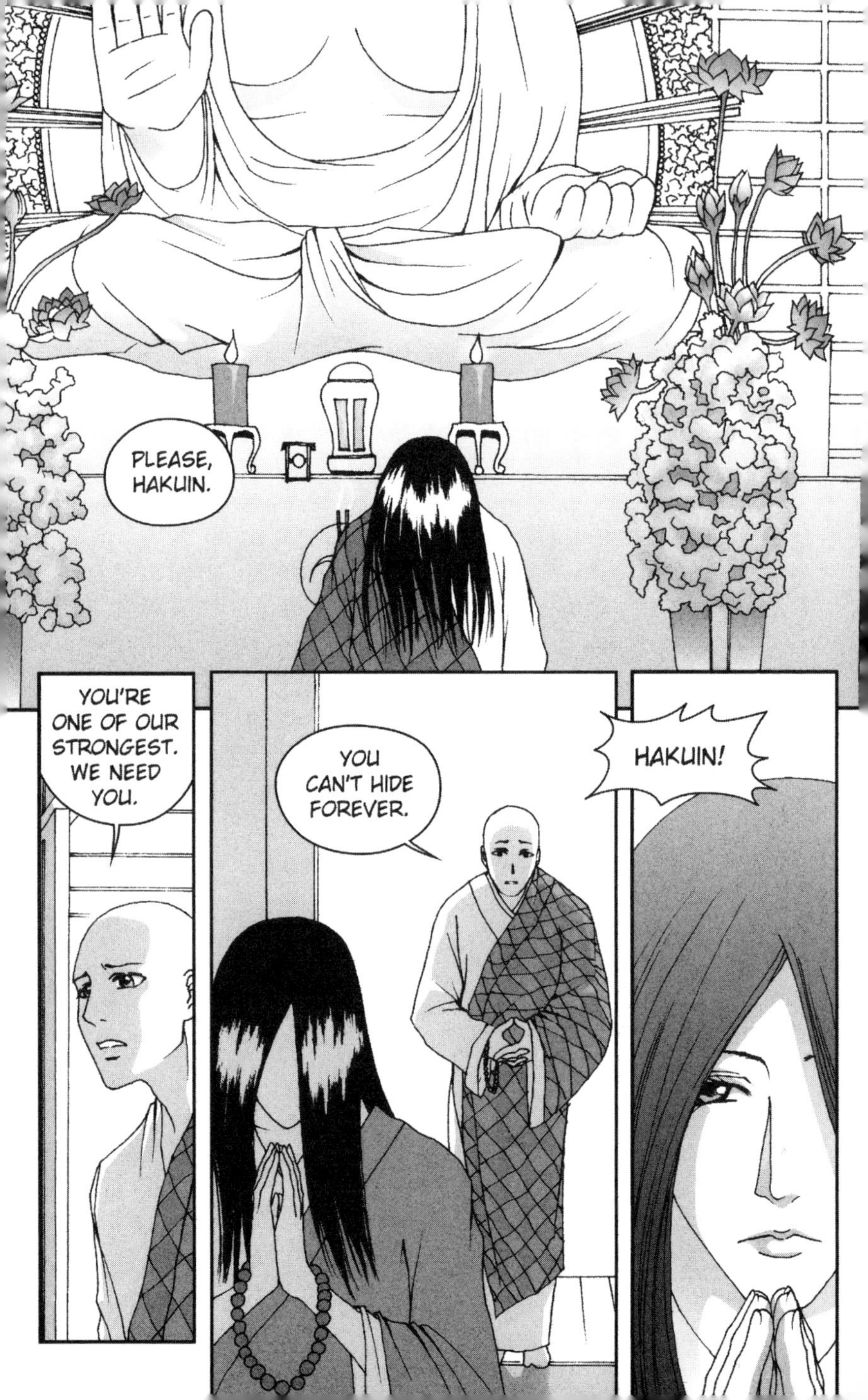
PLEASE, HAKUIN.
YOU'RE ONE OF OUR STRONGEST. WE NEED YOU.
YOU CAN'T HIDE FOREVER.
HAKUIN!

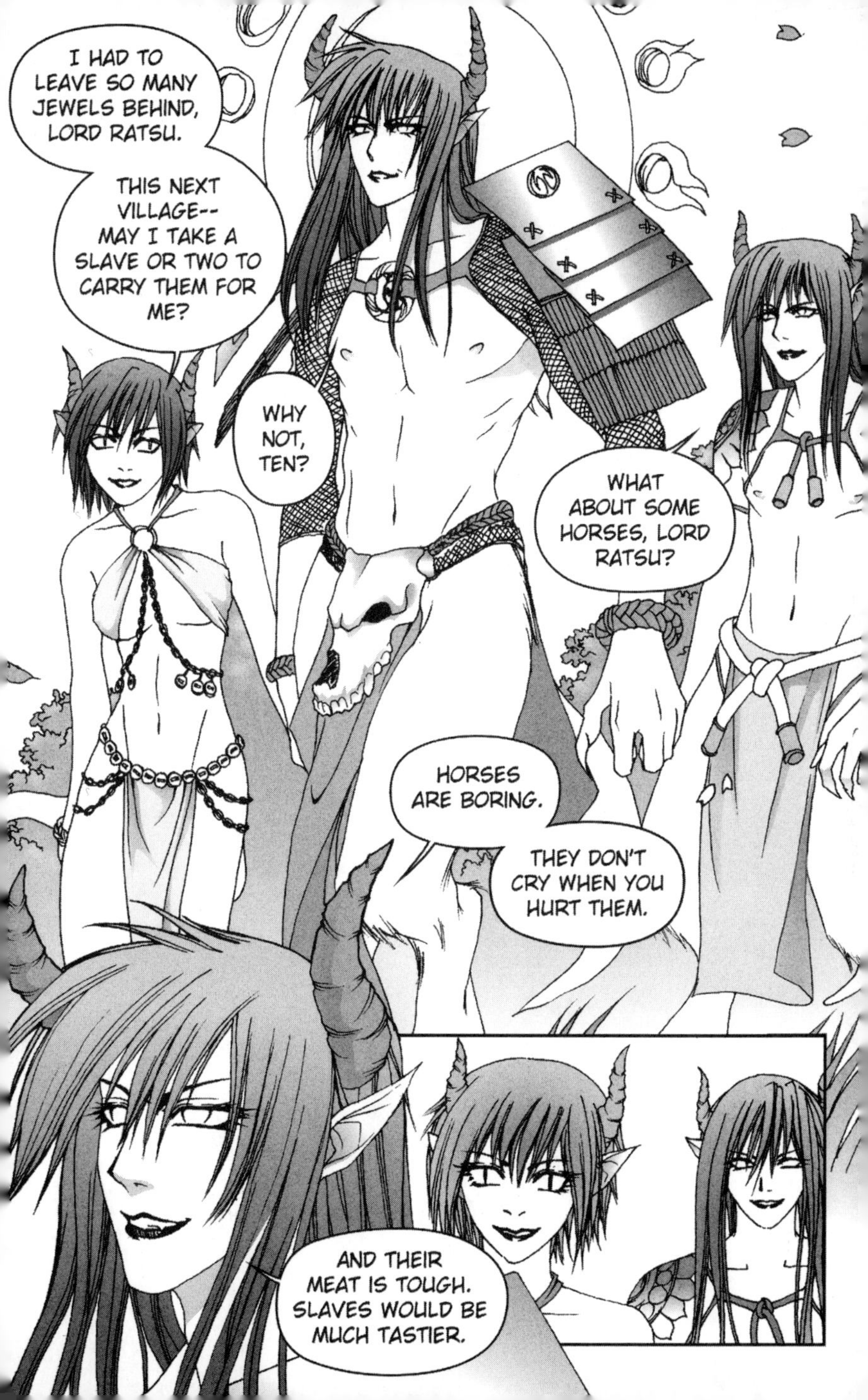
I HAD TO LEAVE SO MANY JEWELS BEHIND, LORD RATSU.
THIS NEXT VILLAGE-- MAY I TAKE A SLAVE OR TWO TO CARRY THEM FOR ME?
WHY NOT, TEN?
WHAT ABOUT SOME HORSES, LORD RATSU?
HORSES ARE BORING.
THEY DON'T CRY WHEN YOU HURT THEM.
AND THEIR MEAT IS TOUGH. SLAVES WOULD BE MUCH TASTIER.

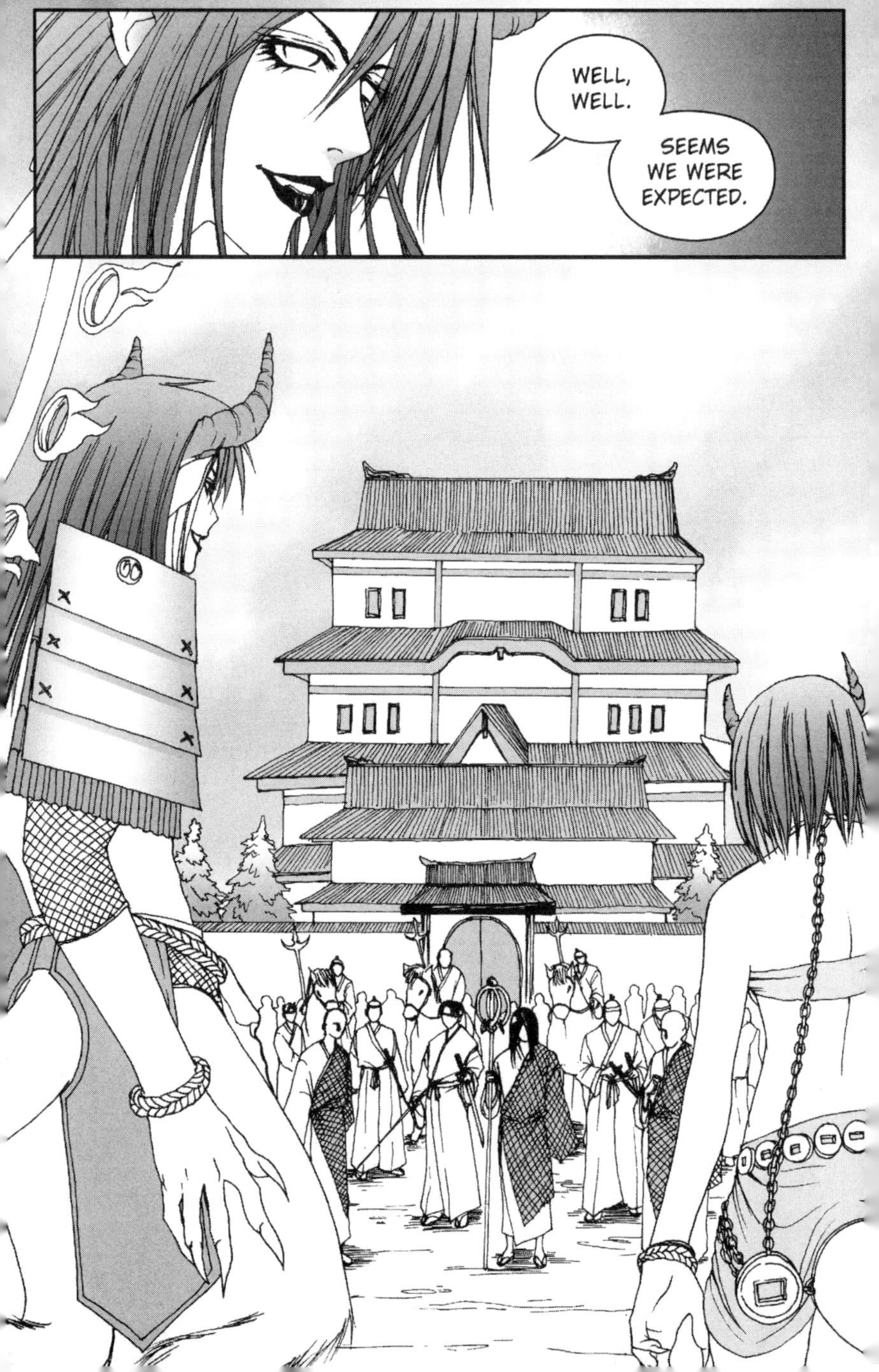
WELL, WELL.
SEEMS WE WERE EXPECTED.

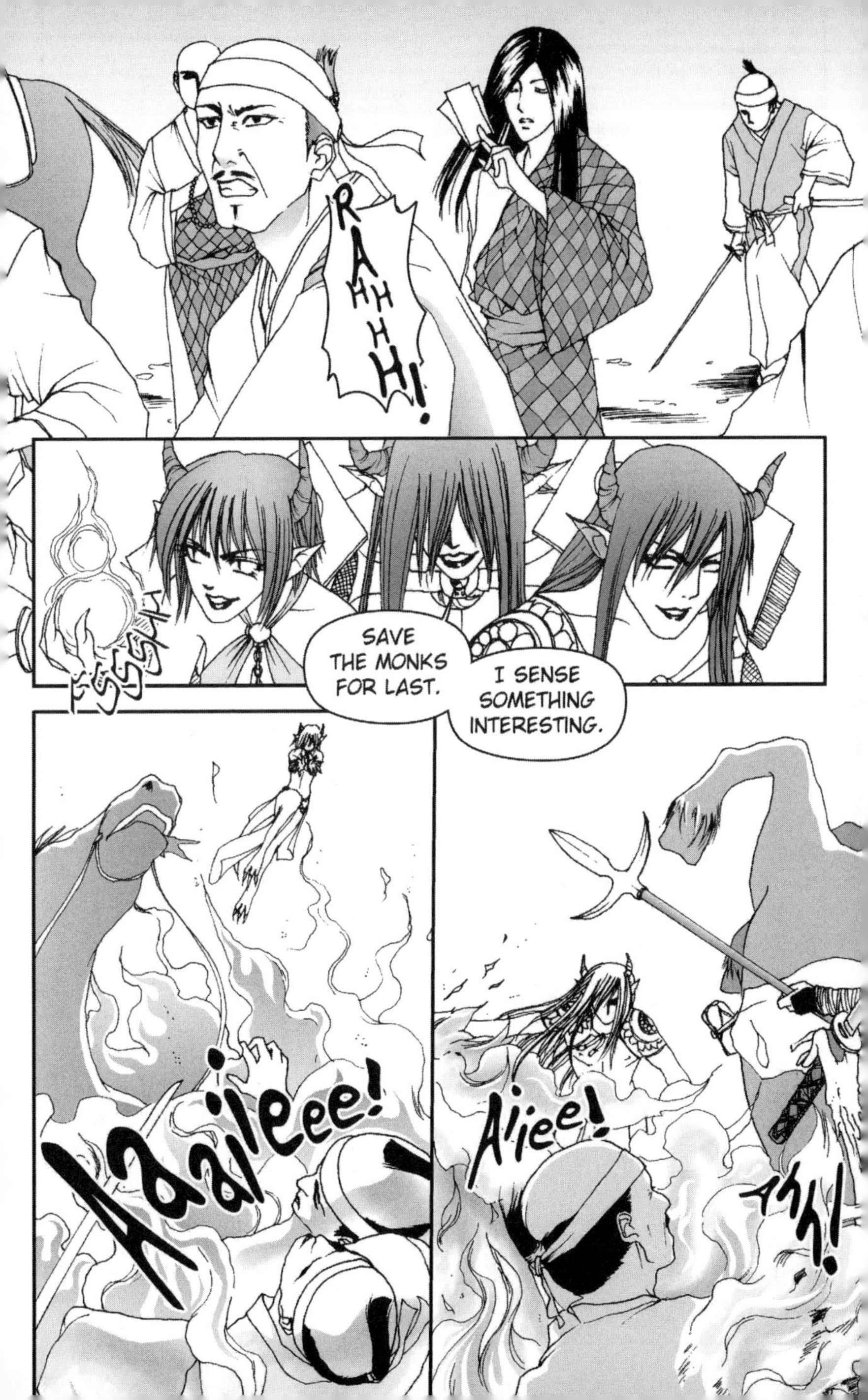
RAHHHH!
FSSSH
SAVE THE MONKS FOR LAST.
I SENSE SOMETHING INTERESTING.
Aaaieee!
Aiee!
Ack!

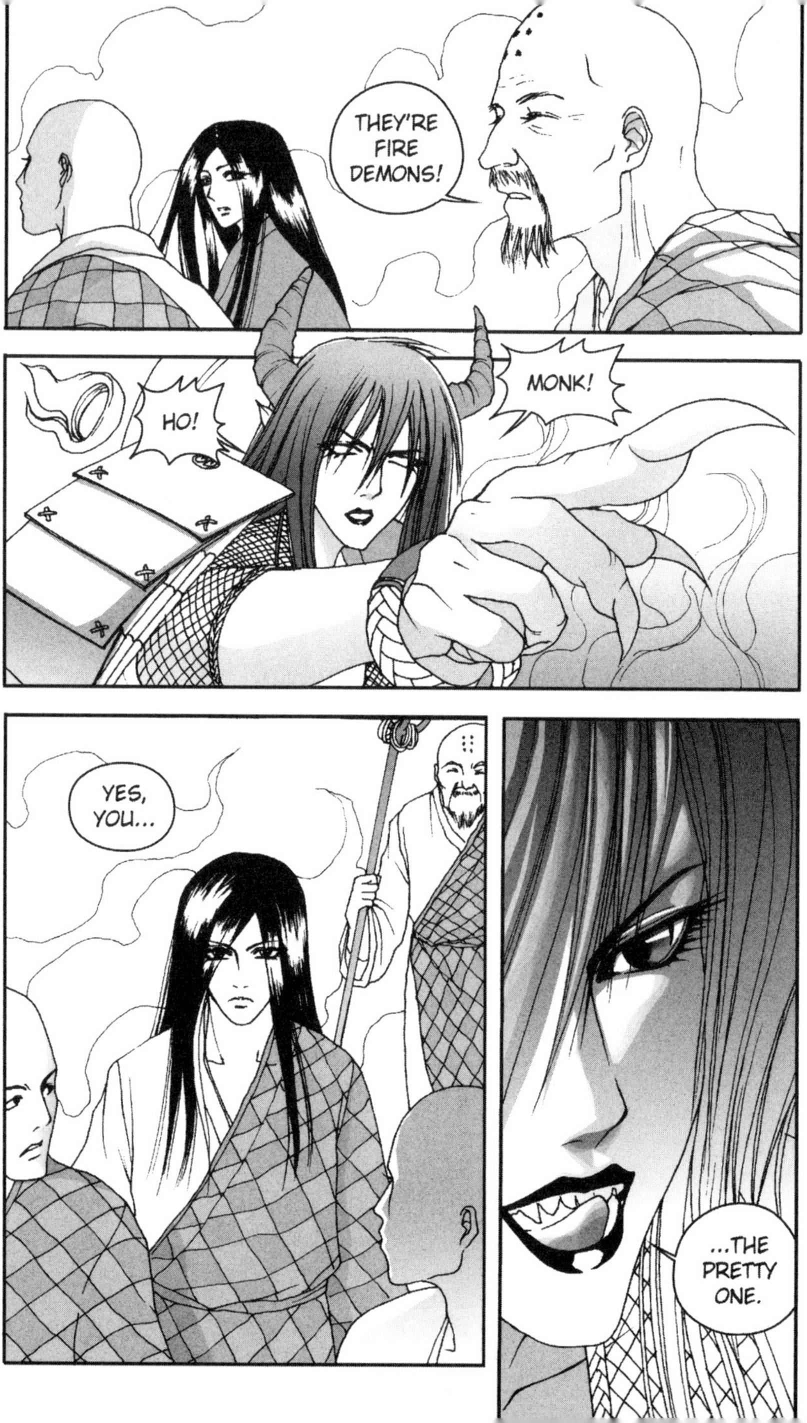
THEY'RE FIRE DEMONS!
HO!
MONK!
YES, YOU...
...THE PRETTY ONE.

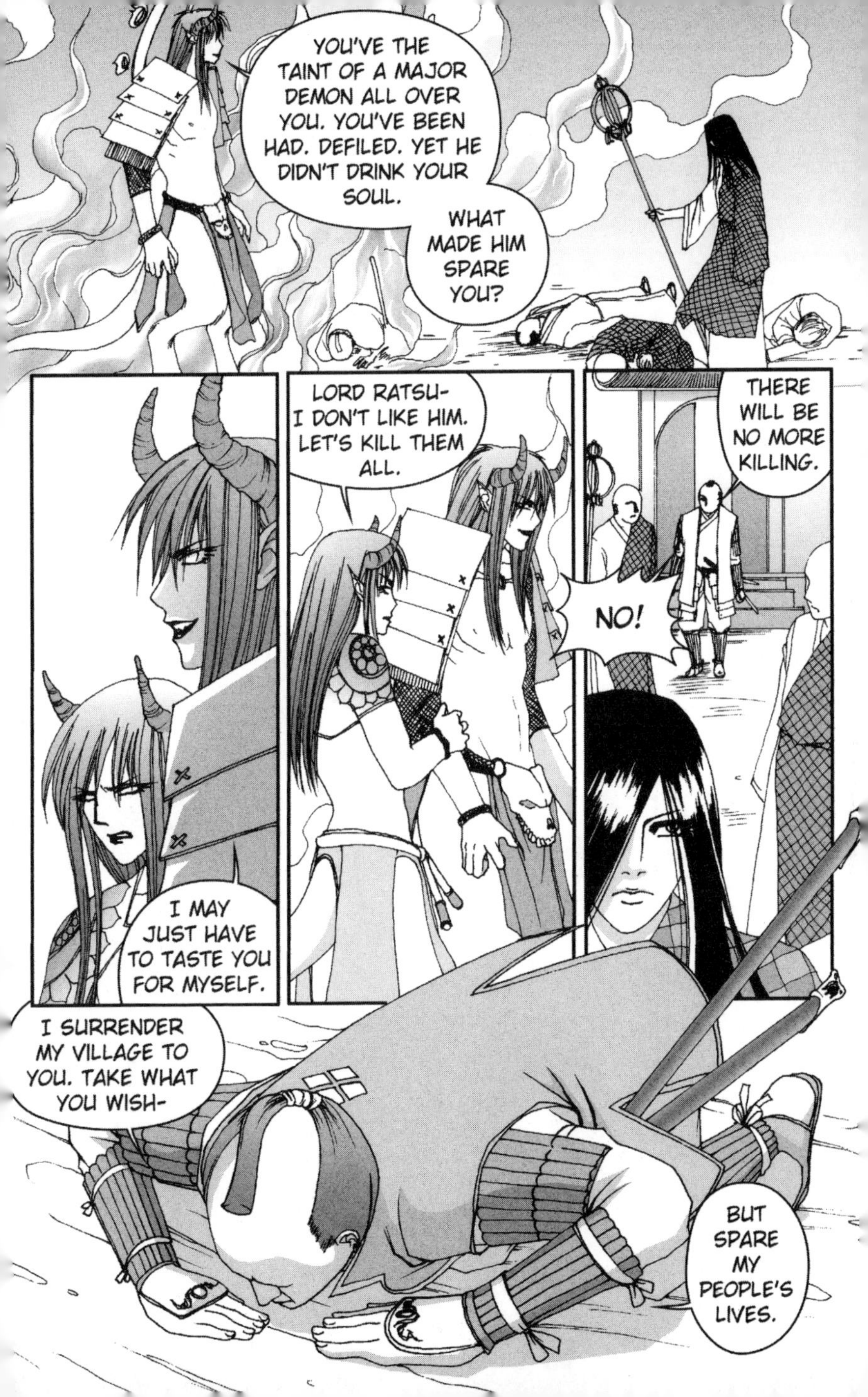
YOU'VE THE TAINT OF A MAJOR DEMON ALL OVER YOU. YOU'VE BEEN HAD. DEFILED. YET HE DIDN'T DRINK YOUR SOUL.
WHAT MADE HIM SPARE YOU?
I MAY JUST HAVE TO TASTE YOU FOR MYSELF.
LORD RATSU- I DON'T LIKE HIM. LET'S KILL THEM ALL.
THERE WILL BE NO MORE KILLING.
NO!
I SURRENDER MY VILLAGE TO YOU. TAKE WHAT YOU WISH-
BUT SPARE MY PEOPLE'S LIVES.

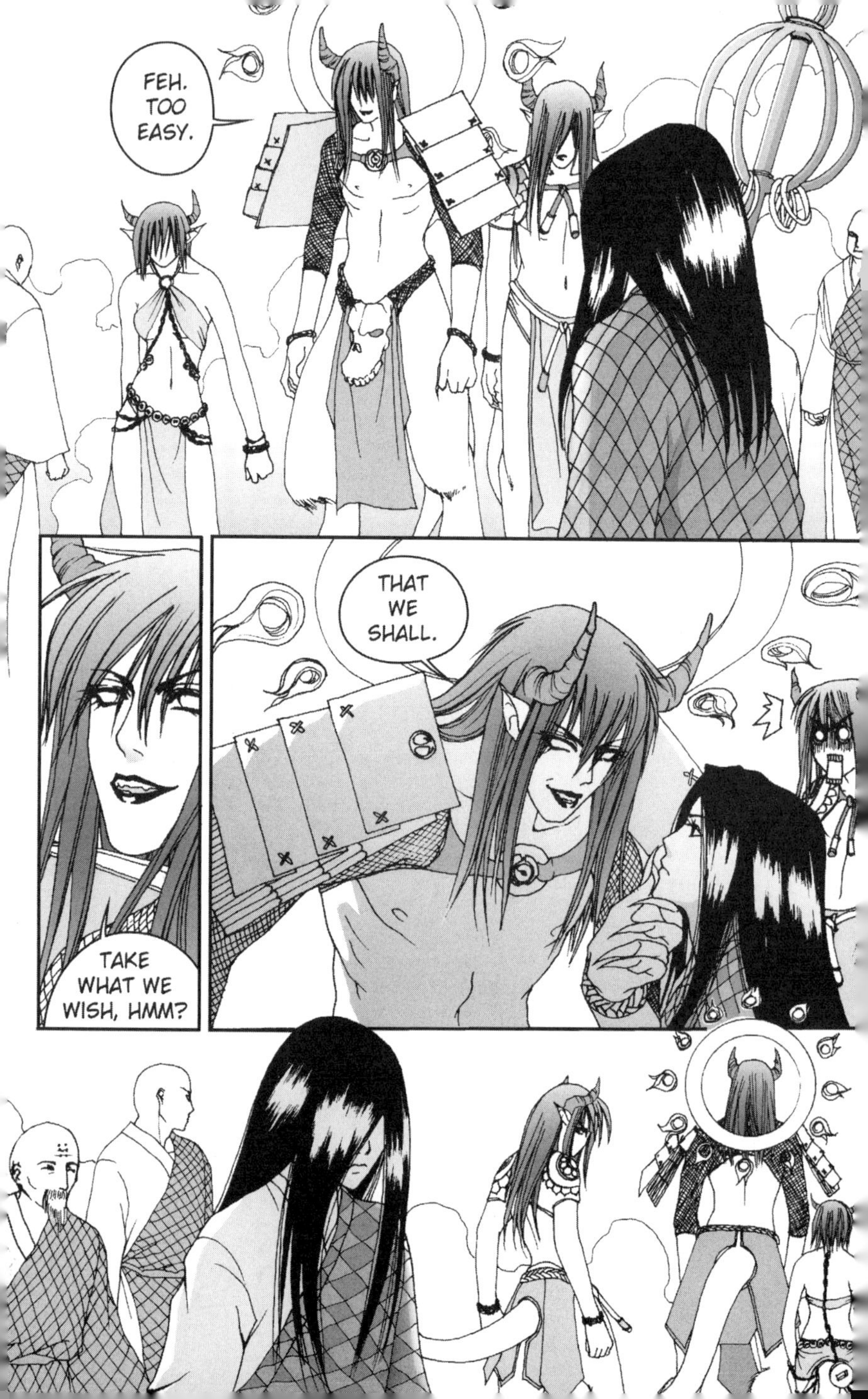
FEH. TOO EASY.
TAKE WHAT WE WISH, HMM?
THAT WE SHALL.

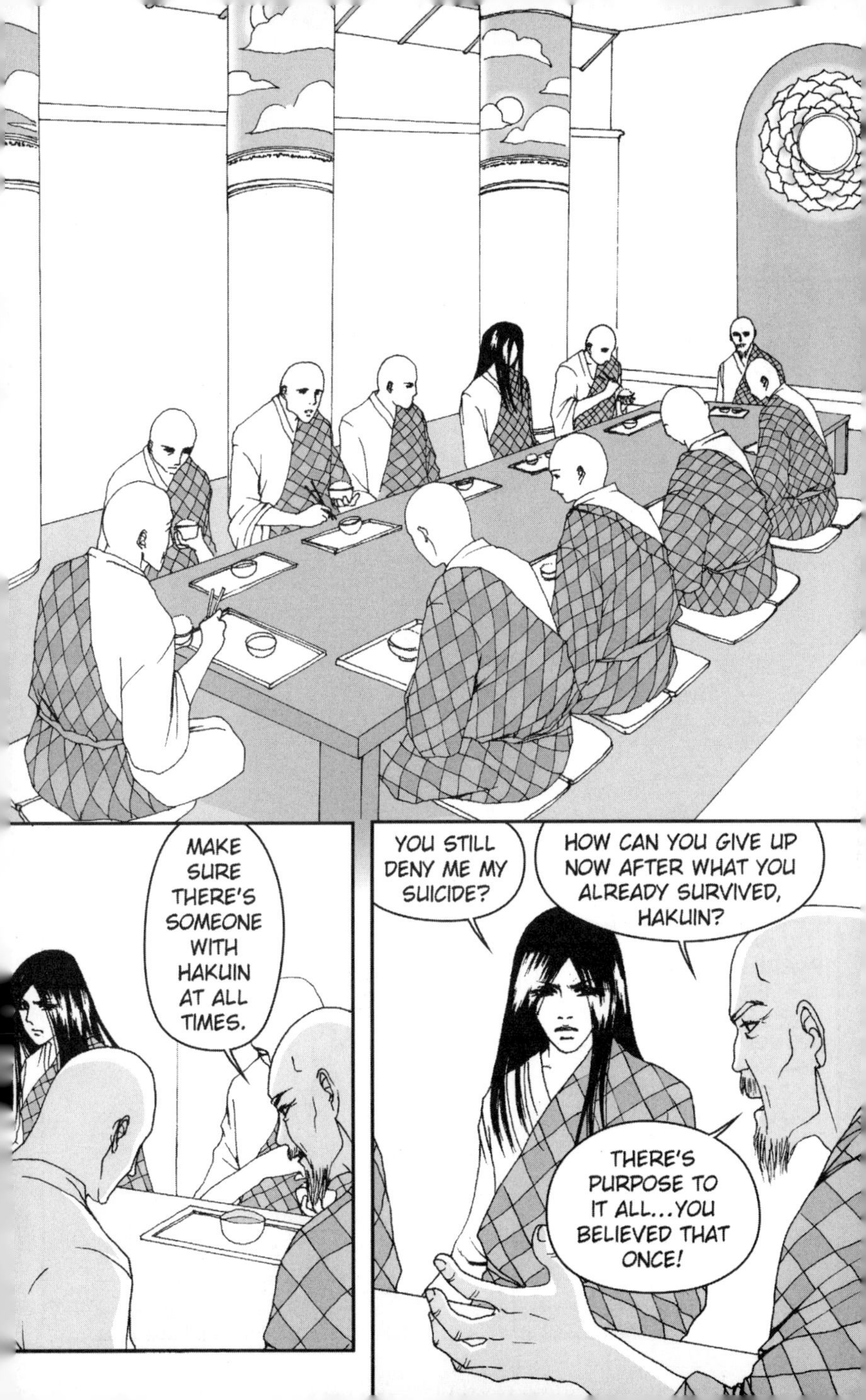
MAKE SURE THERE'S SOMEONE WITH HAKUIN AT ALL TIMES.
YOU STILL DENY ME MY SUICIDE?
HOW CAN YOU GIVE UP NOW AFTER WHAT YOU ALREADY SURVIVED, HAKUIN?
THERE'S PURPOSE TO IT ALL...YOU BELIEVED THAT ONCE!

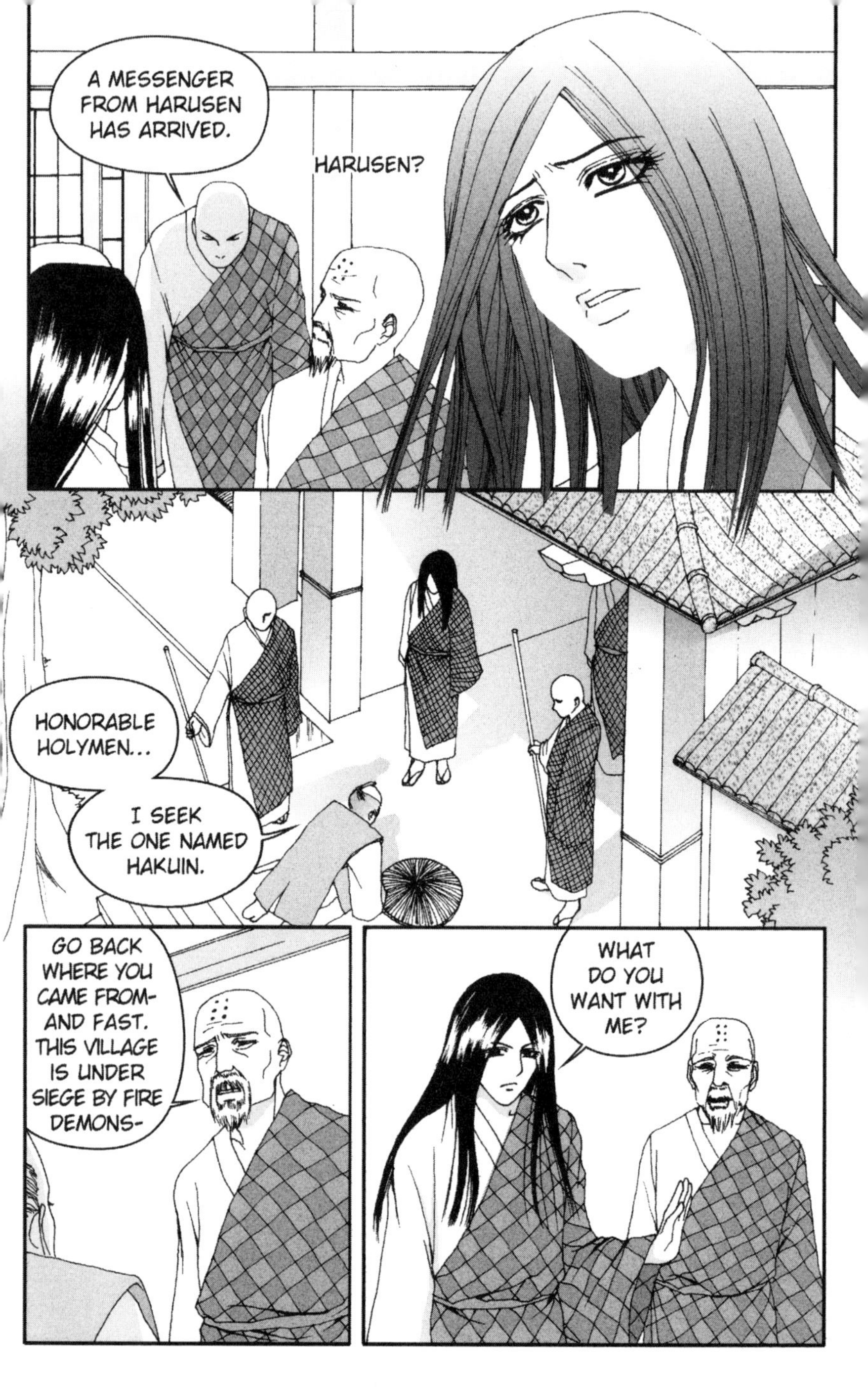
A MESSENGER FROM HARUSEN HAS ARRIVED.
HARUSEN?
HONORABLE HOLYMEN...
I SEEK THE ONE NAMED HAKUIN.
GO BACK WHERE YOU CAME FROM- AND FAST. THIS VILLAGE IS UNDER SIEGE BY FIRE DEMONS-
WHAT DO YOU WANT WITH ME?

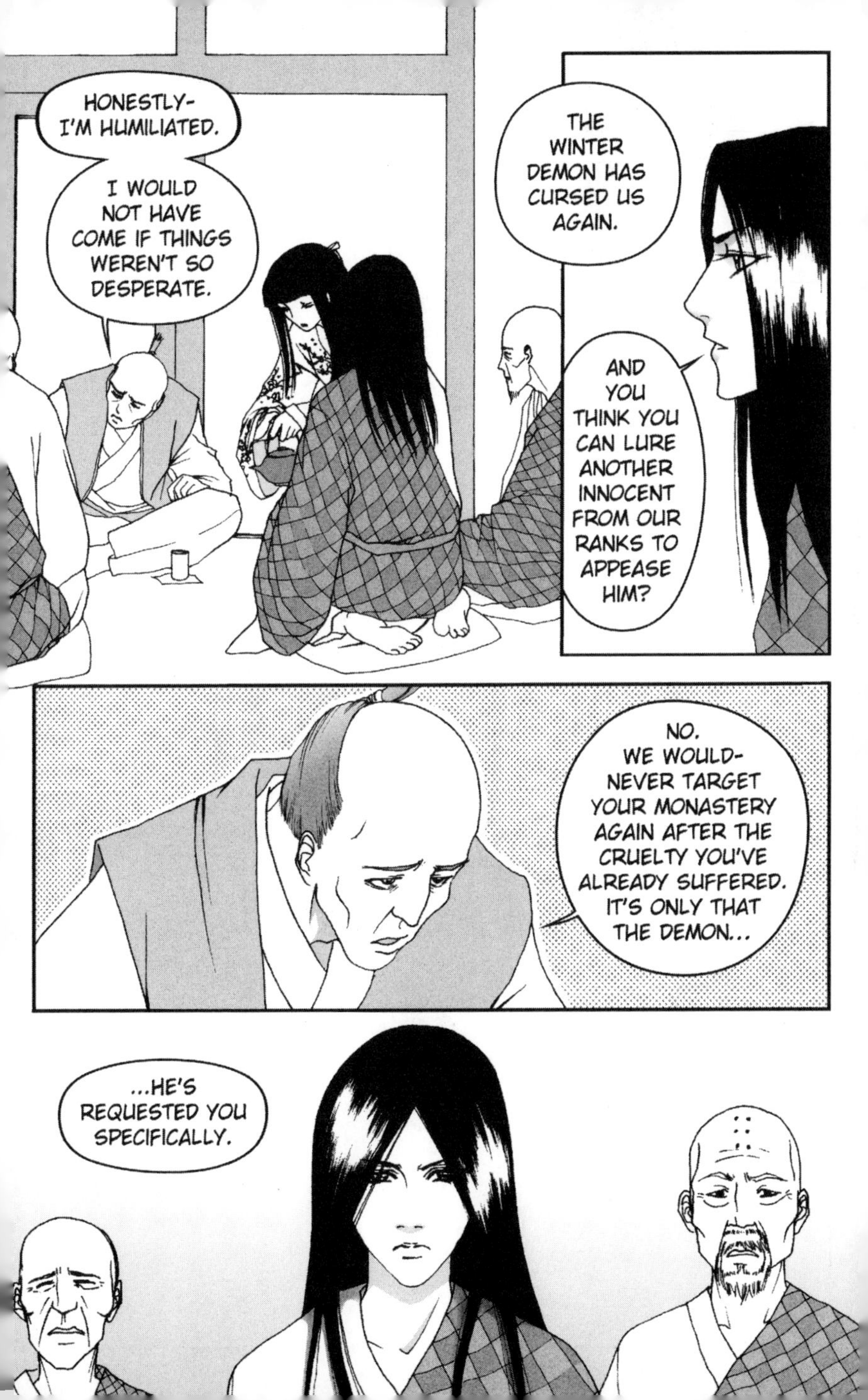
HONESTLY- I'M HUMILIATED.
I WOULD NOT HAVE COME IF THINGS WEREN'T SO DESPERATE.
THE WINTER DEMON HAS CURSED US AGAIN.
AND YOU THINK YOU CAN LURE ANOTHER INNOCENT FROM OUR RANKS TO APPEASE HIM?
NO. WE WOULD- NEVER TARGET YOUR MONASTERY AGAIN AFTER THE CRUELTY YOU'VE ALREADY SUFFERED. IT'S ONLY THAT THE DEMON...
...HE'S REQUESTED YOU SPECIFICALLY.

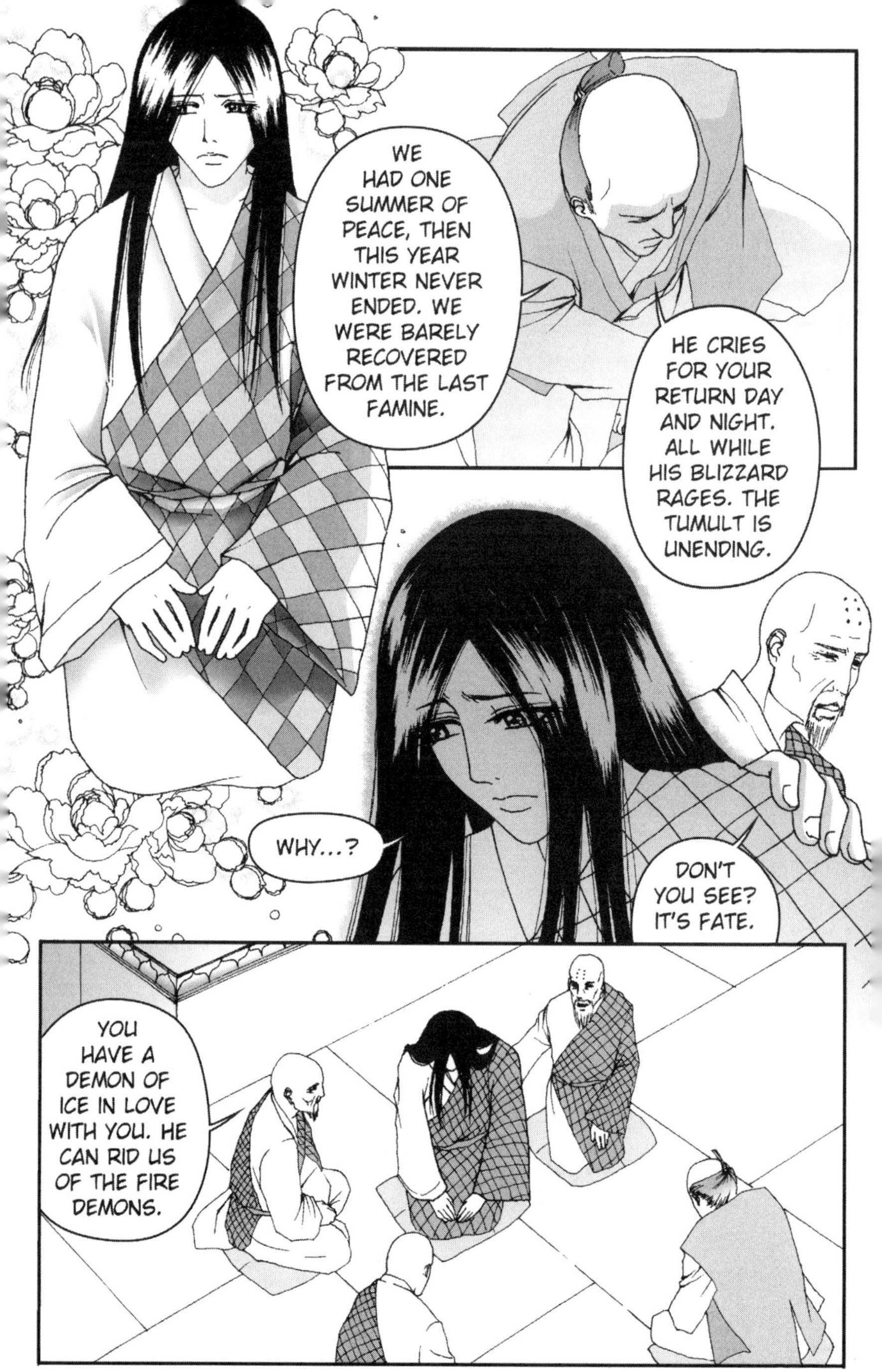
WE HAD ONE SUMMER OF PEACE, THEN THIS YEAR WINTER NEVER ENDED. WE WERE BARELY RECOVERED FROM THE LAST FAMINE.
HE CRIES FOR YOUR RETURN DAY AND NIGHT. ALL WHILE HIS BLIZZARD RAGES. THE TUMULT IS UNENDING.
WHY...?
DON'T YOU SEE? IT'S FATE.
YOU HAVE A DEMON OF ICE IN LOVE WITH YOU. HE CAN RID US OF THE FIRE DEMONS.

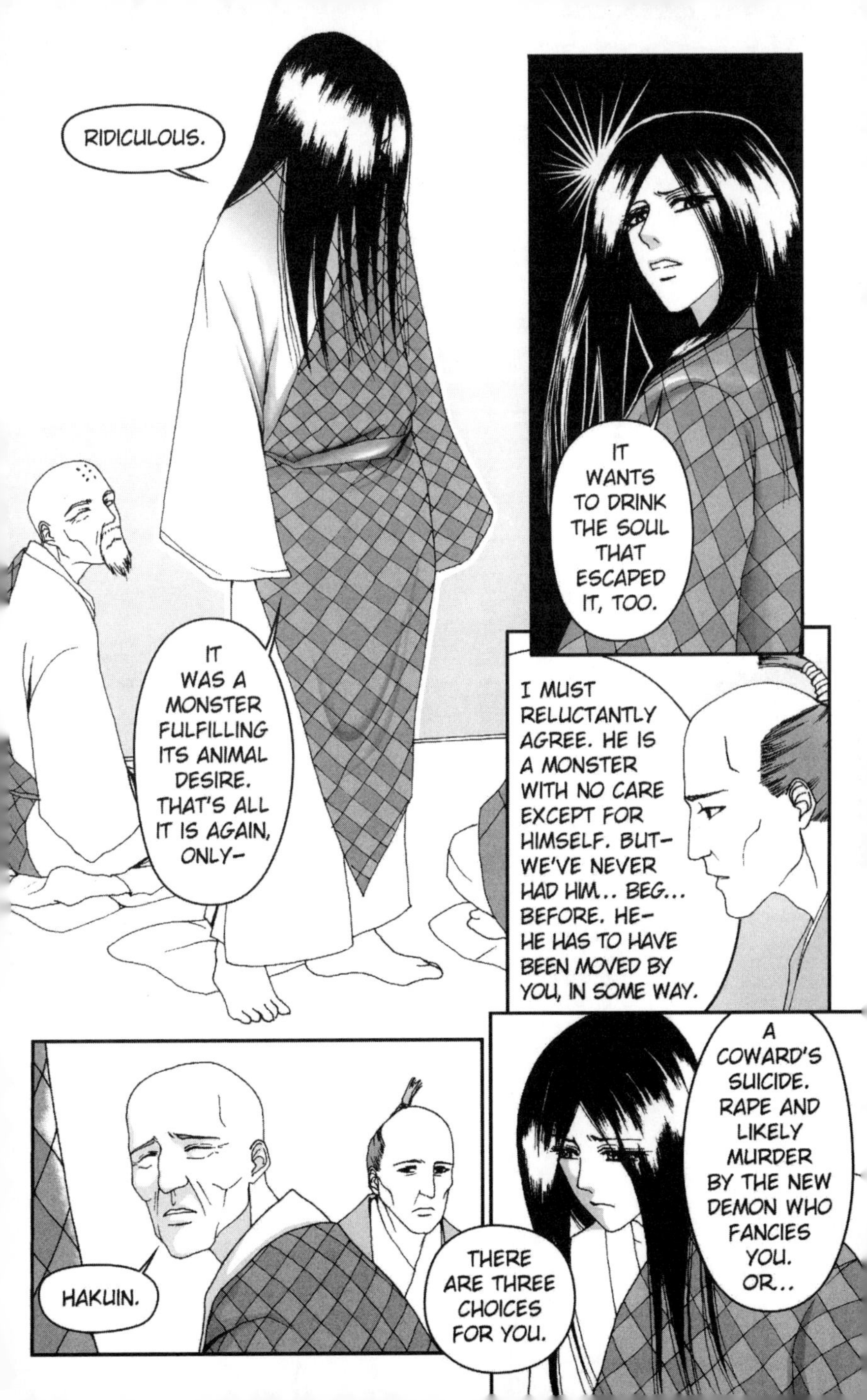
RIDICULOUS.
IT WAS A MONSTER FULFILLING ITS ANIMAL DESIRE. THAT'S ALL IT IS AGAIN, ONLY–
IT WANTS TO DRINK THE SOUL THAT ESCAPED IT, TOO.
I MUST RELUCTANTLY AGREE. HE IS A MONSTER WITH NO CARE EXCEPT FOR HIMSELF. BUT– WE'VE NEVER HAD HIM... BEG... BEFORE. HE– HE HAS TO HAVE BEEN MOVED BY YOU, IN SOME WAY.
HAKUIN.
THERE ARE THREE CHOICES FOR YOU.
A COWARD'S SUICIDE. RAPE AND LIKELY MURDER BY THE NEW DEMON WHO FANCIES YOU. OR..

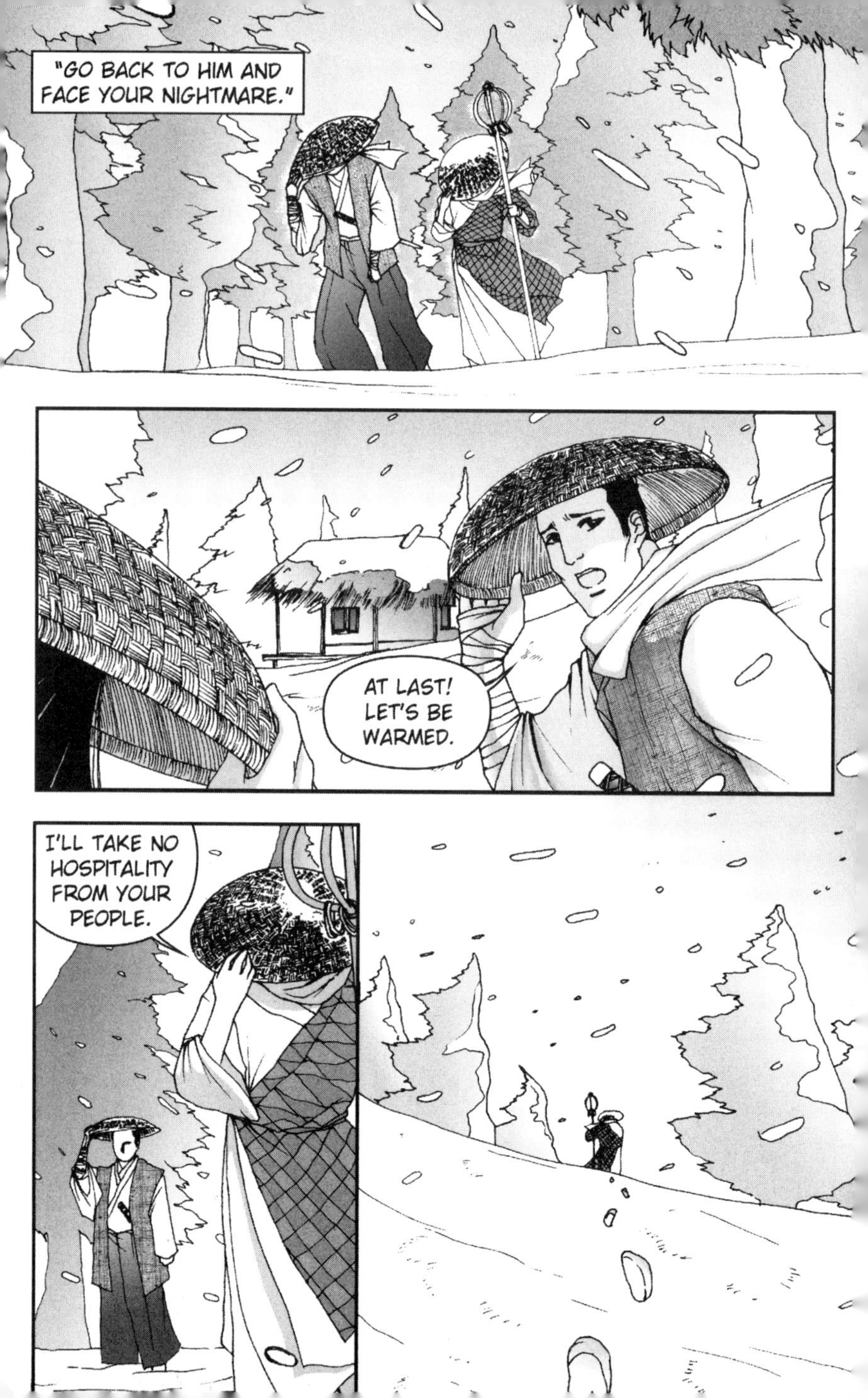
"GO BACK TO HIM AND FACE YOUR NIGHTMARE."
AT LAST! LET'S BE WARMED.
I'LL TAKE NO HOSPITALITY FROM YOUR PEOPLE.

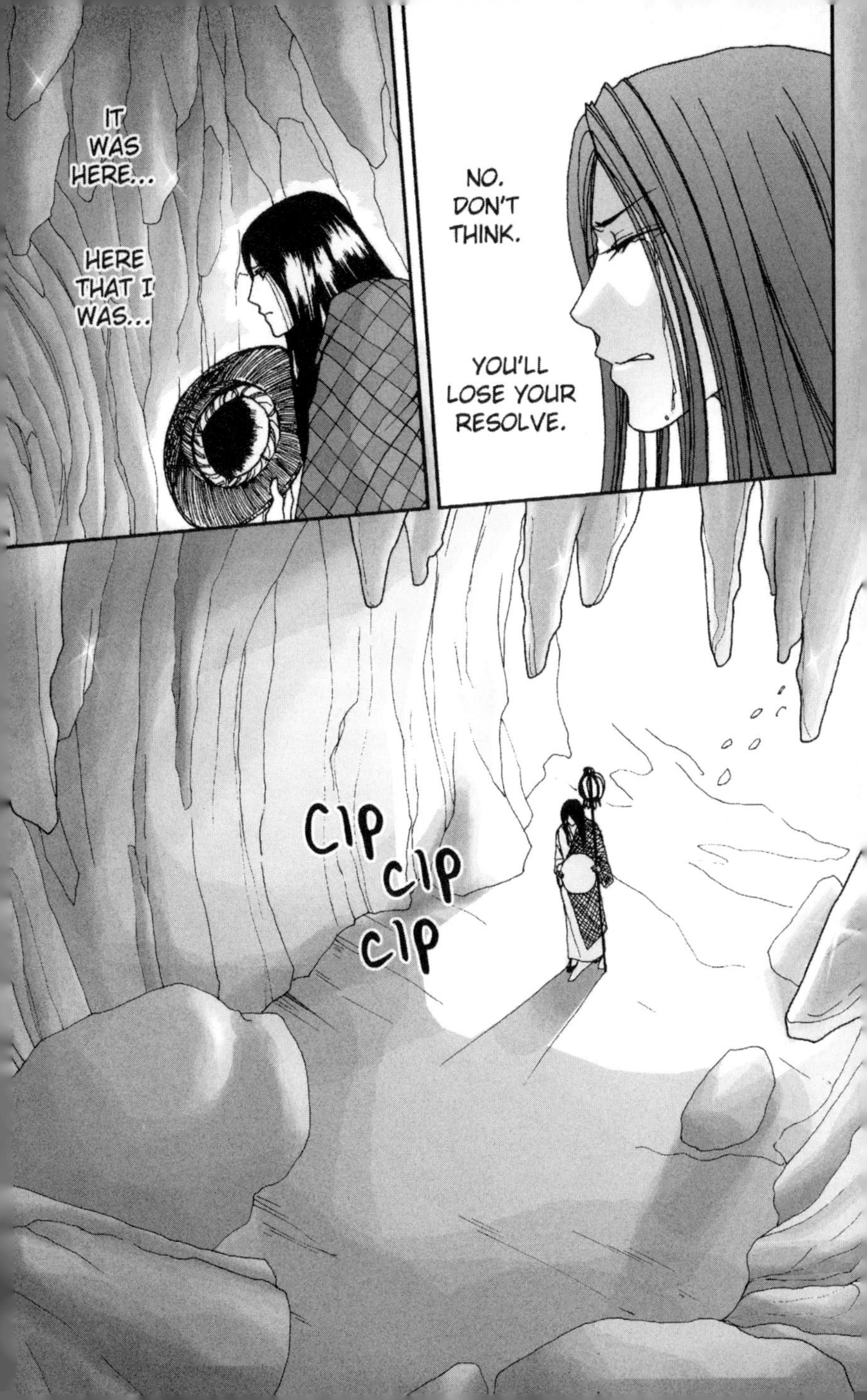
IT WAS HERE...
HERE THAT I WAS...
NO. DON'T THINK.
YOU'LL LOSE YOUR RESOLVE.
CLP CLP CLP

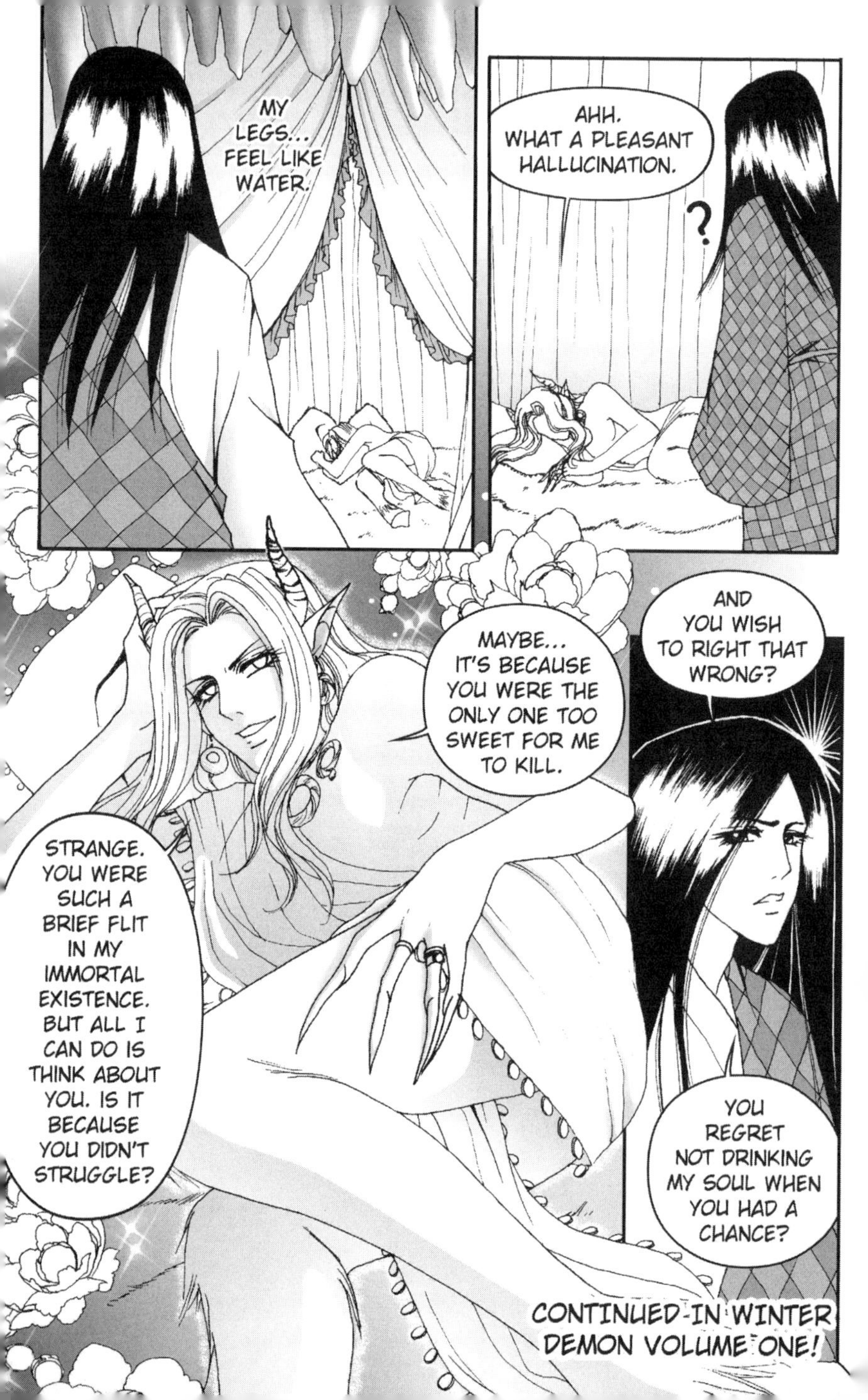
MY LEGS... FEEL LIKE WATER.
AHH. WHAT A PLEASANT HALLUCINATION.
?
STRANGE. YOU WERE SUCH A BRIEF FLIT IN MY IMMORTAL EXISTENCE. BUT ALL I CAN DO IS THINK ABOUT YOU. IS IT BECAUSE YOU DIDN'T STRUGGLE?
MAYBE... IT'S BECAUSE YOU WERE THE ONLY ONE TOO SWEET FOR ME TO KILL.
AND YOU WISH TO RIGHT THAT WRONG?
YOU REGRET NOT DRINKING MY SOUL WHEN YOU HAD A CHANCE?
CONTINUED IN WINTER DEMON VOLUME ONE!

Coming Jan. 2007!

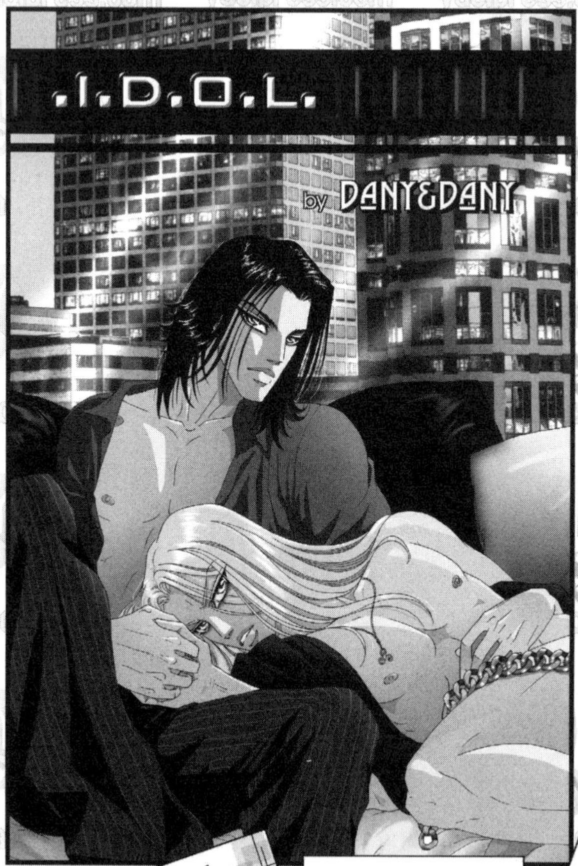
.I.D.O.L.
by DANY&DANY

Idol

by Dany&Dany

The jaded artist David hires the hustler Adam as an art model. This painting finally conveys the passion in David's heart. His model stirs passions of another kind. Acting on these feelings draws David into Adam's dark world of dangerous liaisons and jealous lovers.

THE ENGLISH LANGUAGE DEBUT OF THE RENOWNED ITALIAN YAOI STUDIO DANY&DANY!

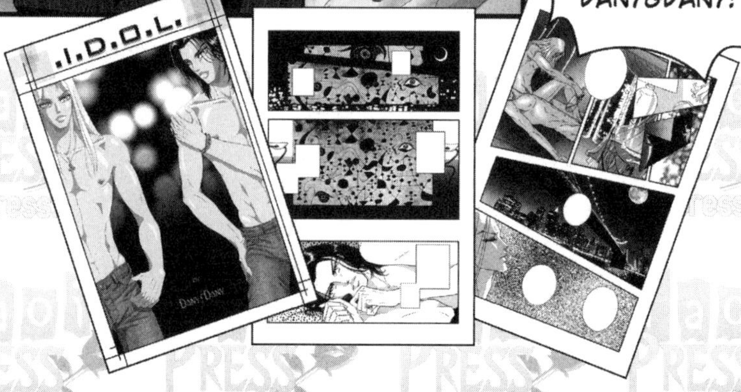
.I.D.O.L.

Coming Mar. 2007!

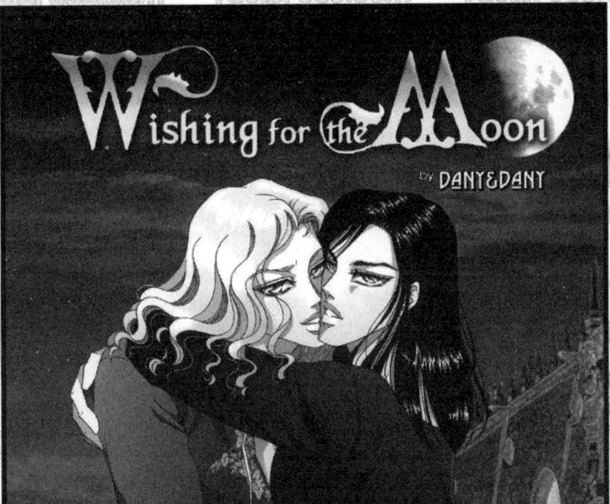
Wishing for the Moon
by DANY&DANY

Wishing for the Moon

by Dany&Dany

Four lives are fatally intertwined behind the scenes of a small Venice theater. An actor, a writer, a theater director and a teenage boy are drawn into a dangerous game of Chinese boxes played partway between dream and reality.

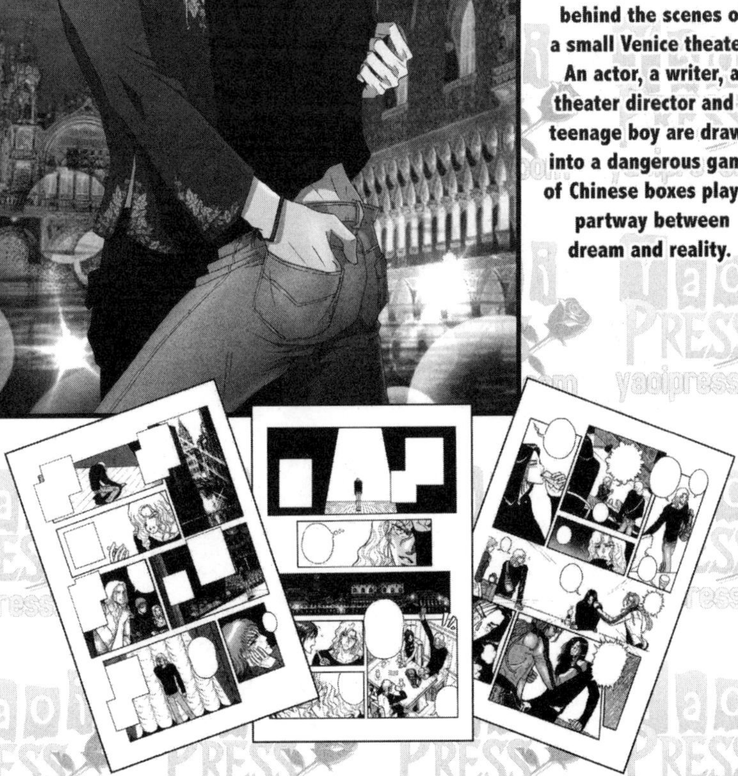

Coming Feb. 2007!

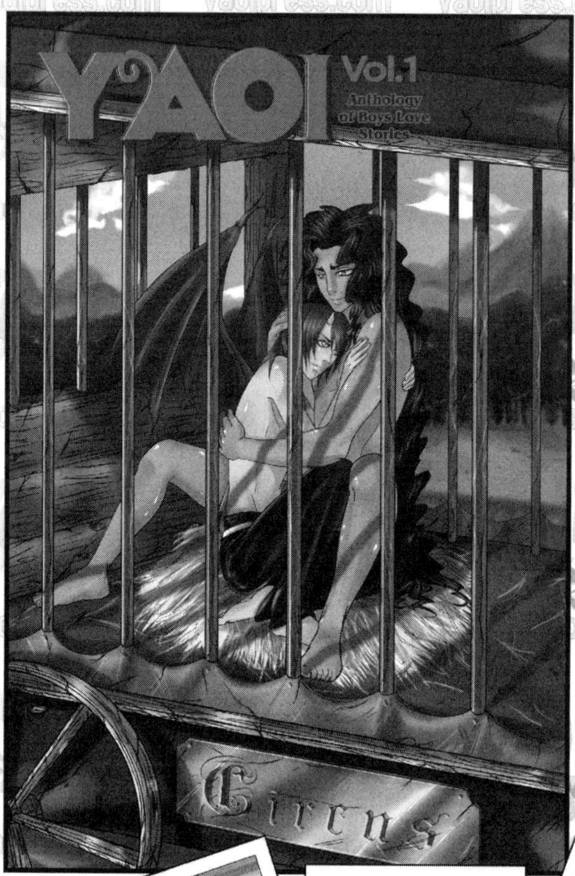
YAOI Vol.1
Anthology of Boys Love Stories
Circus

Yaoi Vol.1

Various Artists

Yaoi anthology of three heart wrenching love stories. First theres romance between prisoners of a medieval circus, then between members of rival Tokyo gangs, and finally, between a cop and a young man who escapes two sadistic hillbilly captors.

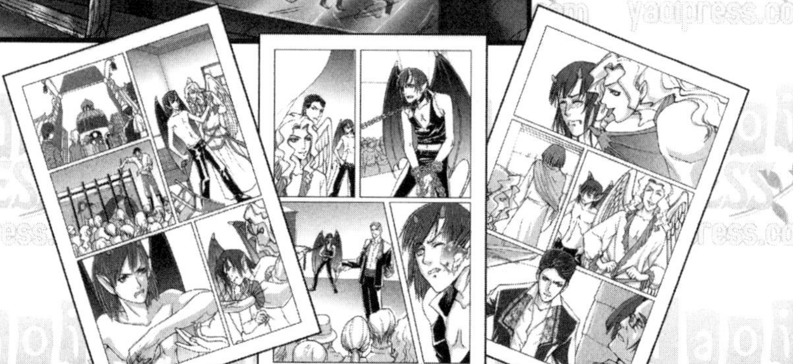